Oracle Hyperion Financial Management Tips & Techniques: Design, Implementation & Support

Peter John Fugere, Jr.

New York Chicago San Francisco
Lisbon London Madrid Mexico City Milan
New Delhi San Juan Seoul Singapore Sydney Toronto

The McGraw-Hill Companies

Cataloging-in-Publication Data is on file with the Library of Congress

McGraw-Hill books are available at special quantity discounts to use as premiums and sales promotions, or for use in corporate training programs. To contact a representative, please e-mail us at bulksales@mcgraw-hill.com.

Oracle Hyperion Financial Management Tips & Techniques: Design, Implementation & Support

1234567890 QFR QFR 10987654321

ISBN 978-0-07-177044-6
MHID 0-07-177044-5

Sponsoring Editor
Wendy Rinaldi

Editorial Supervisor
Janet Walden

Project Manager
Nidhi Chopra,
Cenveo Publisher Services

Acquisitions Coordinator
Stephanie Evans

Technical Editor
Chris Barbieri

Copy Editor
Margaret Berson

Proofreader
Susie Elkind

Indexer
Karin Arrigoni

Production Supervisor
Jean Bodeaux

Composition
Cenveo Publisher Services

Illustration
Cenveo Publisher Services

Art Director, Cover
Jeff Weeks

Cover Designer
Pattie Lee

This work is dedicated to my wife, Courtney. I could not have wished for a better friend and companion. Her support, faith and love keep me going.

About the Author

Peter John Fugere, Jr. has been working with the Hyperion products, specializing with the consolidation tools, for the past 12 years. He joined Hyperion in September 2000 as a Hyperion Enterprise consultant, after having been a customer since 1998. He currently is the vice president and director of a national Consolidation and Reporting Practice. In this capacity he is responsible for assisting numerous clients with development and implementation of financial reporting software solutions. He has led design and project management of several implementations, participating or leading in over 150 HFM implementations of various Hyperion products.

Peter is recognized as a leader within the consulting community. He was one of a team of people who helped Oracle write questions for the 3.2 and 3.4 HFM certification examinations. He has received several awards while working at Hyperion, including Consultant of the Year (2004), before he left to work for Vertical Pitch. In 2010, Peter was awarded an Oracle ACE award for his work with the EPM products.

Peter holds a Bachelor of Arts in Economics from the University of Massachusetts, Amherst, and a Master in Business Administration from Northeastern University, Boston, Massachusetts.

About the Technical Editor

One of the world's experts on Hyperion Financial Management (HFM), **Chris Barbieri** has over 14 years of experience in all phases of design, implementation, and support of consolidation/reporting applications. He has worked with HFM since its inception and is widely recognized as a top authority on HFM functionality, application and system design, and system performance. Chris has led implementation teams at Hyperion and currently at Edgewater Ranzal, where he serves as Practice Director. He holds a bachelor's degree in Finance and Accounting from Boston College, and a Master of Business Administration from Babson College. He has written whitepapers and numerous presentations on HFM, and has been designated as an Oracle ACE for his product evangelism and contributions to the field.

Contents at a Glance

Contents

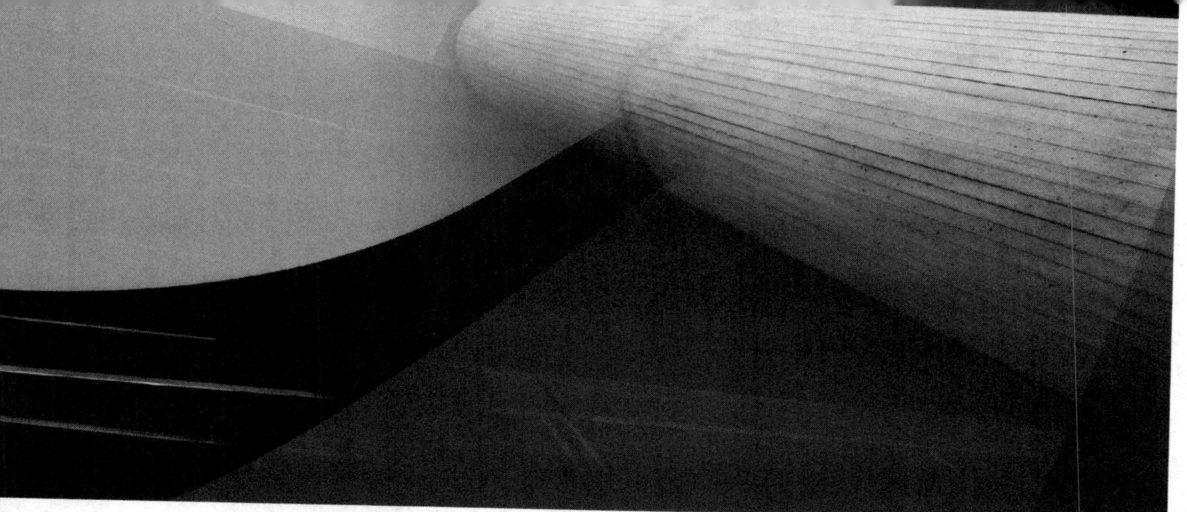

Acknowledgments

I would like to recognize all the people who made this book possible. First, I would like to thank Stephanie Evans and Wendy Rinaldi at McGraw-Hill for helping me so much with this book. Both were so patient and encouraging; they were so great to work with on this. I also want to recognize and thank my friend Dan Gudal for first putting out the possibility of writing a book. I owe a lot of my career, which this book represents, to Dan's support, faith, and guidance. I was lucky to get two amazing technical editors to help with this work. I would like to thank Maggie Reed as one of the technical editors. As absolutely in demand as she is, she was able to find time to help make this possible. I would also like to thank Chris Barbieri, who also worked as a technical editor. Chris and I have worked more closely than most over the past 12 years, and I am so thankful for that. The work he put in on this book was significant, and I sincerely appreciate it. I also want to thank other friends and colleagues who over the years helped me amass the knowledge upon which this book is based: Jim Heflin, who first showed me how to write rules; Bob Nelson and Matt DeCarlo, who always share experiences and have supported me. Finally, I want to thank my family, Courtney, Henri, and Sydney. They were so patient with my late nights, working weekends, and work distractions. Their love and support make everything possible. I love them more than anything.

Introduction

Oracle Hyperion Financial Management (HFM) is a powerful consolidation tool. At the core is a well-designed relational database that provides a foundation for many features. This foundation was built with many new forward-thinking technologies, which have made possible many of the new features and functions clients enjoy today. HFM's web interface allows for faster rollout and adoption. Between the web interface and the database is an application layer. This application layer enables the tool to scale as a company grows and evolves. The rules with which it performs the calculations provide data in ways that are prohibited with many other tools. HFM was built to translate, allocate, eliminate, and consolidate your data with minimal setup. It provides detailed auditing and controls. Alongside the other tools in the Enterprise Performance Management suite, HFM truly is a complete financial suite required for today's reporting needs.

What amazes me when I talk with companies about their consolidation process is how many are using tools that create work, mistakes, and risk. Companies with hundreds of millions of dollars in revenue using a spreadsheet to consolidate are setting themselves up for issues. These spreadsheets are often so complex and convoluted that only one or two key people in the company really understand them. These key people are often so entrenched in managing an antiquated process that they spend little time identifying and resolving real issues. Given the poor data quality caused by using spreadsheets, it is no wonder that data reconciliation and conversion is the biggest part of an implementation. There is little auditing and process control with these other tools. Versioning, tracking, and disaster recovery are impossible with spreadsheets. Some of the most valuable data to a public company is being mishandled.

Companies don't intend to burden themselves during the close. Some companies grow so fast they find themselves with a tool that doesn't work. Excel, for instance, is a tool that is manageable with five legal entities and no currency translation. One day, however, you find yourself with a 25-tab spreadsheet with links that break all the time. Spreadsheets can also hide changes, are difficult to audit, and are rife with mistakes. Spreadsheets create issues for an IT group as well because they are difficult to include in a disaster recovery plan and to back up, and they are not secure. Flat-file databases offer only a small improvement over spreadsheets. Older products, or custom-built databases, only address some of these issues.

Regardless of how you found yourself using a spreadsheet or custom database, there's a better way with better data, and it's Oracle Hyperion Financial Management. Other companies culturally are just slow adopters of technology, trying to keep costs under control or mitigating risks. It can be hard to justify a big investment in something that really isn't part of the core of your business.

Overview

With most every benefit there is some cost. With HFM's flexibility and power, there is a cost of *potentially* making the close process more complex or more complicated. I specifically use the word "potentially," because it doesn't have to be that way. You can benefit from many of the features of HFM without burdening the close process. Many companies use HFM with fantastic results. And since HFM is used so widely to provide consolidation data, many people must be seeing some benefits. Many people use these features and HFM to make their close smoother and improve the work they are doing. The key is obvious; there is a right way to put this tool in place. This book shares the right approach, and the tips that will save you hours, maybe days, of frustration and pain.

This is not an administrator's guide. Oracle did a great job writing that already. This book should augment that guide and the help tools. Where an administrator and user guide tell you *how*, this book should help you understand *why*. For example, if you need to know where to set the ICP member so you can map data to it for your intercompany accounts, this book will not help you. That information is very well documented in the Administrator Guide, help files, and online. But those places do not tell you how other people are using that information to simplify the close, how they integrate with other features, or any tips for making the close easier and more auditable. If you need to understand what suspense or plug account you should define for that intercompany, because it will help with reporting, then I think the following pages in this book will help. I have been working in this field since late 1998. I have been part of projects as small as 15 users, and the world's largest (as of this writing), 3,600 users in 180 countries. Where the Administrator Guide will tell you "what," I will explain "why." I hope you can use my experience in this book to maximize your investment with the Hyperion tools and plan for new uses in the future.

Best Practices

I will refrain, as much as I can, from using the term "best practice." First, it doesn't meet the objective of this book for me, which is to explain why we would do something in HFM. Second, it is completely overused. People will use "best practice" as a way to end the discussion about something with the product. "Because it is a best practice" should not be a giant hammer anyone can use to beat someone over the head with, when they question why they are being told to do something. For example, which would you prefer if you ask the question, "Why do you want to use the balance type for an account when you build an override?" First choice, "Because it is a best practice." Or second choice, "Because the rules are easier to write, it is easier to reconcile, and when we use the balance type for this override, we can translate from one currency to another to another." While you may not understand completely what I was saying in the second option—and you will when you have finished reading this book—you can see that the second response is just not as dismissive as the first answer. It explains why we are doing something.

When I think of the term best practice, I am expecting metrics of how companies benefited from the approach. What is the cost of deviating? What is the cost on the business process? Here is another example of what I mean. Oracle software has functionality that you can benefit from when you connect your application directly to the general ledger system, instead of a data mart. But is it a best practice to always pull from the source (in this case the general ledger) and not pull all of the data from a single data mart? The first question is, what is your book of record? If it is the ledger, do the existing feeds need to remain in place? What is the impact if those feeds are dropped? Will HFM have the full data and detail required for any downstream systems? What is the impact of adding that detail to HFM on the close? What is the effort required to make that change in the data process? In this book, I focus on the principle that the goal to good data integration is to reduce the number of reconciliation points, and the principle that the goal of HFM is to consolidate quickly and have well-defined scope. It does not make sense for a company to replace a data mart with a product like HFM because they will lose the ability to drill back to the ledger detail as the sole reason. Other factors need to be considered as well, like the questions described earlier and the principles in this book.

Contents

While this book isn't written just for people who want to implement HFM for the first time, the flow of this book does follow the lifecycle of an implementation. Before you even get the product in your company, you will likely need to build a case for buying the tool. This book will help you to understand what HFM is, and justify its purchase. And the first and most important part of implementing HFM is having an understanding of how the products work together and how the core HFM application works. Without that understanding of the tools, you will spend more time testing, reworking, and regretting.

Chapter 1, "Designing Your Oracle HFM Application," will cover the critical steps to making sure a project gets off on the right foot. This chapter explains the lifecycle of HFM, from understanding what it is, design and implementation, to ownership and maintenance. This first chapter will start to explain key objectives and provide the foundation for beginning your design. You should leave this chapter with a good understanding of what HFM really does, and what it doesn't do.

Then the chapter will cover key drivers to help identify what should be the goal when embarking on a project using HFM. This chapter covers the team that should be assembled. The phases of the Hyperion implementation are basically the same for any company who has successfully implemented the toolset. They are Requirements and Analysis, Planning and Design, Build, Test, Rollout, and Review. The key to having a good project will be starting the first two phases correctly, providing a strong foundation for your project. The Design part of this chapter will cover the fundamentals of the dimensions and some key considerations when designing them.

Chapter 2, "Tips for Building Your Oracle HFM Application," will cover the major components of HFM. The goal of this chapter is not to redefine what is already in the Administrator Guide, although there are some things that overlap. The goal is to explain how you might get better use from the product by making some simple updates and changes to the design. I will cover many of the tips and techniques you will need to have a great implementation. There isn't any trade secret, proprietary procedures, or magic formula to implementing a successful project. All successful consulting companies use quite similar processes and approaches. What makes a project successful is starting with a clear understanding of what it takes to own the application. Then it is important to know how to make that process of ownership easier, more controlled, and ready for your companies next big change. This chapter covers:

- Workspace
- Defining dimensions
- Starter kits
- International Financial Reporting Standards (IFRS)
- Statutory
- Classic applications
- Enterprise Performance Management Architect (EPMA)
- Calculation Manager
- Member lists
- Grids
- Web Data Entry Forms (WDEFs)
- Process management
- Phased submissions
- Intercompany eliminations
- Intercompany Transaction module
- Line Item detail
- Ownership module
- Equity Pickup Module
- Database management
- Security

Chapter 3, "Rules and Calculations," will explain the basics and fundamentals to share with every client when building an HFM application. Rules are often built with not enough client involvement, and this is a huge mistake. If you are about to begin a project with HFM, you should insist on helping to build the rules with the team. If you do not, the rules will be a mystery for you to maintain and configure later. This experience is critical, because not only will it help you decrypt any rules you have already, but it will also show you how to find errors, resolve issues, look for performance problems, and make them simple and more user-friendly.

The "Rules and Calculations" chapter is the most valuable chapter for anyone working with HFM. I will cover all the VBScript you will need to know. Next, I will give a foundation for writing rules, and cover the basics beyond what is in the Administrator Guide, from each subroutine to the common rules you should find in every application, and how best to add them to the application. I will show the new Calculation Manager, side by side with each example, so you see how the new tools arrive at the same result.

Rules are really critical to a well-performing application, so I have gathered rules from several dozen applications. What I can share from these applications is what works and what doesn't, common mistakes, and formatting. I will also clear up some common misconceptions. The biggest misconception is that writing rules is complex coding. While rules can be complex, the most difficult part of writing rules is for you to simply know where you are pulling data from and where you are writing to. Writing VBScript is not the difficult part. This will be helpful if you are new to HFM or have been writing rules for months. Finally, this chapter will cover how to troubleshoot and handle errors within the rules.

Chapter 4, "Reporting," will cover the core reporting tool, showing best practices and the tricks used to make sure reports are simple to maintain, update, and manage. Reporting is one of the things that will evolve over time at a company. Especially as you find what information you can get from a well-designed HFM application, you will want to improve your reporting. That is almost impossible to do before your first phase, since it is so difficult to visualize what the database will be like. But once that first phase is done, and your project is live, you will see many new options for reports. Unfortunately, most of the team will have moved on, and without some guidance you will struggle to build well-performing reports. This chapter will help you!

I will also show tools that often do not get to be part of the project for the first phase, but will really help you as a user extend your investment with HFM. So, this chapter will cover Charts, and also the Web Analysis tool. Two new relatively new features, Detailed Data and Related Content, are two more ways you will be able to build on this foundation HFM provides.

Not only will this chapter cover the core reporting tool, and how best to design and build reports, but it will also cover two of the newest tools and their use. These tools are Disclosure Management and Financial Close Manager. While these two tools are too new to bring a wealth of implementation experience to these pages, I will cover setup configuration and integration with the HFM product. You can, and should, set your application up in a way that ensures you are ready for these new tools.

This chapter will also cover the use of Smart View. Smart View is the Microsoft Office Add-in tool. Although most people focus on its use with

Excel, I will expand on the other tools in Office. I will show how to create board reports and other filings you might not have even thought possible.

Finally, we will cover some of the really new features like Unstructured Information and Smart Slice, the new features that demonstrate how this product will evolve and offer its users.

Chapter 5, "Data Integration and Testing," will cover the strategy, approach, and implementation for getting your data into HFM and reconciling it. Data reconciliation is, without question, one part of any project that cannot be underestimated. It always takes longer to complete than people imagine or plan for. The biggest reason is that no matter how clean you think your data really is, you will find issues. Sometimes they take a while to identify, explain, document, or just plain figure out how you want to handle the issue. More often than not, either what caused the issue is forgotten, or the people who can tell you about it have moved on. The second reason data reconciliation takes much longer than people realize is that for many of them, this will be the first time they have used a system with 12 dimensions like HFM. There is a learning curve moving from 2 dimensions to the 12 of HFM. It may take a while to even figure out where your data is in the system. The conversations about the different dimensions and how you are using them will start to sink in, as you see them in action at this point.

The core tools of how you will get data into the system are Financial Data Quality Management (FDM) and Oracle Data Integrator (ODI). This chapter will explain the differences between them, and the new tools like Enterprise Resource Planning Integrator (ERPi). ERPi integrates with Enterprise Performance Management Architect (EPMA) and works on top of ODI, and in many cases FDM as well. These chapters cannot cover every aspect of the functionality of FDM. With the growth of FDM, it could almost be a book in itself. But this chapter will discuss how the product should be used and its place as part of an HFM project.

Journals are part of the "Data Integration and Testing" chapter, as are forms and supplemental data. All of these options are manual ways of getting data into the system. I would always tell any client to be sure to minimize any manual data entry, but the reality is that it is often simply unavoidable. People often have to enter data with one of these tools.

This chapter will also cover some of the older tools, such as Hyperion Application Link (HAL) and Data Integration Manager (DIM), explaining what they are, and how to plan to move away from them; also, as you plan to move away, how to ensure that you are minimizing your risk and effort.

HFM also has tools to help get data out of the system. You can use rules to create a data extract, but this is not a decision to take lightly. There is a much maligned tool called Extended Analytics, which actually works very well. I will explain the best way to use this tool and automation of these extracts. This will cover the two main types of data you will want to extract: Elimination and Adjustment data. I will also discuss best practices for integrating with Essbase.

Finally, this chapter will discuss the testing, of which a major part is the data reconciliation. These two main parts of the testing process are Data Conversion and Data Validation. I will define these two and the subtle differences between them. I will explain how best to handle historical data, and approaches to do this. I will cover how to archive an application, and when that is appropriate.

Chapter 6, "Supporting Your Application," will take you past the rollout of your application, and cover the key tasks you need to complete to make sure you are minimizing your effort and maximizing your investment. This chapter will cover the main types of support: IT, administrator, and subadministrators. I will also explain the global support model used by large clients, often called a "Center of Excellence" or COE.

HFM has some product functionality that will play a major role in your decisions of how you will set up your support model. Tools like User Provisioning work in a certain way, so some of your decisions will be made for you, or at least made more difficult to change without this understanding.

I will cover the best approach for implementing Life Cycle Management here. While it is a relatively new tool, there is a way to roll this product out to support and augment your Change Management process.

Task Automation can be used to automate many tasks and processes. Knowing some techniques of how other people have used the product will help identify yet more ways to simplify your close and reduce the manual steps needed during the close.

Supporting your application means being able to help identify errors and what the resolution needs to be. So this chapter covers what the most common errors are, and what could be causing them. Sometimes this is not always obvious. The errors could be in the interface, or found in one of the log files. This chapter will cover the task and audit logs. This chapter will show you how to read these files and the tools you will need to read them. These log files contain incredibly valuable information about the health of your application, but it is, frankly speaking, a cryptic series of messages that are difficult to read.

This chapter would not be complete without explaining how you should be backing up your application, and the log tables you should be maintaining. I will give an overview of the tables and explain how they work to provide the data and structures. This will be important to understand the impact of common tasks like changing an entity label, or moving a structure.

Finally, this chapter will cover the essentials for upgrading your application. What you are really doing, technically and functionally? I will explain why can some people complete and upgrade in a couple of weeks and others spend months.

Chapter 7, "Tuning Your Application," will help you to take the issues you have identified, and identify others, and then resolve them. The most common issues are within the rules file; this chapter will explain how to troubleshoot the types of issues rules can create. I will also explain some of the registry keys and how they impact the core behavior within HFM. Finally, this chapter will explain the process for copying and maintaining copies of HFM applications.

Chapter 8, "Case Studies," will bring all of these chapters together with examples based on real experiences, talking frankly about what worked and didn't work with client applications. While none of these are a real client project, they are absolutely based on those experiences and what was learned during those projects. The case studies will cover shortened close, IFRS, and infrastructure issues. The case studies will also involve various sizes of companies, from 20 users to 3,000 users.

Now that you have an understanding of the flow of this book, let's get into the first and most important topic. Let's discuss what HFM is, and what it will do for you.

What Is Oracle HFM?

When I first worked with Hyperion products, I was working for a larger Boston-based insurance and finance company. The company was planning to demutualize and go public. I was a low-level administrator. We had a very well-known and popular COO who worked just a floor away. I will always remember the time after we had a team meeting with a group of high-powered, Big Four consultants, when he turned to the group of us and said, "If you can't explain your job in a sentence or less, I wonder if *you even know* what you're doing." That statement has always stuck with me.

Not long after that meeting, working very late, I found myself standing in the elevator with him alone. I smiled very politely, because I was pretty sure he had forgotten who I was. Then to break the silence, after only a couple of seconds, he introduced himself and confirmed he had absolutely no idea who I was. I knew he was going to ask. I had thought to myself, "Keep it short." I thought I was ready when he asked, "So, what is it you do here?" I smiled big and proudly said, "I work on the company's financial close software" and took a long pause. Then he said, "...and what is that?"

I wonder what I would have said then, knowing what I do now. Maybe I would say something like, "This Hyperion toolset is going to help get reporting out of this massive company that you can't even think about doing in that multimillion dollar ledger or data warehouse. It is a business-transforming tool, which will change how our subsidiaries communicate with us during the close. It is a tool that will improve our data quality, shorten our close, and lower our audit cost. This Hyperion tool will make your job easier."

Oracle Hyperion Financial Management has helped every company that I have seen implement it with better, more consistent reporting. It has improved the close, yielding better quality of data. And, with decentralizing the ownership of validation and tools like Workflow, you can significantly change the conversation during the close. This means that over time, you can change how people react to issues in the data. End users become proactive and resolve, or begin to resolve, issues before you even need to call them. This will help drive data quality, and improve the quality of work you are doing during the close.

Oracle has made the Hyperion products part of something called Fusion. Fusion is an application suite of products that forms a stack of applications that meet the needs of businesses for reporting. Some key components of the suite of products that are Oracle Fusion are the Middleware, Architecture, and Applications Unlimited.

Oracle Fusion Middleware is a wide group of products that enables and supports a business. It is a very fast and broad group, spanning everything from service-oriented architecture (SOA), portals, and process management to application infrastructure, identity management, content management, and most importantly for this book, business intelligence and Enterprise Performance Management (EPM).

Oracle Fusion Architecture is a standards-based program that defines interaction and interoperability between the applications part of the suite, including middleware and grid infrastructure technologies. As Oracle acquires companies and releases new products and new versions of others, this program ensures that they will interact and integrate as much as possible.

Oracle Applications Unlimited is the group of products that is part of the Fusion suite, but is still being supported by Oracle. This demonstrates Oracle's commitment to its clients and their investments with older products. Instead of simply "sun-setting" these older products, Oracle will continue providing enhancements to current JD Edwards Enterprise One, JD Edwards World, Oracle E-Business Suite, PeopleSoft, and Siebel product lines beyond the delivery of Oracle Fusion Applications.

Oracle Hyperion Financial Management is part of this Fusion suite of products. This means that you can expect to see more integration and expansion of the functionality through the investment Oracle is making. This integration is not only between the Hyperion products, but you will also see a tighter integration between your investments in other systems like your ERP, data warehouse, and subledger systems. This tighter integration not only reduces the cost of ownership, but also reduces integration and reconciliation steps.

HFM loads only balances from these other systems, so this integration provides a level of detail you can't get from HFM alone. You only want to load balances into HFM; it allows HFM to be more responsive and easier to update during the close. For example, allocations that take hours in a general ledger system would take minutes in HFM. In Chapter 1, we'll get into defining the purpose of your HFM application; you should know that HFM is not a transactional system.

HFM can do translation, elimination, allocation, and consolidation better than any other system I have seen. Translation means the calculations required to move an entity from its defined functional currency to the reporting currency if they are different. This includes calculations for the currency translation adjustments, and historical rates for equity accounts. You can modify the methods used for translation as well, so you can use the Current Method, which is used out of the box, or you can use a Temporal Method for hyperinflationary situations, or a modified method for management purposes. HFM is not for revaluation. Revaluation is a process for translating transactions to the functional currency. That process is best done in the ledger. And HFM integrates into that process better than ever; there is no need to burden your close process with trying to calculate detail that doesn't exist in HFM.

Eliminations in HFM can be more detailed than is possible in just about any other system. That is primarily driven by the relationship between two specific dimensions in the tool: Entity and Value. This special relationship allows people to create detail by relationship of parent and child at each consolidation point of an entity rollup. This, when combined with the powerful rules engine of HFM, makes just about any calculation possible.

Allocations can be run as part of the consolation or as a discrete process. And this is one of the places where the power of the rules engine really shows its value. When you understand where data is and when it is available, you can pull values from across the system and spread costs across periods of time or across legal entities. HFM can handle all the key types of allocations: Entity, Account, and Time Periods.

And last but not least, HFM does consolidation incredibly well. Not only does it functionally bring these data values together in a way that speeds reporting, but its integration with tools like Financial Close Manager and its auditing tools puts the natural focus on the close process and those things that make your close work better.

If you are in need of a system that can automate and make systematic many processes you are now doing manually during the close, then HFM can help you. Installing and implementing HFM are important steps to having a world-class close process.

History of Oracle HFM

The company was called IMRS, and it started in 1981. Two men, Bob Thompson and Marco Arese, launched a software company called "Micro Control." Their program was a DOS-based tool that allowed people to pull data together and create reports. It wasn't until 1991 that the Windows-based tool called Enterprise was available. In 1995, Jim Perakis decided the company needed a new name, one that would take the company in an exciting new direction, and renamed the company "Hyperion." It was about that time that Hyperion Enterprise experienced tremendous growth. There was a need to help companies automate and manage their close, and HFM filled it brilliantly.

The name Hyperion was one that the team at IMRS hoped would bring excitement and define who the company was, and where they wanted to go. Hyperion is one of the 12 Titans in ancient Greek mythology. He was one of the gods of light. It was also helpful that one of the new products had "hyper" in the name. We thought it was a much more exciting and interesting name than IMRS, or at least some important people thought so. It was also in 1995 that Hyperion Software Company became public.

In 1998, Hyperion Software merged with Arbor and the combined company was renamed Hyperion Solutions. Changing the name to Solutions was supposed to help prospective clients understand that they didn't just have one or two tools but had answers to help the company drive their business, and find solutions. EssBase is a valuable tool for reporting, and is extremely powerful. The applications of Hyperion Enterprise and Hyperion Pillar were business-focused and easy to implement. All three tools were very different, though. Each had its own security, rules, and even menu format. They could have been built and maintained by different companies.

Hyperion Solutions decided that it needed to reinvent the applications Pillar and Enterprise. Getting away from the flat-file databases each used, using open source or commonly used coding such as ASP and Java, and adding real security became priorities. The idea was for each tool to leverage Essbase. The HFM team could not do it. Planning was able to use it for at least part of the database. HFM needed to sit on top of a relational database like Oracle, or Microsoft SQL. And in 2001, Hyperion Solutions released Hyperion Financial Management.

The team at Hyperion obviously took many of the key concepts from Hyperion Enterprise. They had quite a bit to work with. The Hyperion team took years of experience from before 1991, and the numerous clients, and built a better tool. For example, take the Value dimension; this is the dimension that holds currency, adjustments, and eliminations. The names and concepts were first introduced in an add-on tool for Hyperion Enterprise called "Turbo." It was later changed to "ACE" (Advanced Consolidation Engine). The name change was partly because people who were not really in need of the statutory consolidation Turbo was built for, still insisted their application be Turbo, thinking they were making it faster.

At that time, parts of the technology were brand new for many companies, and ideas about implementation and interoperability were only theoretical. HFM's release came as one of the biggest economic meltdowns in recent memory began, as soaring tech and dot-com stocks fell at stunning rates. Finally, the release of Hyperion Financial Management was a cannibalistic product, meaning that its growth would be at the expense of growing and developing more Hyperion Enterprise business. This was a very difficult time for Hyperion and the future of this tool.

But after months of hard work by some amazing people at Hyperion Solutions, clients were getting HFM in place, and seeing it work. By 2002, Hyperion was seeing there would be references for this product. It was going to work. Planning and Essbase also became successful. One of the biggest drivers of this success was the fact that these products were *source data–agnostic*. It didn't matter at all where the data came from, and it still doesn't. If you can get data out of a system, these tools could load it, aggregate it, and report it. Even companies with strong preferences for SAP or Oracle found themselves deciding that Hyperion would be the reporting tool for this reason. There was no assurance that it would be easy to integrate a non-SAP system, or an in-house custom-built system, but with Hyperion, it just was not an issue.

But the products were still separate; they had separate security, rules, structures, and databases. Even the web interface was using different technology. HFM opted for Visual Basic and ASP pages. Planning was using JSP for its web interface. Hyperion's competition was all too eager to point this out. You would have to have multiple administrators, support structures, and technologies.

Hyperion was quick to point out that each tool had a specific job, and each did it very well. Still the development team at Hyperion worked to bring these tools together. First the front end was updated, creating a common logon and navigation page, common data-loading tool, and expending reporting from one repository of reports across all tools. Second, they updated the back end, creating one tool for managing security, metadata, and task automation. Finally, the tool was able to deliver on its promise. One set of centralized databases, in sync and interrelated, managed from one set of tools, but each flexible to be built for its own purpose. World-class consolidation, planning, and management reporting could be done from a number of combinations of the suite of products, and they could scale as the company or need changed. All of this was to be done without throwing away work and investment that had already been made in the Hyperion products.

Hyperion Solutions made a series of acquisitions that strengthened the offering. In 2003, right after the acquisition of Crystal Reporting by Business Objects, Hyperion Solutions acquired Brio Technology. The BI tools expanded what was possible for the Hyperion team. In 2005, Hyperion acquired long-time Hyperion partner Razza Solutions and renamed their core product Master Data Management (MDM). This would help Hyperion integrate the management and administration of the tools as part of a common foundation they would all use. And in 2006, Hyperion acquired another long-standing partner, Upstream, and renamed their WebLink tool Financial Data Quality Management. The data integration tool that was built on concepts from and for Hyperion Enterprise was to be the key part of a new set of data integration tools for the Hyperion platform. In 2007, Hyperion acquired Decisioneering and incorporated their Crystal Ball software into the reporting suite. The offering had really grown, and they had the customer base to show for it.

On Thursday, March 1, 2007, Oracle Solutions announced they would acquire Hyperion Solutions for 3.3 billion USD. One of the most intriguing parts of this acquisition is that it opened the door of so many SAP-platform-based companies to Oracle software. The ability to be indifferent to what source system you were getting data from was a key driver of value.

Why Use a Consolidation Tool?

Why did so many companies with all these different powerful ERP systems and ledgers need a consolidation tool? Companies that spent millions on data warehouses found the reporting from these systems wanting, and needed a better solution. The obvious answer is that HFM is built for consolidations. It is ready to do basic work on day one.

Companies face challenges now as at no other time in the history of business. Globalization has opened markets, but brought with these new markets varied and ever-changing reporting standards. Scandals, fraud, and cheating have brought more scrutiny to financial statements. Complex securities and tighter lending have made banking in this new economy difficult. On the horizon, new standards like the International Financial Reporting Standards (IFRS) and eXtensible Business Reporting Language (XBRL) offer new challenges and issues to overcome. The truth is that if you are using an Excel spreadsheet, you are taking on risk to your company. That risk far exceeds the cost of implementing and maintaining a system like Hyperion Financial Management.

So besides risk, what are the other reasons to use a consolidation tool? A well-designed and implemented consolidation tool is invaluable to the close. Really, even one that isn't implemented well will help tremendously. HFM does this by having more of the people who are responsible for providing the data work collaboratively to bring the disparate systems within a company together. Take intercompany reconciliation, for example. The fact that HFM has an out-of-the-box report that allows users to view not only the accounts they have going out, but what other people in other legal entities have booked against those amounts, helps the people who are booking those transactions to be proactive. It helps them to work around the clock to improve data quality. But HFM also helps you with things that create reporting issues every day for companies.

Financial Restatements and Reorganizations

HFM with its flexible dimensionality allows for simple and complex changes to the entity structure. You can load the data one time and have consolidation as many ways as you need with different structures and parents. HFM also has a feature that allows for data to consolidate within the same organization differently by period. This is called Organization by Period. The ability of the rules to recognize the different structures, and parent, and values within system accounts, allows HFM to consolidate in a variety of ways. Each parent-child relationship allows for separate storage of elimination and proportional data. Also consider that each entity has four separate places where journals can be posted to the system, including parent members. This creates an opportunity to handle anything that may come up as your reporting structure changes.

Accountability

The power of the relational database allows for the ability to record all kinds of detail about how the system is used. There are audit logs that record how the data changes and who is making those changes. You can also see key tasks your users are doing and when. This not only helps with managing the support of the application, but acts to prevent people from doing tasks that they should not be doing. The security in HFM is advanced, especially compared with older tools like SAP's BPC, Hyperion Enterprise, and tools where security is nonexistent, like Microsoft Excel. HFM records date and time stamps, records the user IDs used, and authenticates the users with a variety of commonly used network security databases. These combinations ensure that the system is secure and your data is safe.

Inconsistent Disparate Structures

Consider a company that over just a couple of years has acquired and merged in a series of business transactions. The chart of accounts of each of these source systems would be different, and you might expect them to be that way. Even companies that work in the same business might have very different accounts and naming conventions. How do you bring together all these systems into one common chart of accounts? HFM has an answer, and it provides auditable and secure source for all of your data.

Mergers and Acquisitions

The Hyperion toolset, when configured properly, allows for the quick and complete integration of other companies' financial data for consolidation. As part of the toolset, FDM allows for feeding of data from any system into HFM. A full trial balance from a merger can take as little as hours to get loaded and fed into HFM. The feed can be traced back to transactional levels of detail and show the mapping used, and how the mapping might have changed from one period to another. Finally, you can add fairly complex validations on your data feed to ensure that the trial balance meets some basic test for completeness.

IFRS: Changing Disclosure Requirements

The new reporting standards have continued to evolve. It is much more common now to see multiple GAAP applications. There have been statutory applications within HFM for years. HFM is not just a US GAAP tool. But as companies try to manage the transition from local GAAP to IFRS, more people are looking to bring these standards into a system that will help reconcile and report on the differences. Tools with limited dimensions, and even more limited consolidation rules, cannot handle these changing requirements. It is becoming more common to see applications that can handle both US GAAP and IFRS in the same application. While you may or may not go this route, tools like HFM give you the option. This type of reporting is a powerful option. In five or ten years, the winds of change will blow through again. When they do, HFM will help ensure that you are ready.

Speak Better to Your Data

For years, companies' consolidation and reporting groups have viewed themselves as the central place where all consolidation work needs to take place, and in doing so, created a huge bottleneck to the close process. Whenever there is an issue, they needed to get on the phone and work to get the sites providing the data to help them fix issues that, frankly, they should be able to fix themselves. Pushing these types of responsibilities out to the sites actually reduces work for the consolidation and reporting groups in the long run, as they are able to take a more proactive approach to resolving issues. And because they are the first to respond, they can better manage the response. They just don't have the corporate group calling them at the last minute with a bunch of "critical" issues.

Simple benefits like being able to programmatically or systematically handle something as mundane as rounding allows people on your team to do things like analyze differences, and not spend their time making sure every report foots, and each report reconciles to each other.

Data quality improves over time as system validations and issues are reduced. This improves the ability to really see what is happening in the business, and make much better decisions.

Operational Data

Better validations allow for many types of data to come together and ensure that they reconcile to each other when brought into the system. That is true for anything you could bring in, but is often done at a minimum for manual data. Text and document attachment allow Oracle Hyperion Financial Management to become the "electronic binder" for all your financial-close–related documents. When HFM is used with Financial Close Manager, you have a central repository for all of your close activities and data in one place.

Costs: Rising Audit Fees

Oracle Hyperion Financial Management and its integration with the other systems in the suite provide a system that is easier to audit, as it is one place to find all your data. This improves your transparency without sacrificing any security.

The ability of HFM to provide basic reporting for journals and intercompany data make the system much faster to audit and to understand. Items like the cash flow statements are stores and validated with the trial balance for the period and kept safely in HFM.

With HFM, you can reduce and replace manual control procedures with automated and preventive controls that ultimately reduce your processing and auditing costs. This includes tasks like eliminations and allocations, to common or repetitive validations within the system.

You Are Ready to Begin

I've covered the history of HFM and defined it. I've also laid out the critical parts of a project, and aligned them with the chapters that are to follow. With this knowledge, you are ready to begin the journey to starting your project. That project may be a new set of reports, adding a cash flow, or a full implementation—so, let's get started.

CHAPTER 1

Designing Your Oracle HFM Application

fter hours of sales demonstrations and information about the products, you are ready to start implementing Oracle Hyperion Financial Management (HFM). The work may seem a bit overwhelming at first, but this chapter will help. In this chapter, we will cover the basics of the full suite of products, implementation strategy, identifying your internal team and consultation partner, what a good timeline would look like, and—most critical—designing the HFM application. A good foundation built during the design ensures success. With these tools you should be ready to take on implementing HFM.

Enterprise Performance Management

Enterprise Performance Management (EPM) is a set of analytic processes and tools that allow a business to identify, track, measure, and achieve goals. Within the EPM group there are several domains. Each domain focuses on a key business process or function. The Oracle tools focus on the most common EPM domains, which include:

- Planning and Forecasting
- Financial Management
- Strategy Formulation
- Supply Chain Effectiveness

The tools Oracle offers are a full suite of products that focus on each process individually or in concert, and they provide the capabilities that management needs to meet its goals. HFM is part of this suite of tools.

The Oracle EPM Suite Overview

Several products make up the Oracle Enterprise Performance Management (EPM) suite. At the core of the suite are three products: Oracle Hyperion Financial Management, Essbase, and Planning. Each product, while designed and built for each of the key EPM domains, also works in concert to integrate the entire process. For example, Financial Management is exceptional for computing complex currency translations, allocations, eliminations, and consolidations. Planning is built for driver-based planning, and managing multiple scenarios such as forecasting and financial business modeling. Essbase is a powerful analytic tool that can handle large volumes of data.

As you can see in Figure 1-1, each core product fills a role between the web tier and the foundation. This is not to say that there is no overlap between these tools. I have seen Essbase applications that include consolidation and elimination. I have worked with HFM applications that have planning, budgeting, and forecasting functionality built into them. However, each product is exceptional for its own focused task.

The three core products all sit on top of the Oracle Foundation. Figure 1-2 shows all of the services included in the Foundation. The core parts I am going to discuss are

- **Oracle Hyperion Shared Services** Shared Services provides a central location to manage user provisioning, lifecycle management, and task flow management for all EPM System products. Also Shared Services includes the Shared Services Registry, which is a central repository that stores and reuses information for most EPM system products installed.
- **Enterprise Performance Management Architect (EPMA)** EPMA allows creating, maintaining, and synchronizing the core applications through a graphical user interface. Enterprise Performance Management Architect works with: Calculation Manager, Planning, Financial Management, Essbase, Profitability, and Cost Management.

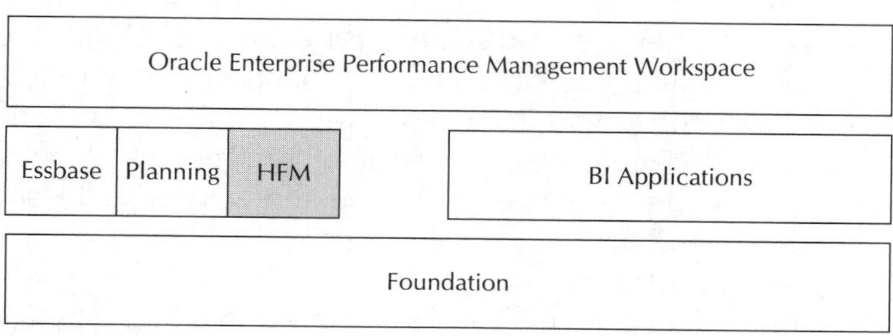

FIGURE 1-1. *The full EPM suite*

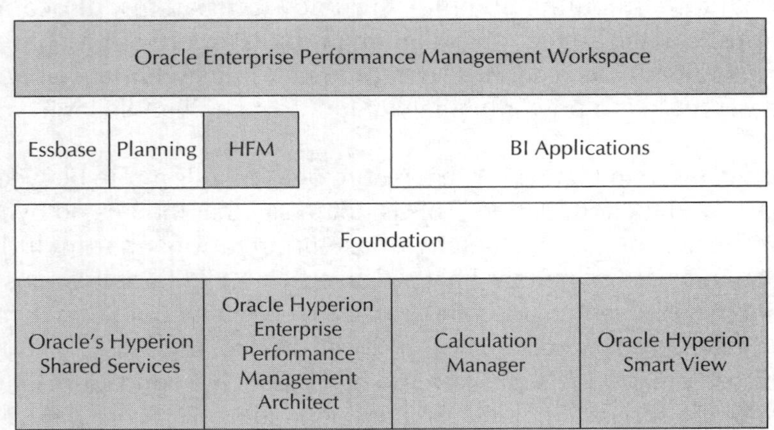

FIGURE 1-2. *The Foundation Services*

- **Calculation Manager** Calculation Manager allows administrators to design, validate, and administer rules in a graphical environment for the core products.
- **Oracle Hyperion Smart View for Office** Smart View provides a common Microsoft Office add-in for Essbase, Financial Management, Planning, and Reporting and Analysis. It can also perform ad-hoc analysis on data from Oracle Business Intelligence Enterprise Edition (BI EE). One of the most underrated features of Smart View is that it is for more than just Excel. Smart View works with Word, PowerPoint, Outlook, and Excel.

You interact with the system primarily through the web. Since there is no local application installed, you can roll the products out to more users. This is just one more way the toolset is able to scale. The primary page users interact with is Oracle Enterprise Performance Management Workspace. The Workspace provides a single place to find and work with the suite of products in a single, multitabbed user interface.

There are newer tools that focus on very specific tasks. For example, the tool Disclosure Management provides an integrated tool for eXtensible Business Reporting Language (XBRL) reporting. Financial Close Manager provides a tool to manage, communicate, and track the entire close process. Financial Close Manager will soon help drive account reconciliation.

The final component to the EPM suite is the financial reporting. There are several tools for reporting, and each one helps serve a purpose. Financial reports work very well for external reporting. Web Analysis, Oracle Business Intelligence Publisher, and Oracle BI EE work best for dashboard reporting.

Define the Scope

Once you have decided what products you will implement, you need to define the scope of the build. The scope is important to determine what you build and when. There are a couple of steps to defining the scope. The first step is to define the critical success factors, or the main purpose of your project. Since each product does something specifically, you should focus on that goal for the project. For example, if you are preparing for an HFM project, you should be focusing on financial consolidations and external financial reporting. You may find you have the bandwidth for adding some budget collection, or management reporting, but your primary focus should be consolidations. This seems obvious, but many people find themselves trying to sell a project internally or trying to make sure they are maximizing the return on this investment. In HFM, people have all kinds of things you would not think of including in a consolidation system. And a lot of them were good ideas. For example, some things that seem like good ideas are unit information, or inventory details. It might be a good thing to add something like this, but you increase your chances for success by tackling that additional piece in a second phase. Successful attempts at being creative to expand value, more often than not, happen after the main consolidation project is completed.

The second step to defining scope is to focus on the core products. If you have purchased more than one product of the EPM suite, you will need to prioritize your implementation. To focus on what products you will be implementing and when, look at your financial calendar and consider what parts to implement during the year. If the budget is due in six weeks, you may be aggressive, thinking you can get Planning in place first. It is a sizable undertaking trying to implement the full EPM suite all at once. Each product not only has its own design considerations, but often impacts different parts of a company very differently. Consider stepping back, consider what products you will be using both tactically and strategically, and plan how you will put these tools into place.

Finally, you need to define your time line. The time you have to implement should help you prioritize what you can accomplish during the implementation. So, if your time line allows, and you have the appetite for having a large project, you could implement the full suite all at once. I would not recommend it. Many people will think that because you expect some economies of having several projects of the same products set, same users, you can save on things like project management. But the risk of having so many tasks, teams, and changes all moving at once outweighs the benefits.

EPM and EPI

One common mistake people make is failing to understand what it means to design an HFM application. It does not mean to re-evaluate the entire business process. Reviewing and redefining the business processes around HFM is expensive and time-consuming, and not required in order to have a good build and a successful project.

HFM is an EPM tool. That tool has functionality that drives how certain processes will function. Using them for other purposes or not as intended creates issues. Using any tool for a purpose it was not intended always leads to some shortcoming. Unless the tool is meeting some very short-term need, why set yourself up for frustration?

EPI, or Enterprise Process Improvement, is not about a tool. It is not even technology-centric. This is an open evaluation of what you do, why, and how you can do it better. This can be a process that takes years, built in stages as the company grows.

While it is important to understand the current business process, and consider what that future state might look like, the future process does not impact as many of the design considerations as you might think. A good design will allow for future requirements. For example, if I asked a hundred corporate controllers to explain the impact of International Financial Reporting Standards (IFRS) on their business in 2003, I doubt I would have gotten one certain answer. Still, applications that were designed well even before that time will be able to accommodate IFRS.

Consider the effort of evaluating and reviewing every process that impacts the close. If you were going to do that, you could also re-evaluate the reports used and the metrics used to measure the business, and consider reorganizing the business. If you use that logic, the scope can easily expand beyond what is really needed to complete a successful project. The building of an HFM application is best handled as a discrete step of a business process evaluation and change effort. Remember, this tool is built to do financial consolidations. And while many business process changes may be things worth doing, they are not required in order to create an HFM application. That is true even for an application that will be used to do all of those transformative goals you may have. A good requirements and design meeting should only discuss those items, so the design team can confirm that the design considers the impact of those changes.

Identify Your Team

Once you have decided on a product implementation strategy, and considered the scope, you need to assemble a team to help implement HFM. There are some key roles you need to fill if you want to be successful. I would group them as internal and external.

The Internal Team

There are four internal roles: Subject Matter Experts (SMEs), an Application Administrator, Infrastructure Support, and a Project Manager. Having these three roles defined internally doesn't guarantee success, but in every implementation that had issues, these roles were not defined. It is also important to define these roles because they will be required to support the application after you go live.

First, a good team will consist of people who understand the business process and are very familiar with the politics and procedures of the business. You will need people who understand the accounting required, including tax, treasury, management reporting, and especially consolidation accounting. These people are Subject Matter Experts. These SMEs should have some minimum time commitment to the project. These people are important to the project because they will help with data reconciliation, training, and support of the application after go-live. When trying to staff the project, this is one role that people often look to staff by hiring temporary resources. I can tell you, no temporary person you hire will know your business and accounting better than the people in your organization. So your project will suffer if you try to hire temporary resources for this role.

And in the unlikely chance you are successful, when the project is over, the people who learned this new system will leave and take this knowledge with them. So, you should look within your organization for these people.

Second, you need to identify an application administrator. This selection is extremely critical to the success of the project. Many projects have overcome seemingly insurmountable obstacles because of strong, bright administrators, and just as many have struggled to get footing within a company because of distracted or overworked administrators. The best people to select as administrators are people with a finance background. Although HFM uses Visual Basic in spots and has scripting, HFM is not a tool used by the infrastructure groups. It is a finance tool. It is much easier to teach a finance person the technical components of HFM than it is to teach an IT programmer the workings of debits and credits. A person with moderate skills in writing a macro in Excel will have all the scripting skills required to administer HFM. This person will own the bulk of the maintenance after the project goes live. They will be critical in maintaining and supporting the application after you have gone live. This role could be broken out by product or by database. The administrators are usually also responsible for data integration as well. It would be wise to plan for having a backup. I would expect this person to spend between one and two weeks per month supporting the application after the implementation is complete.

The administrator should work closely with the IT support team. While the role is not as dedicated as the other roles, the tasks and timing of the infrastructure tasks are very important. The Oracle EPM toolset is complex and has a steep learning curve.

Finally, every successful project has a strong project manager. It is the role of the project manager to communicate risks, track tasks to the budget, and control scope. For some reason, people seem to discount the value this role has in a project. A strong experienced person in this role brings experience about this toolset to the process. Implementing HFM, or for that matter any of the Hyperion tools, is not like working with any other IT project. It is not an enterprise resource planning (ERP) tool, or a custom tool. The Hyperion tools often cross over departments and roles and are wide-reaching. The process for implementing HFM needs to reflect that. You should not make the mistake of underestimating the value of good communication, thoughtful planning, and strong project management. To be successful, the thing to do first is have a plan, and then make sure you are communicating effectively and identifying the impact of the process. These are all things that good project leadership and project management bring to your project.

Your Implementation Partner

The next step is to identify an implementation partner. This part of your team will be easier to find. There are companies who will buy HFM that are lucky enough to have found a person who has consulting experience, or at a minimum has been on several projects and can bring that experience to the team. If your company is not one of those companies, I would suggest having an implementation partner that will give you the best chance of completing the project on time and as close to your intended budget as possible. Besides experience, a strong consulting partner has a network of resources, either internally or across the HFM community, that they can reference to get answers to problems when they come up. I would suggest you look for some key factors when selecting your partner. First, are they certified in HFM? There are several Oracle certifications for different products; it does not help to know Essbase for an HFM project. Second, how many projects has the lead resource worked on? Finally, call their references. You will get some great feedback, hear about pitfalls you won't hear about in a sales cycle, and start to build your own support network for after the project go-live.

Most companies that use HFM are publicly traded, and as such are subject to stringent regulations and reporting deadlines. Look for a partner that can provide a system architecture design that can withstand a single failure of any of the individual components ("redundant services"), or failure of an entire service center (disaster recovery planning).

Do not overlook the value Oracle brings to every project. You need to learn to navigate Oracle support and become familiar with how to get issues logged, tracked, and supported. Not only will this be your lifeline after the project goes live, but it is part of the maintenance you pay for with the product, and you should take advantage of it.

Support from the Infrastructure Group

How much infrastructure support people need to plan for is a very common concern. Especially if you are migrating to HFM from a consolidation and reporting tool like Hyperion Enterprise or Excel, where IT support was minimal or none, you will not be sure what type and commitment of resources you need to plan for. During the project, the times when it is critical to have IT support are: installation, security, testing, training support, and go-live. Now each project is different, but each of those phases typically does not require more than a week or two. If you decide to take on more complex security like Secure Sockets Layer (SSL) at every layer, and use a tool like Hewlett-Packard Load Runner to simulate load on the servers, the times can go much higher. Once you are live, the time needed to support HFM drops off significantly for most all clients. If you are live with HFM and the application is average in size and you have a full-time IT resource supporting your HFM application, then something is very wrong. Most people plan for support to add users, support the change control process, and help with connectivity issues. Many routine tasks can and should be automated. A strong implementation partner will help you set those up.

Create a Project Plan

Once you decide which products you will be implementing, and have pulled together your team, you need to make a plan. Most full implementations of HFM take between five and eight months. During the first month, you establish your requirements and design. The installation, administrator training, and a change control process meeting should also happen during the first month. The second and third month will be focused on build activities. If you are not certain about your design, you can plan for a conference room demonstration or proof of concept. During this time the team will develop rules, create structures (often called metadata), and build reports.

Data should be loaded into HFM as soon as possible. It is important to load data early for two reasons. First, a representative set of data will help the development team determine performance and identify issues during the build. Second, it will help with determining performance issues early in the project.

Once the build has begun, this phase of a project is heavy with data reconciliation. Data reconciliation is very time-consuming, and is the one part of any implantation that cannot be underestimated. The reason this task is so difficult to manage is that, for many users, it is the first time they are working with the software, looking for data, and getting their head around how HFM will calculate the elimination, allocations, and other numbers. This may be the first time the team or users will see data using the 12 dimensions. That learning curve for working with multiple dimensions can take people time to overcome. The second reason data reconciliation can take longer than you would expect is that it is frankly not glamorous work. It can be very tedious. Some people find themselves easily distracted doing data reconciliation. That slows down the work quite a bit.

Once data has been loaded and is being reconciled, then technical testing can start. It is true that data reconciliation is by its nature a test. But you will need to do some other testing to make sure your system is performing well. You need to load data to ensure that you have valid tests. The data does not have to be final or complete, but it should be representative of what the actual data will be once it's complete. You should plan to test when it will not impact data reconciliation, or when data reconciliation will not skew testing results. The length of time required for testing can vary. There are several types of testing:

- **Unit testing** This type of testing is usually not documented, but is required to ensure that each build step is being completed.
- **Integration (functional) testing** This test is a set of common tasks to ensure that each component when brought together works in one application.
- **Performance testing** This testing is at a minimum a baseline of basic tasks on the production server. At best, this test is a full complement of tests simulating activity from remote sites using a tool like Load Runner.
- **User Acceptance Testing (UAT)** This test is either performed by a subset of power users or as a review of training.
- **Connectivity testing** This test is the final test, ensuring that users can access the system by opening the application site in a browser, and security is in place.

After the application has completed testing, the rollout begins. The rollout is the process for getting users to adopt the system. And to have the users ready to take this ownership, you need to train them. This training will happen before UAT or connectivity testing. Training is often completed for administrators early in the project, close to the design meeting. So the best practice is for end users to be trained as close to the UAT as possible. It is best to have users touch the software as close to the training as possible to reinforce what was learned. This makes the UAT much more efficient. Users have an expectation based on training performance, and can use that to make sure the system is working as expected.

There are many kinds of training, enough that one might fill an entire book on that subject alone. The first consideration you need to make is the groups of people who need training. There is the small group of your core team, and these people need to go to administrator training. This needs to happen either before or after the design. If your project has these people intimately involved, they will be trained during the whole implementation. If not, you will need a deep and thorough training for administrators and a developed plan to transfer ownership.

The second type of training is for your end users. There are couple of options here. The most common are

- **Classroom** Have your users come in for a set class. The biggest benefit is that you control the environment. This works great—people are not distracted or getting pulled from training. This option also can cost the most, especially if people are really spread out geographically.

- **The Road Show** Visit each site with a set training program. Creating multiple teams to visit each group helps defray the costs.

- **Train the Trainer** Have a set of super-users train your team. The benefit here is that training knowledge stays in house and the trainers can transition into a support role for your team after the project is live.

The next step is a simulation of the close using HFM. It is called a *parallel*. I would never recommend fewer than two parallels. Users will need that much time to ensure that they can confidently repeat the close in a reliable way. I would also never recommend more than four parallels. Having too many of these simulations creates quite a bit of fatigue within

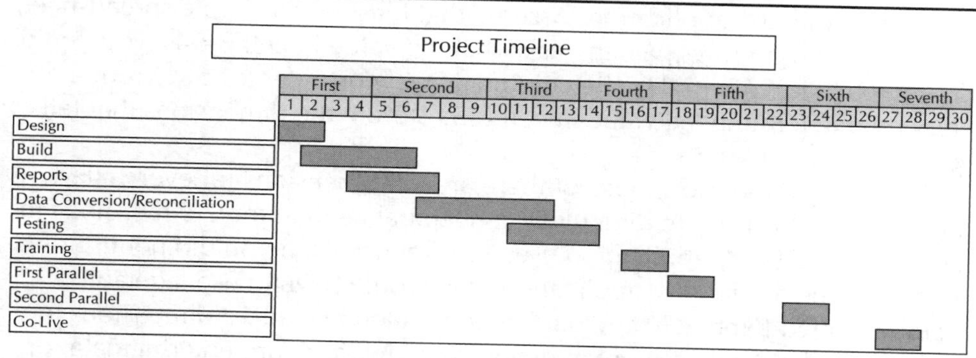

FIGURE 1-3. *A sample HFM project timeline*

the user community. Remember, they have to close the books in two or more systems when these final steps are being completed. It can create quite a bit more work than people realize. You want to have at least one of these parallels happen when you are doing a quarter close and preferably a year-end close, if your process changes at all during these times. Since most people do have processes that are done only during quarter close time, they will include one quarter. You should too. You should also choose a month where the work load is not as high to stop using the old system, and just use this new tool going forward. This is called "go-live."

Although the build is less than a third of the entire build time, looking at Figure 1-3, it is easy to see that the build is the busiest time. You have more going on at that time than during the other project phases.

Dimension Overview

The purpose of this chapter is to discuss topics you would cover during your design meeting. This section should be used to complement the Administrator Guide, not replace it.

You must understand what a dimension is and how they work in order to move forward with a design. Dimensions are the objects we use in HFM to define coordinates within the database. These dimensions define where data is stored within the application. Assume that I just had a simple spreadsheet, with columns and rows. When I ask what the value in cell B-9 is, you could determine that B referred to the column and 9 must refer to row. From that you could determine the value in cell B-9. B-9 are the dimensions that tell you where to find the data.

HFM uses dimensions, except there are 12 dimensions for every HFM application. This is more difficult to conceptualize than the 2 dimensions in a spreadsheet. Every application uses 12 dimensions. If you did not use one of the dimensions in your application, you would have to use a default member called [None]. You would need to reference all 12 dimensions to find data in the database, which includes writing a report, entering data, or writing a rule.

To envision the impact of more dimensions, let's take it up a notch; now picture tabs for the spreadsheet. Now picture multiple spreadsheets all grouped in a folder on your computer. To find a number you need to look at one workbook, tab 3, column C, and row 13. Finding your data in HFM isn't much different than that.

It is important to remember that you must consider all 12 dimensions when designing your application. Many people initially think they will be making the application much easier to use when setting the dimensions up by not using one dimension and trying to make two different dimensions fit into one. It is best to think about what are the slices of data you need to define for your reports, then align them with dimensions and logically lay out how they should align within HFM. If you need to use all 12, then by all means, do not feel restricted.

And scope is still important here. It is important to not try to build for every eventuality. You can't plan for every possible change in reporting, so just focus on the reporting and goals you defined at the beginning of the project.

The 12 dimensions used in HFM are

- **View** The View dimension provides calendar intelligence; for example, Month-to-Date, Year-to-Date, and Quarter-to-Date frequencies. This dimension was formerly referred to as Frequency.
- **Year** The number of years you will use for HFM. The Year dimension provides multiple years of a fiscal or calendar year.
- **Period** The Period dimension provides time periods, such as quarters and months. For example, if you need months, there would be 12 periods of data available for a given scenario in a year.

- **Scenario** The Scenario dimension represents a set of data, such as Budget, Actual, or Forecast. For example, the Actual scenario can contain data from a general ledger, reflecting past and current business operations.
- **Entity** The Entity dimension provides a means to build structures for the consolidation. These can be divisions, subsidiaries, plants, regions, countries, legal entities, business units, departments, or any organizational unit.
- **Value** The Value dimension allows for consolidation, elimination, and adjustments and supports translation, which can include the input currency and parent currency.
- **Account** The Account dimension allows you to build a hierarchy of assets, liabilities, revenue, expense, and so on. Each type of account has a specific behavior.
- **Intercompany Partner (ICP)** The Intercompany dimension represents all intercompany balances that exist for an account. This dimension is built dynamically from the Entity dimension.
- **Custom1, Custom2, Custom3, Custom4** The Custom dimensions provide the ability to store other views of the data, such as products, markets, channels, cash flow changes, balance sheet movement, source of data, or types of elimination.

You will also have to define application settings and aliases to build an application; however, they are not dimensions. All of these dimensions are often referred to as the *metadata*. Metadata is a term used to describe data values that define other data. Technically speaking, the dimensions are all data elements that define data within the HFM application. People often use these terms interchangeably when discussing HFM structures.

Now that you know the dimensions, let's understand how they are built within the application. All of the dimensions are built such that each has its own hierarchy. The hierarchy is a "tree" structure where each member has a relationship with other members. The lowest level of this tree structure is called "leaves," like the leaves on a tree. They are also called "base" members, if you want to think of them as the bottom bricks of a pyramid.

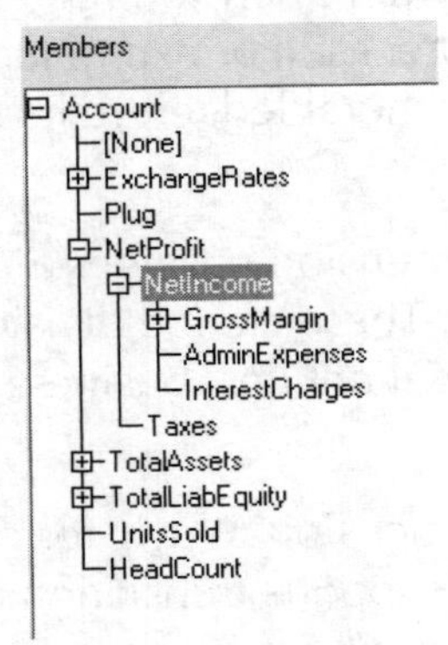

FIGURE 1-4. *A dimension hierarchy*

The tree in Figure 1-4 shows an example of an account hierarchy. The members have "relative" relationships. Some of the obvious ones are "parent" and "child." As in the example shown in Figure 1-4, the child (Net Income) is below the parent (Net Profit.) The child is below a parent. A parent member can have several children. Two children with the same parent are called siblings. Another relationship used is descendants; those are all members below some parent, including children of children. These relationships are one way the tool creates dynamic lists and allows for drilling from one member to another.

Data is entered into base-level members of the dimensions, not into parent members, with very few exceptions. For example, data isn't actually stored for parent account members in HFM. The values for parent accounts are aggregated from their children when the data is brought into memory.

Naming Convention

So you are ready to start adding members to your application metadata. You should give some thought as to what to call them, as it could really save you some time and headaches later. When choosing a naming convention for metadata, I actually have a strong preference about this topic that I bring to every design session. Identify the most common or largest source of data for your chart of accounts, and use that for all base members. This does several things. It simplifies the mapping because you can use the "=" which, simply put, means everything in that dimension maps to everything with the same name. That is only one line of mapping, meaning there is less work that Financial Data Quality Management (FDM) or Oracle Data Integrator (ODI) needs to do to map data values. Even if it isn't your only line of mapping, your mapping work will be much less. Second, this makes it much easier on you and your end users to reconcile. It is much simpler to see an account A7000, and know that it is the same account and means the same thing in HFM as it does in the ledger. Third, a commonly used structure like what is used in the main ledger is typically the largest source of data and is something your users are already familiar with. This familiarity will speed the adoption of HFM within the company. The structures and dimensionality will be something familiar to the end users.

I would also recommend strongly following the Administrator Guide's supported characters. Even when an unsupported character seems to work now, it does not mean that it will still work after an upgrade or patch. Special characters like ampersand (&) can cause problems that are tough to identify early on in a project build. That is why they are unsupported.

Finally, while this will be tough to do if you have never implemented HFM before, you should think about what names will help you while writing rules. People often use prefixes like "CF" for cash flow accounts to help them identify which accounts would be used for the cash flow in a list of all accounts. And while I am on this topic, never use a space in any label. It will make troubleshooting a misspelled label in a rule almost impossible. You can't see the difference in a text file between "Net_Income" and "Net_Income ". (The second one has a space right at the end, and you would never see that in a file.)

You should be consistent when labeling. This will help people follow the system and will speed adoption. Be careful about making the labels too long, though. Remember, you will have to write out some of these names, and the longer they are, the more difficult that will be.

Underscores are supported, and should be used if they help readability. I have found that proper case will do that more often than not, but it is nice to have the option.

Application Profile

When you are ready to create your application and build hierarchies, you need to create a shell for the members to load into. If you are building these members in a Classic application, you will be using the desktop application. If you plan to build these using EPMA, then you should identify only common members to use from the master library, and build other parts separately.

When first defining your application, you need to define some parameters that cannot be changed unless you rebuild the application. You should not plan to rebuild the application for some time, so you should consider something that you can live with. That does not mean you need to plan to live with this forever. There are times when a rebuild makes sense. This book will cover those cases in the support section, but just know these are not parameters you will be updating and changing without some effort. They are Aliases (Formerly Languages), Calendars, View, and Period.

Aliases (Formerly Languages)

Let's discuss aliases first. An *alias* is a set of descriptions, typically by language. These can also be as subtle as the difference between tax and corporate reporting. You can specify up to ten aliases for all of the descriptions within HFM. One of your aliases needs to be English. You can't have an HFM application without English. This should not be confused with localization. *Localization* refers to the language used in the menus and toolbars within the application. The Languages refer directly to the descriptions you would modify for all of your metadata and dimensions. Figure 1-5 shows how you might set that up.

Languages don't have to be an actual language, though. I have worked with applications that have used tax labels for state insurance filing as a language in HFM. They could then report from the same chart of accounts both Securities and Exchange Commission (SEC) and state statutory reports with descriptions.

These languages should not be confused with localization. This is the ability to have the menus in Workspace, HFM, and Smart View appear in different languages. These are determined by demand at Oracle. The localization team fills in strings for each menu item with the appropriate

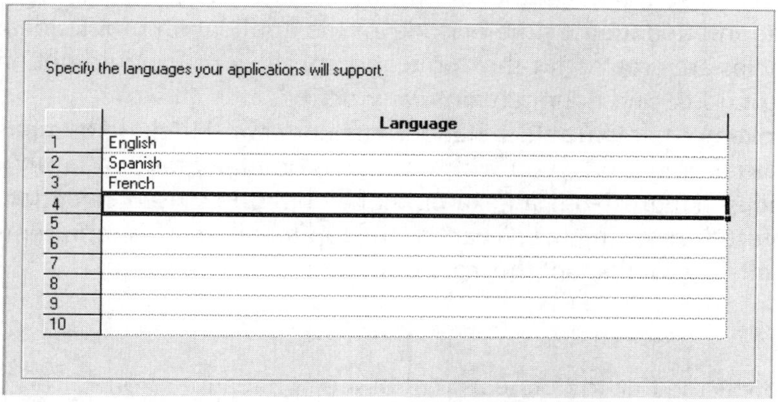

FIGURE 1-5. *Adding languages*

translated term for each of the required languages (Spanish, French, Italian, German, Russian, and so on). These strings are made part of the code so that even the release after a localized release, which should only be US English, still has those strings in the code. The strings are surfaced automatically in the browser—there is a code detection that reads the browser's default language and displays the strings if they are available; otherwise, they display US English. During localization, the product documentation and help guides are also translated.

Experiment with this yourself by adding German, Spanish, or French into your Internet Explorer browser. Go to Internet Options; General; Languages (at the bottom) and add a language (let's say French). Move the new language to the first position and it will become the default. Restart your browser, and then connect to Workspace; you will see the menus in the chosen language if it is one that Hyperion has localized into. For example, French would appear in menus that normally are in English.

Calendars

Next you must define the fiscal calendar. You are given three choices for these to get started: Standard, Custom, and Manually Defined. You can modify any of these when you see them, so I have always found that using the Standard calendar gives a great starting point. You can then modify the names and descriptions of the months here. After you select the type of calendar and update the time periods for the application profile, default frequencies are created for the application profile. You should not have weekly periods, and definitely not daily periods.

For example, if you select Standard calendar and include quarters and months as time periods, you will see yearly, quarterly, and monthly frequencies. Figure 1-6 is an example of a commonly used calendar. Don't get confused by seeing the "Year" as the top member. This represents the sum of all 12 months, not the Year dimension.

View

The View is the first to define as part of the application profile. The View dimension provides calendar intelligence. That means HFM will provide values for the view selected. The most common are Periodic, Year-to-Date, and Quarter-to-Date frequencies. If you set the view to Periodic, the values for each month change are displayed. If you set the view to Year-to-Date, the cumulative values for the year are displayed.

You will have to choose both a label and description for the View members you create. As with many of the dimensions, I would recommend something that could be used in your reports for each. For example, I always use the common abbreviation (MTD, QTD, and YTD) for the label, and the longer description (Year-to-Date, Periodic) for the descriptions. Both are helpful and could be shown in reports.

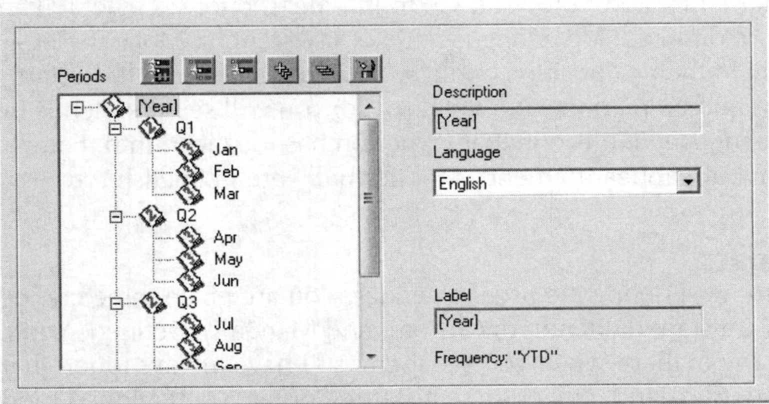

FIGURE 1-6. *A sample calendar*

For each frequency, you can enter a label and description for each language that you previously defined. When editing frequencies, you cannot change the label of the YTD frequency, but you can update the description. It is possible to use more relevant descriptions if they make sense for your business, like "Spring" and "Fall" for a retail company. You should consider what you need in your reports to decide this. There are two system-defined frequencies and corresponding views, Scenario View and Periodic. If you had chosen a Manually Defined Calendar as the time period for the calendar, the Frequencies grid would be empty, and you must update the frequencies. You should enter one frequency for each level of the Period dimension, as shown in the example in Figure 1-7.

Year

The Year dimension seems to spark the most discussion. It is pretty simple; you need only a start year and life of the application. So, it should be a short conversation. Still people struggle with the reality that these aren't changing. At just about every project, this is the point of the discussion when everyone turns to the most junior person and tries to figure out when they will be leaving the company or retiring, and then they want to add one day to that. Figure 1-8 shows an example of how you might set this up.

While there really isn't a performance impact to having more years, there are a couple of things to consider. First, people are going to have to scroll through whatever you decide. Does it really make sense to have many

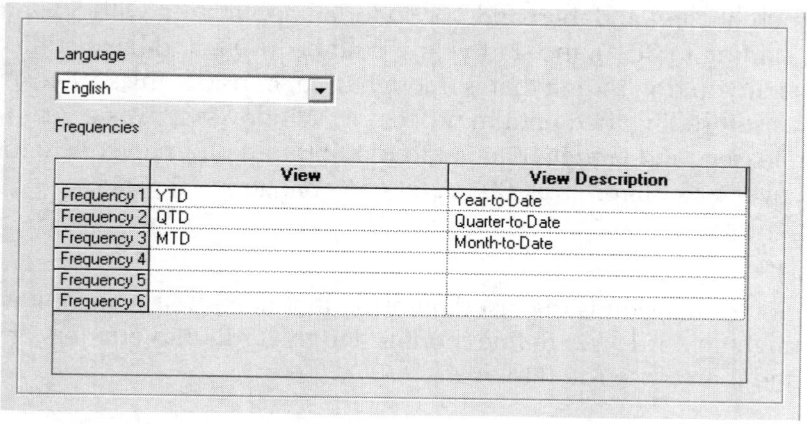

Language

English

Frequencies

	View	View Description
Frequency 1	YTD	Year-to-Date
Frequency 2	QTD	Quarter-to-Date
Frequency 3	MTD	Month-to-Date
Frequency 4		
Frequency 5		
Frequency 6		

FIGURE 1-7. *Frequencies example*

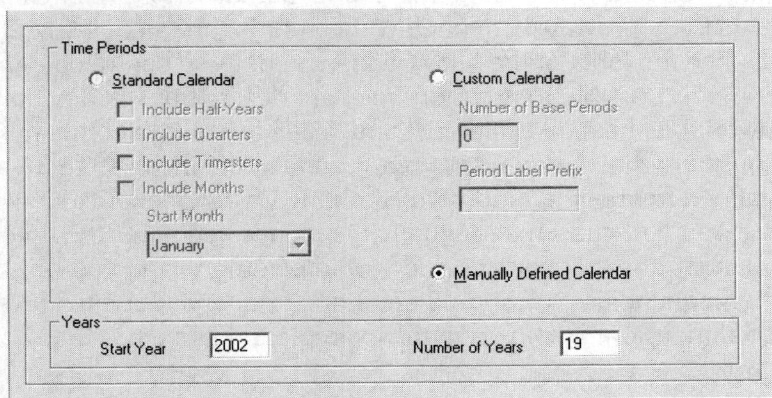

FIGURE 1-8. *Example of years*

years that people will not look at just sitting there to scroll through? Second, open places where data can exist have a remarkable way of finding data to fill them. People fill them by mistake, a rule populates them unintentionally, or test data never gets cleared. That takes up space on the servers and increases costs.

A couple of things to consider here; you can't change the descriptions on years—these years are fiscal, not calendar, years, and you can't add years to the application.

My rule of thumb for number of years is to take the current year and ask how much history, and then add 10. So for an application with 5 years of history starting in 2010, the start year would be 2005, and have a life of 16 years. If you don't think that is enough time, consider this: 10 years ago Intel was still selling the Pentium processor, Windows XP was a year from being released, and Google had yet to top $80 million in revenue (Google earned over $23 billion in 2009). A lot can change in 10 years.

Period

The Period dimension is the last dimension that needs to be fixed. It is also very straightforward. You define months and they roll into quarters or half years, and then those roll into years.

The labeling convention should be like everything else—think of your reports and how you can use both the label and description. I recommend something like in Figure 1-8. You would have a three-letter abbreviation and then the full description.

Finally, you would update the period hierarchy. You will use the time periods and frequencies that you defined. You can make changes to this hierarchy by adding or deleting periods. It really is not a good idea to have a calendar with weekly periods. The performance will be disappointing. I also recommend thinking through whether having a period 13 is really required. Just because it is in your ledger does not mean you need it in HFM. HFM does not need a period 13 to close balances or even to include audit adjustments, so you should question it. Figure 1-9 is an example of how the Period dimension could be set up.

Currencies

Each entity will be assigned a single default currency. By default, HFM can easily translate any entity into any currency in the application. This can also be done by way of triangulation, which is also supported by HFM. The application will triangulate through the default currency you specified in the Application Settings. The application won't translate into every currency automatically. HFM will only automatically translate when it thinks it needs to, and that means when the currency of an entity is different than the currency of its parent. Other translations will require the users to force the translation.

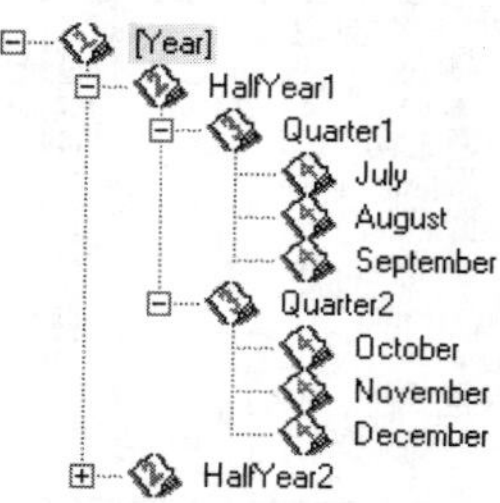

FIGURE 1-9. *Period hierarchy*

While currencies are not a real dimension, when you define currencies, HFM will create members in the Value dimension, Custom1 and Custom2, described later in this chapter. You must provide a label and description for each currency you wish to use. This is another design consideration you should give some careful thought to. You do not want to have to add many currencies later, as doing so has a significant impact on the database. You also do not want to have too many unused currencies, because that can also have a performance impact. I would suggest having all the currencies you do business in now, and those you are certain you will use in the next three years. The labels and descriptions for the currencies should have some logical convention. So consider what your reports require. To that end, it makes sense to use ISO labels and descriptions. As shown in Figure 1-10, use AUD and Australian Dollars, and not something like AUS and Australian $.

There is no need for currencies with the same type (EUR and EUR1 or EUR_old). Since these are really separate dimensions, you can enter several EUR to USD rates, even with the same period, all for different entities.

Application Settings

Once the application has been created, you are ready to start building it. The first step is to define some common application settings. Unlike the profile, these can be changed. It is important, though, to know the impact

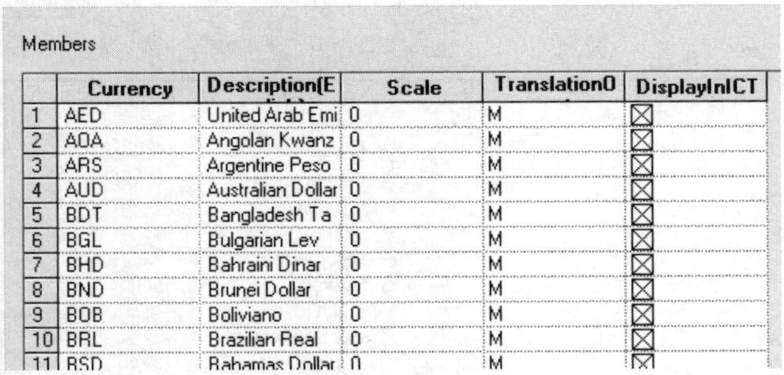

Members

	Currency	Description(E	Scale	Translation0	DisplayInICT
1	AED	United Arab Emi	0	M	☒
2	AOA	Angolan Kwanz	0	M	☒
3	ARS	Argentine Peso	0	M	☒
4	AUD	Australian Dollar	0	M	☒
5	BDT	Bangladesh Ta	0	M	☒
6	BGL	Bulgarian Lev	0	M	☒
7	BHD	Bahraini Dinar	0	M	☒
8	BND	Brunei Dollar	0	M	☒
9	BOB	Boliviano	0	M	☒
10	BRL	Brazilian Real	0	M	☒
11	BSD	Bahamas Dollar	0	M	☒

FIGURE 1-10. *Sample currencies*

of each setting. You will need to come back to these settings once you have defined the accounts. The following list shows some key application settings.

- **ConsolidationRules** This identifies whether consolidation rules will be customized. Specify one of these values: Y, R, or N. Specify Y to use the custom rules written in the Consolidate() subroutine. R will derive the proportional and elimination value in the Value dimension.
  N will use the default consolidation and eliminations. Whenever possible, use R to optimize consolidation performance if your application can use the default HFM consolidation rules.
- **DefaultCurrency** Identifies the default currency for the application. Most applications will use the reported currency of the parent company.
- **DefaultRateForBalanceAccounts** The currency rate account that contains the translation rate to use for Asset or Liability accounts. This is the end-of-period or end-of-month rate.
- **DefaultRateForFlowAccounts** The currency rate account that contains the translation rate to use for Revenue or Expense accounts. This is the period average rate account.
- **DefaultValueForActive** Identifies the default value for the Active account. This attribute is required even though it is for OrgByPeriod applications only. Specify 0 if the child entity is considered inactive by default and will not consolidate into the parent entity. Specify 1 if the child entity is considered active by default and consolidates into the parent. Since most of your new entities will be consolidated, you should choose 1 unless you are building an OrgByPeriod application. In that case you should choose 0. When you choose 0 for Organization by Period applications, no historical periods are impacted when a new entity is added or an existing entity is added to a new parent. Organization by Period has many other considerations covered later in this book.

- **EnableMetadataSecurityFiltering** Metadata filtering is a feature that allows users to see only the members to which they have access, and not necessarily see the entire structure of the database. You can filter on Scenario, Entity, Intercompany Partner (ICP), Account, Custom1, Custom2, Custom3, or Custom4. The default for this attribute is N, but choose Y when you want to limit people's access.
- **FDMAppName** Name of the Oracle Hyperion Financial Data Quality Management application. This facilitates "drillback" from HFM into FDM.
- **ICPEntitiesAggregationWeight** Identifies the percentage of intercompany partner entity [ICP Entities] amounts that aggregate to the [ICP Top] within the Value dimension. It is almost always 1.
- **MaxCellTextSize** Identifies the maximum number of characters that can be used for cell text. You can enter a positive number up to 2,147,483,646, or 1 for no limit. The default of 8000 will be more than enough for most people.
- **MaxDocAttachmentSize** Identifies the maximum number of bytes for any document attachments. You can enter a positive number up to 2,147,483,646, or –1 for no limit. You should consider limiting this as some people will load excessively large files.
- **MaxNumDocAttachments** Identifies the maximum number of document attachments per user. You can enter a positive number up to 2,147,483,646, or –1 for no limit, which is the default as well.
- **NodeSecurity** Enter Entity to check node data based on security access for the entity and Parent to check node data based on security access for the parent. Most applications have Entity. This setting will control who can access the Node of the Entity. These are the value members with square brackets. You might use Parent when another person will be pushing journals or data down to entities earlier in the close process.
- **OrgByPeriodApplication** Specify Y to use Org by Period or N to use only one organizational structure. If you are planning on building complex ownership structures in the entity dimension, you should plan on using Org by Period.

- **SupportSubmissionPhaseforAccounts** If you are planning to submit part of the chart of accounts at different times for process management, you will need to set this to allow for phased submissions. Your options are Y or N, and the default is N.
- **SupportSubmissionPhaseforCustom1-4** If you are planning to submit some of the custom members at different times for process management, you will need to set this to allow for phased submissions. Your options are Y or N, and the default is N.
- **SupportSubmissionPhaseforICP** If you are planning to submit different ICP members at different times for process management, you will need to set this to allow for phased submissions. Your options are Y or N, and the default is N.
- **UsePVAForBalanceAccounts** PVA is a method of translation where the periodic value is translated for each month, and the months are summed to give a year-to-date balance. If you select Y, this translation method would be used on Balance accounts. Balance accounts typically use the VAL method, which is translation at a point in time.
- **UsePVAForFlowAccounts** PVA is a method of translation where the periodic value is translated for each month, and the months are summed to give a year-to-date balance. If you select Y, this translation method would be used on Flow accounts.
- **ValidationAccount** This is required for process management. The validation account must equal zero before a process unit can be promoted or rejected. The validation account also serves as a locking account, meaning that it must equal zero before you can lock an entity. You can specify a validation account for Submission Phase 1 to 9.

Figure 1-11 shows how we would set these application settings up. Now that you have a profile and defined application settings, you are ready to build the rest of your metadata.

Members

	DefaultCurrency	DefaultRateForBalanceAccounts	DefaultRateForFlowAccounts	UsePVAForBalanceAccounts	UsePVAForFlowAccounts	ICPEntitiesAggregationWeight	DefaultValueForActive	ValidationAccount
1	USD	EOMRate	AvgRate	☐	☒	1	1	

Members

	ConsolidationRules	OrgByPeriodApplication	NodeSecurity	UseSecurityForAccounts	UseSecurityForEntities	UseSecurityForScenarios	UseSecurityForCustom1	UseSecurityForCustom2
1	Y	☐	Entity	☐	☐	☐	☐	☐

Members

	UseSecurityForICP	EnableMetadataSecurityFiltering	MaxCellTextSize	MaxDocAttachmentSize	MaxNumDocAttachments	UseSubmissionPhase	SupportSubmissionPhaseForAccounts	SupportSubmissionPhaseForCustom1
1	☐	☐	2048	0	0	☐	☐	☐

Members

	SupportSubmissionPhaseForCustom2	SupportSubmissionPhaseForCustom3	SupportSubmissionPhaseForCustom4	SupportSubmissionPhaseForICP	ValidationAccount2	ValidationAccount3	ValidationAccount4	ValidationAccount5
1	☐	☐	☐	☐				

☐ Disable Combo Boxes

ValidationAccount6	ValidationAccount7	ValidationAccount8	ValidationAccount9	FdmAppName

FIGURE 1-11. *Application settings example*

Scenario

The Scenario dimension is used to identify the type of data that will be stored for all periods, entities, and accounts. It is a version of a projected course. The most common is "Actual." That would be all actual data reported. Other types of data include "Budget" and "Forecast." You could have "Versions" of each. For example you may have Budget1, Budget2, Budget3, and a final budget submission just called Budget. Each of these examples tells a different story of the data in HFM.

You can determine how many you need by asking yourself how many of these versions you review and report on each month. These reports are often called *variance reports*, and they show the differences between these multiple Scenarios.

Like all the other dimensions, the Scenario dimension has a hierarchy, but it is flat. One could have a structure, but it will only serve to help people see the relationship between other Scenarios. You may want to have the "Final Budget" be a parent, and the versions of working budgets are children.

There are some important settings specific to the Scenario dimension that should be considered.

- **ConsolidateYTD** Enter Y for YTD or N for periodic. The decision point here is how should HFM run its consolidation; Org by Period applications will always be periodic.
- **DefaultFreq** This identifies the periods defined in the Application Profile for which data input is valid. For example, Monthly indicates that you can extract input data only in month-based periods.
- **DefaultView** YTD or Periodic. Typically, Budget and Forecast would be periodic and Actual is YTD. This default view impacts rules as its default view.
- **DefFreqForICTrans** Required for Intercompany Transaction Module, this setting identifies the default frequency for intercompany transactions.
- **EnableDataAudit** Y to automatically audit all accounts (even accounts that have EnableDataAudit set to False), or O to audit only accounts with EnableDataAudit set to True. You would choose N to disable auditing for this scenario.

- **MaximumReviewLevel** This attribute is required, but is not used by HFM in any way. You could put any number and it does not impact any functionality. Still, you still need a value from 1 to 10.
- **PhasedSubmissionStartYear** Identifies the start year for phased submissions in process management. This is a new feature of Release 11.1.2.
- **SupportsProcessManagement** Y to enable Process Management, N to disable Process Management, or A to enable Process Management and E-mail alerting.
- **UsesLineItems** Y if the scenario can accept line item detail. This is useful for accounts that require line item detail in Actual, but not in Budget.

Figure 1-12 shows the three most commonly used scenarios and their settings: Actual, Forecast, and Budget.

The next two settings are key settings that need to be considered for setting up scenarios. ZeroViewForAdj and ZeroViewForNonadj are both required attributes that inform applications how to handle missing data. They may be set to either Periodic or YTD, and HFM derives either Periodic or YTD values for missing data accordingly.

Why do you even need these settings? These settings are there simply because you do not want to load zeros into the database. A zero is actually something in the database. A zero takes up space and requires the system to

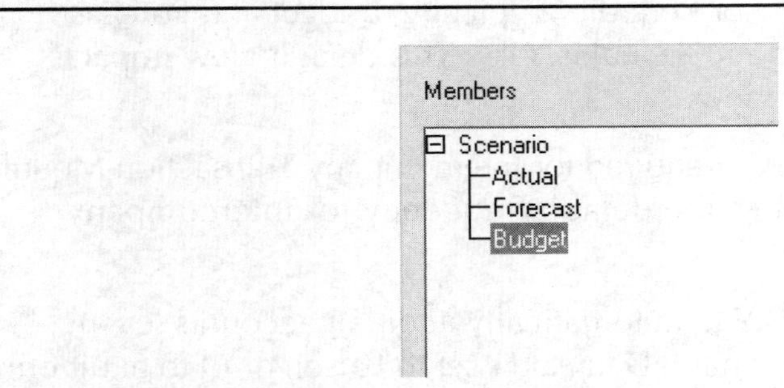

FIGURE 1-12. *Most common scenarios*

handle it, either reading or writing it to the database. Not having zeros in the application will really increase performance.

There is a rare exception when you need to load zeros, and that is when the zero view settings you defined for the scenarios are not valid for all entities; for example, when you have to load periodic data, but the default view is year to date. This would create cases when the periodic change is zero, you need to load that zero so that the year-to-date number is correct. But you really should exhaust your options trying to get the data file in a format that is consistent.

The first difference to note in these settings is that one is for handling Adjustments (journals) and the other is for all other data points.

You should consider how you plan to look at the data; one way is selecting Period view. This is most common for Budget and Forecast scenarios. Let's assume I have selected a Budget scenario that I am viewing periodic. If ZeroViewForAdj or ZeroViewForNonAdj is set to Periodic, HFM displays *a derived value of zero* for missing data, and it is treated as a zero for the current period change. I would see a zero in the database. If I changed my view to Year to Date, HFM displays *a derived value that equals the sum of previous periods' values.* The year-to-date number would suggest there was no change for the month. Looking at Figure 1-13, you can see how HFM populates these numbers.

If you were looking at actual data, you would likely prefer a Year to Date view of the data. If ZeroViewForAdj or ZeroViewForNonAdj is set to YTD, and I was viewing the data Year to Date, HFM displays *a derived zero for the year to date.* That would mean the month change would have to equal the negative of the sum of the prior months, as shown in Figure 1-14.

	January	February
YTD	100	100
Periodic	100	0

FIGURE 11-13. *Period change of zero*

	January	February
YTD	100	100
Periodic	100	0

FIGURE 1-14. *Year-to-date change of zero*

Variance Reporting

For reports that compare two scenarios, for example Actual to Budget data, you have two options for building this. You can either build two scenarios, or build the second view in the custom dimension. Since you only have four customs in the current version, if you are out of dimensions the decision may be made for you. But the advantage of building this type of reporting into a custom over a scenario is that it is easier to manage copying data and journals.

There are some great features in the reports that open many more doors. There are some great ideas for these reports in Chapter 4.

Constant Currency

Similar to the issue with variance reporting, you can make managing the application easier by having Constant Currency Scenarios in a custom dimension over having a separate scenario. It can help to use scenarios to look at Actual data at Budget rates, Last Year rates, and other rates to evaluate the currency impact on your financial statements. That would require adding a scenario and copying data and rates from other scenarios. The other option to creating scenarios is using one of the custom dimensions. The driver for making this decision is simply performance and availability of dimensions. If you have used all your custom dimensions, then it is not an option to use them. If they are available, then you could consider that. So if dimensions are available, you only need to consider performance. The performance impact is that you would potentially double the data within your subcube. This can slow down the consolidation. But there is a big advantage to putting this into a custom dimension: You never have to worry about data in one scenario changing and not flowing into the other translation rates you want to see. Older versions of HFM do not have the newer memory-handling features that minimize this issue.

I would suggest using scenarios, as you have more control over when data is populated into the scenario for evaluation; the special scenario can be consolidated as a separate process.

Entity

The Entity dimension should be used to represent the organizational structure of the business. This is usually done with legal entities, or cost and profit centers at the base level, then consolidating by region, responsibility, or by a defined legal structure. Each entity stores data for the necessary consolidation points. During a consolidation, all the children of a parent are loaded into memory for the system to aggregate all base-level data to store for the parent. This works very well for the structures that are common in consolidation systems. Still, very flat entity dimension structures can experience performance issues due to the amount of information that must be cached. HFM has had many improvements in recent releases that resolve memory issues, and these improvements along with subcube enhancements are discussed later in this chapter. However, versions used before System 9 and applications with large entity structures should consider adding parents, if for nothing else than to improve performance. These additional entities can help make the application more user-friendly, providing more groupings for reporting and drilling on the data.

There are several settings for the Entity dimension to consider when adding new members to the Entity dimension. Figure 1-15 shows a sample Entity. The following list shows the key attributes that must be defined; you should spend extra time understanding the impact of these attributes.

- **Member** Labels are restricted to 80 characters, can be alpha and/or numeric. Don't forget to put some thought into your naming convention.
- **DefCurrency** This is the default currency for the entity. It should be the functional currency of the entity.
- **AllowAdjs** Having this attribute set allows journals to be posted to the value member Entity Currency Adjustment and the Parent Currency Adjustment members. Now with this enabled, it also allows HFM to run

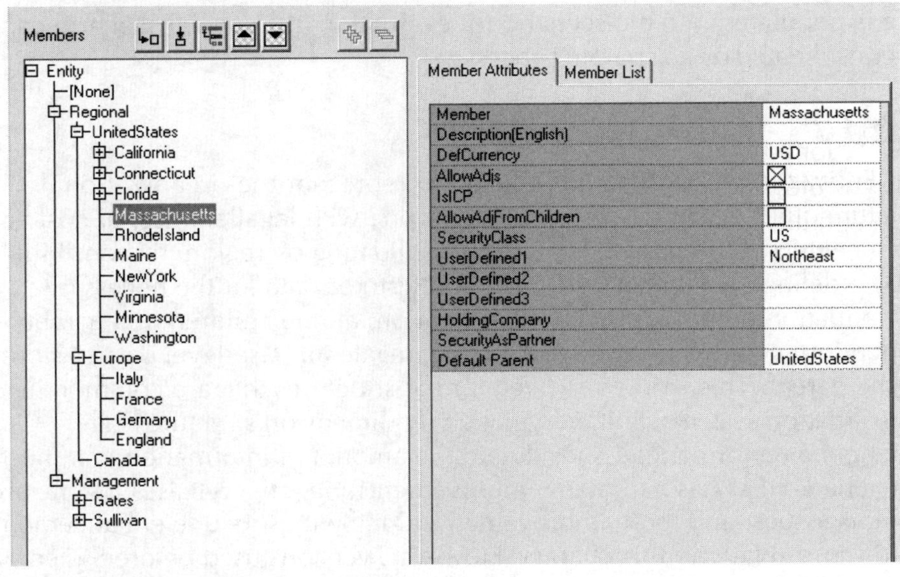

FIGURE 1-15. *Sample Entity*

Sub Calculate there. This feature is not well known, but it can speed your consolidations. If you don't have journals there, there is no need to run calculations on these members.

- **IsICP** This attribute determines whether this entity will be an intercompany partner for any intercompany transactions. Flagging this as Y (yes) will create a member in the ICP dimension, and allow for input of intercompany accounts to an ICP member with the same label as the entity. Selecting R (restricted) will allow for the same conditions as Y will; however, it will prevent people from posting to an intercompany partner with the same label as the entity you are entering data in. This prevents people from recording intercompany activity with themselves. I would recommend using R unless you are certain you are not reporting at the lowest legal entity in the application.

- **AllowAdjFromChildren** Having this set allows journals to be posted to the value member Contribution Adjustment and the Parent Adjustment members.

- **UserDefined1–3** User-defined attributes are used to enhance the flexibility of rules and for creating lists. Rules can be conditionally based upon these fields.
- **HoldingCompany** This field is used to identify the Holding Company for this entity. It can be referenced in the rules. When you are building rules in the system for the consolidation, you will see how this field is critical.

Value

The most important dimension is the Value dimension. It is the part of the product that drives the consolidation in HFM. When you really understand how the Value dimension works, you understand how HFM really does consolidations. It is critical for writing rules. It isn't just how HFM brings the data together, but it tells you how the rules are working to move data up the entity structure to consolidate the data. The Value dimension is a system-generated, system-maintained dimension within HFM. You can't modify it directly.

I say directly because the Value dimension has members based on currencies you add, and you can make some minor changes to default members.

The first thing you notice when you look at the Value dimension is that all of the currencies you add in the application are replicated there. All the currencies in the Value dimension are referenced by something called a *triplet.* A triplet is a grouping of an input member, an adjustment member, and a total. For example, if you had a USD currency you would see for that currency a USD, USD ADJ, and USD Total. You should see a triplet for every currency you have in the application.

So let's talk through the Value dimension. Figure 1-16 is an example of the Value dimension and how data moves from one member to another. Data is loaded only to <Entity Currency>. Every entity has only one default currency. So even though you see all of the currencies in the Value dimension, you can only load to one—the <Entity Currency>. You can make a local currency adjustment in HFM through the journals module in a member called <Entity Curr Adjs>. These two members sum to a total called <Entity Curr Total>. This is also a triplet, and it points to the currency triplet that is the default currency of the entity. If I had an entity with a functional currency of EUR (the euro),

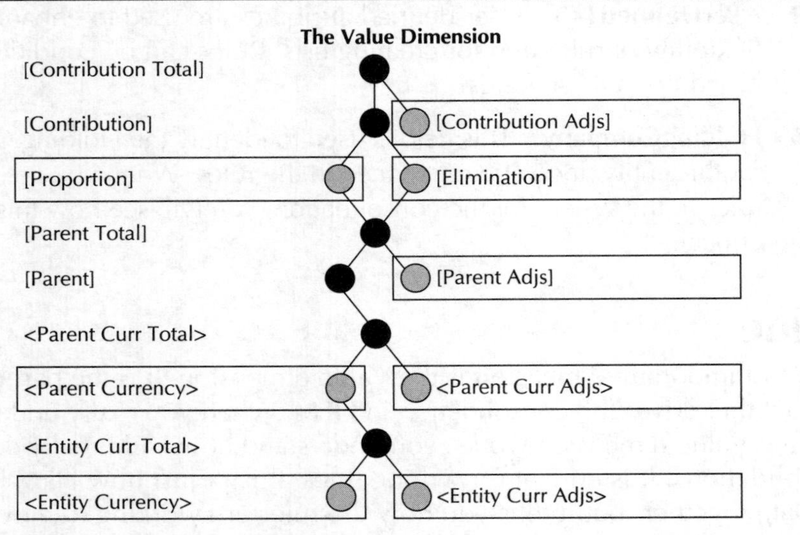

FIGURE 1-16. *The Value dimension*

and I loaded data to Entity Currency, I would see the values I loaded in both the value member EUR and <Entity Currency>. That would be true when I load the data, if I chose EUR or Entity Currency in my load file.

The reason is that the <Entity Currency> and for that matter, all of the value members that relate to the entity, identified by opening and closing angle brackets ("<" and ">"), are just pointers to the currency defined in the Value dimension. They aren't "real" members that store the data. When you load data to an Entity member of the Value dimension, it is valid anywhere the entity appears in the application.

Once we have the functional currency and adjustments completed, we can do translation. We want to translate the entity before we do any other calculations like eliminations or ownership calculations. By default, HFM will translate to the currency of the parent. If local currency and parent currency are different, then HFM will by default have translation. First, the data in the <Parent Currency> is cleared, then HFM takes <Entity Currency Total>, runs the Sub Translate routine, and moves <Parent Currency>. Once the data moves to <Parent Currency>, the Sub Calculate rules are run again.

<Parent Currency> also has an adjustment member you can add adjustment values to called <Parent Curr Adjs>. Those journal values are made in the parent currency of the entity. Both <Parent Currency> and the <Parent Curr Adjust> are added together on the fly to give <Parent Currency Total>. Once you move to the next member, you will notice that the brackets change from angle brackets (< >) to square brackets ([ ]).

The next member is [Parent]. The Parent member defines the first member that is part of the Node. There is also a [Parent Adj] and [Parent Total]. These members are also in the parent's currency, but unlike <Parent Currency>, they are part of the Node.

The Node is the unique relationship between a parent entity and each of its children. For example, if I were an entity that made French bicycles, I could roll up to two parents. I could roll up to Total Bicycles and Total France. Figure 1-17 shows this example.

The eliminations and consoldiation calculations would likely be very different depending which parent it consoldiates. The Value dimension allows this.

The [Parent Total] using consolidation rules, either default or custom, will write values to [Elimination] and [Proportion]. Eliminations occur after any Proportion has been calculated (any non-100-percent consolidations), and the total is stored.

Account

The Account dimension represents a hierarchy of natural accounts. Typically, the accounts store financial data for entities and scenarios in an application. Each account has a type, such as Income or Expense, that defines its accounting behavior. You can use accounts for other types of data, like headcount, units, or inventory. Those accounts typically use other

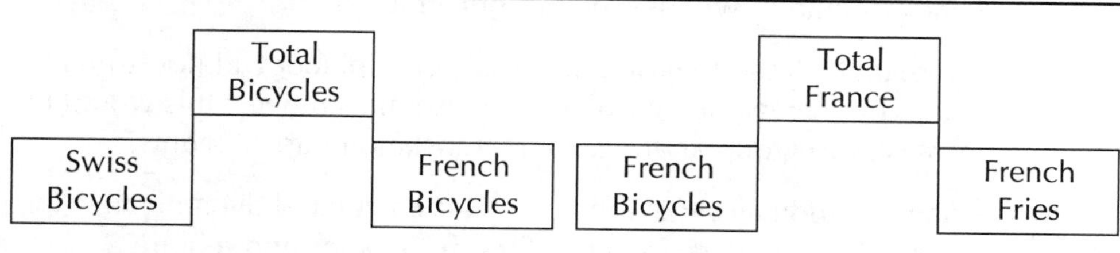

FIGURE 1-17. *The Node, the relationship of a parent and child entity*

types, like Balance. The account type is one of the first required settings after you have defined the label and description.

- **Asset, Liability** Accounts used on the balance sheet; these do not recognize period changes. If you had an asset Cash that had 10,000, it would be 10,000 year to date and 10,000 periodic.
- **Expense, Revenue** Accounts used for the income statement; these accounts do show period change. Revenue was called Income, but they are the same. If you had an revenue account called Sales that had 10,000, it would be 10,000 year to date and the difference between the months for the periodic.
- **Flow** Behaves like an Expense or Revenue account, but will not translate.
- **Balance** Behaves like an Asset or Liability account, but will not translate.
- **Balancerecurring** Allows you to enter data in one period and have it carry forward until the end of the year. If you entered 500 in January, then 500 would appear for all the months after January. This would only carry until the end of the year, and then the data needs to be entered in the next year.
- **Currencyrate** These accounts allow use of currencies in Custom1 and Custom2. A commonly used account would store the end of month rate (EOMRate). Then you can enter a translation rate. The rule of thumb here is to enter the rates as they translate from Custom1 to Custom2. So if you were going to translate a EUR entity to a USD parent, the data would be A#EOMRate.C1#EUR.C2#USD. These accounts are Balancerecurring, so if you don't enter a rate in the next month, it will use the last one entered.
- **Grouplabel** Used to group accounts, Grouplabel will not store a value. You may want a group called "Administrative"; this would be a nice way to group all the tax and translation rate accounts.
- **Dynamic** Indicates that the account is calculated dynamically, "on the fly." The accounts are typically simple ratios and require a special rule.

Once those account types are defined, you need to consider some of the other settings.

- **CalcAttribute** This field allows you to describe the calculations in the rules file that are done for this account. It can be viewed by users in grids and forms. You can enter in plain English what the rule is doing. This feature is not used enough in HFM applications. A well-designed application will include this.
- **DefaultParent** The default parent for the account.
- **EnableDataAudit** Y to enable account auditing or N to disable auditing. To use this functionality, you will need to also turn this on using the Scenario attributes.
- **ICPTopMember** The ICP top member for the account. If you want to prevent entry or usage of [ICP None], this setting can force users to identify a specific intercompany partner when they use this account.
- **IsICP** Identifies the account as an intercompany account. Y will make the account valid for all members of the ICP dimension, N will allow ICP None to be the only valid member for loading data, and R will make the account valid for all members of the ICP dimension except for the ICP member that has the same name as the entity loading data.
- **PlugAcct** Consider this a suspense account for identifying and resolving intercompany matching issues. It is required for accounts to self-eliminate if the consolidation rules are not used.
- **IsCalculated** This should be used on all base calculated accounts; it prevents input and tells HFM to clear data values before rules are run at key points of the consolidation.
- **IsConsolidated** Allows the account to consolidate in the Entity/Value dimensions. If this is not selected, an account will not move past <Parent Curr Total> in the Value dimension.
- **Submission Group** For Phased Submission, this setting will identify the submission group.

- **UsesLineItems** Y if the account uses line item detail and N if the account does not. This also needs to be flagged in the scenario if you want to have line item detail.
- **XBRL Tags** This is a field where you can enter XBRL tags for the account. This setting is not related to Disclosure Management (DM). I would not use it for any substantive XBRL reporting.

Figure 1-18 shows a typical account and the key settings described.

System Accounts

HFM provides a set of accounts that can be used to help with complex consolidation and calculations. These accounts help drive consolidation rules, and that is covered later in the book when Rules are covered in Chapter 3. All system accounts are Balance accounts except for the Active

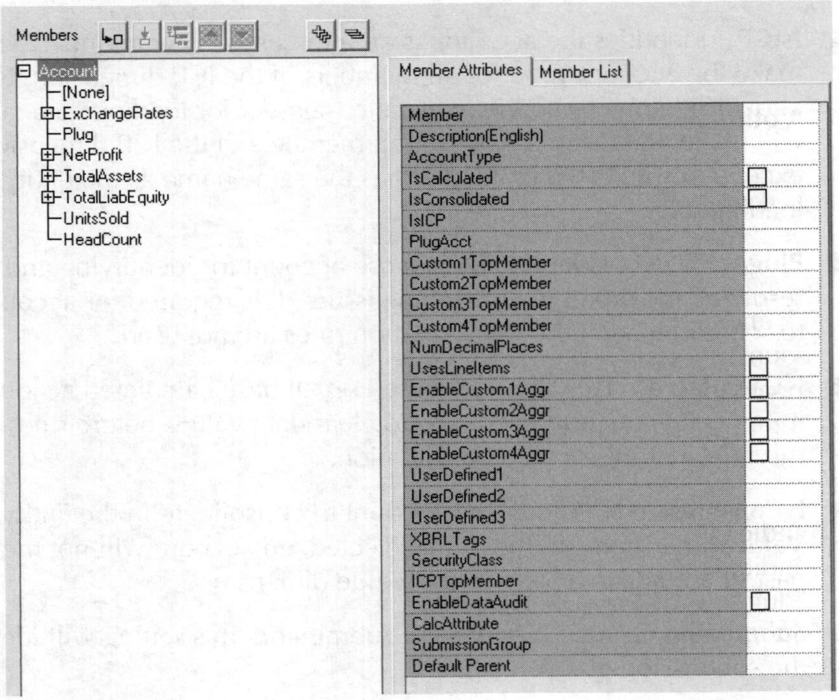

FIGURE 1-18. *The Account dimension*

account, which is a Balancerecurring account. You can modify the description, security class, and the decimal location for system accounts.

- **[PCON]** Percent consolidation
- **[POWN]** Percent ownership
- **[DOWN]** Percent of direct ownership
- **[PCTRL]** Percent control
- **Active** Determines whether the entity should consolidate in the period
- **SharesOwned** Total number of shares owned
- **VotingOwned** Number of voting shares owned
- **SharesOutstanding** Total number or percentage of shares outstanding
- **VotingOutstanding** Number of voting shares outstanding
- **Shares%Owned** Calculated based on above account information
- **Voting%Owned** Calculated based on above account information

Intercompany Partner (ICP)

The Intercompany Partner dimension provides detail for all intercompany balances that can exist for an account. Oracle Hyperion Financial Management can track and eliminate intercompany transaction details across entities and accounts. This dimension is defined when you flag an Entity as an intercompany partner. The member labels will mirror those entities flagged.

Figure 1-19 shows the screen where you will set up an application for intercompany transactions. You must perform these actions:

1. Indicate the accounts that perform intercompany transactions and indicate a plug account for each intercompany account (IsICP and PlugAcct attributes in account metadata).
2. Indicate the entities that perform intercompany transactions (IsICP attribute in entity metadata).

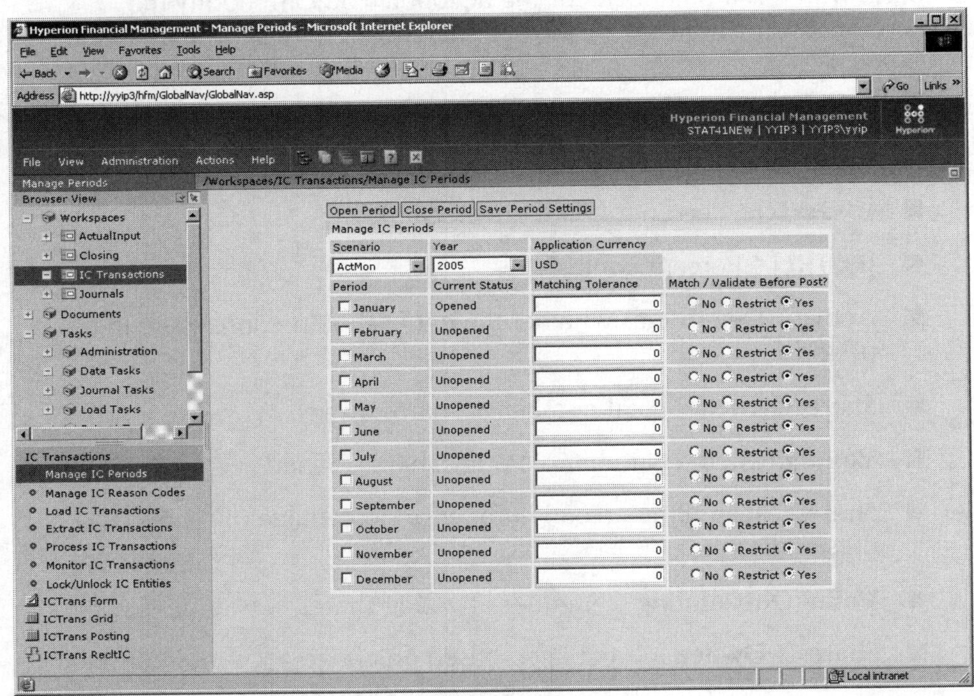

FIGURE 1-19. *Configuring Intercompany*

The plug account created should always be intercompany. It is valuable to see the matching by intercompany partner when trying to resolve a data issue.

Custom Dimensions

In addition to the eight system-defined dimensions, Hyperion Financial Management provides four custom dimensions. You use the custom dimensions to store additional detail, such as products, measurement adjustments, or balance sheet movement. For example, you can have a custom dimension for products associated with your Sales account that you can use to track sales by product.

It is best to think of custom dimensions as another view of the accounts. For example, you may want to view your operating Expense by Function or Department. You may want to see Revenue by Product. In those cases you can put Function and Product in a Custom dimension. Then, by attaching the custom dimensions to the accounts, you create a valid intersection of the account and Custom dimensions. Now in this example, you do not have any overlap of the customs. Revenue is only valid for Product and Expense is valid only for Function. Since there is no overlap, you can put both members in the same Custom member.

To attach them to the accounts, you only need to do two steps. First, attach the top Product member to the Revenue accounts, and the top Function member to the correct Expense accounts. Second, enable Aggregation for each of the accounts.

Consolidation Methods

Consolidation methods are used during the consolidation process to allow HFM to properly calculate the amount that is written to the [Proportion] Node. Normally, there are three consolidation methods you might use depending on the strength of the parent company's control or influence: full consolidation, proportionate, and the equity. The basic principle consists of replacing the historical cost of the parent's investment in the company being consolidated with its assets, liabilities, and equity. You can actually create any names you want, but those are the most common. The methods you define will automatically generate in the [ConsolMethod] system list for the Custom1 dimension. The Consolidation method can be populated either manually through data load or data entry, or populated in the rules, which are based on the ultimate percent control for the entity. Consolidation methods are also used to write to the [Elimination] member.

POWNMIN is a keyword you use for the method corresponding to the Equity method. The settings in this table are used by the Ownership Calculation routine to compute the percentages of control, the ultimate percentages of ownership, and to assign the percentages of consolidation and the consolidation methods for legal consolidation. Using POWNMIN, the percentage of consolidation that is assigned for the Equity Company corresponds to the percentage used in a staged consolidation POWNMIN calculation.

These methods are ways you can consolidate the data in your application. You can build them in whatever way you need to run the consolidation. I have seen some very common ones. I am sure each reader will have seen some twist on each of these, so I will keep the examples generic.

Full consolidation is used when there is majority ownership or control (greater than 50 percent of voting shares) by one parent of its subsidiaries. The two company's financial statements are combined by account, with any adjustments and eliminations. This can mean the consolidated accounts have only part of the values consolidated to a given parent. For example, if you have 100 in revenue, but own 65 percent, you would only see 65 consolidate to the parent. Statement of Financial Accounting Standards (SFAS) 94, issued in 1987, states that majority-owned subsidiaries (more than 50 percent of the voting stock has been acquired), should be fully consolidated and that accounting by the Equity method (generally used for affiliates less than 50 percent owned) is not a substitute for information provided by fully consolidated financial statements.

The Equity method is used when there is minority ownership or control with significant influence (between 20 percent and 50 percent) by one Parent of its affiliates. The Parent entity will reflect ownership of equity with entries to specific accounts, as opposed to all accounts. The equity method is allowable for affiliates less than 50 percent owned as opposed to subsidiaries more than 50 percent owned.

The Cost method is generally used when there is minority ownership or control without significant influence (less than 20 percent of the voting shares) by one Parent of its affiliates. This method is similar to the Equity method, with the exception that entries are put into the system only when dividends are paid.

The Proportion method is used for joint ventures, a method of including items of income, expense, assets, and liabilities multiplied by a firm's percentage of participation in the venture. There is some question of the future of this method with expansion of IFRS.

Other methods such as Joint Venture (JV) or Associate can be used and modified to help with issues you may have. You can create what you need.

Once you have determined your methods and built them into your application, they need to be assigned to the entities. There are a couple of ways to assign the consolidation method to an entity for use during consolidation. The method can be assigned through the ownership console, manually through data load or data entry. The method can also be assigned by the Calculate Ownership routine.

Best Practices for Design Dimensionality

One of the most important design considerations you can make with HFM is thinking about the subcube. In recent releases the product has gotten much better at handling the memory limitations the subcube presents. In releases prior to 4.1, Hyperion strongly recommended a limit of 100,000 records for any one subcube, based on a 12-month Application Profile. This limit was not a hard and fast limit; one could see subcubes larger than 100,000 records completing consolidation without consistently failing or giving an error message. This made it very difficult to identify and resolve these issues. The large subcubes actually bring you closer to the real issue, which is the Maximum Number of Data Records in RAM (MaxNumDataRecordsInRAM) to the 1,500,000 threshold. There is a limit of data records you can load into memory. Each record is about 200 bytes for a 12-month application. That provides the recommended 300 MB for data caching. You can modify this limit by changing the MaxNumDataRecordsInRAM setting in the registry. But this should only be changed if you are sure of the results.

This was a limitation of the memory available in Windows for the service. So the larger the subcubes, or the larger the number of subcubes created, the greater the risk of running into this record limit of 1,500,000. Oracle added some significant improvements, to manage the subcubes, such as 64-bit version of HFM, Lazy Copy, Paging and some options to manage the subcubes in the registry. Since that significant improvement in memory management in HFM, rules issues have become the most common performance issue, more than even bad subcube design. However, large or poorly planned subcubes can still negatively impact performance. The rest of this chapter focuses on the key considerations you must take into account to have a good design.

The Subcube and Its Impact on Your Design

So now that you understand the subcubes are important, let's define what makes up a subcube so you can better design them. The account, ICP, and customs for a period make up the subcube. Data for a different currency, year, or scenario exists in separate subcubes.

Each subcube is defined by the Page dimensions and contains all the members of the Subcube dimensions. The Page dimensions are Scenario, Year, Entity, Value and View. The Subcube dimensions are Account, ICP, Period, Custom1-4. The subcube consists of the stored data records for these combinations of dimensional intersections. That is, it is the actual number of populated records that make up the size of your cubes. You can estimate the size of a subcube by multiplying the number of members in the Account and Custom dimensions to determine all possible intersections. You can determine the largest subcube by finding your most dense entity, usually at the top of your Entity dimension. Data density can have a big impact on the size of the subcubes. For example, you could have 1,000 accounts, and 100 of each custom valid for each account. That is not something anyone would call a large application, but (1,000 × 100 × 100 × 100 × 100) if the subcube had every possible intersection populated, it would be 100,000,000,000. It is easy to see how you could reach a memory limitation doing this.

You can measure the size of these subcubes. First, remember that each record is about 200 bytes for a 12-month application. Then, by using the rules in HFM, you can open a subcube and calculate the number of records.

HFM stores data for these dimensions in three sets of tables (these sets exist for each scenario-year combination per application):

- **DCE (Currency subcube)** Stores <Entity Currency>, <Entity Currency Adj>, <Parent Currency>, and <Parent Currency Adj>. It is also possible for a user to force a translation into another currency triplet, and this is stored here as well.
- **DCN (Parent subcube)** Stores other Value dimension members, the members in the Node. Any value in the Node relates to that specific parent-child relationship, and both the parent and child need to be

identified. This is called out by the additional fields in the tables that identify the parent. So, DCN tables are just like DCE tables but include an additional field for the parent.

- **DCT (Journal transactions)** Stores all journal transactions, they transfer data values to DCE (for <Entity Currency Adjs> and <Parent Currency Adjs>) or DCN tables (for [Parent Adjs] and [Contribution Adjs]) when posted.

There are settings you could modify; however, for most applications you will never need to change them. The default settings work very well. HFM uses an algorithm to identify the least recently used (LRU) cubes and purges them from memory. If you do decide you need to modify these settings, you need to find a balance in the size of the LRU and the amount of memory assigned for data cache. For example, too large an LRU means you hold too many records in memory, putting the system under more memory pressure, which reduces system performance. It is best to consult an expert about these settings, or perform these modifications in a test environment or lab.

Migrating Your Application from Hyperion Enterprise

If you are one of Oracle's long-time customers who have been looking at HFM, you should understand how the dimensions align, and what tools are available for migrating to HFM from Hyperion Enterprise (HE). One of the primary reasons for upgrading from HE to HFM is to gain an increase in dimensionality. There are many similarities from HE to HFM, but HFM offers you 12 dimensions, and HE only 4. In fact, any updates to HE dimensionality mean that you are adding new members to either accounts or entities. This is a technical limitation of a flat-file database, on which Enterprise is based. Figure 1-20 shows how these dimensions align from HE to HFM.

You can see that HE dimensions are aligned into a Hyperion Financial Management application. The Category dimension becomes Scenario and Year. Hyperion Enterprise accounts and subaccounts become the Account, ICP, and Custom dimensions 1–4. Lastly, HFM handles the Enterprise Period dimension using Period and Frequency (for example, MTD, YTD).

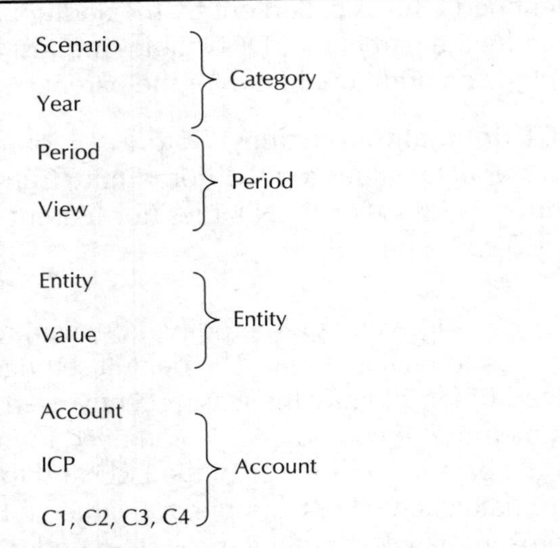

FIGURE 1-20. *Hyperion Enterprise dimensions aligning to Hyperion Financial Management dimensions*

Hyperion Enterprise has a utility to help you migrate your HE application to HFM. It is called Oracle Hyperion Enterprise Extraction Utility. The utility is designed to convert full applications, not just the metadata. First, you may need to upgrade to the most recent version of Enterprise (6.5.1). Then you extract the HFM files from that application. It does work and can save you some time. It produces the application files for you to either update or just load. It is useful in that it brings over the Accounts and Entities and descriptions. Although the utility attempts to place them into hierarchies, this is one place that will need some updating. How well it can do this has a lot to do with the Enterprise structure you start with.

This utility will not do all the work for you, but it is part of HE and will save you some time. The best approach is to redesign the application to take advantage of features offered in the consolidation products.

Conclusion

At this point in a typical project, you should really see some great progress. Following this chapter, you should have a good design, skilled team, strong consulting partner, and plan—you have ensured that you will be ready for the next phase of the project. And most importantly, you have a strong foundation to ensure your success.

CHAPTER 2

Tips for Building Your Oracle HFM Application

hether you are new to HFM or an experienced veteran, you will find a feature or two you can add to your application that will extend the value of your investment. There are many reasons you might not get every feature set up and configured exactly right. Even on the projects where things go very smoothly, you will always look back and want to change a thing or two. One of the most common concerns people have when looking to implement HFM is to be sure they are using the features the way they were meant to be used and using them to their maximum utility. As we discussed in Chapter 1, it is difficult to get everything built for the first phase. Also, if you consider that a project will take you between six to eight months, it is likely that an upgrade has been made available during your project. Or possibly, you have taken a while to absorb the changes the product has brought, or you might have an older version. Regardless of the reason, in this chapter we will cover key components of HFM, and tips for configuring them. If you are new to HFM, you should plan to have the Administrator Guide nearby. We'll highlight the basics, but we won't cover every setting. The product documentation does a good job of doing that. We'll focus on key features, tips for making things work better, explanations of the intended uses, and best-practice approaches.

Workspace

The first topic we'll cover is the Workspace, since it is the first thing you will see after you log in to HFM. The Workspace is the common portal you will use to access all the Hyperion tools through your web browser. If you had any version prior to System 9, you might be thinking Workspace is something else. Workspace used to be a list of commonly used tasks to simplify navigation for end users. What you knew as a workspace is now called a Task List. Workspace is a single web interface for interacting with reports, content, and the EPM suite. By bringing all the different parts of the EPM suite into one place, Workspace makes it easier for you to navigate from one product to another—or when you are ready to add new products, leverage what you know about one to get moving on another.

Taking a look at Figure 2-1, you should familiarize yourself with the key parts of the Workspace.

- **Menu bar** (1) Commands and subcommands that organize tasks and modules.
- **Standard toolbar** (2) Buttons for performing tasks.
- **View pane** (3) Area that provides buttons that enable jumps between panels (each panel having a specific use and corresponding controls) and displays the list of documents and modules. (Hiding this pane provides a larger content frame in which to use Workspace. Select View | View Pane to hide and display.)

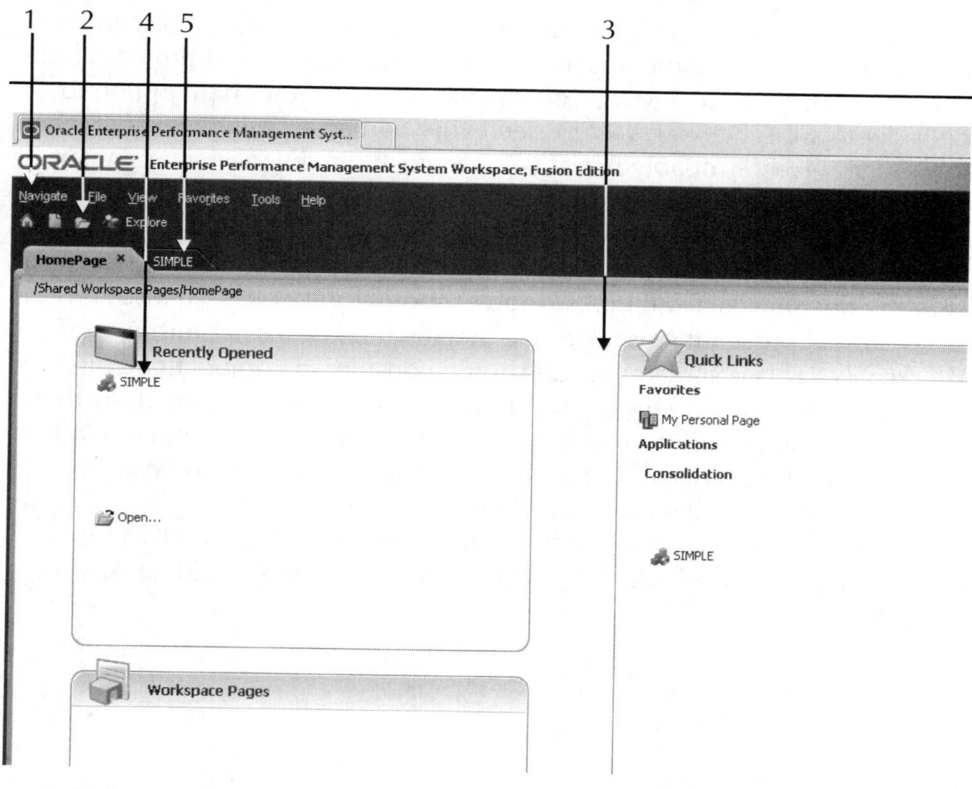

FIGURE 2-1. *The Workspace*

- **Buttons** (4) Buttons for performing module tasks.
- **Document tab bar** (5) Information bar specific to the current module. (If multiple documents are open, the current document tab is highlighted.)

Each application that is open will have a tab, like sheets in a workbook. All of the applications when open will appear as a tab at the bottom of the view pane in the browser. One of the most helpful features to help you navigate is the ability to switch from tab to tab. You can have several tools open and working in the application all in one browser session.

There are some key features you should be aware of in your design. The first is the ability to change the Default Language Selection. You can help users by localizing their HFM experience; even when they speak English or do business in English, this is very important because it can speed adoption of the product. You can also replace the Logon Panel image. This can look nice; it is easy to do and can personalize the application, but provides little value. Removing access to Java client installers is an important option to consider as well. Do you want or need your end users trying to install these tools themselves? Probably not, if you can push out the version you want them using and avoid having the users accidentally create support issues. Users can omit information; for example, "By the way, I installed the Smart View client over what was pushed out," selecting settings other than what is in the default. This can make troubleshooting difficult. You also have the option of preventing users from changing their password through Workspace. This is something you should consider in conjunction with setting up and configuring security. Finally, you can redirect the users to another URL after signoff. This is also a nice option if HFM is not the last step of their close process, but instead the task they need to indicate they completed in a tool like Financial Close Manager.

Workspace is an underrated but critical component of the HFM tool. With it, you can speed adoption of your project and make adding new tools a much easier process.

EPMA and the Win32 Application

In version 9.3, a web-based metadata management tool was introduced. It is Enterprise Performance Management Architect (EPMA), formerly Business Performance Management Architect (BPMA). EPMA enables an administrator to manage, update, create, and deploy HFM, Planning, and Essbase applications within one web-based interface, allowing for a centralized repository of key dimensional elements and controlling data flow between applications.

This new tool will eventually replace the installation of the Win32 (Windows 32-bit) application. In fact, with each release it seems as if there is less and less functionality in the Win32 application. The Win32 tool requires you to extract a file, save it to your desktop, and then open it to make changes. The Win 32 application is simple, and does work well at updating that file, and will allow you to view data within a grid. There is no versioning or controls with the Win32, no reporting on the application changes. It is really quite limited. EPMA uses a graphical interface that provides a visual aerial view into all applications from a single screen. You can create, copy, and synchronize applications from this screen, define properties for one or multiple applications, and reuse or move artifacts from one application to another. With so much more to offer, all clients considering HFM have chosen to use EPMA.

The main pieces of EPMA are the Application Library, Dimensional Library, Data Synchronization, Application Upgrade, and Job Console.

The Application Library provides a graphical view of all applications. From this screen you can see all applications in your environment. From this screen you can see what rules have been deployed to each application, when it was last updated, data flow integrations, and whether it is synced with your Dimension Library. Administrators can deploy, open, delete, synchronize, duplicate, compare, validate, migrate, and reregister applications.

This screen will help an administrator reduce the effort of managing the number of applications. You can share metadata across applications. You could make a copy of an application by using the duplicate feature. Another benefit is that administrators will be able to compare modifications made in the Dimensional Library to an application to determine if those changes should be consumed by the application prior to deployment.

The Dimension Library provides an interface for administrators to view, create, and manage dimensions and hierarchies. The Dimension Library has two views, Master View and Application View.

The Master View is a central repository that contains all dimensions for any application. The Application View is the group of dimensions for a given application. When you create an Application View, the dimensions and member inherit what is in the Master View. Then when an update is made in the Master View, all applications that contain the dimension are automatically updated. Figure 2-2 shows the views together in EPMA.

EPMA allows you to move data between these applications, using Data Synchronization. You can create data movement synchronizations between Hyperion applications in EPMA. It also provides a friendly graphic flow chart of the movement of the data. Figure 2-3 is an example of a data flow in the Data Synchronization tab. The first image shows the screen

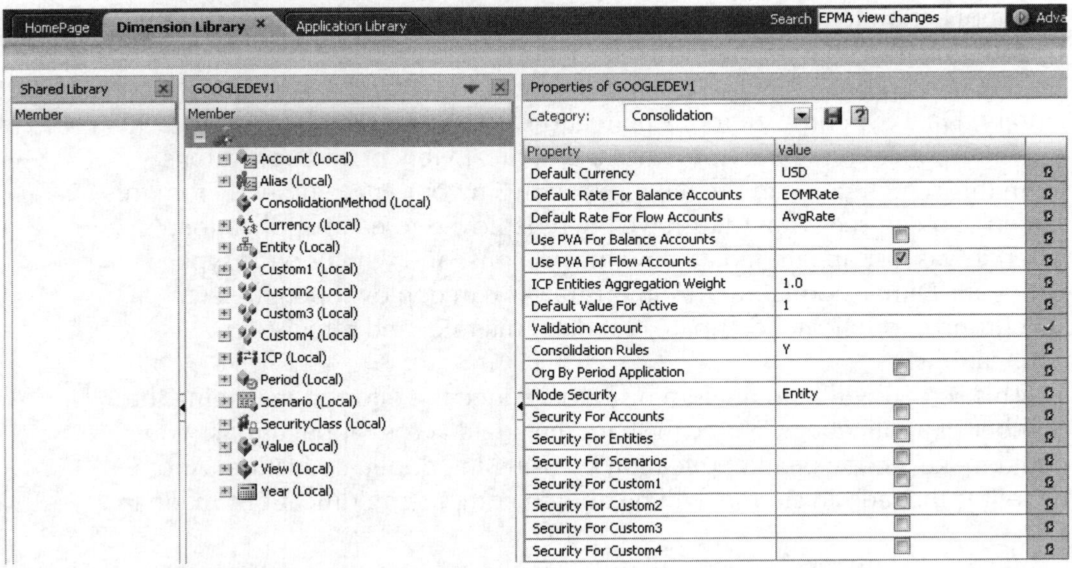

FIGURE 2-2. *Master View and Application View*

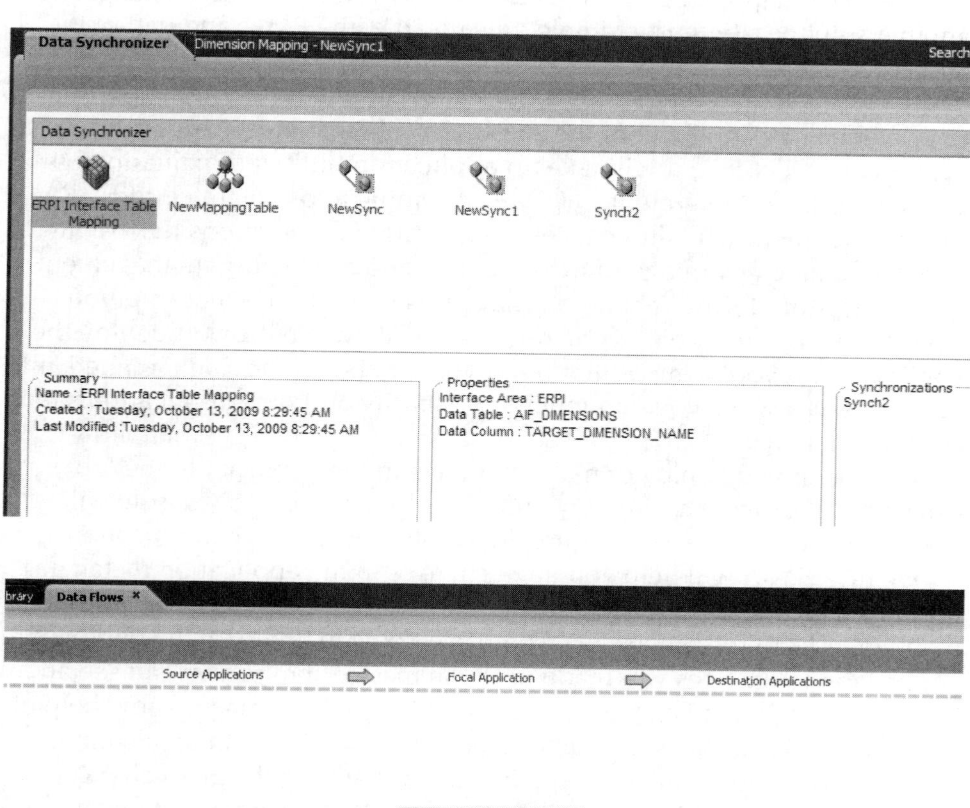

FIGURE 2-3. *Data Synchronization*

you access when configuring the Data Synchronizer. The second image is a data flow, which you access from the Application View. If the administrator has multiple applications that require synchronizing not just for metadata but data, EPMA can accomplish this. However, if you have any complex mapping, or require automation, you might want to explore another solution. But this is simple, integrated with EPMA, and part of the HFM product suite.

There are some other features of EPMA that will be useful. If you have to upgrade your application, the Application Upgrade is a key feature. When you select this, it will take an application built and maintained in Classic mode and migrate it to EPMA. An application migrated to EMPA for redeployment will allow access to upgraded applications right away and start taking advantage of the metadata and application management capabilities of EPMA. When you make this change, the first step you need to make is to update your Application View, before you deploy the application. If you want, at that point you can begin moving members into the Master View, so you can much more easily add new applications and keep them in sync.

Whenever you deploy or make a change in the application, the Job Console will provide a summary and status of the task. Job Console will track activities such as imports, deployments, and data synchronizations.

Finally, EPMA will help you track changes in the application metadata. From the Application View, you can right-click on an application to see a menu of tasks to run, and select Compare. You can compare the deployed application to changes you made or to the master library. You can see an example of the metadata tracking report in Figure 2-4. Imagine how helpful it would be to see changes you are proposing to make to an application, listing them out for a review. If a company has any rigid type of change control, then a report like this will help explain the changes and updates made to the application. It is very valuable, and yet not used as often as I would expect.

When people first use EPMA coming from the Win32 application, the first impression is that EPMA seems less responsive. That is partly because it is running over a network, and as a result there is some latency. When you consider the additional functionality, integration with the Hyperion products, and audit reporting, migration to EPMA should be a priority for any client.

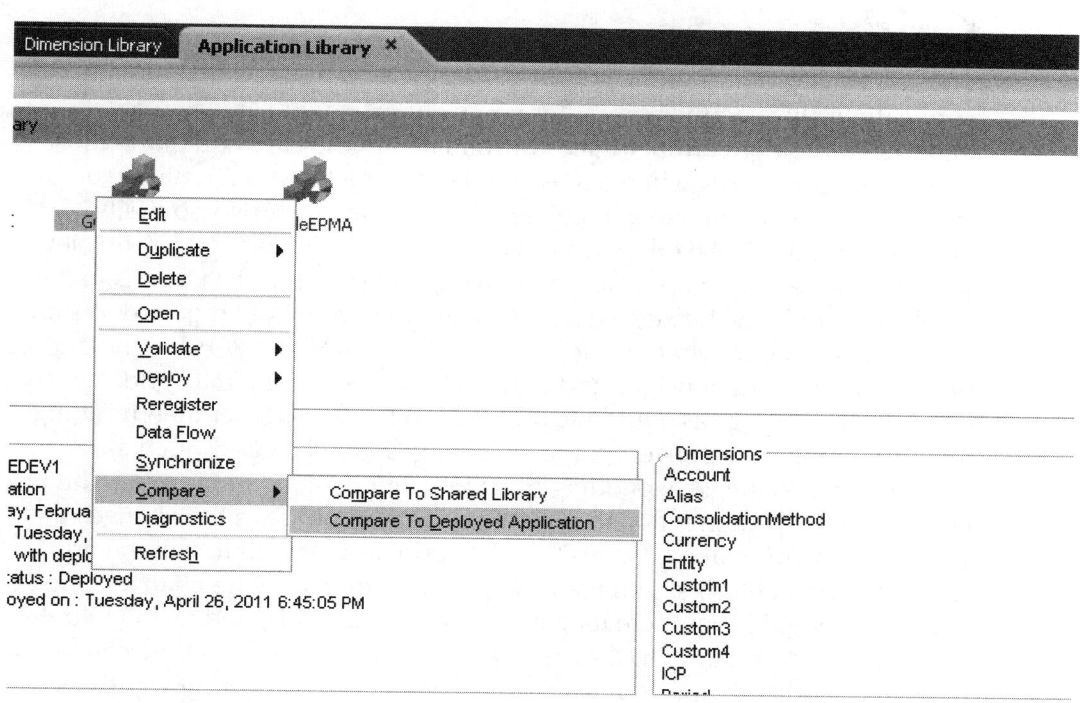

HomePage | Dimension Library | Application Library | **Compare** | Search: EPMA view changes

Dimension Compare Results

Shared Library	Status
Shared Library	
~~Account~~	Removed from Shared Library
~~Entity~~	Removed from Shared Library
~~Scenario~~	Removed from Shared Library
~~Year~~	Removed from Shared Library
~~Period~~	Removed from Shared Library
~~ICP~~	Removed from Shared Library
~~View~~	Removed from Shared Library
~~Value~~	Removed from Shared Library
~~Custom 1~~	Removed from Shared Library
~~Custom 2~~	Removed from Shared Library
~~Custom 3~~	Removed from Shared Library
~~Custom 4~~	Removed from Shared Library
~~Alias~~	Removed from Shared Library
~~Currency~~	Removed from Shared Library
~~Consolidation Method~~	Removed from Shared Library
~~Security Class~~	Removed from Shared Library

Application Compare Summary

Total Differences	19
Property Differences	3
Additions	0
Deletes	0
Renames	1
Removes	16
Moves	0
Shares	0
Includes	0
Excludes	0

Property Compare Results

Property Name	Shared Library	SimpleEPMA
Application Class	Master	Consolidation
Application Description	Master Application	
Application Name	Master	SimpleEPMA

FIGURE 2-4. *Metadata tracking*

Grids

You use data grids to view data in Hyperion Financial Management applications through the web. After you view data, you can calculate it, translate it to other currencies, or consolidate it. Grids are one of the most commonly used tools when accessing data in the HFM web interface, since you can manipulate and change the columns and rows so easily. Dimensions are displayed in rows and columns on the data grid. Grids let you drill into and find the values you need, and research data as it is in the database. Unlike with Excel or reporting, there is very little required to start seeing data in HFM when using grids. The Point of View (POV) of the grid determines what dimensions and data are displayed in the data grid. You can save the settings as a grid file and reopen the grid, rather than resetting the grid settings. Whenever you make changes to a data grid, such as changing grid settings, expanding members, or changing members in the POV bar, it is good practice to select Save Settings, to save the changes that you made. If you make changes to a data grid and attempt to exit the grid without saving changes, you are prompted to either save the changes or exit without saving. I suggest creating a set of common grids, and giving people view rights with security to these grids. Then show them how they can open them and modify them. Your users will then be able to save new grids as "private" that apply to their data and process. It will save them time, and speed up the adoption of this valuable tool.

Organizing forms and grids should be considered when building the application. You can see in Figure 2-5 how you could create folders to organize the grids and web data entry forms. People often break them into some logical grouping, by type or data entered. I always recommend thinking of the end users. If you can think of your end users as groups, then you create much more valuable groups and hence folders to manage the forms and grids. So instead of grouping grids by report type, like "Income Statement" and "Balance Sheet," you should group them by specific categories, like "Northeast Data Entry" or "Data Entry Site." Besides giving your end users fewer places to go hunting for the forms and grids they need, you make managing the logic for these folders much simpler for yourself. For those reasons, it is much more logical to set folders by the key groups or functions than by type of report.

One of the most common issues with grids, especially when starting out with HFM, is how to create a grid that will allow you to find and enter the currency rates. It is simple if you remember this one little trick. Custom1 is your "from currency" and Custom2 is your "to currency." If I were translating

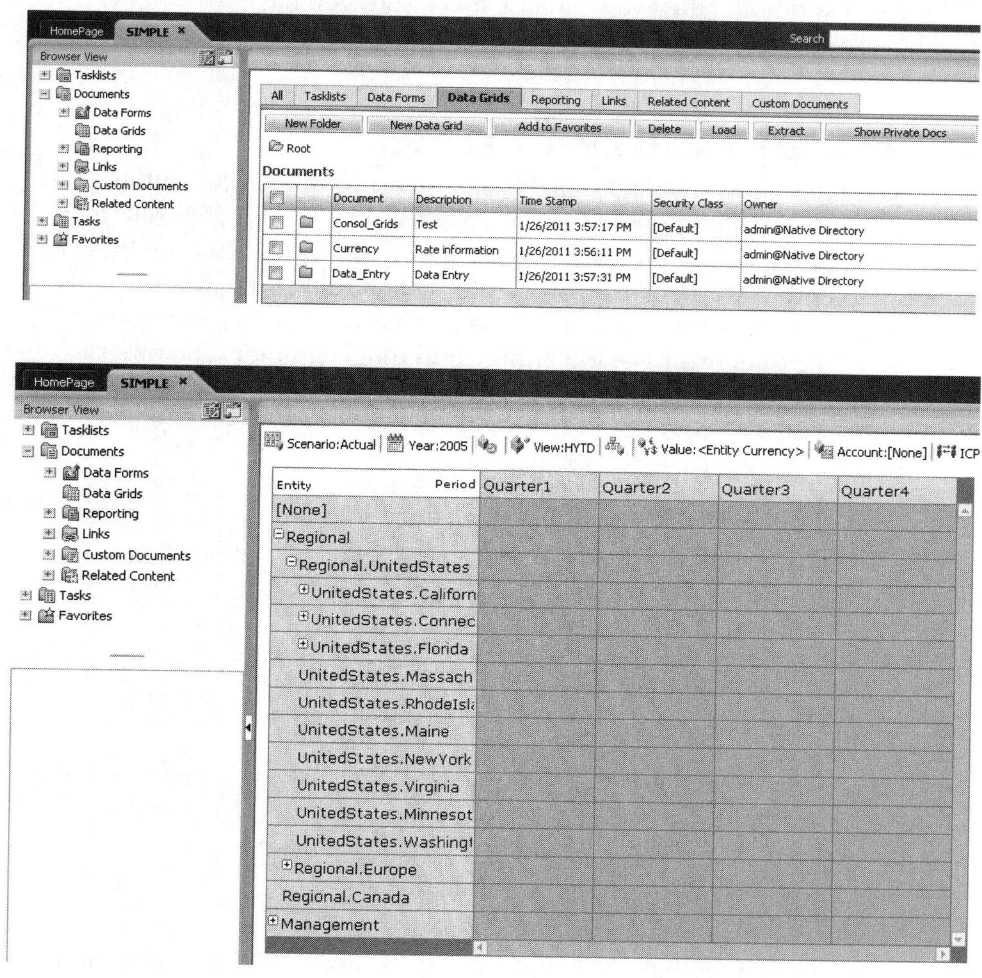

FIGURE 2-5. *Common grid and form folders*

from GBP to USD, then my Custom1 should be set to GBP and my Custom2 should be USD to see the rate. Custom2 is always "to." So you would put your custom dimensions in the rows and columns. You would then need to add the accounts for your currency rates. I prefer to put the Custom2 dimension with the accounts, in either the columns or rows, but Custom2 and accounts together. Why? I like this because if you have many accounts, you will scroll less doing it this way. Finally, make sure you have the "None" members selected for Entity, Value, Custom3, and Custom4.

Web Data Entry Forms

Web Data Entry Forms (WDEFs) are similar to grids, in that they allow you to load data manually into HFM in a web browser. They are different from grids in that they are static forms that cannot be modified. This can be very valuable to end users, because you can further simplify the end-user experience. You can hard-code and hide dimensions, making navigating through the 12 dimensions of the application much simpler. The other design consideration you should give to forms is to make them as dynamic as possible. You should use these year and period functions:

- @Cur
- @First
- @Last
- @Next
- @Prev

The first tip here is: when you are spanning years, always specify Y#@Cur as part of either the row or column definition. For example, to return the correct year if the current period is the last period, you would need

```
C1=Y#@Cur.P#@Cur(+1)
```

The @CUR member will retrieve the current member, with an offset for the month only. With other dimensions, it really doesn't make sense anyway.

You can set attributes several ways within forms. For example, you can set scale, decimals, and point of view in several places. They can be in the rows, columns, and the overall form or even down to a cell. These settings can contradict each other and create conflicts, so there is an order of precedence. So the precedence is defined as

1. Cell Override
2. Row
3. Column

4. Form
5. Default. Default decimals comes from the account, default scale from the entity currency.

When you need to create calculations, you might use SCalc within the dataforms. You use this function to specify calculations in rows, columns, or cells. It overrides the row or column definition. This can create a conflict. It is possible to not only have a formatting conflict, but also a calculation conflict. In those cases, the SCalc overrides the data that may be pulled in. You can reference an SCalc from another SCalc. They run sequentially by row. It is important to always keep these in mind and simplify your approach to these forms. Very inexperienced people will develop a set of forms and give this little thought, making maintenance a lot more work. It is only after the project is complete and there is a change to make to the forms that you appreciate this seemingly small tip.

You never want to choose having users enter data over creating an automated feed from some other source system. Users make mistakes. You want to minimize human intervention as much as possible. Still, in situations where user data entry can't be avoided, Web Data Entry Forms are a valuable tool for entering data, whether it is nonfinancial information, supplemental data like a roll forward or ratio, or a method of last resort for getting an acquisition into HFM. You should use them when the data is not available anywhere else.

A well-designed WDEF will help you make sure that users are entering data correctly. With 12 dimensions, it is very easy for people to enter data in the wrong spot, or in a place that will make reporting difficult. You can make it easier for the end users by defining many of the dimensions for them. You can use these relative members and hard-code other dimensions to make the form as intuitive as possible.

Process Management

After data is loaded into the system, HFM can require users to open grids and reports to ensure the data has passed some set of validations. Then require the users to "sign off" on the data submitted. The system records the user, time and date stamps, and any additional comments. Process Management provides all of this information. It is a valuable and helpful tool for companies to track, validate, and collect signoff on data. Consistent automated validations allow for better auditing and are yet another way HFM helps improve the data quality. If you don't use this functionality, you are ignoring a very valuable tool for your close.

Process Management is one of the modules in HFM that spans multiple areas in the product. You need to configure accounts, application settings, and rules to have it work effectively. It allows you to control access and signoff for each trial balance you have in your application. If you have your months rolling up to quarters or half-years in your application, you need to have promoted the whole quarter or half-year.

Process Management is available only for the input frequency of the scenario. For example, if the input frequency is months, Manage Process is available for January, but not for Q1. If Process Management is enabled for a scenario, validation checks are performed for each process unit as the data moves from one level to the next. Validation checks are defined by the administrator to ensure that the data submitted will pass a set of conditions. And they can be just about anything. Most commonly these are broken out into two groups, Prevent and Detect. (The first application to have these groupings used Hard and Soft, but this was long before Sarbanes-Oxley.) The Prevent validations are the basics, the validations that you want to stop the close because they are not passing. The most common Prevent validation is "out of balance." That means you can prevent someone from promoting and signing off their data if it is not in balance. Other common Prevent validations are: Intercompany Partner (ICP) suspense account exceeds threshold, Fixed Asset roll forward does not tie to Balance sheet, Cash Flow does not reconcile, and Currency Translation Adjustment (CTA) proof does not reconcile. All of these are the types of issues that would indicate significant problems with the data, and the close would need to be stopped. When you set these up, you make Prevent a parent account of all the validation accounts that are ones you want to be in this critical group. Then you make the parent account prevent the validation account in the application settings as described in Chapter 1. By doing this, you would see all the Prevent validations on the Process Management template.

Scenario:Actual | Year:2010 | View:<Scenario View> | Entity:[None] | Value:<Entity Currency> | ICP:[ICP Top] | Custom1

Account / Period	Jan - January	Nov - Novemb	Dec - Decemb
VALIDATION - Validation			
PREVENT - Account must be zero to promote entity			
V_OOB - Your Balance Sheet is out of Balance			
DETECT - DETECT			
[None] - None			

FIGURE 2-6. *Validations*

In Figure 2-6, you can see the grouping of some common validations. The other type of validation is Detect. These are all the validations that are important enough to track, but frankly are not important enough to stop the close. People should still expect a phone call to get them resolved, but these are types of validations for which there may be a good accounting reason. For example, assume that salaries increase for an entity by 20 percent. You may want a Detect validation on something like that. There may be a valid reason why that happened, but it is unusual enough that you want someone to take a look at that and be ready to explain it. Since these accounts are not a child of the Validation account in the application settings, they would not be visible in the Process Management screen. So you would need to create a report to show the validation accounts, and make the review of that report part of a process so that your end users can identify and resolve some of these issues. Some of the Detect validations I have seen are

- Expense validations. Expenses reconcile to the changes on the balance sheet.
- Debt expense. If you have debt, you also have to have expenses related to that.
- Depreciation expenses equal detail in roll forward.

You could have validations that cross both Detect and Prevent. For example, you could have an out-of-balance validation that populates a value of one in an account if the balance sheet is out of balance by an amount over one thousand. You could also have a second validation that populates a value if the trial balance is out by even a penny. The thousand-dollar validation might be a Prevent and the penny might be a Detect. So, now you could have users stop the close when they are out by some material amount, and have them research it, but not stop the close if there is some other amount that is not material. This would give you flexibility to focus on major issues with the close.

When you are promoting your data, it is important to note that you need to have these validations equal zero at Entity Currency Total. So validations that happen after translation are always Detect type.

When building validations, it is always better to create a test than to use some calculation amount. For example, if you are testing for the balance sheet to be in balance, you could either write the amount the balance sheet is out of balance to the validation account, or if the balance sheet is out of balance, then write a "1" to the validation account. It is better to use a Boolean type of number than a result because you could get false positives with an amount. If you have a journal that is causing an issue across entities, creating offsetting out-of-balance conditions between the two entities, the parent would have a passing validation of zero, although two of the children are out of balance. Using the "1" and "0," you would see "2" at the parent validation account. This would tell you that two of the children are out of balance. This is not only more accurate, but much more helpful information.

When you have these two groups, you can work to improve the data quality by moving one account to another. So after a time you may decide that the ICP suspense account issue you were tracking with a validation has been updated, cleaned up, and resolved to the point where you are ready to stop the close when it happens. This approach would let you simply move the account from the Detect parent account to the Prevent parent account. Now, you can treat the same validation as a Prevent validation without modifying the rules. You should make sure the validation was not true or populating a value for any other period before doing this, or you will not be able to unlock or reject any status level.

One last feature I see many people not take advantage of even when using tools like Process Management is maximizing the use of e-mails to notify users of status changes. Since the System 9 version of HFM, e-mail alerting capability has been available in Process Management as a way to improve communication during the review process. The rules in the following list define what e-mail alerts will be sent to the appropriate users.

- The scenario must have the attribute "Support Process Management = A."
- User must have security role access to "Receive Email Alerts for Process Management."
- User must have one of the following security access rights to the "data cell": All or Promote.
- The attribute for the security class is SupportAlert = Y for both Scenario and Entity.
- The user must have either "Submitter" or access to review level before or after the action.
- People with administrator roles do not get these e-mails.

Phased Submissions

There are times when you would not want to promote the entire chart of accounts. You may want to promote the trial balance on one day of the close and then supplemental accounts later in the close. Phased Submissions allows you to do this. It is really an extension of Process Management that enables you to group the process unit into different phases.

There are a maximum of nine submission phases in the review process. This can be defined in the metadata file, both by account, ICP, custom, scenario, and in the application settings. The process defines how it might work differently by period. There are some parts that should always be the same. When you first promote an entity, you want to take from "Not Started" to "First Pass." At this level anyone with rights to the entity can view the data. Doing this can create issues if you need the benefit of limiting people's access to the data until it has been submitted and approved.

Before you set up Phase Submission or Process Management, you should sit down and plan the groups required and the review levels required. The first important point you need to get is that each of the reviews is for each entity. People's first reaction to the limit of ten review levels is often, "only ten!" But then they realize that is ten for each entity, and a structure with several levels can have dozens of review levels. Then it hardly seems like a limitation. So by each entity, consider who needs to submit, approve, and promote at each step for the consolidation.

In Figure 2-7, you can see the groups by entity you will need to identify. You need these groups to identify the proper security classes, and both the Process Management or Phased Submission groupings, and to complete the work in security. You can see I have identified first the process by entity, then account phases. This could also be applied to the ICP and customs, but would result in more groupings. None of the members inherit submission groups from parents or from their children. The next step is to open the metadata file and set the application and dimension metadata attributes to use submission phases. Set the UseSubmissionPhase application attribute to Y, and set SupportSubmissionPhaseForAccounts, SupportSubmissionPhaseForCustom, or SupportSubmissionPhaseForICP attributes if required. You display and manage submission phases using the Manage Submission Phases task in Security.

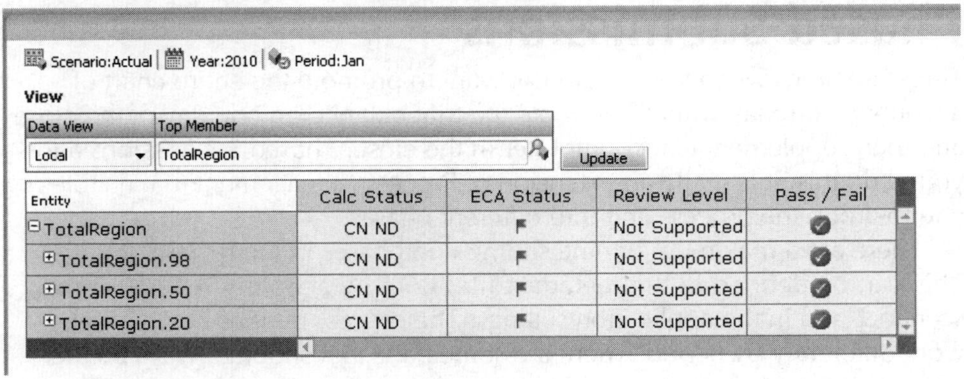

Scenario:Actual | Year:2010 | Period:Jan

View

Data View	Top Member
Local	TotalRegion

Update

Entity	Calc Status	ECA Status	Review Level	Pass / Fail
TotalRegion	CN ND		Not Supported	
TotalRegion.98	CN ND		Not Supported	
TotalRegion.50	CN ND		Not Supported	
TotalRegion.20	CN ND		Not Supported	

FIGURE 2-7. *Sample Process Management grouping*

This task is available when you have UseSubmissionPhase selected and you have the either the Administrator or Review Supervisor security role. You can select 1–9 based on the grouping defined from your planning.

You can then assign submission groups to the phases. The default for Submission Phase 1 is the keyword ALL to indicate all groups. All groups belong to Submission Phase 1 until you change their assignment.

The last step in configuring this is to do some testing. There are really two approaches; either recruit some key users to test the approach in a test environment, or create some test IDs to validate with. I would suggest some testing, however; it is critical to making sure the security is working as you planned.

Phased Submissions and Process Management change the conversation of your close. Instead of calling and asking people if they know they have issues with their data, give them the tools to find and resolve the issues themselves. You won't need to call a site and ask them, "Did you know?" because they will already be working on the resolution. That type of work is incredibly valuable during the close.

Intercompany Eliminations

HFM uses the Account, ICP, and Value dimensions to process Intercompany (ICP) matching and eliminations. This functionality matches values between ICP accounts that share a common suspense account (plug account), automatically creates eliminations at the proper entity levels for each intercompany account, and writes unresolved differences into the specified suspense account (plug account). The first concern people have is that HFM is somehow plugging the data in the consolidation. It actually isn't working quite that way.

In Figure 2-8 we show how this elimination works. For each intercompany transaction that is eliminating, HFM will create both sides of the entry that offsets the data value from the intercompany account, and intercompany partner. That offsetting amount, though, is written to the plug account. If the entries do in fact match, then the debit and credit for each side of the intercompany match would net to zero. For example, if you had one entity with an intercompany payable and one with an intercompany receivable,

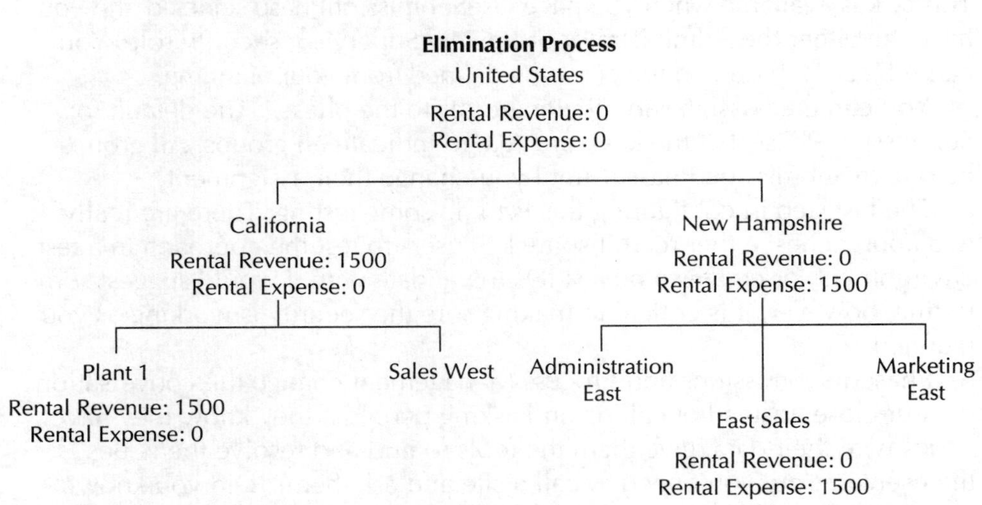

Entity	Value	Account: SalesInterco	PurchasesInter	IntercoDiffPL
California.1000	<Entity Currency>	500		
	[Elimination]	-500		500
California.Plant1	<Entity Currency>		600	
	[Elimination]		-600	-600
UnitedStates.California	<Entity Currency>	0	0	-100
	[Elimination]			

FIGURE 2-8. *Intercompany example*

when each entity reaches the common parent, when the elimination should take place, there is an entry in the Value dimension for that account that offsets the amount in the account eliminating. At the same time, HFM also writes a value for each offset it created to the suspense account or plug account.

For intercompany matching and elimination functionality to work, several interdependent features must be properly enabled:

- Intercompany accounts must be flagged as IsICP.
- Accounts flagged as IsICP must have a PlugAccount specified. If an account is flagged as IsICP but no PlugAccount is assigned, it will consolidate but will not eliminate.
- Entities that can engage in Intercompany activity must be flagged as IsICP. When an entity is flagged as IsICP, it is automatically added to the ICP (Intercompany Partner) dimension. Only entities that are part of the ICP dimension are valid choices for Intercompany accounts. When flagging entities, you should always flag the lowest level at which your intercompany data is available. That should be the base entity. You can flag parents, but be aware that if you do use parents and wish to reorganize your entities, you will need to have the entities that are flagged as intercompany continue to be the lowest level of your new structure. Not doing this will cause your eliminations to fail. Whenever possible, you should try to make them ICP entities as base members, but when this is not possible, know the impact.

The ICP dimension represents the ICP Partners, which an originating entity can post an entry against (for Intercompany flagged accounts). This is a reserved dimension that is used by HFM to track and eliminate Intercompany transaction details across the Account dimension and related Custom dimensions. Accounts that are matched and eliminated in HFM are typically set as outlined in the following list and in Figure 2-9.

- The IsICP attribute should typically be flagged as R for all Intercompany accounts. This will allow an entity to have ICP transactions with all ICP entities, except with themselves. As well, the [ICP None] member can be selected. Values entered to [ICP None] represent third-party activity and will not eliminate.

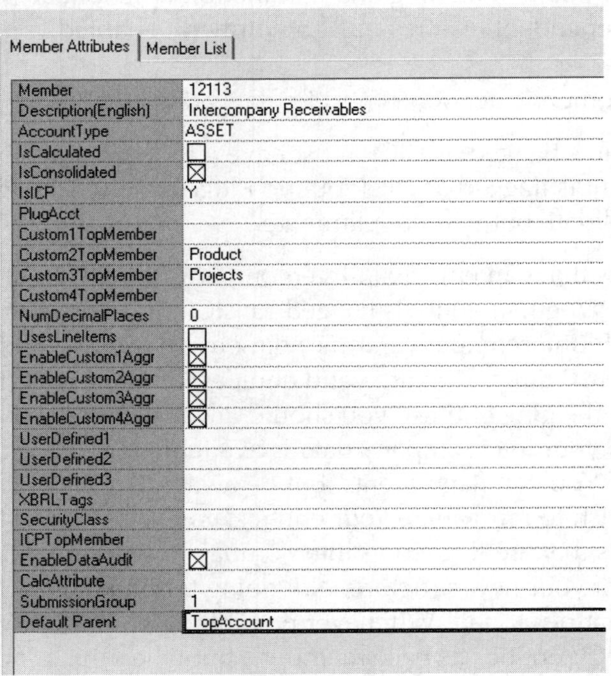

FIGURE 2-9. *Intercompany account settings*

- Plug accounts will be used only for automatic elimination processing and should never have data loaded into them through FDM or Journal Entry. All plug accounts should be flagged as IsCalculated to prevent any possibility of manual input. A plug account should be used for each intercompany match. So you should not have Payables and Receivables share the same plug account as your Intercompany Sales.
- Plug accounts should be flagged as IsICP so that out-of-balance mismatches can be easily detailed by Intercompany Partner.

- Most intercompany and plug accounts will set the ICPTopMember attribute to [ICP Top]. This will allow input into the [ICP None] member. You could avoid using NoInput rules by using [ICP Entities] as the ICPTopMember.
- Built-in system Intercompany matching reports are available to view and track intercompany transactions at any time through the HFM web site.

There are some great reports that really help with viewing intercompany reporting that are ready to view "right out of the box" with HFM. Ironically, the issues people have often involve two problems. First, the formatting of the reports is pretty static, even though the reports can pull in quite a bit of data. If you have a very specific format, and find you are inflexible, then you will have an issue with the report. The second issue is pulling a large volume of data. I have to question any report that tries to pull data from every entity. How valuable is that report? When someone wants to sit and tick and tie each intercompany match on a report, he or she has not followed the guidelines outlined in the preceding list. If I use an intercompany for *each* match, as outlined earlier, I could look at that suspense account from the top parent entity and validate that it in fact has a zero balance. Then drill down to ensure that each match was done correctly as you move down the organizational structure.

The biggest reason to use the system ICP Report is that it ignores security for the intercompany accounts. So each person can see matching balances even though they don't have access to the offsetting amounts. Reports and Smart View do not offer this. This feature can be really helpful to get people to take ownership of the intercompany matching process, which usually reserved for the corporate consolidation team.

Figure 2-10 shows the new user interface for creating an ICP Report.

1. The first sections define the Name, Description, Style Sheet, and Security Class for the report.
2. Select the appropriate Entity and Partner selection. You will only see entities flagged as ICP here.

Overrides for generation of Intercompany Reports

- Place a check next to the values you wish to override when printing the selected reports.

HFM_IntercompanyDefault.xsl

Override POV: Actual 2010 Jan <Scenario View> <Entity Currency>

Entity: Partner:

Suppress Matches: Matching Tolerance: Matching Tolerance (Percent)

Suppress Reversed:

Suppress Details:

Suppress Customs: Custom1 Custom2 Custom2 Custom2

Scale Factor: 0

Decimal Override: 0

Member Display: Label Description

Plug Account Display: Summary

Group By: Custom1 Custom2 Custom3 Custom4 Do not Group

OK Cancel

ICP Report 4100 Matching

Scenario: Actual
Year: 2005
Period: October
View: Periodic
Value: <Entity Currency>
Suppress Reversed: No

Entity: Connecticut.4100
Partner: California.1000
Suppress Matches: No
Matching Tolerance: 0
Scale Factor: 0
Decimal Override: 0

Date: 9/28/2005
Time: 2:35:14 PM
User: RREILEY1\rreiley
Plug Account:
Suppress Details: No

Entity	Partner	Account	Custom1	Custom2	Custom3	Custom4	Entity Amount	Partner Amount	Difference
4100	1000	SalesInterco	Network	[None]	[None]	[None]	1,500		
1000	4100	PurchasesInterco	Network	[None]	[None]	[None]		1,000	
4100 1000							1,500	1,000	500

Grand Total 500

FIGURE 2-10. *ICP matching report*

3. Select the Suppression options:

   - **Suppress Matches** You can specify tolerances as well.
   - **Suppress Reversed** Removes transaction matching to the same account.
   - **Suppress Details** Shows a summary.
   - **Suppress Customs** Just shows accounts and not custom detail. If you suppress customs in this report, then you should add your top custom member to the intercompany accounts in the script. This will match only at the top custom members, instead of showing each custom, which could be many more rows.

4. Select Display options:

   - **Scale Factor** Sets scaling.
   - **Decimal Override** Select the number of decimal places displayed.
   - **Member Display** Display label or description or both.
   - **Group By** Allows for grouping of transactions by a Custom dimension. Note that this also provides subtotals by the selected custom dimension.

5. Select accounts to be used in the report.

You could just select a plug account, so if you have each match by a single plug, the report would be much more valuable.

A new feature in HFM System 9 and later provides for much faster ICP reports by improving how translation is done for the report. Consider that the intercompany reporting has to be done in a common currency. Also consider that it is almost always the parent currency, so that means the consolidation is complete and the translation is done. However, there are times when you might want to see the report in another currency for the matching. HFM used to do this translation on the fly, but now that is only an option, and the default is to translate using the Sub Translate routine. The Sub Translate routine is much more accurate than the on-the-fly translation.

It would have all the special rules and translation calculations you might need as well. Also, the on-the-fly calculations are sometimes slow, and when you bring in a lot of data, can really slow the report creation. In newer versions of HFM when the ICP report is run in a different currency, by default the system uses existing translation logic Sub Translate in rules and commits changes to the database. So when your Entity Currency does not have a status of OK, you will get an error since the calculation needs to run on <entity currency> before any Sub Translate can be run. In older releases, the translation is just done on the fly using default translations (no Sub Translate) and is not stored, so you will not have this issue in prior releases. If in your application, as in most U.S. applications, the base entity rolls up to a USD entity, and the ICP report is run most often in USD, the newer code would be much faster for the ICP report to run since the data would most often be in an OK status for USD.

If someone did choose another currency to reconcile the ICP, the HFM would generate a new set of data records in some other currency. Since both are considered on the fly, no values are written back to the database in either case.

You can change how the ICP system report translates by following these steps:

1. Open the Registry and find the following key:

   ```
   KEY_LOCAL_MACHINE\SOFTWARE\Hyperion Solutions\Hyperion
   Financial Management\Server\SystemReports
   ```

2. Under the SystemReports registry key, add a DWORD value named IcmSystemReportTranslationMode.
3. Set this value to either: 1-Use SubTranslate or 2-On the Fly(no Sub Translate rule).

If you set up the intercompany eliminations correctly in HFM, and have your users using the intercompany matching report, they will be proactively driving resolution of the issues that can slow down the close. This is yet another tool where HFM can change the conversation of the close, where people are asking, "Did you know?" or "What is this?," to more statements like, "I already started resolving this" and "You will see the update soon."

Intercompany Transaction Module

HFM allows users to enter and post intercompany transactions to the application. This chapter will cover some of the basics and design considerations you should have when using this module. Adoption of the Intercompany Transaction module (ICT) has been slow in the United States. There are a couple of reasons for this; first, the natural position for the intercompany matching process is further upstream in the close process; second, you need multiple systems to provide the detail required at the same level; third, it has to provide more value than seeing balances alone reconcile. Since many U.S. companies continue to settle cash and intercompany in U.S. dollars, reconciling intercompany at local or transactional currencies is not as pressing an issue. This is still a very valuable tool, especially if you have many intercompany eliminations and a weak process for reconciling and matching the data.

In your application as part of the setup, the administrator should also create a list of valid Reason Codes to explain why certain transactions are not matched. These Reason Codes will only need to be set up once in the application, and they are available to use in any periods. You can manually create the Reason Codes or load them from an ASCII file. The Reason Codes should be something informative. As you begin to list out the codes, you should also consider the types of issues you will see. Some you can resolve quickly, others are exchange-rate-related, and still others are related to specific process issues you may have. Consider grouping them as you list them out. It will make adoption smoother, and help users think about what are the next steps during the matching process.

There are two ways to enter the transactions. Either you can manually create the transaction, or if the transaction information comes from an external system, you can load the transactions file directly into the application. The important thing to remember when designing the application is that the data need to be at the correct level. You may be loading data by account, by two or three custom members, and by intercompany partner. When you're doing that, it is not a good decision to assume users will be able to key that in. First, they will make mistakes. Second, the volume of data manually entered could become a bottleneck in the close process, putting deadlines at risk.

Like other modules, the Intercompany Transaction module has a rule section. Transaction rules are written in the Sub Transactions routine, and specify the accounts in the application that support intercompany transactions. Cell intersections defined here are read-only in web grids and data forms. Only a subset of rules are used in this section:

- HS.SupportsTran "*POVExpression*"
- CalculateExchangeRate
- CalculateRate
- CreateInputCache
- IsAlmostEqual
- IsZero

When defining the process for having users enter data into HFM, you want to identify what they will be doing in each step. I recommend thinking through the functionality, and asking questions to understand how best to support the process in place. It helps, though, to start the conversation with what the most common steps are or steps other people use when using this tool. The most common to consider are

- Opening an IC period for starting the IC Transaction Process
- Creating IC Transaction details
- Matching IC Transaction details
- Posting IC Transaction details
- Monitoring IC Transaction process
- Making additional changes after IC Transactions have been posted
- Running matching reports
- Performing drill-through from account balance
- Locking entities to prevent future update
- Closing the IC period to prevent any more IC Transaction changes

Once the data is in and matched, you can use the Monitor Intercompany Transactions feature to track and report the intercompany transaction matching process. Assuming you have several ledger systems, the whole process can be time-consuming to ensure that all transactions are entered and matched successfully. The Monitor Intercompany Transactions feature enables the administrator to easily find out which intercompany partners have started their intercompany transactions process. The entities are links to Intercompany Transactions Monitor Detail information. Clicking an entity on the screen opens a window that displays the number of posted and unposted transactions by status, such as Matched, Mismatched, or Unmatched.

You can also configure e-mailing for the Intercompany Matching, as for Process Management. The e-mailing functionality is available throughout the ICT module. If you are unable to reconcile the differences in the matching report, you may want to send an e-mail alert to the Partner Entity. Another possible usage of e-mail alerts may be in the Monitoring screen. During the Monitor process, you can identify entities that have not yet begun their IC process. You may want to send e-mail alerts to the users who are responsible for the entities to remind them.

Line Item Detail

In Hyperion Financial Management, you can provide detail below the account level, called line item detail (LID). A user can create detail below the displayed account with custom descriptions for each line added. It can be used for only certain accounts, as defined by the administrator. The first thing to consider with line item detail is that it does not consolidate. This makes reporting on it a bit of a challenge. If you are collecting data from many base entities, and there is detail there, you would have to pull all of those entities into a report to get the information.

Most of the major enhancements to line item detail were done in the releases before 4.0, and it has not changed very much since then. As always, once you set an account up for LID, you can only load at the LID detail.

Line item detail has a specific rule that can help with the close process, GetNumLID—returns the number of lines entered for LID. You can use this to test if detail was provided for an account, but not to see the details. But you can't use the data in LID for calculations in HFM.

When making a change to cells that have line item detail, which includes deleting accounts, changing the default view or other settings, you will need to extract the line item detail, then delete it completely from the application. Then you can make your structural changes and reload the line item detail.

I suggest using line item detail for things like top ten customers and asset names. Knowing that the data will not consolidate should help you identify what is good information to enter in this feature.

Organization by Period and Structures

When deciding to write rules for customizing the consolidation, you will very likely need to use the Organization by Period (OrgbyPeriod) functionality. This enables the most recent consolidation structure to coexist with past structures in the same application. Organizational structures can change for many reasons, including acquisitions, disposals, mergers, and reorganizations—all of the reasons we are modifying the rules in our consolidation. Although there appears to be a spread between the use of OrgbyPeriod and consolidation rules, this is wrong. If you have consolidation rules, then you likely require the use of Organization by Period. If you choose not to use OrgbyPeriod, you will require rules to fix what the system should handle for you. The Default Frequency and Default View do not affect consolidation; however, they do affect rules. Zero View for NonAdjust and Zero View for Adjust as well as Consolidate YTD will also impact data and rules. These Default View settings tell HFM how to handle missing data in the next period, if there was data in the prior period. So, the Default View affects rules for numbers in flow type accounts (Income, Expense, and Flow). For example, in a Periodic scenario you would need to specify W#YTD on the right side of the expression to retrieve YTD numbers in a Sub Calculate routine, but the inverse would be true for a YTD scenario.

Here are the recommended Organization by Period settings:

- **Default Frequency** MTD
- **Default View** Periodic
- **ZeroView for Non Adjust** Periodic
- **ZeroView for Adjust** Periodic
- **Consolidate YTD** No

These settings allow for the proper consolidation of numbers on both a periodic and YTD basis based on the active and inactive members as they could be defined with Organization by Period.

How Organization By Period works is basically by having Financial Management have the entity appear twice in the organization, and then with the use of a system account, Active, determining the active or inactive consolidation status of a child into its parent. For example, the entity appears twice and you tell HFM which of the two would consolidate.

The Active account uses the Intercompany dimension to store data about its children at the parent level. Children that correspond to ICP members for which the Active account is equal to 0 are considered to be inactive children and are not consolidated. Children that correspond to ICP members for which the Active account is equal to 1 are considered to be active children and are consolidated. The DefaultValueForActive attribute controls the status of children for which the Active account is blank. So, every parent-child intersection does not have to be flagged as active or inactive. By default, every child is active in relation to its parent unless otherwise specified.

Basically there are two main groups of structures you might see in the Entity dimension to support complex consolidations. The first is *flat*. There is one parent and several children, and a holding company. Looking at Figure 2-11, you can see what that structure might look like. The approach here simplifies the consolidation. There are no subgroups and steps that you need to do. The focus here is on the total consolidated company.

This second type is called a *staged consolidation*. The focus here is being able to see consolidation levels. Figure 2-12 shows us what a structure might

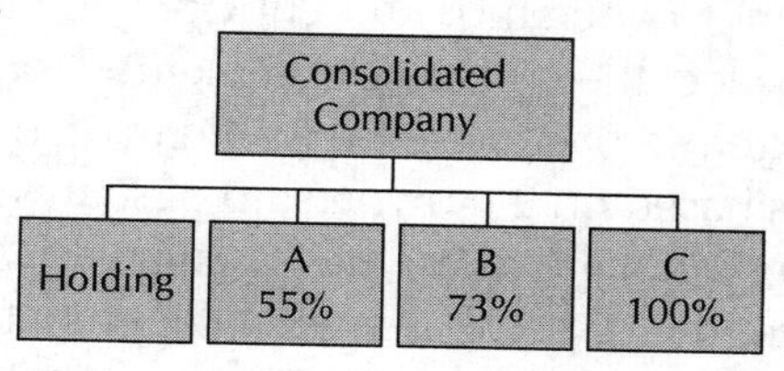

FIGURE 2-11. *Flat structure*

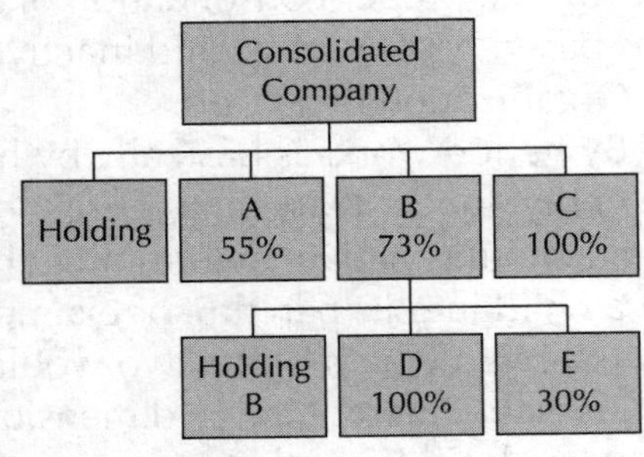

FIGURE 2-12. *Staged structure*

look like. It is important to point out that each level of ownership has a holding company. That will allow the system to record the investment and eliminations correctly.

I would recommend thinking about what your structure needs to be in order to accomplish your reporting. This can get very complex, especially if there are two passes of consolidation rules at each level. This is called a Double Staged or Equity Pickup.

Ownership Module

The Ownership module of HFM allows users to provide ownership information in HFM, and show total and ultimate ownership information, calculate the correct methods of consolidation, and report on that information. You do this in the Ownership Management module by entering ownership information for entities, such as Percent Ownership, Percent Consolidation, and Percent Control. You can also select the consolidation method for the entity and select whether the entity is active or inactive. HFM can also calculate certain ownership percentages based on the ownership of shares of entities provided. Using a specific subroutine in the rules, the Calculate Ownership task on the Ownership Module uses the direct share percentages that entities own to calculate the ultimate ownership and control percentages. One important thing to note with these accounts is that the names they use are *reserved*, meaning they cannot be used anywhere else in the application. Figure 2-13 shows an example of an ownership structure in the module.

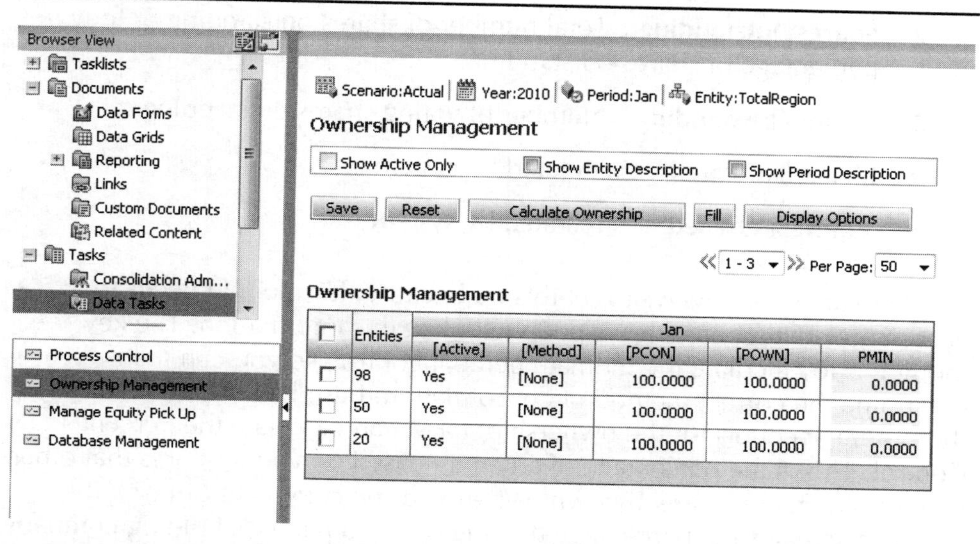

FIGURE 2-13. *Ownership module*

The following are the system accounts HFM uses to provide this information:

- **[Active]** Consolidation status of a child into its parent
- **[PCON]** Percent of an entity that consolidates to its parent
- **[POWN]** Percent ownership based on the shares of the entity that are owned
- **[DOWN]** Percent of direct ownership
- **[PCTRL]** Percent control based on the voting shares of the entity that are owned by other entities
- **SharesOwned** Total number of shares owned
- **VotingOwned** Number of voting shares owned

- **SharesOutstanding** Total number of shares outstanding or the percentage of shares outstanding
- **VotingOutstanding** Number of voting shares outstanding
- **Shares%Owned** Calculated by system
- **Voting%Owned** Calculated by system

There are several ways to set this up because this module needs to accommodate the many ways people look at this information. The key, though, is to calculate the ultimate percent control, so you can then determine the correct method of consolidation. Based on the information in the system accounts for the ownership, HFM can calculate the Percent Control. This is the percentage of an entity based on voting shares that other entities directly or indirectly own. When you select Percent Control, the system calculates the percentage that the selected parent's holding company controls of each dependent based on the shares information stored in the Voting%Owned. You can load this ownership information just like any other data, although you do have to select the Include Ownership Data button.

So once the system has the correct ownership percentages and the values it needs, you can determine the correct method for the consolidation. When a company owns another company, you have to determine how the owned entity will be presented. For example, a common method is Equity. The Equity method has the owning company present its equities as an asset. This method in HFM is also the set of rules that determine how data will consolidate data from an entity to its parent. The system determines this method based on the percent control and the available consolidation methods in the Consolidation method metadata table if the UsedbyCalcRoutine is enabled. You can't just add them to the rules. If the entity is a holding company for the parent, then for that holding company the rules will not use the percent control. Instead, it will use the method that has the IsHoldingMethod enabled. The rules that are required for each method and sample methods are covered in the rules section of this book, Chapter 3.

I ask people to consider, when building reports to view the data, that the data is stored in ICP members for those accounts. If you require better or easier reporting, you can build reports to show this information. If you do, you may want to create some holding accounts that make the reporting of this information easier. You need to make sure you do a couple of things when doing this. First, use new account names, not anything already defined in the system. Second, have the rules run for a place in the structure that do not consolidate, like the Proportion node of the Value dimension.

If you are building any consolidation rules for HFM, you should not hard-code the methods or assign them using an approach that excludes this module. You can plan for the future and growth of the company regardless of how complex your rules become, if you incorporate this tool as part of your project.

Equity Pickup Module

Equity Pickup is a method of re-evaluating the investments owned by a holding company, allowing the parent to realize changes in equity. This results in the holding company's balance sheet showing the current value of the corresponding share in the equity of the subsidiary. Investments are normally shown at historical or acquisition cost. But an invested company has a value that can vary based on the profit and loss they are incurring. The Equity Pickup adjustment offsets the historical cost in local currency, showing the actual value of the equity owned. The Equity Pickup adjustment is not unlike the Equity method described in the "Ownership Module" section of this chapter.

You can calculate the adjustment by simply taking the direct ownership percentage multiplied by the equity of the entity owned and then subtract the investment in the parent. The administrator or users can enter the percentage of ownership into the Equity Pickup module. Once this information is in the system, you can calculate the adjustments. You could just use a regular account and build this into the rules without using the Equity Pickup module, but the module does some specific things to help. In fact, if you have a system older than Fusion when this was first available, you may not be using this feature. And you might be thinking, these rules are complicated enough, and if it works why open a can of worms? Well, there are some nice advantages here when it is set up correctly.

The format and form allow you to much more easily get the information into HFM in a way that helps create the adjustment. As in other modules discussed, there are special rules. Equity Pickup rules specify the owned entity, owner entity, and percentage of ownership. There is a section of the rules that run specifically for the Equity Pickup from the module. In this section, you can specify how this will be calculated. The Sub EquityPickUp uses the Percentage Equity Pick Up (PEPU) function to get the percentage of ownership form the Equity Pickup table. You can run these rules from the Equity Pickup module. Another nice feature is that the system will impact these entities by pairs. So when there is a change in status in the calculation of the owner, the owned or any Equity Pick Up (EPU) descendant of the owned, you will see that rules need to rerun to update the adjustment. Once the rate has been pulled, you are ready to calculate the adjustment. Let's assume you have an entity owned (Keene) 75 percent by some parent (Boston). You would need that 75 percent in the system. You would also need to see that entity Keene was bought for $1,000,000. That would be recorded in the Boston set of books and loaded into HFM. But since Keene has been growing over the last year, it is really worth $2,000,000. The adjustment is (75% *2,000,000) – 1,000,000 = 500,000. This reflects the actual value of Keene, which is 75 percent of the $2,000,000.

So if you have Equity Pickup adjustments, and you can use this module, you should. It helps report, track, load, and calculate the values you need, and make this adjustment much easier to manage.

Database Management

Database Management is a module in HFM that allows administrators to perform some critical tasks. They are Copy, Clear, and Delete Invalid Records. These tasks are often critical to application maintenance, but they also impact the close process and other features you might use. For example, some people will consider using rules to copy actual data into the Forecast scenario. This will work fine, but consider that you will have rules to do this, and since you don't want them running all the time, you need a flag account to turn them on and off, and you need to watch scope, making sure they run correctly. It is enough in this book that there is a whole chapter dedicated to defining rules and setting them up, Chapter 3. So why not consider using this feature that is ready to run right away, and is flexible and secure with very little setup work?

Copy and Clear are two intuitive options. While there are some special considerations for system accounts and line item detail, these features work just about as you would expect. One thing I always point out to people, though, is what the Derived data means. When you select this option, it will pull parent and calculated accounts. Derived data is also parent entities, all data at this level. When using Clear, there are two things that seem to surprise people. You cannot clear any cells that contain line item detail, and you cannot clear locked data.

The Delete Invalid Records feature scans an application for invalid records and allows you to remove them. You must be an administrator to do this. Running the Delete Invalid Records process puts a huge impact on the database, network, and Financial Management environment. So, this feature should not be run during heavy usage periods, and never during the close. But this does not mean it should not be run. Older applications could have a significant amount of data that cannot be cleared any other way.

This happens in the database when you have an entity or scenario where you loaded data and then delete it. The data that was associated with the member still resides in the table. For example, you may have an entity called France. And when created, France is given an entity ID of 10 (because it is the tenth entity created). Then within the tables of HFM, all the data loaded to France is represented by France with this ID. You could find the field when you look at the tables and locate the EntityID field. All the data loaded will be broken out by record and given an EntityID of 10. When you delete the entity, the only thing removed is the association between France and 10. The data records remain. This is to make the speed of the metadata loads acceptable. Running all the possible validations could really slow the loads down. Over time, as metadata is changed, some of the existing records in the database will become invalid.

There are two types of invalid records. The first are what I have already described. These are invalid metadata members. These are members that existed at some point and were populated with data. Renaming or deleting these members orphans the data in the database. This type of invalid record can be deleted safely by using Delete Invalid Records. The second type are invalid intersections. This type is created when there was a relationship between the metadata members that was valid and is no longer. The members are still valid in the application, but the relationship where the data is populated is no longer valid. Most commonly it is when there are changes to the CustomXTopMember relationship, and less commonly moving a parent-child relationship. This type of invalid data is not currently removed by any HFM functionality. The only way to resolve this issue is to rebuild the application.

Rebuilding the application as an option is not appealing. You lose Process Management information and audit trails and have to reconcile the database. It should not be taken lightly. The best option is to be aware of this, and clear your data *before* you make the metadata changes. Depending on the types of the invalid records in the database, and how successful Delete Invalid Records is in deleting them, rebuilding the application could be your only option. Since invalid records are extracted, the data extracted is clear of invalid data.

You may be asking why Oracle didn't add this validation for the metadata load. The reality is that validating every possible intersection is not reasonable. There is a big impact to metadata loading when the existing validations run. You can see the impact when you try to load a file that has many errors or validation checks. Anyone who has tried to load an entity reorganization without unposting all the journals can tell you that the file seems to take forever to load. When there are no errors, loading is quick. Because of this impact, one validation in particular is excluded when metadata is loaded into HFM. It is the validation to check for invalid records.

I recommend that customers delete invalid records every couple of months, especially after significant changes to metadata. While doing this task is relatively safe for the database, if you have never done it, or it has been a while since you've done it, it can take a long time to complete. So be sure to do this during a down time for the application and never during the close.

Security

You have your application structure defined, but before you start loading data into the system you need to think about security. Maybe you don't want to have anyone looking at anything they want, or maybe you do. But your security model needs to plan for this, and plan for what you will have in the future. I suggest you start with thinking about the data you have as a first starting point for security. Without data, many of the other objects in HFM provide little value. A grid is not important if you cannot see any data. Some people want to limit what structures people can see.

Oracle HFM Security

Security in HFM is important for more than just the obvious reasons. Security settings are critical for many reports, forms, and features. Setting security is a very fine line between giving access to too much data, and limiting the functionality to a point where you limit your potential return on your investment. Ultimately, the decision of how tight or restrictive you want the security to be is up to you. HFM will allow for most dimensions and objects to be secured. It can be done by user and by group. The first thing you should take away from this chapter is how not to make the security a nightmare to maintain and own. The second thing is to realize that the security can also be configured in a way that enhances some functionality.

Let's just start with some security basics. There are some key features you should be familiar with. Security within Hyperion Financial Management is composed of the following objects:

- **Users** People who need access
- **Groups** Users with common rights
- **Roles** Common tasks each group might use
- **Classes** Tags assigned to metadata items

Now we have some key terms defined. We need to discuss how a user gets access within HFM. Users have two processes they must pass to get access to data and objects in HFM. They are authentication and authorization.

Authentication is the process of validating that the user is in fact a valid user and has provided the correct credentials. You can have HFM do this process against other systems that are external to HFM, like Lightweight Directory Access Protocol (LDAP), NT LAN Manager (NTLM), or Active Directory (AD). This is commonly called external authentication. When using these external systems, none of the password information is sorted within HFM. Authentication gives the users access to them by authorization.

Authorization is the process in which the application determines, based on classes and roles, what objects and data the user can view. This next process is controlled through User Provisioning in HFM. When you are authorized, the system determines, for example, whether you have modify rights to an entity and grants those to the person. This step of creating how users are granted authentication rights occurs when the user is Provisioned. Provisioning is managed through the User Management Console, and is defined at the user or group level. That would be when you add a user to HFM and select what rights the user has. You could, for example, have a class called TOTAL COMPANY. That class might be attached to the top entity. If you give someone view rights to that class, they could view the entity. So, take a step back and follow through how a user would get access to that data. First, they would enter their logon information and get authenticated. The external security database ensures that the user exists, is current, not locked out or suspended, and the password is correct. Then those credentials are handed to the User Management Console, where the application determines the user was given view rights to anything with the TOTAL COMPANY class. That class could be attached to many objects, but in our example it just attached to the top parent entity. Now the user can see the data.

There is a class called Default. For members that do have a class, the Default class is used. Most users will have to have access to this Default class.

A user can have rights from being a member of a group or individually. When there is a conflict, the user will get the least restrictive access. So it is best to keep these separate. In other words, you should use either groups or individuals for an object or roles in HFM. Not doing so will create a maintenance nightmare. As a rule, I would recommend that groups are best used for roles, and individuals are best assigned to classes. Organization here will keep you from making the security a maintenance nightmare.

Groups are helpful when you have many users with the same rights, like for roles. When you have many users with unique rights, groups are not helpful.

I like to start with a spreadsheet to keep all this organized. This is a trick that has been used as far back as Hyperion Enterprise, but has evolved with the new tasks and still works for HFM. I will list my users along the rows, and the columns are grouped with classes and rows. You should decide what dimensions you want to secure at this point. Almost every application secures entities and scenarios. That is because most people look at their data by legal entity and scenario. You may have modify rights to an entity in

Budget, but only view rights to the same entity in Actual. So consider that you may not just want to secure a dimension by giving access or not, but you may also want to secure just by the type of access. I would list those dimensions across the top, and put as subgroupings my classes, as shown in Figure 2-14.

Next, you will need to start thinking about the roles by group that you want to create. You should think generally at first. What are the main roles you have for the system? Maybe you have an administrator, maybe a reporting-only user, someone to manage just security? You should list those roles across the top of that spreadsheet as well. Now you need to start refining these groups. You can start with these user groups. I would start another list. I would put all of my tasks along my rows, and the roles I defined along my columns. For all of the products you have defined, list the tasks you will need to update by role. You can use that list to update the role groups with tasks that make sense. Once you have the role groups defined, you can add users to these groups in the User Management Console. If a user was added to the administrator group, they would have the right assigned to that group. And obviously the same is true for the user group.

So, now that you have your role groups defined and built, you are ready to have the users given rights to the classes. You will first need to determine what are the classes based on the dimensions you decided to secure.

Hyperion HFM User to Group Cross Reference

		Scenario Class		Enity Class		Role	
USER ID	**USER NAME**	**Group 1**	**Group 2**	**Group 5**	**Group 6**	**Group 7**	**Group 9**
		Admin	**Admin**	**Cawse**	**Kuching**	**Thailand**	**AsiaPacific**
	User 1						
	User 2						
	User 3						
	User 4						
	User 5						
	User 6						
	User 7						
	User 8						
	User 9						
	User 10						

FIGURE 2-14. *The security template*

Before you start assigning users and creating anything, you should first decide on a naming convention. First, if you had only two groups, you might just have HFM_PARENT and HFM_BASE. Each group would be assigned rights appropriate for them.

Finally, you are ready to define the classes for your application. HFM security relies on security classes in the same way Hyperion Enterprise used them, if you were familiar with those. If you are not, a *class* is a code or tag attached to metadata and other application objects (forms, grids, system reports), and users are granted access to the classes. I always use the same name or label of the metadata item that is being secured. This may sound confusing at first. But this actually makes giving rights to the class easy. You will find later that when you give someone rights to France, it is easy to find the France class. To create classes, you can either populate the field in the metadata file, or if you are using EPMA, there is a specific dimension in the Dimension library for Security class. Once the member has been created in this dimension, you may assign it to the Entity, Data Source, or Scenario dimensions. When you assign rights to a class, you have to determine what rights you are giving for that class:

- **All** Full read/write access to the data or objects.
- **Read** Read rights to the data or objects.
- **None** No rights at all.
- **Metadata** Overrides the Metadata Security filtering by allowing the member to be seen in a pick list, though the user will be unable to view the contained data.

Please note that administrators have "All" access to every class and therefore do not need to be assigned rights to any classes. There is a Default role; users who do not have any other role should be given access to the default role. This should not be confused with the Default class.

You can also secure objects.

- HFM objects: Grids, forms, journals, task lists, and journal reports
- Workspace objects: Financial reports, folders, and any other documents stored in the Explorer repository

- EPMA objects: dimensions
- Object-level access in HFM
- All HFM application objects, including Data Forms, Data Grids, journal entries, Journal Reports, and so on, will be available for all users to modify, subject to their role access.

Now that the data is secure, you need to decide at what level you want to secure objects within HFM. You can control access through the Explore menu in Workspace. Typically objects, documents, and folders are accessible by all users.

The WORLD Group is a special group, used in Workspace. WORLD contains all users that are visible to Shared Services, both Native and External. Use this group to simply grant all users with View access to all folders and files. Leave other settings at their defaults.

When you are ready to define the classes you need for objects outside the HFM database, you can open the spreadsheet you have been using to define the security and add a new parent group, next to the dimensions for the "Objects." As shown in Figure 2-15, you can see how this will help you maintain your security. Then you will decide for each user what security classes they will have access to for the groups of objects, and how they will access them. The object groups can be even further defined by type. For example, you may have SEC and Management reports, which have different classes, and hence different security rights.

Oracle FDM Security

Since FDM is such a critical part of most HFM implementations, it is important to include the security impact of FDM as well. Since FDM functionally is different than HFM, the security is quite a bit different.

There are two securable components of FDM:

- **Object** Controls access to web menu and form items (objects). The application menus, menu items, forms, and form components are referred to as objects. Each application object is assigned a default role (access level). These defaults are based upon an average FDM implementation and can be customized. As in HFM, FDM application objects employ "metadata" filtering based on the role assigned.

Hyperion HFM User to Group Cross Reference

		Scenario Class		Enity Class		Role	
USER ID	USER NAME	Group 1	Group 2	Group 5	Group 6	Group 7	Group 9
		Modify	View	Modify	View		
	User 1	ACTUAL		Americas	AsiaPacific	Power	
	User 2	ACTUAL	PLAN	Americas	AsiaPacific	Power	
	User 3	ACTUAL		Americas			View
	User 4	ACTUAL	PLAN	Americas			View
	User 5	ACTUAL		Americas			View
	User 6		PLAN	Americas			View
	User 7		PLAN	Americas	AsiaPacific		View
	User 8	ACTUAL	PLAN	Americas			View
	User 9		PLAN	Americas			View
	User 10		PLAN		AsiaPacific		View

FIGURE 2-15. *A completed security tracking sheet*

- **Location** Controls access to FDM locations and data. Each user must be assigned to at least one location or more. A user must be assigned to a default location even when only assigned to one location.

The first step is to group the users by security role. You can then assign security roles to FDM objects. Then you can assign the users to roles and locations. A user can be assigned multiple roles, which are location-specific. Users should also line up with the locations you have assigned, and be given access by location. Every user (including administrators) must be assigned at least one default location.

There is a fixed set of 11 predefined security roles within FDM, and they cannot be changed. They are, in order of access permission:

- Power (Full Admin Rights—required to run workbench, provides complete access to the application)
- Intermediate 2 through 9
- Basic Reviewer
- Basic Reviewer and Submitter

When a user is assigned a user level, they have access to every object that has been assigned that security level and higher. For example, if a user is assigned Intermediate-5, that user would have access to each object that has Intermediate-5 through Intermediate-9, and All Intermediate. All Intermediate should never be assigned to a user. This security class is intended to be assigned to FDM objects only.

Conclusion

Whether you are new to HFM or a grizzled veteran who has seen many changes with the product, there are many functions and new features that are changing the way the product is used by everyone. Some of the tips and setup that many consultants prefer to use will help you. After reading this chapter, you should have a good understanding of many of these features and whether they make sense for you to put in place.

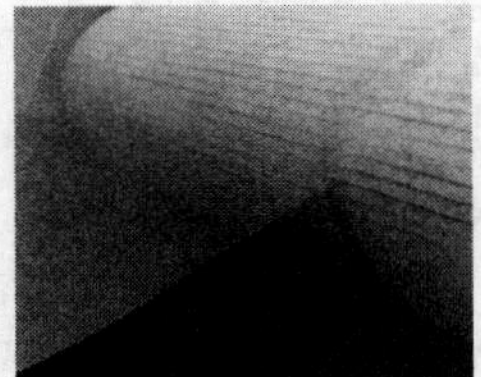

CHAPTER 3

Rules and Calculations

Structures and hierarchies alone will not provide the detail and data the application needs to provide full consolidated numbers. The way you can add this into HFM is by using rules. Rules are an incredibly powerful and flexible way to add calculations to the application.

There really is not any part of HFM that can do more to make your project more valuable and more customized than the rules. Unfortunately, poorly written rules are most often the reason for poorly performing applications. No other part of this tool impacts everything else in quite the same way as rules do. Rules that are not done correctly can make every part of HFM—grids, forms, reports, security, lists, even logging on—a real chore. However, when rules are done well, they can reduce reconciliation, prevent errors, automate many data tasks, and bring the most value to your project. This potential for problems and issues scares people. But you don't have to be afraid. I want this chapter to set you free! You will be free to look at the rules and really understand what is going on, make changes, and own this incredibly valuable and misunderstood part of the product.

In this chapter, we will cover the basics of sound rule writing. We will cover the core functions you must know, and the basics of Visual Basic scripting (VBScript). We will go through some examples that you could and maybe should use in your application. Then finally, we will discuss the new graphical rule builder for the Oracle EPM suite, Calculation Manager. We will discuss how the concepts used in VBScript translate to this new tool. Finally, I will show you how to migrate your rules file for Calculation Manager. Whether you are new to HFM, or you are going to migrate from an older application, you can be the rule expert you need to be.

Overview

The purpose of the Rules module is to perform many of the calculations that are required for preparing the close data. Many of the calculations you will need are subtotals and aggregations. But all of those values you will need are calculated automatically from what you built in the hierarchies. Still, there are more calculations you will need to do, and those are things you will build in the system. For example, you will need ratios, cash flow, validations, translation rules, investment in subsidiary eliminations, and so on. These are the calculations you will build in rules. Many people new to HFM are used to doing these calculations offline, and then loading them to a journal or adding them to a spreadsheet. Obviously this is error-prone, risky, and time-consuming. The rules in HFM allow you to perform these calculations programmatically as part of the consolidation, making them easier and more auditable. While HFM will do some calculations "out of the box," just about all applications have rules.

I really enjoy working with the rules. The biggest reason is how powerful the rules are. It is exciting to see an issue that someone is struggling with, spending days sometimes working through during the busiest time of the accounting calendar, minimized or eliminated with a set of rules. Why is it so powerful? Not only do you have the toolset Oracle provides, but a lot of the tools provided by VBScript. This lets you do things like complex currency translations, and calculating the foreign currency impact by account line, if you choose. You can automate a big part of your cash flow. You can validate your data. You can completely customize the consolidation. It drives everything you want HFM to do.

Rules run when certain conditions are true. For example, if translation has occurred, then rules for overrides would need to run. One of those conditions might be if the entity has specific shares owned or controlled. We call those *methods* in HFM, and a method would determine how data would consolidate. These consolidation methods integrate through rules with the user interface. Before we go into any detail about how to do this, consider how helpful that could be. You could consolidate parts of your trial balance by each relationship of parent and child, and build that to run programmatically as part of your calculation of the database.

Rules are often the "black box," meaning a complex secret no one really knows or understands—or worse, a source of extreme anxiety. It seems as if writing rules in HFM must be some dark art taught by holy monks and you need some kind of HFM guru to help with even basic things. It really isn't, but I have thought a lot about this. Sure, it could be a potential for disaster; people get scared thinking they could corrupt the database, or bring down the servers. That could happen. But since you will have good backup procedures in place (right?), and it is easy to restore the database, you should not be that afraid. Also, as we discussed earlier in the book, good change control and testing in development environment make that risk small. I think part of it is fear of VBScript. Looking at it for the first time, it seems like a complex foreign programming language that accounting people were never meant to understand. The truth is: this is the same programming language people use to write macros in Excel. And no one is afraid of Excel. But quite possibly the biggest reason people are afraid of HFM rules often has to do with how they are developed during the project. It is too easy for most of the team to not be part of the rules development. You absolutely have to be involved with writing the rules. Do not let your consultant come in and build in a room alone and just let you know when they are done. There is not one part of this tool that lends itself to a turnkey type of implementation, and rules are the best example of this.

So rules aren't meant to be confusing, scary, or complex. They aren't based on complex script, and most accountants should be able to build this skill. And rules are important for performance and functionality. So, now are you convinced that you need to know rules?

VBScript for Oracle HFM

All the rules are written for HFM in VBScript, unless you are using the Calculation Manager tool. Then they are built graphically. At the time this book was being written, not many people have migrated to Calculation Manager, so it is likely that you will still need to know the basics to migrate, maintain, or build your rules. Calculation Manager has a script object that uses VBScript. Also, if you want to see the VBScript that Calculation Manager is generating, it is helpful to know. Other tools like Financial Data Quality Management (FDM) use VBScript as well, so this is important to know.

What Is VBScript?

Here is the first misunderstanding about HFM. The rules are not written in Visual Basic. They are written in something called VBScript, owned and developed by Microsoft. VBScript is a lightweight active scripting language. It is a subset of the Visual Basic language, and uses similar concepts like procedures, constants, variables, user interaction, array handling, date/time functions, error handling, functions, objects, and string manipulation.

Here is the second misunderstanding about HFM: It does not use the full toolset available from VBScript. There are many functions you can't use. For example, anything that requires user interaction, like a message box, will not work in HFM rules.

HFM does give you something else, though. There is a full set of tools that Oracle provides. All of these begin with an "HS." This is the *name space*. It stands presumably for Hyperion Solutions. All this does is allow any functions and objects to be written without concern if someone else uses the same name. For example, Oracle may have a tool that has a function called EXP, and so does Hyperion. So which one should VBScript use? This "container" keeps the functions and objects grouped.

Objects are important to an object-based programming language. Everything is about the objects and how they work. These are typically structures that contain methods for doing something within HFM. Each object is represented by elements of the Hyperion Financial Management application. For example, Account, App Settings, Entity, and Scenario are all objects. These all have different functions they can do.

Generally, you write rules by using the functions within objects. *Functions* (or methods) represent actions that a rule can perform, such as returning a setting. Each of these functions sometimes needs an argument passed to it. The argument varies, and you should check with the guide to be sure you are providing what the function needs to return some expected result.

So, let's put this together. Let's assume you wanted to know the default currency of a specific entity. You would write a rule like this:

```
Hs.Entity.DefCurrency("E#SpecificEntity")
```

Hs is the namespace, Entity is the object, DefCurrency is the function, and E#SpecificEntity is the argument. Note that to define the dimension in the argument, HFM requires the dimension label and a number sign (#).

One exception to this rule is when you do not refer to a specific object. These functions are part of the class. They are obviously not part of a specific part of HFM; for example, NoInput. This is a rule you would use in the NoInput section, but it is not something that is defined by an Entity or Account.

It is important to note that the rules run sequentially. This means the rules run in order from top to bottom *within* a subroutine, excluding any conditions or calls. However, they might not always run from top to bottom. They may have statements that make the rules jump around.

The simplest way to determine what functions and objects are available is either to refer to the Administrator's Guide, or to use the Function Wizard that is available in the Rules Editor. In Figure 3-1, you can see how the Rules Editor shows you the objects available, and the functions you can use for each.

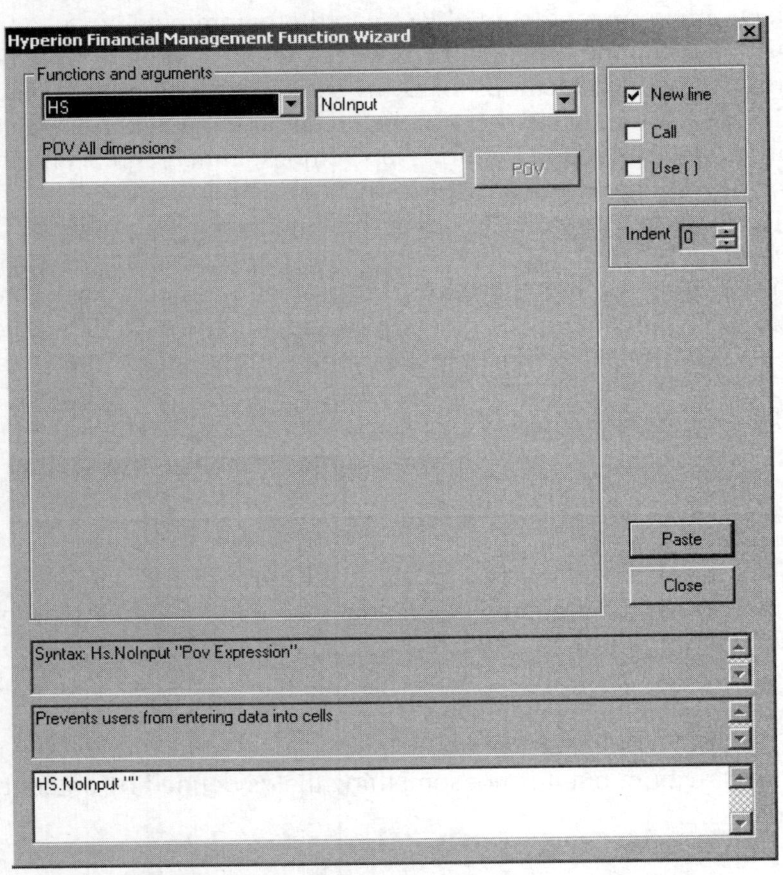

FIGURE 3-1. *The Function Wizard*

Formatting

One of the most important things you can do to make your rules readable and helpful is to make sure they are properly formatted. There are some simple rules you should always follow without exception. All of the examples used in this chapter include sound formatting, and should be your standard. The rules of good formatting are

- **Use proper case** Function names are not case-sensitive; for example, hs.entity, or Hs.Entity, or HS.ENTITY are treated as the same. Still, it is a best practice of VBScript style to be consistent and to capitalize judiciously. Proper case throughout the rules file makes it much easier to read.
- **Always comment** Add comments to any line of code explaining what you are doing and why. Use the apostrophe at the beginning of the comment to make sure that the comment is not interpreted as part of the rules. If this is done in a VBScript editor, the comment should turn green by default.
- **Remember that indentation is critical** This is especially true when using any nested statements or conditionals. Those statements are explained later in this chapter in the section "Conditionals." Indentation should be done for any scripting, even scripting objects in Calculation Manager.
- **Name your variables and constants properly** All variables should be named useful names.

Formatting the rules also means using the underscore (_) and colon (:) symbols. When using the underscore, you are telling the script that the line ending with an underscore is continuing on the next line. For example:

```
strAccount = HS.GetCell ("A#7999.C1#Sales") + _
    HS.GetCell ("A#7999.C1#Marketing")
```

The colon allows you to combine two lines. For example:

```
strSalesAccount = "A#7999.C1#Sales" : strMktAccount = "A#7999.C1#Marketing"
```

I think it is important here to underscore the importance of comments. You will not remember a year or two later why something is quite the way it is, but comments will help keep you from making the same mistake again. Comments can help provide a new administrator with detailed information, such as what needs updating or regular maintenance, if you add a new cash flow account, for example. Finally, they can help remind you what needs to be considered for an upgrade or rebuild.

Variables and Constants

Variables and constants are used to hold values or expressions. Think back to your ninth-grade algebra class. In the equation 2 + y = x, y is the variable. See, your teacher was right—this may prove useful yet. Variables can have any name. So "y" or "x" is a valid name. But they should be named something that makes sense. Consider which of the following is easier to follow. 2 + y = x or 2 + strVariablePercent = strPercentMarkUp. I would say you can understand more from the second equation than the first, even without knowing the context. Add a line of comments, note the proper case, and you are on your way to well-formatted descriptive rules.

A *variable* is a value that changes depending on parameters and when it is used.

A *constant* will not change, regardless of when it is used or changes in the application. You will need to declare constants at the beginning of rules files. You declare them right away because they don't change. Constants are available to all procedures at all times. But other than these differences, they are to be used just like variables.

You should follow some guidelines when writing rules, and one of the simplest things to do to keep yourself organized is to have a naming convention. I like to use a prefix. The prefix is something that helps me remember what is in the variable. I might use "str" or "s" for a string, or "bln" or "b" for a Boolean (true or false), and "nbr" or "n" for number. Then, using proper case, I use a descriptive name for my variable. So, for a number from Net Income, my variable might be called "nbrNetIncome." I can see that variable name anywhere in the file and know what the variable is for and what it is. Compare that with "x": If I see just "x," who knows what it stands for?

What also helps is knowing what you are going to use the variable for. We have two types of variables in HFM: replacement variables and execution variables. *Replacement variables* are typically used for constants like static strings (for example, topC1=".C1#TopC1"). This variable might change, but it is replacing some part of a string. *Execution variables* are typically used for situations in which a variable is populated or reset during some condition or rule (for example, sPOVEntity = HS.Entity.Member). The point of view changes constantly and what would be written in the variable would be updated accordingly.

There are some other rules for variable names that you must follow. They must always begin with a letter. They cannot contain a period. Finally, variable names cannot be longer than 255 characters. You should avoid keywords such as "HFM," "Entity," and "Account" when naming variables. These names are reserved and could cause problems.

All variables in HFM are implicitly defined by default. That means you don't have to declare a variable before using it. Most rules files work fine without changing this. But there is a slight risk in not considering it. In fact, my recommendation for descriptive variable names makes this more of a potential problem. Assume I am using a variable that has the ownership percentage of an entity called strOwnershipPct. And later in my rule file I write something like this:

```
"A#EquityElimination = A#Sales" * strOwneshipPct
```

Do you see what is wrong? It is subtle. Okay, check the spelling of the variable name. It is misspelled. But since the variables are not explicitly defined, the script assumes this must be a new variable and just moves on. The problem is that you would never catch it. However, if you add the text "Option Explicit" at the beginning of your rule file, you would get an error as the file started to run because you would need to declare the variable before you use it. So if you add the following line, HFM knows this is the variable you intend to use.

```
Dim nbrOwnershipPct
```

If you are familiar with programming, you might ask, why don't I need to tell the script the type? The reason is that all variables by default have the Variant type. All that means is that there is a small step the VBScript engine performs to determine what it should do to store the data.

A Variant behaves as a number when you use it in a numeric context and as a string when you use it in a string context. So when you are using a variable that is storing a number, VBScript assumes that it is numbers and stores the data as a number. Or, if you are using a variable that is storing some string of data, VBScript treats it as string data. Of course, you can always make numbers behave as strings by enclosing them in quotation marks (" "). This Variant type actually makes many further distinctions. Although the type of variable doesn't change, the way the value is stored in the variable can change.

Since the variables will determine on their own what the type needs to be, you need to make sure you avoid letting the variable use a type that HFM is not expecting for that member. For example, if you use a rule that checks whether the year is 2010, then HFM could see that as something different than "2010." When you use the quotes, the number 2010 becomes a string "2010." When HFM runs into this problem, you will get a Type Mismatch error. So if you do get this error, double-check that the variable you are testing is correct.

Table 3-1 shows the subtypes of data that a Variant can contain.

Some of the most common variables are

```
strPov_entity = HS.Entity.Member                'current entity
strPov_parent = HS.Parent.Member                'parent of current entity
strPov_scenario = HS.Scenario.Member            'current scenario
strPov_value = HS.Value.Member                  'current value
strPov_year = HS.Year.Member                    'current year
nbrPov_period = HS.Period.Number                'This is the number not the name
is_parent_cur = HS.Value.IsTransCur             'are we at Parent Currency
is_parent_cur_adj = HS.Value.IsTransCurAdj      'are we at Parent Currency Adjust
is_base_ent = HS.Entity.IsBase("", "")          'is this a base level entity
Nones = ".I#[ICP None].C1#[None].C2#[None].C3#[None].C4#[None]"
Tops = ".I#[ICP Top].C1#TOTC1.C2#TOTC2.C3#TOTC3.C4#TOTC4"
'     A variable to start translation and consolidation rules from one location
      StartYear = "2004"
```

In Calculation Manager, the variables are a little different. Although behind the scenes all of this applies, when you set the variables up in the

Subtype	Description
Empty	Value is 0 for numeric variables or a zero-length string (" ").
String	A variable-length string that can be up to approximately 2 billion characters in length.
Boolean	True or False.
Byte	Integer in the range 0 to 255.
Integer	Integer in the range –32,768 to 32,767.
Currency	A value from –922,337,203,685,477.5808 to 922,337,203,685,477.5807.
Long	An integer in the range –2,147,483,648 to 2,147,483,647.
Single	A single-precision, floating-point number in the range –3.402823E38 to –1.401298E–45 for negative values; 1.401298E–45 to 3.402823E38 for positive values.
Double	A double-precision, floating-point number in the range –1.79769313486232E308 to –4.94065645841247E-324 for negative values; 4.94065645841247E-324 to 1.79769313486232E308 for positive values.
Date (Time)	A number that represents a date between January 1, 100 to December 31, 9999.
Object	Contains an object.
Error	Contains an error number.
Null	Variant intentionally contains no valid data.

TABLE 3-1. *Data Subtypes That a Variant Can Contain*

system you need to determine if the variables are substitution or execution variables. Take a look at the group of examples above. The variables that change depending on the point of view are the execution variables. They are populated when the rules are run and depend on where in the structure they run. The "Nones" variable is a substitution variable. This variable replaces a string or some other part of the rules. This is very valuable if you want to avoid typing the same thing over and over again.

Assigning Values to Variables

You assign a value to a variable like this:

```
strSuperHero ="GreenLantern"

i =10
```

The variable name is on the left side of the expression and the value you want to assign to the variable is on the right. Any time you refer to strSuperhero, you will get the value of "GreenLantern" and i has the value of 10. Using the quotation marks lets VBScript know it is assigning a string and not another variable.

In Calc Manager, the syntax is similar except that a variable is presented in braces, such as {i}=10. Of course, the braces are removed during the VBScript rule generation.

It is possible to set one variable equal to another. In the preceding example, you would have something like this:

```
strSuperHero =strGreenLantern
```

Headers for Variables

Since constants need to be defined at the beginning of the rule file, you should start your rule file with a header. A *header* is just a section of the file that contains the variables and constants you plan on using throughout the rest of the file. In Figure 3-2, you can see how constants might be set up. Obviously, your file might be different depending on what you need. Create a constant that represents all the "None" members of the ICP and Custom dimensions and use this constant within the Exp formulas.

There are some commonly used variables like current POV members for the POV dimensions. You might have a variable called strPovEntity. That would be your point of view entity. You could test that to make sure you are running rules where you intend. These can act as triggers for your conditional statements.

```
'
'|
'| Custom defined Rules
'| Application: Common Rule file
'| Updated: March 25, 1971
'| Authors: Peter Fugere
'|
'
'Routine is executed when user calculates or consolidates data.
Sub Calculate()

   '*************************************************************************
   'Populate variables that represent the Point Of View and entity status

   sPov_entity = HS.Entity.Member                  'current entity
   sPov_parent = HS.Parent.Member                  'parent of current entity
   sPov_scenario = HS.Scenario.Member              'current scenario
   sPov_value = HS.Value.Member                    'current value
   sPov_year = HS.Year.Member                      'current year
   sPov_period = HS.Period.Number                  'This is the number not the name
   bis_parent_cur = HS.Value.IsTransCur            'are we at Parent Currency
   bis_parent_cur_adj = HS.Value.IsTransCurAdj     'are we at Parent Currency Adjust
   is_base_ent = HS.Entity.IsBase("", "")          'is this a base level entity
   sNones   = ".I#[ICP None].C1#[None].C2#[None].C3#[None].C4#[None]"
   sTops    = ".I#[ICP Top].C1#TOTC1.C2#TOTC2.C3#TOTC3.C4#TOTC4"
```

FIGURE 3-2. *Header of the rule file*

So now you can create and populate a variable, but how long does the value stay there? When you declare a variable within a procedure, the variable can only be accessed within that procedure. When the procedure exits, the value stored in the variable is removed. These variables that exist within a Sub procedure are called *local variables*. You can have local variables with the same name in different procedures, because each is recognized only by the procedure in which it is declared, but I would only do this if the variable serves the exact same purpose. If you don't do that, it will be easy to get confused.

When you declare a variable outside a procedure, all the procedures on your page can access it. You can look at the constants as an example of how these are used. In Calc Manager, the variable scope is declared as part of the variable. The choices are "rule" or "rule set."

Strings

A string is a series of characters enclosed by quotes. For example, "Tom Brady" is a string. What makes a string very helpful is that it can be broken up. For example, "Tom" and "Brady" are now two strings. When I add the ampersand (&), I can make the two strings tie back together. In this way, "Tom" & " Brady" is equal to "Tom Brady".

Notice that I have a space in the "Tom Brady" string. That's why my " Brady" started with a space. It might be glossed over when you read it, and is even harder to find in the scripting. For that reason, we would never use spaces when we can avoid them. In this case, we would use the underscore, "Tom_Brady".

There is a whole toolset of functions that helps you bring these strings together. The following are some frequently used string functions:

- **Mid** Pulls values from the middle of a string.
- **Len** Returns the length of a string.
- **UCase** Makes a string all uppercase.
- **LCase** Makes a string all lowercase.
- **Left** Returns some number of characters starting from the left.
- **Right** Returns some number of characters starting from the right.

Arrays

An *array variable* is used to store multiple values in a single variable. The simplest of these is with just a single element. So, if you were to declare this array, and it had 50 members, it would be something like this:

```
Dim states (49)
```

The number in the parentheses is 49 intentionally. It is not because I am ignoring Alaska. We start counting at zero, so this array contains 50 values, and is fixed. You assign data to each of the elements of the array like this:

```
states (0) = "New Hampshire"
states (1) = "Massachusetts"
states (2) = "Rhode Island"
```

The concept of an array can be difficult to envision (especially for accountants), so I tell people to think of a spreadsheet. You are putting a value in each row. Then, the values can be retrieved from any element using the index of the particular array element you want.

```
GraniteState = states (0)
```

You can define more elements, up to 60. For example, let's assume we want an array that will contain addresses. Multiple dimensions are declared by separating the numbers in the parentheses with commas. Let's create one with room for the street, city, state, and zip code.

```
Dim Address (9,9,9,9)
```

This address array would allow you to store 10 addresses, all with different streets, cities, states, and zip codes.

Sub Procedures

A "procedure" is how you separate the code into smaller groups. There are two types of procedures; the function, which can return a result in an assignment statement, and the subroutine, which cannot.

The Sub procedure is a series of statements that begin with a "Sub" and end with an "End Sub". This procedure can be "called," meaning there is a Call statement that tells the script when to run the statements in the Sub procedure:

```
Call Golf ( )
Sub Golf ( )
     ... Some golf rules...
End Sub
```

Function Procedures

The *function* is a series of statements, enclosed by the Function and End Function statements. The only difference is that it returns a value. It returns a value by assigning a value to its name.

```
Function myfunction ( )
      some rules
      myfunction = result of the rules
End Function
```

This function, when called, returns the result of the rules that ran, in the variable called myfunction.

How to Call a Procedure

There are different ways to call a procedure. You can call it from within another procedure, on an event, or call it within a script. It can be as simple as

```
Call CashFlow( )
```

Inside the parentheses, you can specify arguments to give to the function or Sub procedure. It could be a point of view, a variable, or value. Take this example and assume that the cash flow was only to run for certain entities. You might want to test what entity the rules are running on. You would add that to the Call statement.

```
Call CashFlow(strPovEntity )
```

One thing to consider is that when you call a subroutine or function, each argument can be passed by reference or by value. "By reference" (ByRef) will allow the called procedure to change the value of the variable. This is valuable if you want to change the value in the variable or not. The change persists after the procedure is called. "By value" (ByVal) will mean that any changes that the called procedure makes to the value of the variable will expire after the procedure is called. If you do not specify, the default is ByRef.

```
Call CashFlow(ByVal strPovEntity )
```

Conditionals

Conditional statements control when parts of your script run. There are many kinds, including iterative and conditional Do loops, If-Then-Else statements, and Case statements. They are decision points for your rules. They allow to you control what rules run and on what part of the database. You have four options of which ones to use.

- **If statement** Executes a set of rules when a condition is true.
- **If...Then...Else statement** Selects one of two sets of rules to run.

- **If...Then...ElseIf statement** Selects one of many sets of rules to run.
- **Select Case statement** Selects one of many sets of rules to run.

If...Then...Else

The If...Then...Else statement is what you would use if you want to test whether a condition is true and then run some code. If you want to execute only one statement when a condition is true, you can write the code on one line:

```
If x = 10 Then strAccount = "A#7999"
```

If you want to execute more than one statement when a condition is true, you must put each statement on separate lines, and end the statement with the keyword End If:

```
If x=10 Then
    strAccount = "A#7999"
End If
```

If you want to execute a statement if a condition is true and execute another statement if the condition is not true, you must add the Else keyword:

```
If x=10 Then
    strAccount = "A#7999"
Else
    strAccount = "A#8999"
End If
```

In this example, the first block of code will be executed if the condition is true (if x is equal to 10), and otherwise, the other block will be executed.

If...Then...ElseIf

You can use the If...Then...ElseIf statement if you want to select one of many blocks of code to run. In the following example, consider that if the first condition is true, the rule exits the statement.

```
If x > 10 Then
    strAccount = "A#7999"
ElseIf x = 10 Then
    strAccount = "A#8999"
End If
```

Select Case

You can also use the Select Case statement if you want to select one of many blocks of code to execute. First we have a single expression or condition that is tested. The value of the expression is then compared with the values for each Case in the structure. If there is a match, the block of code associated with that Case is executed. Unlike the If...Then statement, it will not exit the conditional until all of the cases have been compared.

```
Dim strPovEntity
  strPovEntity = Hs.Entity.Member("")
  Select Case strPovEntity
  Case "France"
        ... some rules
  Case "USA"
        ... some rules
  Case "Japan"
        ... some rules
  End Select
```

Looping Statements

Looping statements run the same block of code a specified number of times, in a loop... hence the name.

In VBScript, we have four looping statements:

- **For...Next statement** Runs a set of rules a specified number of times.
- **For Each...Next statement** Runs a set of rules for each item in a collection or each element of an array.
- **Do...Loop statement** Runs a set of rules while or until a condition is true.
- **While...Wend statement** Runs a set of rules while or until a condition is true. However, it is important to note that the Do...Loop statement provides a more structured and flexible way to perform looping.

For...Next Loop

Use the For...Next statement to run a block of code a specified number of times. Typically, here you would be looping through a list or a certain number of times.

```
For x= 0 to 9
  some code
Next
```

The For statement looks to the counter variable (in this case it is x), to determine its start and end. The Next statement increases the counter variable (x) by one. You could use the Step keyword to increase or decrease the counter. In the next example, you can see how the Step keyword is used.

```
For x=2 To 10 Step 2
  some code
Next
```

If you wanted to decrease the value, you would use a negative Step. So in the next example, instead of increasing, it decreases by 2:

```
For x=10 To 2 Step -2
  some code
Next
```

Finally, when using a list of some sort, you will need to determine the start and end of the list, especially since the iteration values (start and end) are evaluated only once, before the loop begins. The Ubound function determines the highest available subscript for the indicated dimension of an array. The LBound function determines the lowest available subscript for the indicated dimension of an array.

```
For x = LBound(MyArray) to UBound (MyArray)
      some rules
Next
```

Finally, you can exit a For...Next statement with the Exit For keyword.

```
For x=1 To 10
  If x=5 Then Exit For
  some code
Next
```

For Each...Next Loop

A For Each...Next loop repeats a block of code for each item in a collection, or for each element of an array. This is valuable to have when you do not want to define the upper and lower boundaries of the array.

```
For Each x In arrayList
        Some rules...
Next
```

Do...Loop

If you aren't sure how many repetitions you want, use a Do...Loop statement. The Do...Loop statement repeats a block of code as long as a condition is true, or until a condition becomes true. You use the While keyword to check a condition in a Do...Loop statement:

```
Do While x >10
  some code
Loop
```

You can use the Until keyword to check for a condition while working through a Do...Loop statement. The Until statement tests a condition then exits the loop when the condition is true.

```
Do Until x =10
  some code
Loop
```

If x is greater than 10, the code inside the loop will never be executed. In the following example, the loop would run if x equals 10, but only once.

```
Do
  some code
Loop Until x=10
```

If you do not want to use the Until statement, you could just exit at any time by adding an Exit Do statement.

```
Do Until x=10
  x = x-1
        If x<10 Then
                Exit Do
        End If
Loop
```

Sub Procedures

There are some main Sub procedures that run as part of the normal consolidation. Each of these routines are called as the data works its way through the Value dimension. All of these will be in your rules set within Calculation Manager, but only need to be in your rule file if you are using them. The main groups are

- Calculation
- Translation
- Consolidation
- Allocation
- Input
- NoInput
- Dynamic
- Transactions
- Equity Pickup

Calculation

Generally these rules are rules that impact the accounts, but aren't aggregations that you could build into hierarchies. Since the Calculation routine runs so many times for each entity, you can do more here, like overrides for temporal translation, re-creating repeating adjustments for consolidation, complex statistical accounts like days sales outstanding or return on assets, and much more. These run when the user selects Calculate, Force Calculate, or run implicitly as part of [Force] Calculate Contribution, Consolidate, or [Force] Translate.

Translation

The Translate routine allows you to change the standard translation of the system. The out-of-the-box translation will accomplish what you need for most of your accounts, but you would build any exceptions in this routine. For example, you would expect that the Asset and Liability accounts would use the end-of-month rate for translation, but assume you have assets that you would like to translate at a historical rate. You would do that here.

Translation rules run when:

- During consolidation there is a difference between parent and entity currency.
- If a user runs a Translate or Force Translate.
- When a user runs the intercompany matching report for entities that do not have matched currencies.

Consolidation

The out-of-the-box consolidation is very basic, so any changes would need to be added here. When you decide to turn this on in the application settings, remember you must add all the default rules, but those are provided to you in the sample applications.

Allocation

Allocation rules allocate data from one entity to a list of entities. However, they do not consider currency and are very sensitive to the POV from which they are run. For these reasons, you don't see many applications use this routine, so you can opt to use the Calculate routine instead.

Input

Input rules allow input at the Parent entity level, entity currency Value dimension, but not parent customs or accounts.

NoInput

The NoInput rules prevent input. These rules do not run as part of the consolidation, so if they are not written well, they will impact other parts of the system. So be careful with looping here. There are some limitations to these rules:

- You can only use the NoInput and List functions.
- For the List function, dynamic, fixed, and system lists are supported.
- Remember there is no current point of view, so you can't test for the scenario being "Actual."

Dynamic

Dynamic rules define dynamically calculated accounts. You want this because you can take some ratios and metrics out of the consolidation, and secondly, you can create ratios that give the right values for parent members. For example, a normal account would add the children to a parent. If two expense accounts had .5 in each, they would sum to 1.0 at the parent. But you would not want a ratio to do that. You would expect that the parent recalculates the correct amount.

Let's say you wanted to have a return-on-investment ratio in your application. If you took the income on a year-to-date basis divided by the investment, you would have the YTD number. But you would need to recalculate it to get the correct periodic number. You would not be able to take the difference in the months to get the periodic change. Dynamic accounts let you do this.

There are some limitations for these rules as well:

- You can only use base accounts.
- You can't use data from another Dynamic account.
- You must stay in the current Scenario, Year, and Entity.
- You can have different calculations for each view in the system.
- HS.View.PeriodNumber is the only HS statement that can be used in an HS.Dynamic calculation.

Transactions

These rules support the Intercompany Transactions module. Cells supporting transactions are read-only in web grids and data forms.

Equity Pickup

These rules specify the owned entity, owner entity, and percentage of ownership for the Equity Pickup module. These rules run for the current year, period, and scenario, for a given entity at <Entity Currency>.

The Value Dimension

The Calculate, Translate, and Consolidate subroutines execute when called as the data moves along the Value dimension. Take a look at Figure 3-3, and follow the data as it moves through the Value dimension—noting how and where each of these subroutines are called.

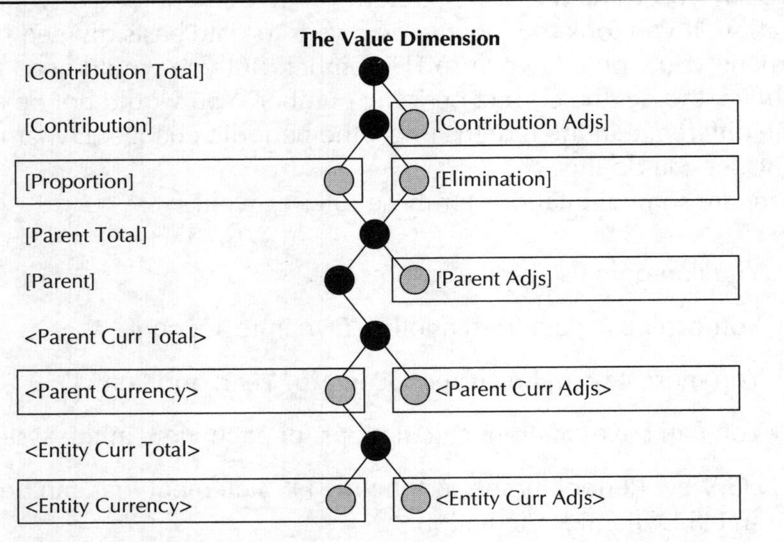

FIGURE 3-3. *The Value dimension*

Take a look at the base members of the diagram in Figure 3-3. The first three members are all Entity Currency. There is an input, an adjustment, and a total. This group is called a triplet. Notice that there is one for Parent Currency as well. In fact, there is one for every currency in the application. If you had EUR for a currency, you would see EUR, EUR Adj, and EUR Total as members of your Value dimension.

First, data in all accounts that are flagged as IsCalculated in the metadata are cleared in EntityCurrency and then in EntityCurrAdjs. Then the Sub Calculate() routine is executed on EntityCurrency and then on EntityCurrAdjs. The data sums up to EntityCurrencyTotal. If the parent and entity currency are different, the next step is that the data in ParentCurrency is cleared before data moves from EntityCurrencyTotal to ParentCurrency. Then the default translation is applied to all accounts from EntityCurrencyTotal to ParentCurrency, and then the Sub Translate() routine is executed from EntityCurrencyTotal to ParentCurrency. Then the Sub Calculate() routine is executed on ParentCurrency. All accounts are flagged as IsCalculated in ParentCurrAdjs, and the Sub Calculate() routine runs for that member.

The data moves from ParentCurrencyTotal to Parent, and as this happens, we see the brackets change. The data is leaving the entity and moving to the node. At this time, data is copied to all parents of the entity in this node. It is at this point that the data is in the relationship between the parent and the child. We call this relationship the *node*. The Sub Calculate routine does not run at Parent. However, all accounts flagged IsCalculated are cleared in ParentAdjs, and then the Sub Calculate() routine is executed. The data sums up to Parent Total.

Before data can move from Proportion and Elimination, all data is cleared. Then if the application is not using custom consolidation rules, default consolidation and eliminations complete; otherwise, the Sub Consolidate routine runs here. This writes data to both Proportion and Elimination. Next, the Sub Calculate() routine is executed on Proportion and Elimination.

Proportion and Elimination sum up to Contribution. Accounts flagged IsCalculated are cleared in ContributionAdjs, and the Sub Calculate() routine runs here as well. Finally, the sum of Contribution and ContributionAdjs is put in ContributionTotal.

The next step is that the parent entity takes the sum of all the children's ContributionTotals and writes it to the parent entity, EntityCurrency, after data is cleared. Then this process runs for the parent entity, until all entities have been done.

Understanding the Subcube

What is the subcube? A *subcube* is a unit of data based on the point of view. The 12 dimensions in HFM can be grouped into page dimensions and subcube dimensions. The subcube dimensions are Account, ICP, Custom 1–4, View, and Period. Page dimensions define the data in the subcube; they are Scenario, Year, Entity, and the Value triplet (Currency, Adjustment, and Total).

A *data unit* is a subset of the subcube. A subcube will contain all periods within a year and Scenario, and the entire triplet of the value dimension. The data unit will only contain the current value member and period.

As you will see as we dive into the rules and functions of HFM, it is important to know which cubes you are updating, and what your point of view in the application is. These page dimensions will help you define scope, improve performance, and help you build efficient and well-performing calculations.

Writing a Rule

So now you have the basics of the dimensions and VBScript, and you are ready to write some rules. But where should you start? How do you express what you want rules to do in the rules file? When you are sitting down to write your first rule, don't think about functions and objects.

I have a method that I use and share when I am teaching rules. I call it the "commentary approach." The best way to start writing a rule is to think about what you want the rule to do, not think about what functions or tools you need. This works best for even the most complex rules. It will help you think through what you want the rules to do, before you start writing any code. For example, "I want a rule to pull Net Income down to Current Retained Earnings." Then think about what scope you want to add to limit this rule. For example, "This rule should run at base entities."

The words you use will dictate the parts of your rule. Action words like "write, do, open, pull," or "get" are words that mean the rule is doing something. For Calculation Manager, as discussed later, this would identify the object. For VBScript, this could be an "object.function," or just an object. For example, HS.Account.PlugAccount or HS.Exp both are doing some action. *Condition* words like "if, when, consider, only, look for," or "loop through" all indicate that you are adding some conditional test.

So if I wrote on the board, "I want a rule to pull Net Income down to Current Retained Earnings, and run only at base entities," I can see my action is "to pull" and my condition is "only." If I started writing this, it would look like this:

```
Is this entity a Base Entity?  If so, then...
     Make Retained Earnings equal Net Income
End
```

The next step is to add the accounts from the system:

```
Is this entity a Base Entity?  If so, then...
     Make Retained Earnings equal Net Income
A#RetainedEarnings = A#NetIncome
End
```

I might add another test to make sure I am pulling from Entity Currency only:

```
Is this entity a Base Entity and Value is Entity Currency?  If so,
then...
     Make Retained Earnings equal Net Income
     A#RetainedEarnings = A#NetIncome
End
```

Taking what we built so far, you are ready to start writing rules. So now look at Figure 3-4, and see how we take this text and add the rules to make this work.

Next we will cover most of the actions you can do in HFM. These actions are the objects and functions that Oracle provides to help pull and write data to HFM. The toolset Oracle provides has many things you can pull and get from the database to help you write your rules. If you are not sure if you can do something you write out, use the Function Wizard. Whatever the rule you want to build, I am sure there is a way to do it, but you might need to be creative.

```
Sub Calculate
	If HS.Entity.IsBase("","") = True And HS.Value.Member = "<Entity Currency>" Then
		HS.Exp "A#RetainedEarnings = A#NetIncome"
	End If
End Sub
```

FIGURE 3-4. *Writing your first rule*

Whether you plan to write a rule in VBScript or in Calculation Manager, the commentary approach will help. In Calculation Manager, each line of the rules shown earlier will be an object in the rule or a line of commentary. For example, "Is this entity a Base Entity and Value is Entity Currency? If so, then…" is a conditional statement you would drag over from the left panel and drop on your rule. You would then add the two conditional tests. Having the commentary helps you map out what the rule should be doing. Make sure you have thought out a detailed commentary while building the rules. That is important regardless of what tool you use to write the rules.

If you are really stuck and not sure where to turn, there are some great samples of rules in a Sample Apps folder, which you can find wherever the Win32 application was installed. Within that folder are examples both in Classic script and for Calculation Manager.

HS.Exp Function

So now let's get into the functions and objects. How do you convert what you want the rules to do into the functions and objects? The first step is to understand some of the basics, and how key functions work.

The most important function is the HS.Exp. Without question the HS.Exp function is the most frequently used. This is the function that writes data to the database. You use the HS.Exp function with an account expression to assign values to the accounts.

HS.Exp expects a destination on the left-hand side and a source on the right-hand side of the equal sign. Looking at Figure 3-5, see how by using the account dimension, you can specify the destination and the source for the rule. The example shows that Net Income (A#NetIncome) is being written to Current Retained Earnings (A#RetainedEarnings).

```
Sub Calculate

        HS.Exp "A#RetainedEarnings = A#NetIncome"

End Sub
```

FIGURE 3-5. *The HS.Exp rule*

You can also use more dimensions like the Custom dimensions and the Intercompany Partner. If I specify those on both the right and the left side of the equation, I am picking one cell to pull from and one to write to. In Figure 3-6, you can see what happens if we add all the Custom dimensions to each side. While this is very deliberate, meaning we are pulling exactly what we want and writing exactly what we want, this rule is long and prone to misspelled words and errors.

Before we go on, let's review some of the tips we discussed earlier in the chapter. First, we can create variables that hold the commonly used Top members and None members. You will find there is some string of Custom and Top members you will be pulling constantly from the database. In this example, let's create two.

```
strNones = ".I#[ICP None].C1#[None].C2#[None].C3#[None].C4#[None]"
strTops = ".I#[ICP
Top].C1#Regions.C2#Customers.C3#TotalC3.C4#Balance"
```

Now, if I break the string using the ampersand (&) and quote ("") characters and insert the variables I created, the rule would look like Figure 3-7.

```
Sub Calculate

        If HS.Entity.IsBase("","") = True And HS.Value.Member = "<Entity Currency>" Then
            HS.Exp "A#RetainedEarnings.I#[ICP None].C1#[None].C2#[None].C3#[None].C4#[None] =
A#NetIncome.I#[ICP Top].C1#Regions.C2#Customers.C3#TotalC3.C4#Balance"
        End If
    End If
End Sub
```

FIGURE 3-6. *The HS.Exp with customs and ICP*

```
Sub Calculate

strNones = ".I#[ICP None].C1#[None].C2#[None].C3#[None].C4#[None]"
strTops = ".I#[ICP Top].C1#TotalProducts.C2#TotalC2.C3#TotalC3.C4#TotalC4"

        If HS.Entity.IsBase("","") = True And HS.Value.Member = "<Entity Currency>" Then

            HS.Exp "A#RetainedEarnings" & strNones & "= A#NetIncome" & strTops

        End If

    End If

End Sub
```

FIGURE 3-7. *HS.Exp with variables*

If this were the first page you opened to and you started reading this rule, you might think it is starting to look complicated. But it really isn't. By just adding the Custom dimensions we want to pull from and write to, we made the rule seem more complicated, but it is still just doing that one thing: pulling data from Net Income and writing it to Current Retained Earnings. All the rules do this; each concept is very simple, and it builds on itself. Each part is simple; all the parts together appear complex.

Now why would we want to be so specific with the right- and left-hand side of the equation? The reason is that the HS.Exp function is pretty smart, and does some very helpful and powerful things. The destinations we covered, Account, ICP, and the Custom dimensions, are the only members supported on the left-hand side of the equation. But on the right side, we have so many more options we can use to make sure we are calculating the right numbers. We can use other dimensions like Entity, Scenario, Year, Period, and Frequency. These are all the page dimensions of the subcube.

When you pull period and years, you have the option of using, in addition to the dimensions you created, some Dynamic or Relative members. They are relative in the sense that based on the period or year you are in, they could change. Some examples are Prior and Last. Obviously Last would always be the last member regardless of the period you are in, but Prior would change. In March, Prior is February and in December Prior is November. There is another member called Cur. And what make this member special is that you can offset it. Cur-2 means the current member less two. These are more ways to make the HS.Exp function pull exactly what you need. But what if you need to change the data before you write it back?

HS.Exp will allow you to use math operators to perform calculations in the database. Figure 3-8 shows how you can multiply one account by the value in another account. You can use all of the standard math operators on the left-hand side of the equal sign. Here I have changed the accounts. I am now taking the Net Income and multiplying it by the amount in the Percent Mark Up (PctMarkUp) and writing it to the Income Mark Up account (IncMarkUp). I could add, subtract, multiply, and divide.

It is also worth noting that these follow the standard order of precedence as well. All the rules in HFM do. They are

- First, perform any calculations inside parentheses.
- Next, perform all multiplications and divisions, working from left to right.
- Lastly, perform all additions and subtractions, working from left to right.

```
Sub Calculate

strNones = ".I#[ICP None].C1#[None].C2#[None].C3#[None].C4#[None]"
strTops = ".I#[ICP Top].C1#TotalProducts.C2#TotalC2.C3#TotalC3.C4#TotalC4"

    HS.Exp "A#IncMarkUp" & strNones & "= A#NetInc" & strTops & " * A#PctMarkUp"

End Sub
```

FIGURE 3-8. *HS.Exp and operators*

You can also use other functions with HS.Exp. You can pull members; for example, you may want to show sales by cost center. That might look like this:

```
HS.Exp "A#AvgSales = A#Sales/HS.Entity.NumBase(NH)"
```

So, are you convinced this rule is the single most important rule yet? Well, hold your thoughts for possibly the most impressive part of the HS.Exp. This rule can pull from many members and write to one, it can pull from one member and write to many, and it can infer dimensionality and create detail in the calculation. This rule lets you specify what members you want to bring from the source to the destination.

If no member of the Intercompany Partner dimension or of a Custom dimension is specified on the left side of the equal sign, the HS.Exp places data in each valid intersection of the account and the dimension. If you do not specify a destination account, Hyperion Financial Management will insert data into all accounts that are valid for the current point of view. If a member of a dimension is not specified on the right side of the equal sign, then there are several possibilities:

- If a dimension has only one member, then the HS.Exp gets data from the intersection of this member and the source account.
- If a dimension has only one valid intersection with the source account, then the HS.Exp gets data from this intersection.
- If a dimension has several intersecting members with the source account, then the source intersection of the data is determined by the left side of the equation.

Assume you have a couple of rules that are pulling from one account and writing to another. Figure 3-9 shows what data values will be pulled in HFM. Notice that since both Account3 and Account4 have the same custom dimensions, and the rules in the following example do not specify what Custom1 dimension should be pulled from Account4, the rules use what was defined on the left-hand side of the equal sign. Twenty is pulled for each Chips and OLAP.

```
HS.Exp "A#Account3.C1#Chips= A#Account4"
HS.Exp "A#Account3.C1#OLAP= A#Account4"
```

	Account3	Account4
[None]		
Allcustom1	90	280
TotalBusiness	90	280
Hardware	20	60
Network		10
Chips	20	20
Computers		30
Software	70	220
Applications		40
DataWarehousin		50
Ebusiness		60
Olap	70	70

FIGURE 3-9. *The left side drives the equation.*

Now notice what happens when the custom dimension is defined on the right-hand side of the equation and not on the left. Let's just take the preceding example and move Chips and OLAP. Take a look at Figure 3-10; since one member is specified as the source, the HS.Exp assumes that you want to write to all intersections of Account3.

```
HS.Exp "A#Account3 = A#Account4.C1#Chips"
HS.Exp "A#Account3 = A#Account4.C1#OLAP"
```

It is actually much worse than it looks. Because what really happens here is: First, 20 is written to every intersection, and then it is overwritten with 70. Not only is this wrong, but it is horribly inefficient, a double whammy.

This mistake is commonly called *data explosion*, and this is as bad as it can get in HFM. Think back to the subcubes; they are only as big as the data you load into them. Well, if you load zeros and stray data, the subcubes get big for no reason. That slows the entire system down to a crawl. Performance will be terrible. The only way to completely fix it is to fix the rules and rebuild the application. Data explosion is so serious that you will want to make sure you

	Account3	Account4
[None]	70	
Allcustom1	560	280
TotalBusiness	490	280
Hardware	210	60
Network	70	10
Chips	70	20
Computers	70	30
Software	280	220
Applications	70	40
DataWarehousin	70	50
Ebusiness	70	60
Olap	70	70

FIGURE 3-10. *The same formula reversed*

always spell out as much as what makes sense for your rules. I always use the customs and ICP. I always think of scope. You should too.

This also makes the case for being very deliberate in defining your custom dimensions. All too often, I see general ledgers that have poorly written validation rules. That allows users to create new account strings, or combinations of accounts and other dimensions. So, instead of fixing them in the ledger, people take the lazy route of just opening up the HFM application to allow for loading all these intersections. Here is the problem: Not only do you have useless data in bad spots, but it makes the potential for an issue like this more likely. It impacts other things too, like reporting, validations, and data mapping.

So while HFM will give you the flexibility to omit dimension members, do this only when you intentionally want the rules to run for all intersections. Any time you use one dimension on one side of the equation, use that same dimension on the other side.

The HS.Exp function is the most important in the toolset. It is used so much, and is so powerful, you will want to really understand it, and think about where you are pulling data from, and where you are writing it to—the most challenging aspect of writing rules.

GetCell Functions

While the HS.Exp writes data, the HS.GetCell function is used to retrieve data from the database. You will need to pull values from the database to either test if a number is valid, or to see if you should perform a rule. The most common way to use these numbers is to populate the variable with numbers:

```
SomeVariable = HS.GetCell("POV")
```

You can specify all of the same values you can for the HS.Exp on the right-hand side of the equal sign here too. You can use all 12 dimensions, mathematical operators, relative members, and other functions.

The following example assigns to the dData variable the amount stored in the intersection of the Sales account dimension:

```
Dim dData
dData = HS.GetCell("A#Sales.I#[ICP None]")
```

Some of the most common HS.GetCell functions not only pull data but also pull test values, so you can more easily test conditions. Other HS.GetCell functions pull special types of data.

- **GetCellNoData** Tests if there is no data in the cell
- **GetCellRealData** Tests if the data is derived
- **GetCellType** Returns the cell type
- **GetRate** Returns currency rates
- **GetNumLID** Returns line item detail

While all these functions will return a numeric value from the database, GetCellNoData and GetCellRealData will also return a Boolean variable. You can then know more about the data you are about to use for the calculation, for example, if it is derived. Now why would it be important to know if the data is zero or derived? There are a couple of reasons. First, you need to make sure you are not writing zeros back to the database. You want to avoid this, because it bloats the database and affects performance. Second, you need to make sure you don't divide by zero in VBScript. It is undefined and will produce an error. So make sure you are checking the denominator in any functions, to be sure it is not zero.

You might notice that all the rules will seem to "pull" data. This means the rules look to other data units and write to the currently open data unit. For example, I would have a rule that says, "If I am in the France entity, then take the Corporate entity operating expense divided by current number of heads." You are pulling data from Corporate and writing in France. You could not say, "When in the Corporate entity, write the operating expense out to each entity divided by its heads." This is a subtle difference.

There are only a few exceptions in rules where we are allowed to "push" data to another place. Those exceptions are

- **HS.Con** Writes data to [Proportion] or [Elimination] of the current entity, or any of the current entity's siblings.
- **HS.ImpactStatus** Changes the calc status of another entity (though not a child), or another scenario or year, but will not write a data value.
- **HS.Alloc** Writes values to base members of the current entity, and can only be invoked in Sub Allocate.

Scope of Rules

When we talk about scope in the rules file for HFM, we talk about two things. We talk about variables and when they expire, and we talk about limiting when rules run in the application.

If you get the right answer, it does not mean your rules are written efficiently. Most applications have some part of the rules poorly written. When rules that don't need to be on are on, that affects performance. When you write rules, think about when the rule needs to run. You need to think about implicit dimensions of the statements. Then you should be using conditional statements to limit the rules as much as possible. You should ask yourself, "Does that ratio need to run at every level? Or even every base?" If you only report on it at the parent level, then limit it to run only there.

Some people are afraid the users will be confused if the values aren't everywhere. Believe me, they will be much happier if the application is fast and accurate than if they looked for a useless piece of data and didn't see it. Don't think your users care if it is everywhere; ask them if you are not sure. Look at every report and determine what needs to be in the application.

You need to use the conditional statements from Visual Basic to limit where the rules run. For example, use the If…End If statement to limit execution to base entities. Rules that only need to run for base-level entities don't need to be rerun for parent level entities.

Also, you should consider using the If…EndIf statement to limit execution in the Value dimension. Not only do you need to limit execution to base entities, but it is also frequently useful to limit execution to <Entity Currency>. Otherwise, execution will take place through all levels of the Value dimension that are stored. Look at the example in Figure 3-11 and see how just by adding two scope-limiting rules, the potential number of times the rules run decreases. If you think that the Value dimension will run Sub Calculate eight times for every entity, and then there could be several parents for one entity, by adding these rules you can decrease the number of rules by a factor of hundreds.

Then you should compartmentalize your rules. That means instead of having a large section for the cash flow, put all the cash flow rules in their own section, inside a Sub procedure. Then call the procedure from the main part of the rules file. This makes it easier to debug the rules later, because you can turn off large parts of the code. It also makes it much easier to move

```
Sub Calculate

    If HS.Entity.IsBase("","") = True And HS.Value.Member = "<Entity Currency>" Then

        strNones = ".I#[ICP None].C1#[None].C2#[None].C3#[None].C4#[None]"
        strTops = ".I#[ICP Top].C1#TotalProducts.C2#TotalC2.C3#TotalC3.C4#TotalC4"

            HS.Exp "A#IncMarkUp" & strNones & "= A#NetInc" & strTops & " * A#PctMarkUp"

    End If

End Sub
```

FIGURE 3-11. *Limiting scope*

large parts of the code between applications. Most good Visual Basic editing tools will even go so far as to give you the option to jump from each of the Sub procedures.

Consolidation Rules

Aggregation is the process of taking the data from one entity and adding it to the data of another to get a value for the parent. *Consolidation* can involve intercompany data, ownership percentages, different types of consolidation, and so on. In HFM, this process is so much more than just adding up the numbers. Consolidation is accounting for the relationships between legal entities, and HFM does this very well.

Methods

It turns out that there are several ways companies can create relationships, new companies, or even buy other companies. So let me first explain what these relationships are. Business combinations are basically grouped by method of combination into three types: mergers, consolidations, and acquisitions.

A *merger* is the combining of two or more companies when there is some exchange of stock, cash, or other payments, where the acquiring company survives and the acquired company ceases to exist as a legal entity and surrenders its stock. For example:

Company A+ Company B = Company A

A *consolidation* results when a new corporation is formed when two or more corporations exchange voting stock. The acquired corporations cease to exist as separate legal entities. For example:

Company A+ Company B = Company C

These first two basically result in new groups of legal entities. While they may present other problems, like getting data, and new reports, the new groups do not mean that you are going to consolidate any entities differently than any other. All entities are fully owned and controlled.

An *acquisition* is when a company buys most or all of the voting stock of another corporation to assume control of the target firm. The acquired company would remain a separate entity. This type of relationship results in entities that have different ownership and control and need special accounting treatments applied during consolidation. "Control" means something very specific here. Control is the ability of an entity to direct the policies and management that guide the ongoing activities of another entity. For purposes of consolidated financial statements, control involves decision-making ability that is not shared with others.

In HFM there is an option to add something called a method. These methods are ways you can consolidate the data in your application. You can build them; however, you need to run the consolidation. There are some very common ones I have seen. I am sure each person will have seen some twist on each of these, so I will keep the examples generic.

Full consolidation is used when there is majority ownership or control (greater than 50 percent of voting shares) by one parent of its subsidiaries. The two company's financial statements are combined by account, with any adjustments and eliminations. This can mean the consolidated accounts have only part of the values consolidated to a given parent. For example, if you have 100 in revenue, but own 65 percent, you would only see 65 consolidate to the parent. Statement of Financial Accounting Standards (SFAS) 94, issued in 1987, states that majority-owned subsidiaries (more than 50 percent of the voting stock has been acquired) should be fully consolidated and that accounting by the Equity method (generally used for affiliates less than 50 percent owned) is not a substitute for information provided by fully consolidated financial statements.

The Equity method is used when there is minority ownership or control with significant influence (between 20 to 50 percent) by one Parent of its affiliates. The Parent entity will reflect ownership of equity with entries to specific accounts, as opposed to all accounts. The equity method is allowable for affiliates less than 50 percent owned as opposed to subsidiaries more than 50 percent owned.

The Cost method is generally used when there is minority ownership or control without significant influence (less than 20 percent of the voting shares) by one Parent of its affiliates. This method is similar to the Equity method, with the exception that entries are put into the system only when dividends are paid.

The Proportion method is used for joint ventures, a method of including items of income, expense, assets, and liabilities times a firm's percentage of participation in the venture. There is some question of the future of this method with expansion of IFRS.

Other methods, such as Joint Venture (JV) or Associate, can be used and modified to help with issues you may have. You can create what you need.

Once you have determined your methods and built them in your application, they need to be assigned to the entities. There are a couple of ways to assign the consolidation method to an entity for use during consolidation. The method can be assigned through the Ownership console, manually through data load, or data entry. The method can also be assigned by the Calculate Ownership routine.

Organization by Period and Structures

When deciding to write rules for customizing the consolidation, you will very likely need to use the Organization by Period functionality. This enables the most recent consolidation structure to coexist with past structures in the same application. Organizational structures can change for many reasons, including acquisitions, disposals, mergers, and reorganizations—all of the reasons we are modifying the rules in our consolidation. It is unusual to see an application with custom consolidation rules that is not using Organization by Period. Because of the way Organization by Period and Periodic consolidation handle "no data" values or missing values, it is a best practice to use these when building statutory rules.

Financial Management will have the entity appear twice in the organization, and then with the use of a system account, Active, it can determine the active or inactive consolidation status of a child into its parent. The Active account uses the Intercompany dimension to store data about its children at the parent level. Children that correspond to ICP members for which the Active account is equal to 0 are considered to be inactive children and are not consolidated. Children that correspond to ICP members for which the Active account is equal to 1 are considered to be

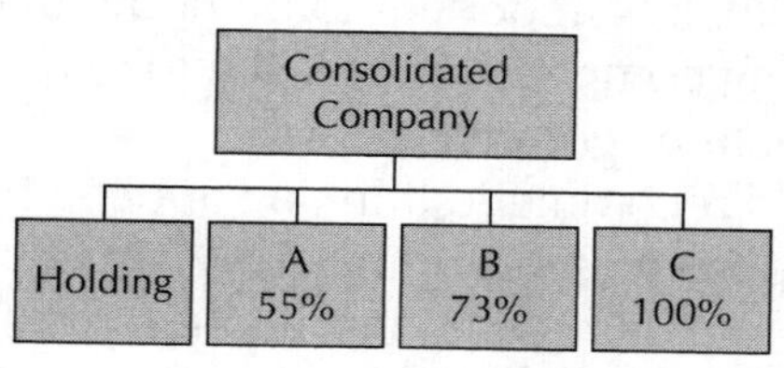

FIGURE 3-12. *Flat structure*

active children and are consolidated. The DefaultValueForActive attribute controls the status of children for which the Active account is blank. So, every parent-child intersection does not have to be flagged as active or inactive. By default, every child is active in relation to its parent unless otherwise specified.

Basically there are two main groups of structures you might see in the Entity dimension to support complex consolidations. The first is flat. There is one parent and several children, and a holding company. Looking at Figure 3-12, you can see what that structure might look like. The approach here simplifies the consolidation. There are no subgroups and steps that you need to do. The focus here is on the total consolidated company.

This second type is called a staged consolidation. The focus here is being able to see consolidation levels. Figure 3-13 shows us what a

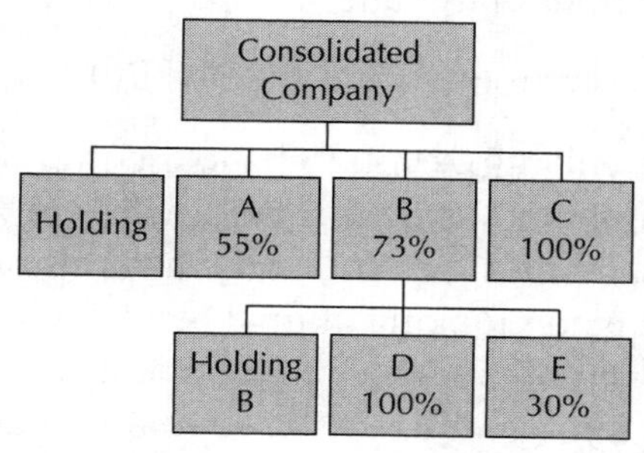

FIGURE 3-13. *Staged structure*

structure might look like. It is important to point out that each level of ownership has a holding company. That will allow the system to record the investment and eliminations correctly.

In this case, I would recommend thinking about what your structure needs to be to accomplish your reporting. This can become very complex, especially if there are two passes of consolidation rules at each level. This is called a Double Staged or Equity Pickup.

HS.Con

The foundation of the consolidation rules is the HS.Con rule. This rule in the consolidation section moves data from the Parent Total member to the Proportion and Elimination members of the Value dimension. Like the HS.Trans function, the HS.Con accumulates the values it writes to the database. So if you write a value of 10 to the same date intersection twice, the value you would expect to see is 20. So in a sense, this rule is transactional by nature. The HS.Con statement has three parameters:

- **Destination** Unlike with the HS.Exp rule, you don't have to specify the source. The reason is: since you have to run this for all members of the subcube, HFM will know the point of view of the record it is currently processing. Valid Value dimension members in the destination point of view are [Proportion] and [Elimination]. The destination entity does not have to be the same as the source entity. So you could write eliminations to a sibling, for example, a holding company or partner elimination.
- **Factor** Most commonly this is PCON, POWN, or PMIN.
- **Nature** HFM will allow you to have the transaction written to a system audit trail, and using this field will give you a description of what the transaction is for. You can leave this blank. The audit trail is very helpful when looking at final results; you can see the breakout for each of the HS.Con statements by nature. As of Release 11.1.1, the Nature parameter is used to automatically generate a journal entry label, and is visible within the journal entry module.

If the destination is not defined, then the data will be written to the same account as the source in the current entity's Proportion member. Typically, people use a variable to hold the factor; here, we are holding the percent consolidation.

```
dPCon = HS.Node.PCon
HS.Con("",dPCon,"")
```

You can specify the value dimension when writing to the Elimination member. Note the percent consolidation value (PCon) is negative. That will create a reversing entry. This is helpful when we want to decrease an account, like an intercompany amount that is eliminating.

```
HS.Con "V#[Elimination]", -HS.Node.PCon(""), ""
```

OpenDataUnit Functionality

When writing rules in the consolidation routine, we need to start by opening the current data unit. Specifically, we need the full set of data for all accounts, ICP, and custom dimensions for the current Parent Total member. Fortunately, HFM provides a function to give us that information.

```
Set DataUnit =HS.OpenDataUnit("S#Scen.Y#Year.P#Per.E#Ent.V#Val.W#View")
```

If you do not specify any of the arguments, the OpenDataUnit returns the current point of view. And as you can see in the preceding example, we want to take that set of data and store it into a variable called DataUnit. A nice feature of being able to call other data units is that we are able to view data from other entities and periods, and so on, and loop through them.

GetNumItems

Now that you have the set of data, you need a way to know how many data records are actually there. If you know how much data is there, you can set up a looping statement. Luckily, we also have a function to help with this as well. The GetNumItems function will return this number for us.

```
vNumItems = ConsUnit.GetNumItems
```

So we need to store this number in another variable, which I have called vNumItems. Now we are ready for our For…Next loop to retrieve each item so that it can be dealt with individually.

GetItem

So when we are looping through all the members, we will need a way to know what are the account, ICP, and customs for each data value we are working with. That is handled by the GetItem function. This returns the data value, account, ICP, and custom.

```
Call ConsUnit.GetItem(i, vAccount, vICP, vC1, vC2, vC3, vC4, vData)
```

All of the arguments to the GetItem function are variables. For example, vAccount will return the account label for the data value stored in vData. Each member only returns the label and not the dimension identifier, like "A#".

Put It Together

This is as complicated as it gets, so if you can follow this you can handle just about anything in rules with HFM. Let's go line by line in the example. Take a look at Figure 3-14 and follow along. If you need an example of this rule, find your folder called SAMPLE APPS with your installation of HFM. There are examples of applications with rules you can use.

1. First, we define some variables: *MyDataUnit, lNumItems, dPCon*
2. Next, we open the current data unit. Notice we don't define any dimensions, so it pulls the current ones.

   ```
   Set MyDataUnit = HS.OpenDataUnit("")
   ```
3. Now we put the percent consolidation into a variable (typically this is 1 for 100 percent):

   ```
   dPCon = HS.Node.PCon("")
   ```
4. Now get the number of data values we need to loop through:

   ```
   lNumItems = MyDataUnit.GetNumItems
   ```

```
Sub Consolidate() 'consolidation rules (if app does not use default this section is used to consolidate

    Dim MyDataUnit
    Dim lNumItems
   Dim dPCon

    Set MyDataUnit = HS.OpenDataUnit("")

   dPCon = HS.Node.PCon("")

    lNumItems = MyDataUnit.GetNumItems

   for i = 0 to lNumItems-1

      ' Get the next item from the dataunit
    call MyDataUnit.GetItem(i, strAccount, strICP, strCustom1, strCustom2, strCustom3, strCustom4, dData)

      ' See if this is a consolidatable account
     If HS.Account.IsConsolidated(strAccount) Then

         ' Proportionalize this account
         call HS.Con("",dPCon,"")

         ' see if we should eliminate this account
         call Eliminate(strAccount, strICP)
     End If

   next

End sub
```

FIGURE 3-14. *Default consolidation rules*

5. Here is our looping statement, for each record:

   ```
   for i = 0 to lNumItems-1
   ```

6. Now we get the item labels and data value for the individual record:

   ```
   Call MyDataUnit.GetItem(i, strAccount, strICP, strCustom1,
   strCustom2, strCustom3, strCustom4, dData)
   ```

7. Now we can do any work we need to on this one value. First, see if this is an account that we should consolidate.

   ```
   If HS.Account.IsConsolidated(strAccount) Then
   ```

8. Then, using the HS.Con function, write to the Proportion member times the percent consolidation.

   ```
   call HS.Con("",dPCon,"")
   ```

9. Check to see if we should eliminate this account:

   ```
   call Eliminate(strAccount, strICP)
   ```

10. Then we are done:

    ```
    End Sub
    ```

Elimination

Before we move on from consolidation rules, there was one big part we didn't cover. It is the Elimination subroutine. We sent the account and ICP members from the data record within the data unit to a Sub Eliminate routine. That is where we will test to see if it is to be eliminated. Let's walk through these rules, and take a look at Figure 3-15. This was taken right from the Sample Applications provided with HFM. You could take this rule

```
Sub Eliminate (strAccount, strICP) 'intercompany elimination rules

   Dim CanEliminate
   Dim strPlug
   Dim dPCon


   CanEliminate = TRUE
   NegatePlug = FALSE

   If (StrComp(strICP, "[ICP None]", vbTextCompare) = 0) Then
      CanEliminate = FALSE
   ElseIf (HS.Account.IsICP(strAccount) = FALSE) Then
      CanEliminate = FALSE
   ElseIf (HS.PARENT.ISDESCENDANT(HS.PARENT.Member,strICP) = FALSE) Then
          CanEliminate = FALSE
   'ElseIf (HS.PARENT.ISDESCENDANT(strICP,"") = FALSE) Then
      'CanEliminate = FALSE
   Else
      strPlug = HS.Account.PlugAcct(strAccount)
'HS.Parent.IsDescendant("I#[ICP Top]", "")
      If (strPlug = "") Then CanEliminate = FALSE
   End If

   If CanEliminate Then

      dPCon = HS.Node.PCon("")

      call HS.Con("V#[Elimination]",-1*dPCon,"")

      call HS.Con("V#[Elimination].A#" & strPlug,dPCon,"")

   End If

End Sub
```

FIGURE 3-15. *Default elimination rules*

as it is, without any modification, although you could remove the commented lines for ElseIf and HS.Parent. These rules provide a great starting point for building something more complex.

1. We start again here by defining some variables we plan to use:

```
CanEliminate; NegatePlug; strPlug; dPCon
```

2. Now we want to make sure the variables have the correct values for us to start:

```
CanEliminate = TRUE
NegatePlug = FALSE
```

3. For each of the next tests, we will now look to see if they fail. If they fail, we know the account can't eliminate, so we will put a "False" in the variable CanEliminate.

4. Here we are checking to see if the ICP member was identified; if not, it can't eliminate:

```
If (StrComp(strICP, "[ICP None]", vbTextCompare) = 0) Then
CanEliminate = FALSE
```

5. Here we check if the account is an ICP type; if not, it can't eliminate.

```
ElseIf (HS.Account.IsICP(strAccount) = FALSE) Then
CanEliminate = FALSE
```

6. Is this the first common parent? We test that by checking if the ICP member is a descendant of the parent.

```
ElseIf (HS.PARENT.ISDESCENDANT(HS.PARENT.Member,strICP) = FALSE) Then
CanEliminate = FALSE
```

7. This is the way we used to check first common parent, but should be changed to the method in step 6.

```
'ElseIf (HS.PARENT.ISDESCENDANT(strICP,"") = FALSE) Then
'CanEliminate = FALSE
```

8. Now we need to check if there is an intercompany plug account; if not, it can't eliminate.

```
strPlug = HS.Account.PlugAcct(strAccount)
If (strPlug = "") Then CanEliminate = FALSE
End If
```

9. Now if we get past all of that and the CanEliminate variable is still True, then we can eliminate.

   ```
   If CanEliminate Then
   ```

10. We get the percent consolidation here.

    ```
    dPCon = HS.Node.PCon("")
    ```

11. Here we write the elimination entry to decrease the intercompany account, and write an offset to the plug account.

    ```
    call HS.Con("V#[Elimination]",-1*dPCon,"")
    ```

12. If the intercompany entries match, the plug account should net to zero.

    ```
    call HS.Con("V#[Elimination].A#" & strPlug,dPCon,"")
    ```

13. And we are finished!

    ```
    End Sub
    ```

After you put this rule in the application, the system will do the default elimination. Consider if you had two entities, A and B. Each had an intercompany balance with the other. A has a $500 receivable with B. B has a $550 payable with A. (Yes, they don't match, but don't jump ahead.) In Entity Currency they book the amounts. These rules will at the Elimination node write a two-sided entry for each. Let's assume we also have a plug account that has an account type of Asset. At the Total.A Elimination member, the rules will write a credit to AR decreasing it to zero, and eliminating it, and writing a debit to the plug account. At the Total.B Elimination member, the rules will write a debit to AP decreasing it to zero, and eliminating it, and writing a credit to the plug account. First, let's look at Figure 3-16 and see the accounting. Each entity has a double-sided entry and the values are eliminated.

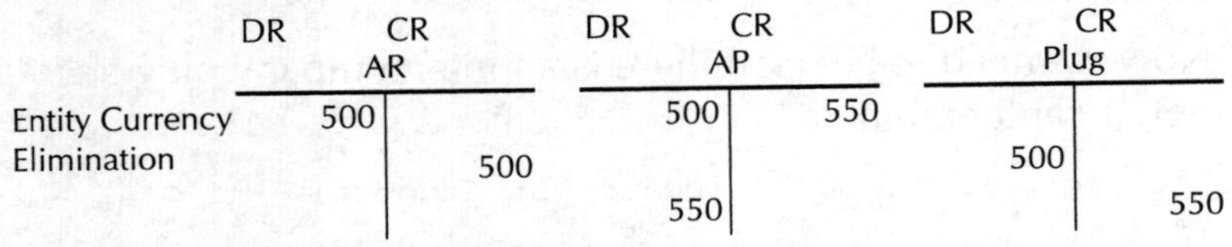

	AR DR	AR CR	AP DR	AP CR	Plug DR	Plug CR
Entity Currency	500		500	550		
Elimination		500			500	
			550			550

FIGURE 3-16. *T-accounts*

	Total		
	A		B
Entity Currency			
AR	500		
AP			550
PLUG-Asset type			
Elimination			
AR	–500		
AP			–550
PLUG-Asset type	500		–550

FIGURE 3-17. *Elimination entry*

Now within the rules, you can see where each of the values is entered. The elimination values HFM calculates make sure the Contribution value dimension member is net of the intercompany activity. And the sum of the offsetting entries in the plug accounts should net to zero. It is when they do not net to zero that you know you have an intercompany out of balance. As shown in Figure 3-17, each account is treated correctly depending on its account type. HFM knows when to increase or decrease, or debit or credit, based on the accounts type.

This can be very helpful as you build complex eliminations, since HFM will help make sure that as you create offsetting entries, each side is booked correctly based on the account type you are writing to.

Error Handling

Okay, it didn't work out, the rules aren't working, or worse, you are getting an error. What do you do? First, you need to identify what is an error and what isn't. Sometimes the only way to really isolate where a rule is failing is to start taking parts of the rules out of the system and start adding them back until you find the error. This can be tedious, and doesn't always give you enough information to fix the file.

When you load the rules, HFM will check for errors, but only when it gives you an error does HFM tell you right at the top of the header. It tells you the start of the load and whether HFM could identify any issues.

```
Load started at: 17:27:30
Number of Errors: 0
Number of Warnings: 0
```

So what does HFM do when it can't tell you if there is an issue? You will see a mess of lines in the rule's error log.

```
Line: 665, Information: Validation was not performed
HS.Exp "A#92000.C2#07904" & _
        "A#92000_PL.C2#07904"
Validations are not performed on line of code with line continuations "_"
Line: 242, Information: Validation was not performed
If HS.GetCell("A#1000" & right_value) > 0 Then
Validations are not performed on lines of code with variables in them.
```

When rules are really tough, you may need to see what the rules are doing by each line or step in the process. When that happens, you need to use a Write to File routine. This Write to File procedure will create custom log files that you can use to tell you exactly where your issue is. Now take a look at the Write to File routine in Figure 3-18. You would need to simply paste this to the end of your rule file. Then when you want to create a log entry, you would add the line:

```
Call WriteToFile("Something you want to see as a string")
```

```
Sub WriteToFile(txtStringToWrite)
    Dim fso,f
    Set fso=CreateObject("Scripting.FileSystemObject")
    Set f=fso.OpenTextFile("c:\ruleslog.txt",8,True)
    f.WriteLine txtStringToWrite & " " & Now()
    f.Close
End Sub
```

FIGURE 3-18. *Write to File*

You can put the point of view, the numerator, and denominator of a complex ratio, or the value in a ratio. You might need to see the times it is taking a rule to run, to isolate problems. You have many options, so this is a valuable tool. One word of caution: never use this rule in a production environment. It will severely impact the rule's performance, especially if left unattended.

When you get to the Calculation Manager tool, you have a much better tool called *error logging*. Why is it better? You can much more easily time the execution of rules to measure execution time to help during the design and test phase. In the formula grid, you can also include information to be logged during rule execution time. The log file will be stored in the Server Working Folder for you to access. This just like the Write_To_File routine in VBScript. You activate this logging by selecting the Enable Logging check box on the Property tab. This is selectable for each object. Double-click on the Logging icon on the first row of the grid to view sample log information. You can optionally enter a condition for the log so that the system will only log the information if the condition is met. You would view this data in the log file.

Complex Rules Issues

As you could tell, you can take rules anywhere you want in the system. But as I love to say, "Just because you can do something doesn't mean you should...." So what are some complex rules you should dive into, and what are some you should pass on trying to get into HFM?

Invest in Sub

The Holding Company has investment accounts on its books that need to be eliminated. The equity in the holding company does not get eliminated. This is the Investment half of the famous "Investment-Equity" elimination. Percent Consolidation (PCON) for a holding company is generally 100 percent and Percent Ownership (POWN) for a holding company is generally 100 percent. Consolidation rules are written to reclassify investment into the investment plug account.

The Subsidiary Companies have equity on their books that roughly offsets the investment on the Holding Company's books. This is the Equity half of the famous "Investment-Equity" elimination. As a general rule of thumb, companies owned between 51 and 100 percent are considered Subsidiary companies. PCON for a subsidiary is 100 percent. As mentioned previously, POWN is generally between 51 and 100 percent. Where POWN is less than 100, the remaining percentage is owned by a minority. Consolidation rules are written to reclassify Equity times PMIN (100-POWN) into Minority Interest and the rest (Equity times POWN) into the investment plug account. If both halves tie out, the investment plug account will zero out.

Good Ideas

Days Sales Outstanding and Days Payable Outstanding are both great rules to add to the HF application. Other rules you should consider are Share Information, Supplemental Schedules, and Data Required for any external reports. If you want to see a full set of rules that are good to have in your application, please review Appendix B. In that section is a full set of common rules with examples.

Bad Ideas

There are some new things that just should not be in rules and in some cases not in HFM at all. Someone once told me, "My car can go 120 mph, but that doesn't mean I should go 120 mph." Can you do some of these things in HFM, sure, but should you? I will now ask why not? Once the person who set this up leaves, can you really manage it? Or have you just created a 120mph, out-of-control monster?

Revaluation

Revaluation is the process of translating transaction detail and writing a foreign exchange component to the operating expenses of the trial balance. This process is transactional in nature; HFM captures balances.

The problem is that HFM just doesn't have transactional detail. Even if you could get most of the detail into the application, you won't be able to capture each transaction and each possible rate. Any process that needs transactions should be avoided. Remember HFM just has balances, so don't try to make HFM a transactional system. You will be disappointed.

Rounding

I have never seen an application where rounding works well. And frankly, when someone is convinced this data should be in the database, I know they do not understand the purpose of HFM.

When attempting this, people take the approach that they have to create a member for each consolidation point for which rounding can take place. Since every external report is required to foot, that could mean dozens or hundreds of members that hold data that is not of any real financial value. It requires rules to figure differences. These rules impact performance. They are never easy.

Here's another reason not to do this: Consider what impact your rounding rules would have on updating structures in HFM. You have taken away one of the real benefits of HFM, being able to update your structures, and made it a risk.

It really doesn't work well. You can't get every rounding error, so now you find yourself thinking the system is doing something that it can't do consistently. Then a report goes out wrong.

Finally, reports are just a better place to handle this. They are better because you can determine what line to plug the rounding amount, and make reports that are easier to foot across and down. Since there are other products that offer an intelligent rounding in their reporting tools, I would expect Oracle has something similar in the works. And if this smart rounding did ever materialize, you would feel just terrible ripping out weeks of work to use it in HFM.

Extracting Data

It is possible to take the Write to File routine used for resolving errors and write large parts of the database to a flat file to import to other systems. This is another really bad idea. First, when the rule is running, it has to open a file and close the file. That can slow the rules because that takes time. It is sometimes referred to as "single-threading the rule file," or making the rules do one thing at a time.

Consider that you can extract data from HFM with extended analytics, and then ask yourself why you would ever do this.

Tax Provision

The only reason you should consider not doing the Tax Provision calculation in HFM is that there are so many tools that do this calculation better than HFM can do it. I think you need to ask yourself if the calculation you are trying to put into the system is really the right place for it. If you do tax provision in HFM, then you need to extract data, reload to the ledger, and then reload to HFM. How many times could that happen during the close? Circular data flows are always problematic.

Waterfall Allocations

When you need to pull data from parent entities or other entities off in other parts of the organization, you can create problems. The problem is that you cannot know for certain the consolidation order of the entities. It is possible the destination entity may run and pull values for the allocation before the source entity has calculated.

Consider that a rule you want to add could make your close in HFM much more difficult, and that isn't the purpose.

Writing Rules in Calculation Manager

Now we can dive into writing the rules within Calculation Manager. Everything covered in this chapter builds up to using this new tool from Oracle. Calculation Manager is a graphical rule-building tool that will create calculations for HFM and Planning. Calc Manager is a powerful tool for developing and administering rules for HFM and Essbase.

The biggest benefits of using Calculation Manager are

- Common interface to design calculation rules. Easier to maintain for administrators.
- Easy way to create complex financial calculations. Doesn't require quite as much coding knowledge.

- Graphical flow provides better understanding of calculation process and a more transparent way to explain calculations to auditors or for documentation purposes.
- Reusable rules to share among applications. Shared objects can be used in multiple situations and multiple applications.
- Central repository of all calculation objects. Templates allow for the faster creation of the most commonly used rules and the benefit of leveraging best practices.
- Custom folders for easy navigation.

This is the future direction for Oracle products, so if you are building a new application, it should absolutely be built with Calculation Manager. Calculation Manager will create a visual flow of the rules, and this is a real value. So learning how to manage script only for any new project would really be a disservice.

So let's begin by logging on to Hyperion Workspace and navigating to Calc Manager. Once in Workspace, the navigation path is Navigate | Administer | Calculation Manager. Figure 3-19 shows us the main screen, and this is where we will build all the rules in Calculation Manager.

Five views are available for navigation of calculation objects:

- **System view** A hierarchical view of objects by application and by calculation type.
- **Custom view** Rules objects grouped into various custom folders. A folder can contain rules objects from any application.
- **List view** List of objects. You can sort by object type, by name, and by application in the List view.
- **Deployment view** Allows you to see the rules and sets to be deployed (loaded) into the HFM application.
- **View pane** Allows you to see and modify the rule you are working with from panes within the screen.

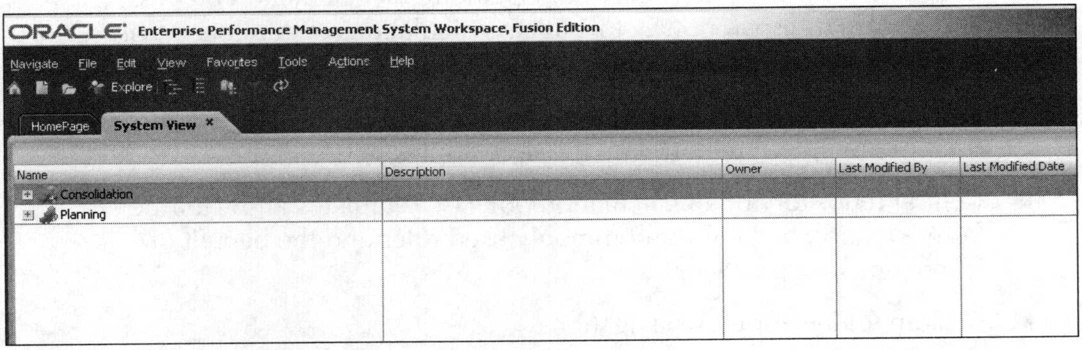

FIGURE 3-19. *Calculation Manager*

To use Calculation Manager, you need to use three objects: the Components, the Rule, and the Rule Set.

- **Component** Formula or script statements
- **Rule** A group of components, as well as conditional and looping statements
- **Rule Set** A group of rules

Components are smaller pieces of a larger rule. They are grouped as two types: a formula component and a script component. Figure 3-20 shows how we would define the beginning of the formula component. Then once we have that defined, we would define the component. Take a look at

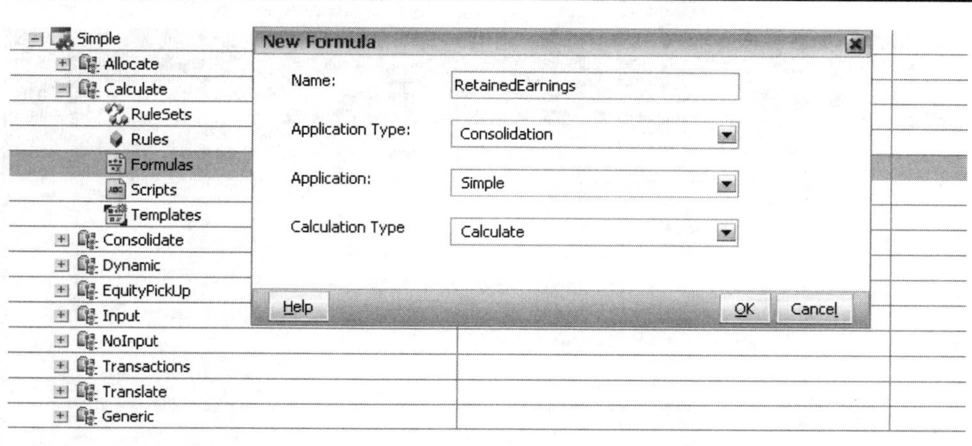

FIGURE 3-20. *Creating a formula component*

Figure 3-21 and notice how the component is basically what we learned to write in the scripting.

- A *formula component* is a collection of formula calculation statements. When you use the formula calculations, you can easily see each of the arguments in the user interface.
- A *script component* is a collection of valid VBScript statements. Think of script components as an easy way to reuse code. Typically, they are written as small stand-alone pieces of code, meaning that all variables and functions are included.

Writing rules is easier in Calculation Manager. For example, the @EXP can be omitted from the formula. You can just say A#RetainedEarnings = A#NetProfit. This makes developing the rules more intuitive and less about syntax.

Rules are objects that have several calculations, either formula component or script component. They also can contain a conditional

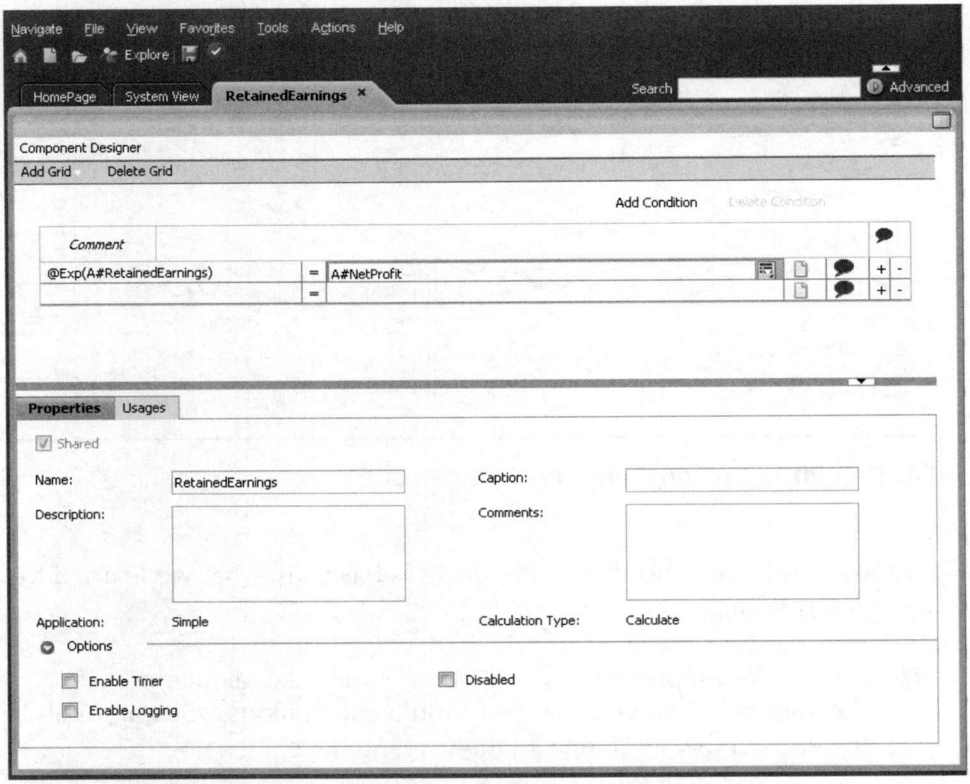

FIGURE 3-21. *Formula component*

object or a loop object. Figure 3-22 shows us how the components are grouped to show a rule.

Rule sets are simply collections of rules or other rule sets. The rule sets execute in the order that appears in the Rule Set Designer. They are grouped by calculation type (all Calculate rules would be in the type Calculate), however. Generic objects can be part of any calculation type objects. Think about how you might name the rule sets. A good naming convention will

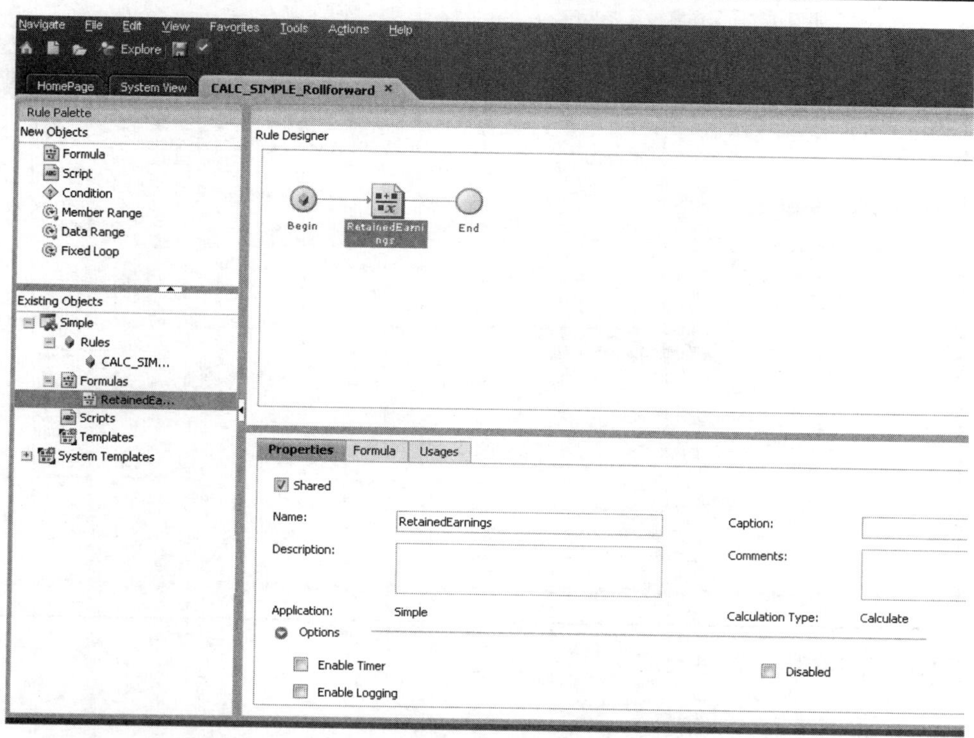

FIGURE 3-22. *Rule*

have the application name, date, and version. Figure 3-23 shows the grouping of rules as a set.

Each rule set will have a primary or main rule. This rule will take the place of what used to be the main Sub procedure. For example, the Calculate Sub procedure typically contains a few rules but is used primarily to define variables and call other Sub procedures.

But to start writing a rule in Calculation Manager, you want to stick with the "commentary approach." Put down in plain English what you want to do. For Calculation Manager, you will be building this graphically, so you should use something like Word or Notepad to write your commentary. Really think about what you want the rules to do, because you can use this to help build your commentary. It might be something like this:

> *"I want a rule to write a value to a validation account when there is a value in my out-of-balance account."*

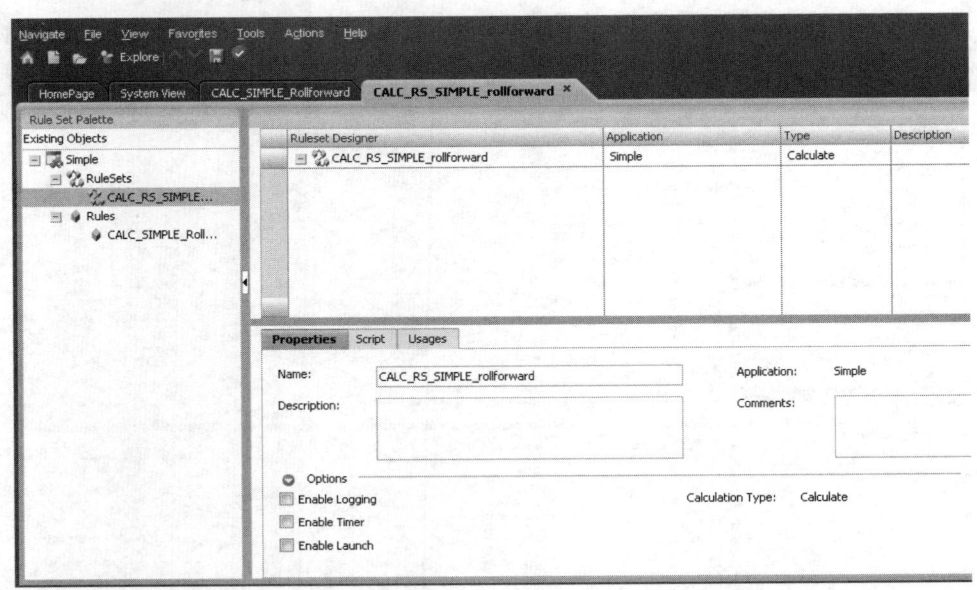

FIGURE 3-23. *Rule set*

So then ask yourself what is the condition you need to test? Here it is: *"when there is a value in my out of balance account."* So, this should be thought of as

"If there is a value in my out-of-balance account"
  "write a value to a validation account"
"end"

Now add the accounts you are using in your application:

"If there is a value in my out-of-balance account"
```
If OutOfBalance <> 0 Then
```
write a value to a validation account
```
          V_OOB = 1
```
"end"
```
End if
```

Now before we start in Calculation Manager, identify the basic part of this rule. What is the object of this rule? This one is pretty straightforward. Writing the one to the database is the object. An object can be a script or a function, as we described. But you can break that down by looking for the action that needs to be done. What will the rule "do"? Here it is writing a value.

So once you have built your script object, you need to put that into a rule. The rule is a set of conditions around the object or objects. Here we only have one condition. Drag and drop it into the flow diagram to look like Figure 3-24.

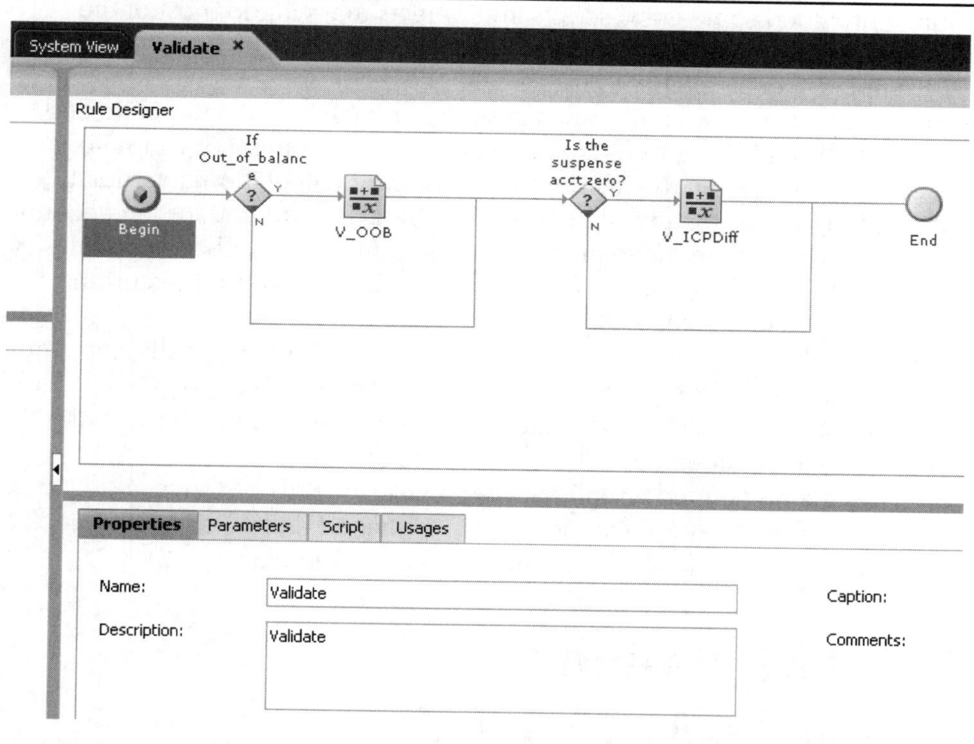

FIGURE 3-24. *Basic Calculation Manager rule*

Syntax is a bit different than with VBScript, but all of the functions are there, and will be familiar to the HFM veterans. When you are done writing a rule and you want to see what Calculation Manager will generate, you can select the End icon, at the end of the rule, and one of the tabs will be Script. If you select that tab, you will see the whole rule in VBScript. This can be very helpful when trying to troubleshoot or work through an issue.

You can refer to the Administrator Guide and the sample applications to make sure the attributes you used are correct. Now load the rule, open a grid, and see the rule pull your data. You can validate that the rule is working here.

I would suggest until you are comfortable writing rules in Calculation Manager, use the sample applications as examples to guide your building. Oracle provided some good scripts and objects that will do most of the basics.

Templates are available to use as well. I have found these very helpful when you have many similar rules to write. You can build a template and use that without having to re-create the basics every time. For example, instead of hard-coding the account in the rule for calculation, a template can be designed using a Design Time Prompt (DTP) variable for the account definition. Then when the template is dragged into a flow chart by a rules designer, the user is prompted for the account to be used for the current instance of the template.

The last thing you need to consider is your variables. Typically, they are grouped in two types: replacement and execution variables. This is just like in the script. In Calculation Manager, though, you need to declare your variables in the dialog box before you use them.

To access predefined templates, right-click on "Rules." Once you give the rule a name, the graphical designer is launched. In the Existing Objects window, you should find a list of the pre-existing templates.

Rules Migration in Oracle HFM 11.1.1.3

So when you are ready to migrate your rule file, you will need to do a bit of preparation work. However, it doesn't have to mean a complete rewrite of your rules. If you have very complex rules, you really should get a string consultant to work with, someone who can bring some experience of migrating to the effort. But if you have pretty standard rules, you can try to run the Rule Migration tool.

The interface is simple, as shown in Figure 3-25.

The path information is simply the source and destination of the files. The system will continue to create the corresponding rule set per calculation type. Within each rule set, the system will convert each Call statement as a separate Rule object. Within each rule object, the system will also split the statements into various component objects based on the comment line specified within the script. As we use a lot of comments, this should not be a big issue. You will need to rewrite the comments.

The first option is the Conditional Object option; don't bury the conditions inside formula objects. The best practice here is placing conditions in their own object.

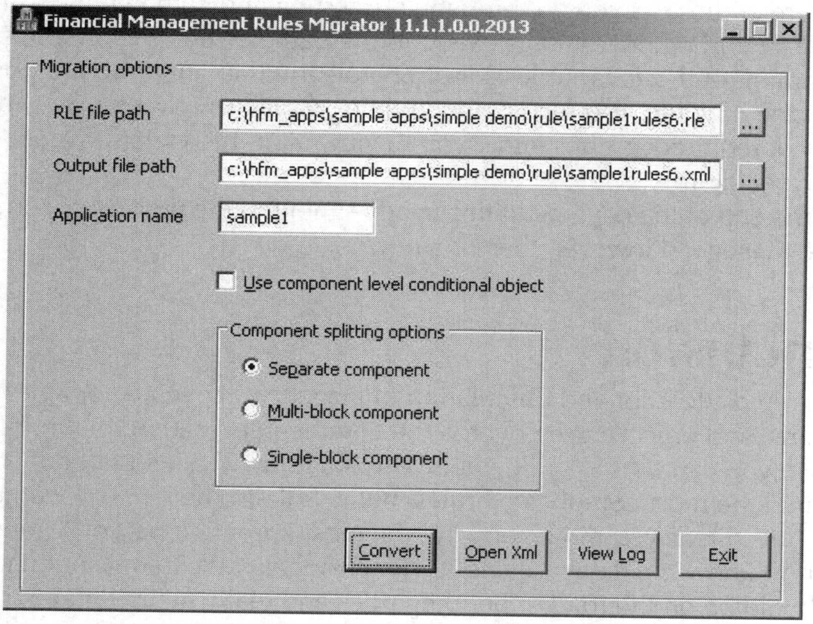

Financial Management Rules Migrator 11.1.1.0.0.2013

Migration options

RLE file path c:\hfm_apps\sample apps\simple demo\rule\sample1rules6.rle

Output file path c:\hfm_apps\sample apps\simple demo\rule\sample1rules6.xml

Application name sample1

Use component level conditional object

Component splitting options

Separate component

Multi-block component

Single-block component

Convert Open Xml View Log Exit

FIGURE 3-25. *Rules Migrator*

There are three options available for the user to convert based on the comment line specified:

- **Separate component** The utility creates a separate component per comment line. This is generally the style of formatting and component/object relationships that should be used as best practice.
- **Multiblock component** The utility creates one component with multiple blocks of calculation statements. This works when you have several related calculations, especially if they share variables.
- **Single-block component** The utility creates one component with single blocks of calculation statements. There will be no separation based on comments.

All constant variables are converted as replacement variables. You might add more of these as you go through your testing and commenting. All other variables will be converted as execution variables with type as string. The naming of these variables should be cleaned up after you are done converting. I would also recommend putting variables into groups. While this is not required, groups allow you to view all of the variables associated with a specific rule.

At the end of the day, the utility greatly simplifies the process of converting to Calc Manager. However, there is still work to do.

Conclusion

We covered VBScript and Calculation Manager; we covered variables, functions, and objects. We covered the commentary method of writing rules, so you can start to build your own functions. This will not only help you build the most complicated rules, but it will also help you document them. But still, as you move forward, the most important part of writing rules is to know the database and its dimensionality. With this foundation, you should be on the road to building rules and really maintaining your application.

CHAPTER 4

Reporting

he application build is under way, and you can start to see how the application is coming together. But you will need to build reports to get the data out, in some useful kind of way. The report writing should even really happen before you have the first period of data reconciled. The reason for this is the amount of time it can take to write reports. Not because of the way Financial Reports works, but more because of the way reporting can evolve when people see the data available. It is at this point that scope can change, and you can see risk to the project.

This chapter will cover how the different reporting tools work together, some best practices for building reports, and how to take on large reporting projects. Like the rest of this book, the goal here is not to tell you the basics, or to train you for these tools. The goal here is to give you a strategy for building, and developing, provide best practices, and guide your work. There are things you can do to save yourself time and aggravation. And specifically for reports you have to build, there some very important things you can do.

Overview

The first thing you should do, and I would even propose doing this during the design meeting, is to gather your reports; that is to say, ask yourself, "What are you trying to build?" This system should be focused on the reports and detail you want to get out of it. The structure of your database should be built to support the reporting you need to do. The main goal of a system like this always includes good reports. You would do yourself a favor to think about your end product first. In fact, the more reports you have, the more important this is to do.

There are several tools that will allow you to build reports. The first tool is Financial Reports (FR). These reports are typically the monthly book that comes from the printer every month. They are reports that are run for many members with the same view, like a balance sheet. Web Analysis (WA) reports are the dashboard-type reports, quick snapshots or dashboards of information. There is very little information in these reports relative to the others, although they may have some of the most valuable information needed to run your business. There are Smart View and Ad Hoc reports. These are the reports you can't build for people, as they will be created as needed. There are System Reports, which include journal reports and intercompany matching reports. There are also Support and Audit Reports, which include the users on the system, task audit, data audit, and system messages. Finally, there are the Security Reports: configuration changes, security changes, role access, class access, and role inheritance reports.

The focus of your report building will be on Financial Reports. These are the reports that need to be built from the metadata in your application. These reports should be considered the purpose of your application. In fact, when you want to add members and dimensions, you should consider how each addition impacts the reports you build. This is critical.

So now that you have the reports, create an inventory. An inventory is a list of each report, what the reports you need to build are, and who owns each. You can and should group them by priority. What are the reports you need to build first? Which reports are nice to have? And no, you cannot have 100 reports all with a priority of "High." The more reports you have, the more important this is. When you've gathered the reports, decide what the right tool is for each. Each report is better served by one of the tools. Is the report a Financial Reports report? Is the report a Web Analysis report?

This organization is critical to any significant reporting project. I am shocked when people start building reports without having defined the scope. This is not just because it is so difficult to manage the scope without knowing what work there is to do, but also how can anyone build a database without a sense of the reports needed to run the business?

Oracle provides several tools for building reports. The main tools, and the ones most clients use, are Financial Reports, Web Analysis, and Smart View. Coming soon is a new tool called Oracle Business Intelligence Enterprise Edition (OBIEE). OBIEE is Oracle's current direction for dashboards and reporting.

Oracle Business Intelligence Enterprise Edition (OBIEE) is a set of enterprise business intelligence tools. It includes a query and analysis server, an ad-hoc query and analysis tool, interactive dashboards, proactive intelligence and alerts, real-time predictive intelligence, and an enterprise reporting engine. It will be nice to have a common and comprehensive tool not only across the Hyperion toolset, but across all of Oracle's deep database stack.

Financial Reports

Financial Reports (formerly Hyperion Reports) delivers formatted, high-volume, production-quality reporting across the enterprise. These reports are the type that is often needed for books or filings. Financial Reports provides a graphical interface for rapid report creation. A library of reusable report components simplifies and streamlines report creation and maintenance: data grids, text, charts, graphs, and images. Something as simple as the company profit and loss statement, balance sheet, and cash flow are common in Financial Reports. Figure 4-1 shows the main report repository you see when you log in.

Financial Reports is a scalable, cross-platform report server that facilitates easy deployment to large user communities. Dynamic report

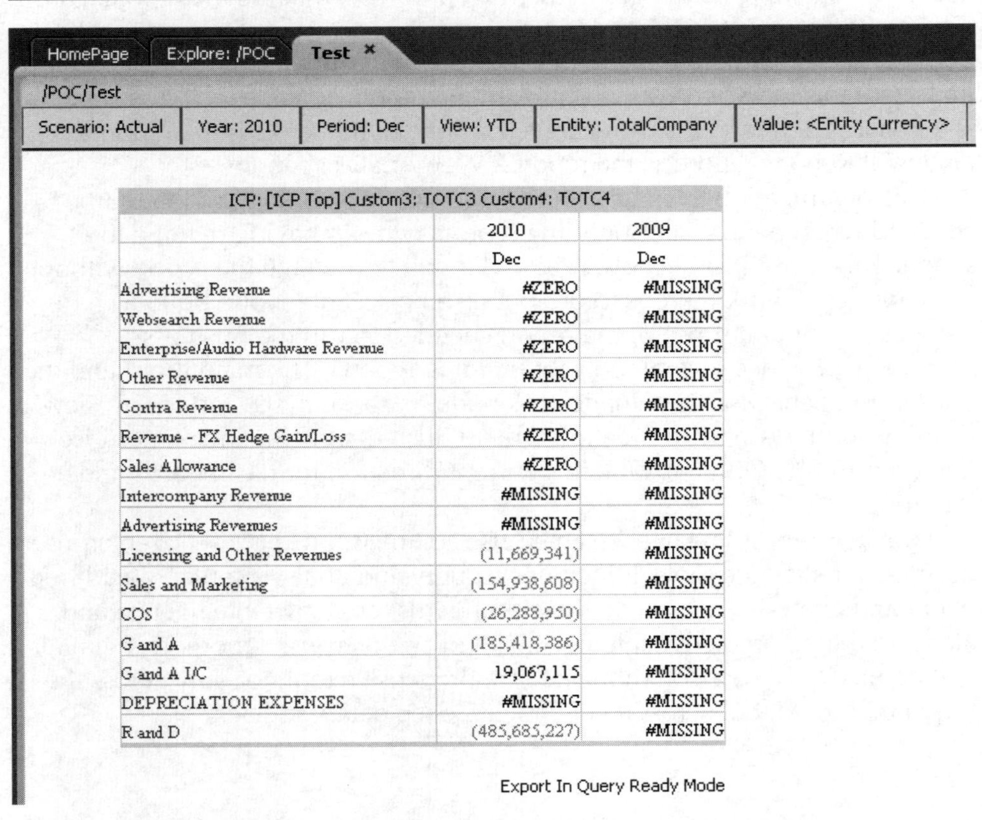

ICP: [ICP Top] Custom3: TOTC3 Custom4: TOTC4		
	2010	2009
	Dec	Dec
Advertising Revenue	#ZERO	#MISSING
Websearch Revenue	#ZERO	#MISSING
Enterprise/Audio Hardware Revenue	#ZERO	#MISSING
Other Revenue	#ZERO	#MISSING
Contra Revenue	#ZERO	#MISSING
Revenue - FX Hedge Gain/Loss	#ZERO	#MISSING
Sales Allowance	#ZERO	#MISSING
Intercompany Revenue	#MISSING	#MISSING
Advertising Revenues	#MISSING	#MISSING
Licensing and Other Revenues	(11,669,341)	#MISSING
Sales and Marketing	(154,938,608)	#MISSING
COS	(26,288,950)	#MISSING
G and A	(185,418,386)	#MISSING
G and A I/C	19,067,115	#MISSING
DEPRECIATION EXPENSES	#MISSING	#MISSING
R and D	(485,685,227)	#MISSING

FIGURE 4-1. *Financial Reports*

scheduling ensures that users have easy access to timely, relevant, and complete business-critical information.

Financial Reports includes these key features:

- A flexible range of output options. The output options are actually a key differentiator for FR: the fact that PDF, HTML, and book outputs are available is a competitive advantage.
- Scalable, cross-platform, server-based report generation.
- Graphical, object-based report creation with simultaneous access to multiple Hyperion data sources, like Essbase, HFM, and Planning.
- Reusable report objects across multiple reports.
- Book creation to bind groups of related reports.
- Dynamic command-line scheduling for automated reporting.
- Support for asymmetry in both columns and rows.
- Dynamic expansion and point-of-view modification at run time.

Since this is a book about tips and tricks, here are a few tips for reports, before the discussion turns to best practices for implementation and design.

- As with just about everything else in this tool, you need to think of a standard naming convention for your reports.
- Minimize your use of prompts. If you leverage grid POV to users POV, you will have better reporting. (Prompts add additional clicks, and the default value may be a member the user does not have access to.)
- Discourage users from previewing the user's POV.
- Back up your reports by exporting the repository often. (This is needed to be synchronized with the Database restores.)
- Make your reports specific, and not dumps of the entire database. They will run faster and work better. See the discussion of the "report from hell" in the section "Report Performance Basics" later in this chapter.

You can make your reports more dynamic, and consistent, not only in appearance but in formatting, by building more links. As you prepare to create links, you should make sure you decide where you will store your images and files; if you move the directory where the linked objects exist, then all links will be broken.

- Always link to company logos and commonly used images.
- Create standard row and column templates and link them to other reports (example: P&L and BS rows).
- Create standard headers and footers and link them.
- Create a starting report or template to create all new reports from and leverage the Save As function to build new reports.

The goal of any report writer is to make reports as maintenance-free and as dynamic as possible so there are no more reports than needed. This approach is better for users as well, since they will have fewer reports to scroll through while hunting for the ones they need.

When building a report, you should consider how you will pull the detail into the columns. If I were building a report that needed to show elimination detail, but all within one column, I might do that as follows.

- **Column A**-Entity: Children of Cur, Value USD Total
- **Column B**-Entity: Children of Cur, Value Elimination (this column is hidden, since it could be several members)
- **Column C**-Sum (Column [B]): Custom header, but with a custom header called Elimination
- **Column D**-Entity: CUR, Value USD Total

Another thing to take away from this discussion of reports is to note that instead of making several reports with static entities in columns, I used the current entity as reference. This would allow the users to leverage their POV. You should always use "CUR" whenever possible.

I would suggest changing the color of the hidden column header; in this case column B as it is hidden. This way, anyone else, for example the other admin/report designer, knows right away this is a hidden column when looking at the report in the designer.

If you have the elimination member represented in the columns, metadata can change and the report will always foot. When designing reports, always make sure data will foot when adding across columns and rows.

Rounding

I should start with what the differences are between scaling and rounding. Scaling is making the number appear as thousands, or millions. For example, 1,234,567 shown in thousands would be 1,234,000. What to do with the 567 is rounding. Typically, people will "round up" for this, so 1,234,567 scaled to thousands and rounded would be displayed as 1,235. The problem this can cause is that numbers scaled and rounded in a report will create reports that might not foot. If you have rounded numbers, you might want to consider how to deal with this.

Before I dig into rounding in reports, I should explain that this is just math. Most people who are looking at a financial report understand that when they are looking at them. When a report says "in millions," they know there must be some rounding somewhere. I strongly believe the purpose of the reports should be to provide as much information as possible. That said, when you push rounding into a line on the report somewhere, you are making one line of the report wrong. Now some people are fine with that because they view the line they will plug rounding into not as valuable a line of information, like "other expenses."

The reality is that with rounding, every approach is technically wrong. Any approach that is used will have some number that is "wrong." Since people tend not to like the "well, that is too bad" approach, I offer three ways to handle rounding. The three approaches have increasing levels of maintenance, but are tailored for a specific audience. The two issues are footing down, and footing from one report to another.

The other thing that can complicate the report rounding is rounding for rows and columns. It can be tricky to make sure the rows and columns are working the way you are expecting if the report is very complicated, but not impossible.

Assume you have this in your application:

A - 50
B - 50
Total- 100

The first is to just scale the data as it is in HFM. These reports should only be used for internal reporting; those should be easy to define.

Option A (scaled to 100):
A - 1
B - 1
Total- 1 (note that this line does not foot)

So while this option does not foot, most people understand that is because of rounding and can handle that. But there is almost no maintenance for this approach. And you never have to worry about reports footing from one to the other.

The second approach it to make the totals calculations in HFM. The reports will always foot, though. This approach should be used for one-off reports, and for internal users.

Option B (scaled to 100):
A - 1
B - 1
Total- 2 (This line is calculated, but note this line does not tie to the database.)

The third approach is to make a summary line a calculation in HFM. The reports will always foot, and will be easier to reconcile from one to another. This approach should be used for the smaller set of reports used for external reporting.

Option C (scaled to 100):
A - 1
B - 0 (Now this line is calculated, but note this line does not tie to the database.)
Total- 1

The trick to the Option C approach is to not just sum in the report. If you can use a list or dynamic member from the database and then compare that to the total, you add a validation right inside the report. Then with conditional formatting, you would then add some text to flag when these amounts exceed what you would expect for rounding (maybe .5). So if metadata changes, you can show the report has an issue.

Report Performance Basics

You want to build reports that have good performance. But what is *good* performance? It is a relative term. Report performance varies for every report, installation, and design. It depends on the load on the servers, other processes going on, and other software running during the day. It also depends on the people running the reports. What is acceptable for one person may not be acceptable for another. Fifteen seconds may seem fast for one person, and unbearable for another. So how do you define "good"? The exact time will vary, but you need to determine what is acceptable for a given report under as close to ideal conditions as possible. Take your key reports, maybe 5 to 12 and run them with no one logged on, no other processes running, on the local network or on the server. You want to measure the time each of these reports takes to run. Now you have a base line. If you have a report that takes 5 seconds to run under these ideal circumstances, and then if you are running it while the consolidation is running over a WAN, it takes 15 seconds, you have an idea of what the issue is.

When you call support and tell them the system is "slow," that doesn't give them a lot to work with. If you call support and say, "The report took 5 seconds and now takes 15 seconds, and by the way this was over the WAN," now they should have some starting point.

Whenever I see a report with hundreds or thousands of columns and rows, I ask, "Do you really need this as a report?" Usually when people have reports like this, they are compensating for some other issue. Otherwise, explain to me why someone would need so much data. They might be aggregating it or rolling it up another way, doing some calculation. You need to ask if there is a better way to do the work they need to do. The answer is often "yes." HFM and Financial Reports can take the work of pulling the data and doing calculations off people's plates and give them the ability to spend their time analyzing the data.

Suppose you have a report that pulls every entity, multiple value dimension members, multiple scenarios, and multiple years. Since performance is based on the number of subcubes brought into memory, this much data will create the "report from hell." It will take forever to run, and it will slow the system. Worse yet, how valuable is it really? Even people who swear they need this data will eventually break down and tell you it isn't very valuable. You see, Financial Reports are driven by the dimensions, not just the ones that contain data. These reports cannot be data-driven: the program cannot go and find subcubes that have data—it must look everywhere and present what it finds, or doesn't find.

The first report you should build is the reporting template. You should define as much of this report as you can. You should build default fonts and formatting. You should use your logo, and build the first parts of the report. Figure 4-2 shows you a great way to start building your report. People like

/Users/admin/Reports/CashFlow

Scenario: Actual | Year: 2011 | Period: Feb | View: YTD | Entity: Total_Company | Value: <Entity Currency>

Total Company
Period: Feb-2011 Currency: USD
Submitted: 20-Apr-11 20:03:27

ICP: [ICP Top] Custom1: TOTC1 Custom2: TOTC2 Custom3: TOTC3 Custom4: TOTC4			
	2011	2010	2009
	February	February	February
Operating Activities, Cash Flows Provided By or Used In			
Net Income	-	-	-
Depreciation and amortization on PPE	-	-	-
Amortization of intangibles and other	-	-	-
Stock-based compensation	-	-	-
Excess tax benefits	-	-	-
Deferred taxes on earnings	-	-	-
Other	-	-	-
Accounts receivable	-	-	-
Income taxes, net	-	-	-
Prepaid revenue share, expenses and other assets	-	-	-
Accounts payable	-	-	-
Accrued expenses and other liabilities	-	-	-
Accrued revenue share	-	-	-
Deferred revenue	-	-	-
CASH FLOWS FROM OPERATING ACTIVITIES:	-	-	-
Investing Activities, Cash Flows Provided By or Used In			
Purchases of property and equipment	-	-	-

FIGURE 4-2. *Sample report template*

to put the company logo on the report, and it is a nice touch to add to your template. Be careful here with the logo image you select. If it is very large, it can really impact the performance of your reports. You should take some time to find a size that looks good, and yet is as small as possible.

Create as much as you can common for the reports set you are going to build. You should remember the practices described earlier in this section, and use links, create a common object to start with. This makes development easier since you can start with this and make changes to this template, and then use the Save As command to create the template.

When you have the template, you should save it as one or more template reports. Then export the reports from the Workspace and save them to a secure location that is backed up regularly. When you wish to create a new report using the template, import the desired design file and start the report build. You would do this because if there were ever an issue with the repository, all of the copied reports would be lost. If you import the design every time, the resulting report is not related to any other report, and is independent of any issues with another report.

Once you have the first templates and sample reports built, you should build a structure that will help you in your build. You do not want to build too elaborate a folder structure. But you should group the folders by reporting users who use the reports, as shown in Figure 4-3.

Okay, the example here is simple. But you can run with this idea. You could group the reports by type, or by user, or by phase of the close. You should also group your report objects by type, like having a grid folder or logo folder.

Even if you schedule regular backups, there is no way to restore a single report that was mistakenly deleted, or modified. You can restore everything or nothing. So it is another best practice to do the following while in development. You should always export the reports from Workspace, and save them in a safe location. There would not be data in these reports, so it should be a concern. But if you do this and if you have an issue, you can restore the individual file.

Financial Report Design

When you build reports, you have a grid to which you can add objects. The objects are grids for data, text boxes, and images. There are some limits to the number of objects you can use. Within a grid, you never want

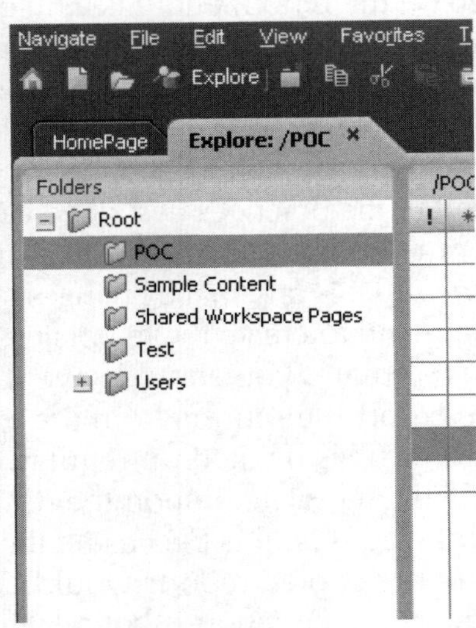

FIGURE 4-3. *Sample folder structure*

to have more than 2000 rows or columns. If you have more than that, the report may not run at all. I have found that if I have more than 100 rows or columns, the report will be noticeably slower than other reports.

The following table lists metrics by dimension to be used as a guideline for determining common terminology with regard to report size.

Dimensions for the Report	Small	Medium	Large
Number of row dimensions	1	2–4	4+
Number of column dimensions	1	2–4	4+
Number of expanded rows	<100	100–1,000	1,000+
Number of expanded columns	<10	10–15	15+
Potential size of report	<1,000	20,000	100,000

NOTE
Limiting or reducing the number of expanded row dimensions is recommended.

If you understand the proper usage of formulas and how reports use the columns and rows, you can save time building your reports. You can use the two methods at the same time:

- **Cell** Cell formulas are valid only for the cell where that formula was entered. You simply click on the individual cell in the grid that will receive the cell formula.
- **Row/Column** Row and column formulas are valid for the entire row/column. This is preferred, because these formulas perform much better. You would click on the row or column header on the grid and enter the formula in the property sheet.

You can make references to row cells from columns and vice versa, from column cells to rows. Let's say you put in the row [A] – [B] / [10]. The reference to the A and B column is called a cross reference. This is not a good practice to use. Cross references are difficult to use and will create errors if the reports change.

As you build the report, you will want to watch how you add functions and formatting. This is another reason why the template you create is so important. Each operation happens in a sequence that can supersede something you think might be controlling the formatting or functions.

Hyperion Financial Management data sources will return #MISSING or #ZERO for cells without data. To minimize the impact of this in existing client reports, the default behavior is to ignore #MISSING in formulas. You can change this setting in the hr_repserver.properties file.

Best Practices for Reports

There are some good practices to follow when writing reports. It starts back when you created your design. You should be thinking of the reports you want constantly through the design process. You need to design your application to support the reports rather than the reverse. When you build structures and hierarchies, they should support the reports you need. Your totals and subtotals should be parent members in these structures. You want to build calculations in the system that support the reports. Why have the report calculate a simple ratio every time it is run, when you can build that in the database and calculate it one time when you consolidate? Think about it like this: What is easier to pull, one number or two or more numbers, do a calculation, and then have some special formatting? What if you have a hundred reports, and you have to change the ratio in each? It just makes sense to build as much as you can in the database.

That doesn't mean you want to build every calculation in the database. There are some that do make sense to build into the report. You need to have a well-performing application, or even the best reports will be slow. Rounding and scaling are great examples of something that should be in a report. Financial Reports has a great set of functions and formulas you can use, too.

You also don't want to have too many cells in the report. Look at your reports before you suppress any cells, and count the members reports will call from the database in all the rows. Multiply the number of members in each row dimension by each other and then multiply this number by the number of columns. If you're using expanded segments in the columns or rows, use the number called at run time. This is the potential total number of cells. If you are in the tens of thousands, this is a large report.

So, a report with very few calculations and data cells performs better than one with a lot of calculations and data cells. That seems almost too obvious, right? But you need to think of each report in the context of "good" again. If a report is pulling a lot of data and the users know it, they will usually give it a little more time to run before getting frustrated. So, large reports that could create performance issues are a balancing act between providing the data required and performing well.

If the report is just unbearably slow for the data required, then you need to come up with some other options. You could create a snapshot report. If it doesn't have to pull all the data and calculations, then you would expect it to be faster. You could run these snapshots during off-peak hours, or before people get into the office, using a scheduler.

Another option is to break the report into small reports. When there are really big reports, with hundreds of rows and columns, there are also likely some other issues or processes that can be improved. When that is the case, you might find the report wasn't really the issue.

Other options are

- Make the report smaller by using the point of view or prompts instead of lists and page dimensions.
- Look to limit the number of cells you call and suppress.
- Increase the number of print servers.
- Remove conditional formatting and suppression.

Fat Rows and Columns

A *data segment* is a row or column that retrieves data from a database. The data segment is considered "expanded" when the resulting grid contains two or more rows or columns when viewed in the report. A *fat row* is a single row that contains multiple members or lists within it.

Expanded data segments often use lists to show the many members, and are referred to as "fat" rows or columns. When a single data segment is a row or column that remains a single row or column when shown in the viewer, it is referred to as a "skinny" row or "skinny" column. You might use both in the same grid.

When possible, use expanded or fat rows and columns. Not only is the performance better, but this is a great way to make you reports more dynamic. Since the fat columns and rows often use lists like "Base" and "Descendants of…", as the structure changes in the database, the reports will automatically update. You don't have to worry about adding a new account, and then having to update your entire repository of reports. However, when you're using fat columns and rows, the formatting is very limited. You can't change it by each member. So if you need to produce detailed formatting for each data rows or columns, you need to use single data segments.

This is not like "Allow Expansions," which is useful in its own way. Figure 4-4 shows an example of an expansion. This feature shows a grey triangle at the beginning of the account, which tells us that it can be expanded. This allows a report developer to create fewer reports because they can be summary and detailed. This provides the report user with an ability to drill down on a dimension at run time, finding the detail they need.

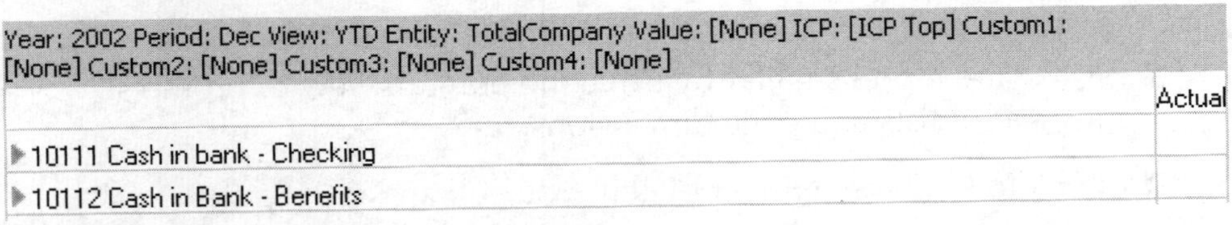

Year: 2002 Period: Dec View: YTD Entity: TotalCompany Value: [None] ICP: [ICP Top] Custom1: [None] Custom2: [None] Custom3: [None] Custom4: [None]	
	Actual
▶10111 Cash in bank - Checking	
▶10112 Cash in Bank - Benefits	

FIGURE 4-4. *Expansions*

Good Design Tips

If there is only one dimension selected, do put it in the rows or columns, or page axis. No, it does not add to the number of cells called, but when the query is made, the report needs to take that into consideration and is slower.

Cross-axis references are when you refer to columns from rows, or vice versa, when you refer to rows from columns. You should avoid using this when possible. You should consider using a cell reference instead.

If you have a formula that repeats for each cell in a row or column, use a row/column formula. If you have different formulas that need to be performed on each cell, use a cell formula.

Parentheses allow you to define the order of calculations. Using these unnecessarily will slow the report down. They cause extra evaluations within the report-writing calculation engine.

Conditional Formatting and Conditional Suppression

Conditional formatting and suppression can affect performance, depending on the size of the report and how often it is used within the report. Certain values, like label and description, will have less impact. But this is something that when used excessively can slow the report.

Member Selection

When selecting your members, double-click on the corresponding member name on the property sheet or double-click on the Member Name from the corresponding cell on the grid. This will show the dimension selected for editing, and allow you to specify that the member selection be separated into multiple rows or columns. You can specify this option by marking the check box on the bottom-right corner.

Member selection is more efficient when selecting what is defined rather than what is not defined. So use the "not" operator sparingly.

Using the Grid POV

If the dimension will change but is set to one member, it should be in the User POV. If the single member will not change, then it should be in the Grid POV or Page Axis. For example, a report may need to run for several entities, but will always show entity currency. Then the entities will be selectable in the user POV and the value dimension will be in the grid POV.

Every time the User POV changes, the report will retrieve data from the database. The Page Axis obtains the data up front once. So if you have many members in the Page Axis, performance will be poor.

Best Practices for Cell Text, Documents in Reports, and Commentary

Adding attachments and documents in HFM and reports is pretty easy. This capability has been available since the version 4.0 release, so it is pretty stable. In fact, the only place where people go sideways trying to set this up is not being careful and deliberate in where they attach the documents. You need to have a member where you can always be sure to find the documents. Do not let people put this information just anywhere in the data base.

You can attach a Microsoft Word document, Microsoft Excel spreadsheet, or XML file. To attach or extract any custom documents to or from the server, you must be assigned the Manage Custom Documents security role. You absolutely should set the size limit for document attachments and a maximum number of document attachments by user when you create an application. This will keep users from filling your database with too many useless files. MaxDocAttachmentSize sets the maximum number of bytes for the size of document attachments up to 2,147,483,646 bytes. MaxNumDocAttachments sets the maximum number of document attachments per user up to 2,147,483,647. You can enter a value of –1 for both of these to have no limit, but that is not recommended.

Anytime you have a significant total in a report, it is not a bad idea to build a validation in the report. For example, if you are calculating a total, then pull the total from the database and calculate the difference. You can then use conditional formatting to tell the report to suppress the text if the result is zero. The text might just be something as simple as "This report does not reconcile." Every report should have some check. This will help you with data reconciliation.

Books, Batches, and Bursting

One thing that will improve the use of your reposting tool is understanding how Financial Reports can help with report distribution. Even if the reports run quickly, it will not help you if people are clicking constantly to run each report. The Financial Reports tool provides great ways to generate and group the reports for distribution. They are Books, Batches, and Batch Bursting. When you create one of these in Workspace, you just have to create a new document. Figure 4-5 shows the options you have when creating a book.

A *book* is basically a group of reports and snapshots. This allows users to generate the group of reports as one exercise. The book runs a group of

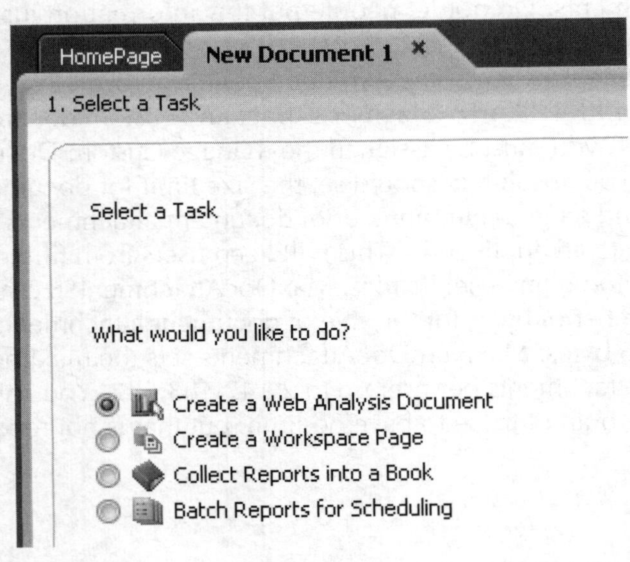

FIGURE 4-5. *Book options*

reports at one time. The book can also be configured to run for different points of view or for a group of members. The book can also run individual reports for a list or set of members. For example, you could see a book with only two reports in it, but the book has those reports run for all entities.

Batches are used to group and run groups of reports or books. This can be printed, using either HTML or PDF as an output. The batch process can also e-mail users the exported output.

Batch Bursting allows you to run more than one batch. The batch bursting can run batches for different members of a dimension, e-mail the reports, and save the reports in a set of folders, all with one step. A Bursting Destination File contains the default settings for the batch, and can be created to override default settings assigned to the batch.

Books

Once you have a group of reports, creating a book containing those reports will allow them to run at once. The New Document wizard will help you create a book. You would select File, New, Document. In Figure 4-6, you can see in the system how you would select the reports to add to a book. In general, a book contains one or more reports that are generated for a

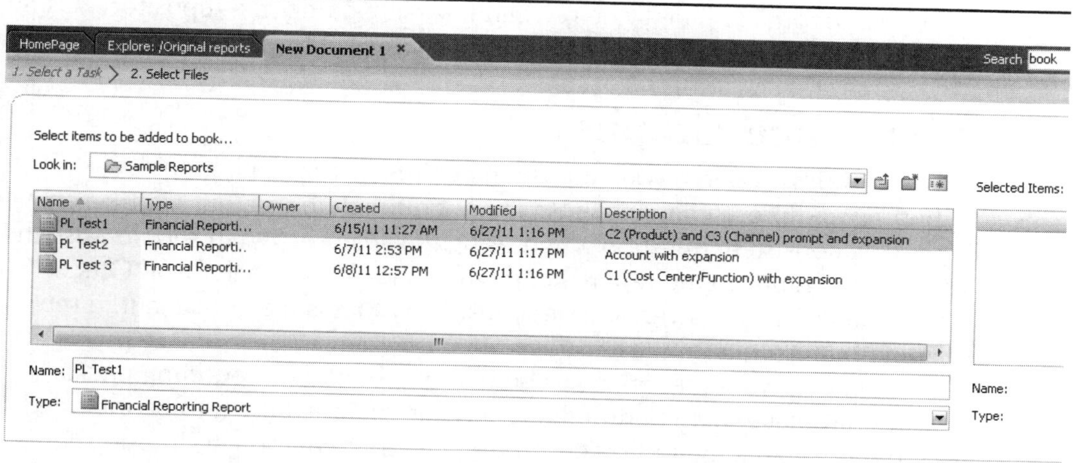

FIGURE 4-6. *Creating a book*

particular Point of View (POV). The POV typically contains the Entity, Year, Period, and View dimensions. Another feature of the book is that it will generate a Table of Contents for each report.

If you find a book is running too long, consider making the book a snapshot. It will not be dynamic, but it will be much faster for users to view.

Batch Process

Batches are basically a way to group reports for distribution, printing, and automation. The output generated by running a batch can be sent to a printer or to the repository, and you can export both as HTML and PDF files. The batch process can also e-mail users the exported output. You can select a number of exports options for your batch job. They can be extracted as snapshots, or as static reports that are saved in the repository, PDF files, and HTML. Why not have a batch run to get your reports to your users after the database is done consolidating? It would make your reporting much more proactive. You can also have a batch of reports e-mailed to someone.

When you schedule batches, you can select bursting options to run reports for multiple members. For example, in a batch scheduled to run for two entities, A and B entities, you can send the output for A to user@oracle.com and send the output for B to mgr@oracle.com. Just remember, you can only use one dimension to specify your distribution target.

Great reports do little to help when they sit waiting in a repository. Using books and batches will help get the information out to your team.

Charts and Graphs

When building reports, you can use the charts to help with graphical reporting and presentations. These are not difficult to use, but people seem to have a consistent question when using this feature. When should I use the charts and graphs in the reports, and when should I use Microsoft Office functionality? The answer is: it depends. Now that is the consultant in me coming out, isn't it?

When you want the reports to be part of a book or a reporting package, you should make them part of the reports. If you need them to be included in the report package in PowerPoint or Word, then you can import the report. If the graph or chart will only ever be in one report that is best served as part of a presentation, in a tool like PowerPoint, or a document in a tool like Word, then you can build it directly in the Office document. The reason is simple. If you have any changes to the grid or chart—you can do it in one place, as opposed to many. This reduces your maintenance.

Web Analysis

Web Analysis was formerly known as Hyperion Analyzer and before that Wired for OLAP. This was a tool built for Essbase, and then later enabled for HFM. The tools should be used for simple dashboards. The first thing to keep in mind when building this type of report is that you need to have a design already conceived. Do not fall into the trap of asking what the tool can do, and only getting, "Well, what do you want it do?" as an answer. If you can define a set of dashboards and reports at the outset, you can build a better application to support these reports.

If you are planning to invest in some dashboards, you might want to consider Oracle Business Intelligence Enterprise Edition (OBIEE). OBIEE will become strategic to HFM reporting in future releases.

If you are familiar with this tool for Essbase, then you should know HFM requires that every dimension must have a selection, unlike Essbase. Figure 4-7 is an example from the Eden application that came with the installation. This sample application has some great examples.

Best Practices for Web Analysis

There are limitations to Web Analysis. For example, when pulling data from HFM, web analysis will not support suppression for zeros and no data. If you want to have fast-running reports, then you should follow these performance guidelines:

- No more than four (4) data queries (reportdatasrc) per report.
- No more than 100,000 cells returned on a query (reportdatasrc).
- No more than four (4) OLAP selection/subscription controls that have "dynamic" enabled per report and should only contain a maximum of 5,000 members for each.

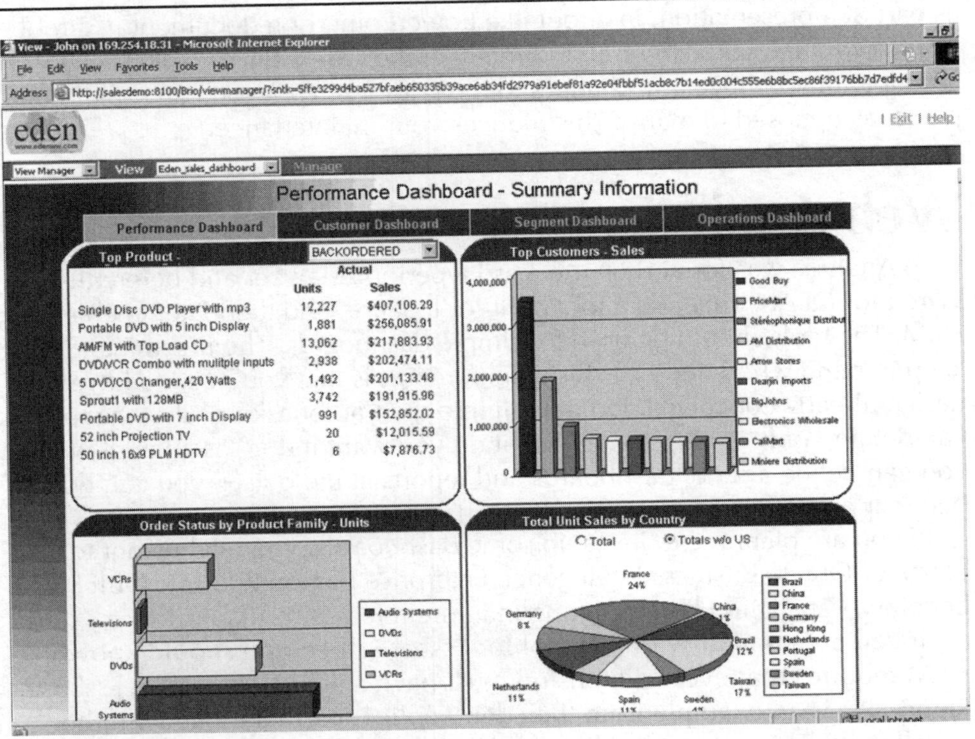

FIGURE 4-7. *Web Analysis example*

- No more than four (4) "set depth" levels for multilevel combo boxes or four (4) dependant subscription controls.
- No more than .5MB of total size of graphics on a report. This includes graphics used on pinboards.
- When LROs or EIS drill-through reports are not necessary, then disable the Show LROs Indicators (Grid API) to improve performance.
- When using advanced member selections (for example, descendants, children, and so on) to apply database formatting on a database connection, limit the use on small outlines to no more than 10,000 members.

- No more than 1,000 pages on a query (reportdatasrc).
- Printing a report in the Studio Client with a large number of Pages (for example, hundreds or thousands), printing may fail due to the large number of pages to compile in memory. To resolve this, reduce the number of pages printed in the report to a more manageable amount.
- No more than twenty (20) Traffic Lighting definitions with a maximum of seven (7) levels per reportdatasrc.
- No more than twenty (20) Show/Hide definitions per reportdatasrc.
- No more than twenty (20) Calculations per reportdatasrc.
- No more than twenty (20) Data Formatting definitions per reportdatasrc.
- Only one (1) Retrieve Top/Bottom per reportdatascr.
- No more than twenty (20) Restrict Data conditions per reportdatascr.

Smart View

Smart View for Office provides the framework to integrate the Hyperion Suite with Microsoft Office. Hyperion Smart View for Office replaces the existing spreadsheet add-ins for Financial Management and Planning. This is not just an Excel tool. Smart View really integrates with the whole Office suite, including Word and PowerPoint. Ad-hoc content can be retrieved using the Smart View add-in, across the Hyperion and BI+ offering.

One of the newest features of Smart View is the new Query Designer. This will help users define "what is the data set" they need to pull from the application. This is another tool that, while fairly intuitive, is also new. People who administer HFM for companies need to look for ways to extend the value of the functionality of HFM within their companies. Get people to look at the data in ways that help them, as quickly and efficiently as possible. This is a feature that helps do that.

People who use the tool that was the predecessor to HFM, called Hyperion Enterprise, will tell you how valuable a tool Hyperion Analyst is. This is not to be confused with Web Analysis. This is an Excel-based tool that allowed you to drill and interact with the data. Once users have access to it, they are able to work with the data in new and better ways. Smart View takes this functionality and adds something to it. It is called Ad Hoc and it allows users to:

- Create a grid
- Zoom in and out within a dimension
- Nest dimensions within columns and rows

End users of HFM absolutely need to understand how this works and be shown this tool so they can take full advantage of the system. Earlier in the chapter I talked about very large reports, and needing to look at what people are trying to do. Very often having your end users understand what ad-hoc analysis can do will reduce the need for people to try and pull the entire database into a report. They can build a spreadsheet made more for a specific purpose, and focus the data set to just what they really need.

Best Practices for Smart View

The users' experience of Smart View is the result of performance on the application server, web server, LAN, and ultimately the Smart View client. Best results are obtained when you monitor performance across the system to identify the bottlenecks and address them first. Performance issues are most commonly associated with large workbooks that have many links to the database called HS.GetValue statements. Look at Figure 4-8 as an example of what these statements look like. Ad-hoc queries are much more efficient than functions, so you should use those when performance is an issue. But sometimes the functions are preferred, for a number of reasons. For example, they are much more familiar to former users of Hyperion Enterprise.

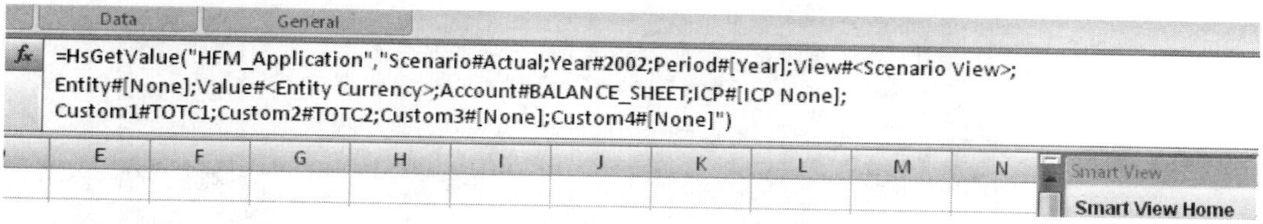

```
=HsGetValue("HFM_Application","Scenario#Actual;Year#2002;Period#[Year];View#<Scenario View>;
Entity#[None];Value#<Entity Currency>;Account#BALANCE_SHEET;ICP#[ICP None];
Custom1#TOTC1;Custom2#TOTC2;Custom3#[None];Custom4#[None]")
```

FIGURE 4-8. *HS.GetValue statements*

Obviously you can reduce the number of these links, and that will help. But once you have exhausted that, there some other suggestions that can help improve performance. These suggestions will also help you design your workbooks to maximize performance.

When you set up the workbook, it is a best practice to create a common point of view section. Here we can define dimensions for the functions to run. Since there are 12 dimensions in HFM, it seems to make sense to put all 12 in this section. Figure 4-9 shows how this section would be set up. You would start by selecting the manage POV menu option. The POV Manager window will appear, which you can define your point of view in. Unfortunately this increases the size of the workbook, increases data sent to and from the server, and prevents Smart View from using POV caching efficiently. You should set certain dimensions that will not change within the sheet to the Background POV, and put only those dimensions that could change from sheet to sheet in the workbook. You do this in the POV Manager.

Like all reports, grid and form, your Smart View workbook will update faster if you call fewer subcubes. Remember that the subcube is basically defined as all the records where Scenario, Year, Entity and Value are the same. The more combinations of these you have, the more subcubes you call. As subcubes are loaded into memory on the HFM application server, you may need to monitor memory usage, the Task Audit, and general server performance during a Smart View refresh.

When you do need to build full trial balances by every entity, there is a much better option to do this inside Financial Reports, not in a Smart

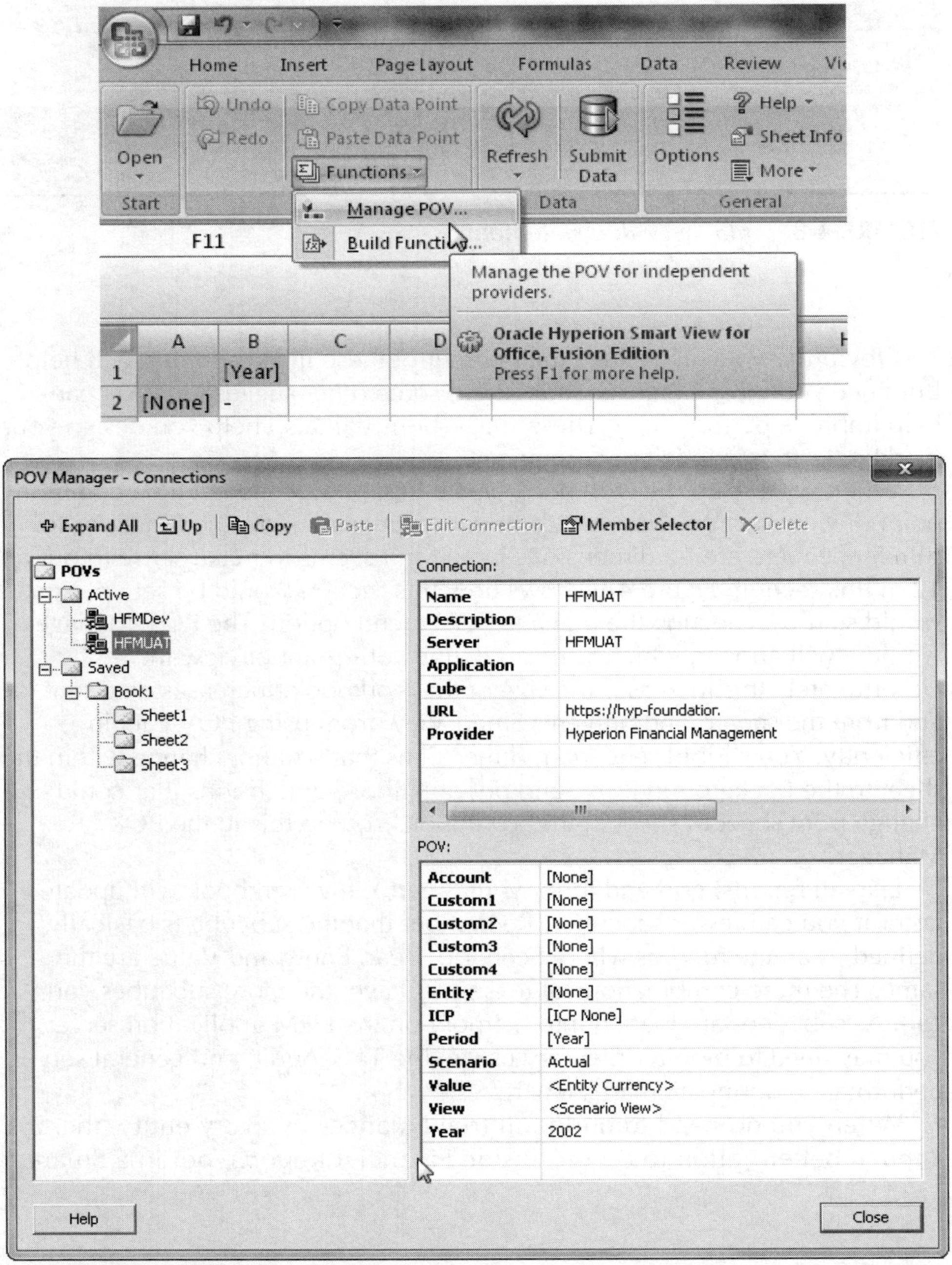

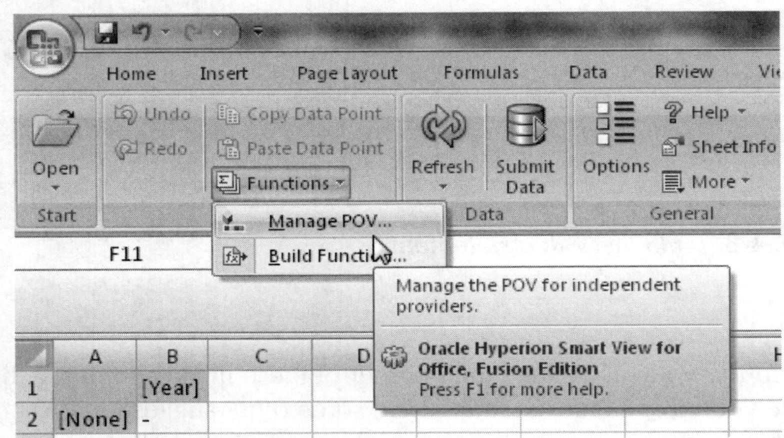

FIGURE 4-9. *SmartView Point of View*

View spreadsheet. There are limits within Excel that make it not a good option for doing this. Older versions of Excel have a 65,000-row limitation, for example (versions of Excel 2003 and earlier). That alone makes it undesirable to re-create the database. Even the newer versions of Excel (version Excel 2007 and later), that do not have this limitation, are still not tools that are well suited for anything more than ad-hoc reporting. The workbooks become large and unwieldy. They are typically not part of any backup and disaster recovery. They have very limited security. And perhaps worst of all, they allow people to keep different versions of the data. When people are taking so much data into Excel, one needs to identify why and resolve that issue.

With each release of HFM, performance improvements are made everywhere. Sometimes issues can be eased by simply upgrading. For example, Smart View 9.3.1and later use HTTP compression to reduce network traffic. This will help with refresh times, so make sure you have the latest version of the tools.

Within the options for Smart View, there is a built-in feature that will compress the Excel file size, by compressing the stored metadata information from HFM. This will make the Excel file smaller. The workbook size compression does not impact performance; however, the data compression on the network can improve performance, where the network throughput is an issue.

The second place you should look to upgrade is the client machine, since the majority of the time spent during a refresh is on the client. Not only does the client machine have to pull the values, it also has to recalculate them inside the spreadsheet. Often just adding RAM to the client machine will help ease the problem. Any guidelines for hardware are the lowest you can have and expect the software to work. Remember that "required" is different than "recommended," and that is also different than "preferred." If performance is an issue, you need to identify what is preferred for the client machine and use that as your base line.

The most valuable advise I can give with regards to Smartview is to remind you that this is a reporting tool and not a database extract tool. Do not try to pull so much data from HFM in excel that the spreadsheets are huge and slow. This is not what this tool is meant to do.

Connection Manager

The Connection Manager enables users to manage their data source connections. Users can add, delete, and modify connections per Excel instance. These connections have no relationship to worksheets. Users can establish multiple connections per Excel instance. A connection is a communication line between the user and data source regardless of whether the data source is connected or disconnected to the provider server. Visually, you can tell whether a data source is connected or disconnected by viewing the icon next to the data source name in Connection Manager. From the Smart View panel, you can manage data source connections, access data and task lists, and create reports. Figure 4-10 shows the Connection Manager.

The Smart View panel is displayed by default on the right side of the Microsoft Office application. You can move, resize, or close the Smart View panel from the down arrow in the title bar.

Smart View operations in Microsoft Office 2007 applications are available through ribbon commands. The Smart View ribbon, which contains commands for common Smart View operations, is always present. When you connect to a data source (other than Oracle Hyperion Reporting and Analysis),

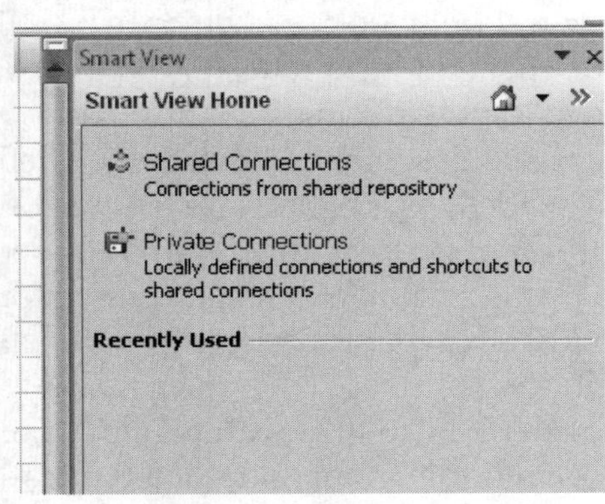

FIGURE 4-10. *Connection Manager*

the corresponding data source ribbon is also displayed. For Oracle Hyperion Planning, Fusion Edition, Oracle Hyperion Financial Management, Fusion Edition, and Oracle Hyperion Enterprise, when you enter ad-hoc analysis, the data source ribbon is automatically replaced by its ad-hoc version. Each ribbon displays only the commands permitted for that data source, mode, and Office application.

Linked Views and Dynamic Data Points

Since release 9.3, Smart View allows users to copy data points and move them from one Office component to another. You can move these data points between PowerPoint decks, or Word or Excel files, and they can be sent to any user who has Smart View. When you are viewing the data point, it appears just like any other number. But it isn't. That user can refresh the value and drill into the data point, and then see its dimensionality and see the detail behind it.

The other amazing thing about using this feature is how simple it is to use. You open an Excel ad-hoc query, highlight what you want to copy and paste, and then select Copy Data Points from the menu. You can then paste them using the same menu option. It is very easy.

When building documents that have references to data, it is a good idea for reports that require financial data to build these links instead of hard-coding the number into the report. Numbers will change and users can run a refresh in their own Word documents. This is a powerful feature.

Then you can have these dynamic data points maintained only in Word and PowerPoint. If you copy and paste data points within Excel, the data points are not linked to the Excel grid. You can use Word or PowerPoint tools to change number formatting.

Smart Slice

A Smart Slice, which is new in 11.1.2, is a reusable perspective of a data source. It is composed of a single member and any combination of single members and filters. Think of this as just a part of the data available for more detailed query. You can set preferences specified for the Smart Slice as well. Any operation that can be done in Smart View can be done within the confines of a Smart Slice. Smart Slice boundaries can be as inclusive or exclusive as required to make the Smart Slice useful for data analysis.

Smart Slices are created by administrators and stored in the Provider Services layer, where they are available to all users with the proper privileges. You can create Smart Slices for a variety of needs, by any dimensions you have built. Users create queries from entire Smart Slices or from a subset of data. These queries and subqueries can be stored as part of Excel, Word, or PowerPoint documents on their local machines. Think of this as a way to help users navigate the 12 dimensions of HFM to find data they are commonly using in the system. A Smart slice will start them where they need to start looking in the system, making the users more efficient and productive.

You should use the new Smart Slices when you can. It will help users navigate to the data they need, and do it in a very efficient manner. And when your users find data easy and helpful, this will speed adoption of the system.

Related Content

Related Content allows a designer to create links to Financial Reporting documents, Oracle Hyperion Interactive Reporting and Oracle Hyperion Web Analysis documents, and custom URL links. This is very valuable. You want to limit the times a user has to click, and this is one of the ways you can actively control that. Users can drill to a related content link to a URL or another report.

When you build your reports, you group them by priority. To really make the most of this tool's functionality—think about the work flow. If you are really thinking about the tasks, then lay the reports out by detail. The summary report should be at the top of the list, and the detailed reports flow from that. Create links that users can intuitively click through. Your reports should have a natural flow from one report to another. Users should be able to navigate from one report to the next as they apply to the close process. When sitting down to define the reports, consider how they relate. Why not have the fixed asset roll forward linked to the trial balance? Consider linking the AR aging to accounts receivable, since when people view the accounts receivable, they might have questions about aging. You could link sales by customer to the revenue line on your profit and loss statement.

Related Content can be specified on Image, Chart, and Text objects. The link is applied to the entire object. Chart and Image objects with Related Content can be clicked to point to the Related Content link. For Text objects with related content, the entire textual content is marked as a hyperlink. When you click that hyperlink, the Related Content link is followed.

One good example of Related Content is when viewing Validations. When validations were described earlier in this book, we discussed how you might have Prevent and Detect validations. The Detect validations would be on a report for users to view and be aware of issues. This is one of those ways we get the users to take ownership of their data and drive the resolution of issues. In this report, you can show validations the users need to resolve. When they click on the validation, it can take them to the report that details the issue. For example, you could have a validation that flags an out-of-balance condition with fixed assets on the roll forward. When you click on the roll forward, it takes you to the roll forward with the issue. This makes it much more intuitive for the end users to navigate the system.

Line Item Detail

Since the release of HFM 2.0, you have been able to have Line Item Details by data cell within HFM. This lets users create detail below the account level. They can also add descriptions to each of the lines. Unfortunately, since this information is so unstructured, you won't see it consolidated.

You will need to set this in two places, the Scenario and accounts. The system will then take the combination of the flags set at both the Scenario and Account levels and determine what the correct requirement needs to be. The most restrictive of these settings prevail. For the descriptions, you need to have between 1 and 80 characters, and you can use any characters.

So if you decide you want to use this, but need some help with ideas on how to add this to the application, take a look at the sample data form scripts that are installed with Sample Applications for Financial Management. The files are located in the Sample Apps folder in the directory where you installed Financial Management. One last comment about LID: cell text and line item detail are not exported to the star schema within extended analytics.

Annotations

Speaking of collaborative functionality that helps users communicate and improve data quality, HFM and the reporting tools support Annotations. Annotations are a tool that allows users of reports to make comments on the reports, from simple notations to full-fledged threaded discussions. If you know Hyperion Enterprise, think Data Extend on growth hormone and steroids. It is very cool.

This is a great tool. You can get people to get a jump on commentary, add notes, and do some other commentary that you could not do easily in HFM before. There is full support of annotations in Books, and read-only support of annotations in snapshot reports.

They are easy to find. From the Workspace View menu, you control the display of annotations in reports with the Show Annotation command. A list of all annotations in a report can be viewed in the Annotations main window. In PDF Preview, the annotation will read like footnotes. There are numeric references to the corresponding annotations as footnotes, but they are specific to that report.

The Annotation text function returns the requested information about an annotation within a grid object. The Footnote text function returns the requested information about footnotes within a given report object. Don't confuse these grid objects with grids in HFM. Annotations are only stored in the Financial Reports repository, not in the HFM database. This means you can't access Annotations from the objects built in HFM. This includes Grids, WDEFs, Smart View, or other reporting tools.

This is another great way this tool changes the conversation of the close. You don't have to send e-mails with pages and circled numbers and pen scratching on them. Users can see the comments people are making, and this helps you understand the numbers.

Before you start using Annotations, you should consider it as part of a group of tools that will help you gather and collect comments and text. Cell Text, and the ability to upload documents, are other tools. Annotations are best for quick comments, and dialog between users of the reports. Cell Text is best for comments and notes in the system. Uploading documents are best for backup and supporting details. When you have significant commentary, you will find putting too much in HFM a real burden. Remember, this system is a consolidation system and not a document repository.

IFRS and Multi-GAAP Reporting

IFRS is coming to the United States. We just don't know what it will be when it does come. It could be exactly as it is in the rest of the world. But the truth is that many countries really did need something better and closer to U.S. generally accepted accounting principles (GAAP). Does the United States really need to change that much? For so long, the U.S. economy has been so big and so powerful that even good systems needed to anchor to what companies did in the United States. However, in the wake of a massive economic recession, started in the United States, is the rest of the world content with business as usual? I suspect not, and I also think something will change. IFRS is sweeping the globe in the aftermath of the global financial crisis. Governments around the world are pushing this change.

What is IFRS, and why should you care? IFRS stands for International Financial Reporting Standards. IFRS is a global set of accounting standards developed by the International Accounting Standards Board (IASB), which is an independent accounting standards body, based in London. Global companies need to move to IFRS because doing so will reduce compliance costs. Local statutory financial reporting in a number of foreign countries is moving to IFRS as well. Since the best practice for these changes is to have at least five years of data, people have begun work as early as 2007 for IFRS.

IFRS is intended to be a more principles-based set of standards rather than the rules-based approach of US-GAAP. The two systems (IFRS and US-GAAP) differ conceptually on a number of points. They are

- The way pre-operating and pre-opening costs are reported
- The fact that IFRS prohibits the use of LIFO for inventory valuation
- Borrowing costs
- Fair value
- Revenue recognition
- Extraordinary items
- Cash Flow (indirect is preferred)

Even the reporting you will be required to submit will change—the formatting and presentation of data will change. And while it is still not completely clear what exact detail will be required, the changes that are known are not something you can manage in Excel, or even in Hyperion Enterprise. The U.S. Securities and Exchange Commission (SEC) recently issued its proposed roadmap for conversion from US-GAAP to IFRS. Mandatory reporting under IFRS will begin in 2014, 2015, or 2016, depending on the size of the issuer, and provides for early adoption in 2009 by a small number of very large companies that meet certain criteria. With compliance beginning in 2014, you should have started in 2009 to manage this change. The SEC says it will decide in 2011 whether to hold to that schedule. But do you want to risk waiting?

HFM can help as part of a full IFRS migration. While some of the changes have a much more significant impact on the ledger and other systems, HFM has specific functionality that can make IFRS transition easier. HFM has been used for years to do multi-GAAP reporting, so IFRS is not completely uncharted waters. Many companies in Europe and Canada have already moved, and their experience provides some guidance for companies in the United States.

With a major change like IFRS, you have to look at the project both tactically and strategically. The move to IFRS is not an HFM issue in the sense that this hits so many parts of your business process that you cannot look at this move narrowly. HFM can help with the tactical change; that is, creating a short-term option that bridges the current system of accounting you are doing now to whatever the future holds for IFRS.

The methods we would use to do this have been used for several years by companies—companies with large global presences that required being able to report multiple GAAP statements. This has been used for local statutory as well. You can imagine how valuable it would be to take data that is provided for US-GAAP and layer local statutory adjustments on top of that information or load statutory data alongside the GAAP data for reporting.

There are three main approaches you can take; they are the customs, scenario, and entity approaches. Each approach is basically using HFM dimensionality to provide both views of data, and by design, a method to reconcile the data between the two. The custom scenario makes use of the custom dimension. Custom dimensions can be used to help segregate and identify different types of data, such as data that is loaded from the G/L (SAP, JDE), JE adjustments, calculated data, manually input data, automated eliminations, and data loaded to supplemental PL accounts from business warehouse. This is commonly called using the custom dimension as a "DataType Dimension." Also, the DataType dimension can be used to separate IFRS adjustments so that historical results that were loaded as US-GAAP can be adjusted to meet IFRS reporting. The advantage of using this method is that the actual data remains unchanged for history. It also allows you to very easily move from one method to the other by simply changing what member you load your primary financials to. This approach provides for fairly simple reporting and usually has a low to moderate impact on the rules and reports.

The second method is the scenario approach. This method uses the scenario as a way to keep a second set of books within HFM. This is a better approach when the data need to be loaded from another source completely. That means, you will not have US-GAAP to IFRS adjustments, but instead will have a whole new set of data to load and consolidate. This has a low impact on the rules and reports, but will require some considerations for mapping and loading the data. For example, how will you handle beginning balances and opening periods? When will the new reporting start? People who have been through data integration for a project will tell you how much work this really is.

The entity approach is a great approach for situations where you see significant issues with converting the data during the consolidation. For example, a company that makes use of proportional consolidation will have to change that, and creating a new structure helps them do that more cleanly. The entity approach is also good when you are collecting US-GAAP to IFRS adjustments at parent levels for new groups. For example, you may not have details for a group of entities as they are grouped, so you need to create new groupings for these adjustments.

Accounts are not really a good option, and here is why. This approach would be to basically have two complete sets of accounts. This option creates two big drawbacks; you need to have a completely new set of accounts to maintain, and you are loading data from two sites into the same entity. Now if you are doing this approach for statutory, and you are just grouping the accounts in a new hierarchy, that can make sense. But you will find that is not really required for the whole trial balance but just for sections. So even when doing this for statutory reporting, you don't have to create a whole second structure.

With good planning and an understanding of the options and impact, you can leverage your HFM application to help make the migration to IFRS smooth.

Financial Close Manager

Financial Close Manager (FCM) enables you to define, execute, and report on the interdependent activities of a financial close period. It also provides monitoring of the entire close process and provides a visible, automated, repeatable system of record for running close processes. This is truly a unique product since this is the first tool that can do this for the entire close process starting before the ledger even closes. This is important to HFM because of how important HFM is to the close process. At many companies HFM is, in fact, the book of record. A tool that manages the close of those books is of critical importance. Figure 4-11 shows the main calendar view.

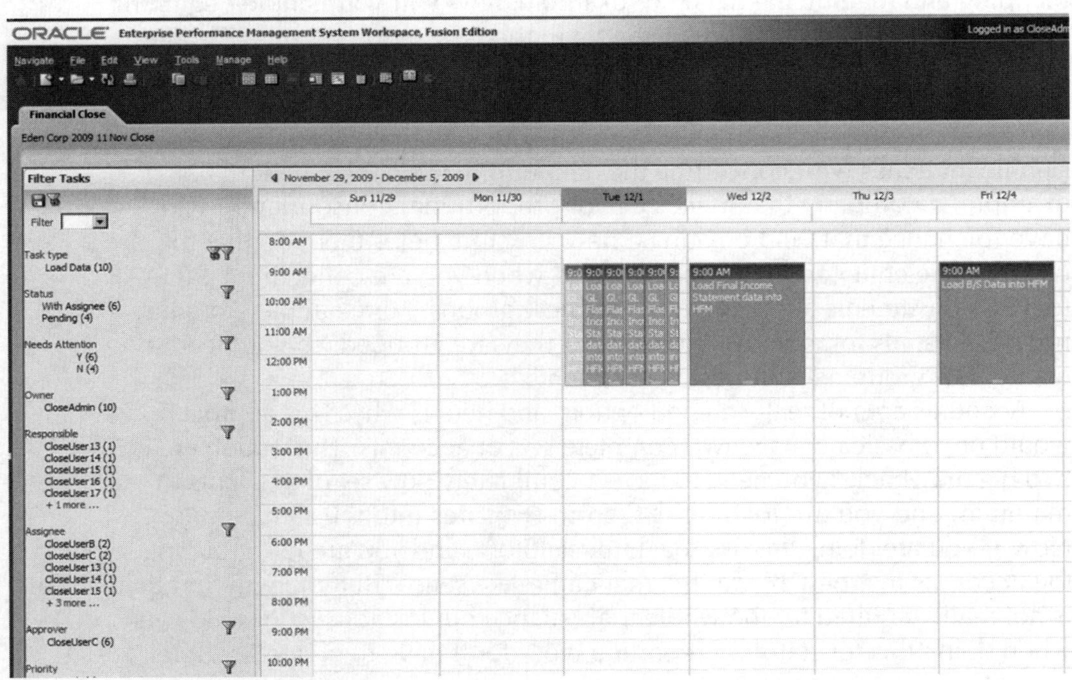

FIGURE 4-11. *Financial Close Manager*

Some of the key benefits of FCM are

- Executive-level dashboards and ad-hoc reporting provide instant real-time insight into your close processes.
- Creates one system to control the close.
- Automatically updates status and flags which tasks are at risk or behind schedule.
- Allows for e-mailing to users notifications.

FCM allows for detailed Process Monitoring; you can track the close process each step along the way. This encourages continuous improvement to the close process, because you can identify what your bottlenecks are. Why does it take five days to close the books? Is it because all sites really need five days, or does one site have some issues that are costing your company time and money?

The reporting FCM provides gives you insight into the close process. Both dashboards and ad-hoc reporting provide "real time" visibility into the close processes. You can see each step of the close as it updates automatically, then identify where you are at risk.

FCM provides an Active Financial Close Calendar. This shows you all the details and the tasks required for the financial close process. You can view this data as a Calendar view, Task List view, or Gantt view. This can be customized for each user.

The Task Management supports multiple task assignment types so you can identify what types of task you have ahead of you. You can build them as task hierarchies, create dependencies, and group them.

The important design consideration here is when building an application that uses FCM, you need to document each process as an individual thread. From that you can identify each person who touches the process and identify their role. That will help you build the flow and configure the e-mail alerting. For HFM, it will help you integrate the HFM processes into FCM much more cleanly.

As Financial Close Management continues to mature, there are some features you might look forward to:

- Extended EPM Integration
    - Planning
    - Essbase
    - Data Relationship Management
- Extended ERP Integration
    - PeopleSoft
    - E-Business Suite
- Extended GRC Integration
- Account Reconciliations improve the close by controlling the account reconciliation process
    - Automatically identifying reconciling differences
    - Integrating all relevant information into one application regardless of source
    - Ensuring policy compliance
    - Managing reconciliation process

Disclosure Management

Disclosure Management (DM) is a tool that integrates with the Office products to help you create, edit, and submit eXtensible Business Reporting Language (XBRL) documents for submission to a regulatory agency. This is another big change coming to the way companies report. The days of writing your SEC submission on hard copy are fading. It will need to be provided electronically through the SEC website.

Because DM integrates so well with HFM and Smart View, you can spend more time validating the information and less time gathering it. As data changes and the commentary updates, you can update and modify your tagging in real time. Figure 4-12 shows Disclosure Management tagging.

A tool like this takes the risk out of preparing the XBRL filing. While many companies have elected to outsource this effort, a last-minute change for them is just not possible. Many companies ask for days of time to ensure they can update the filing before sending it back. In the meantime, as you pore over the data in your system, you understand more. You realize that maybe there is more to the story of the numbers. Having a process like XBRL in the house allows you to update the filing. It gives you more control

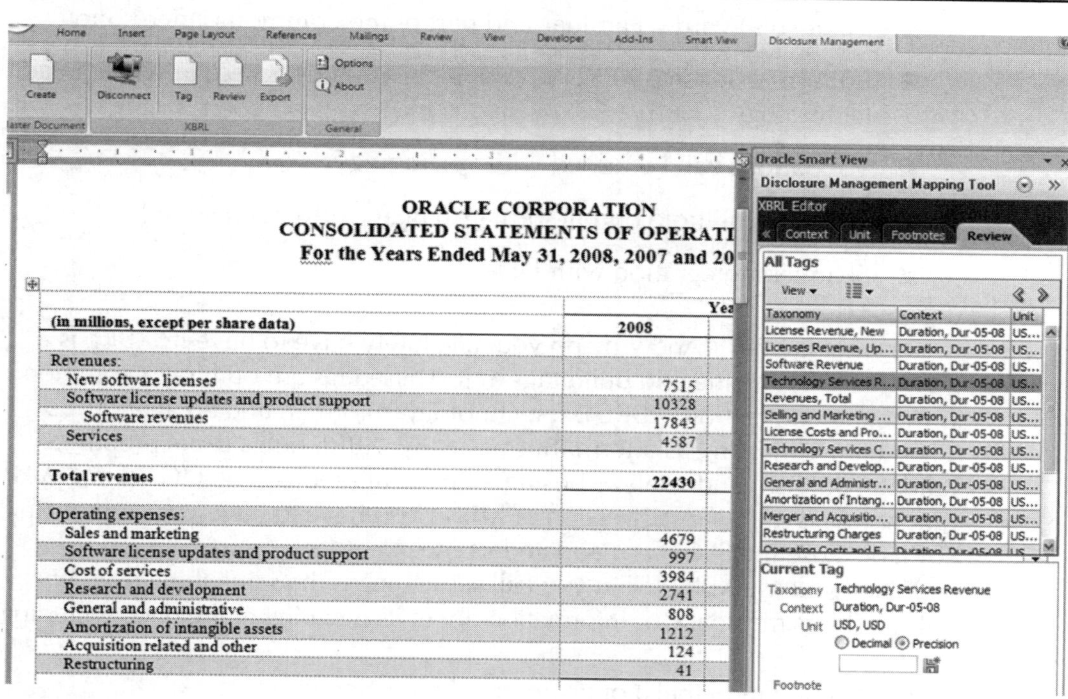

FIGURE 4-12. *Example of XRBL tagging for Disclosure Manager*

and minimizes risk. So why not just ship it out? You have more control and less risk. Risks like

- Errors leading to restatements
- Late filing
- Insider leaks
- SOX noncompliance

There was XBRL reporting in releases of HFM before the release of DM. But frankly, the type of reporting you could do with it is very limited. Disclosure Management provides a complete XBRL creation and management solution. Some other features are

- Microsoft Word – Familiar and part of the common Office suite
- Built-in, extensive XBRL reporting capabilities based on widespread technology
- Validations can be added with versioning
- Supports multiple output formats (Edgar, XBRL, and so on)
- Seamless integration with HFM

So what is XBRL? And why do you absolutely have to have it? XBRL is a way to take a data file and build tags in it. These tags are built on a common format and convention. XBRL is a technology, a format, and an agency. So this is a bit confusing as a term. But basically, XBRL helps users prepare, validate, publish, and analyze business financial reports. The UGT (US-GAAP Taxonomy) is a US-GAAP version of XBRL. You have to have your reports in XBRL because the SEC has mandated its use.

When you use XBRL, what you call something is the same thing everyone calls it. This is metadata, or information about its meaning of the data, including

- Name (and labels) of its financial reporting concept
- Reporting context

- Reporting period
- Reporting entity
- Currency (or other data value type)
- The data value itself

To get started with XBRL, you need to have a taxonomy. The XBRL taxonomy is a finite description of the data about the data that you will be reporting. This is the tags and system you will use to identify the data. You can update and modify your taxonomy with DM. This allows you to add extensions to your taxonomies, and easily adapt to the evolving XBRL standards.

XBRL (eXtensible Business Reporting Language) functionality allows you to create XBRL instance documents. The instance document contains information specific to a single "report." One of the first things it has, though, is the Taxonomy, which defines the meaning of the data. The Instance Document needs to have the Taxonomy. The Taxonomy is like a dictionary for the tags; it contains the definitions for the various reporting periods, kinds of numbers, financial reporting facts. Each fact is tagged with:

- The name of the taxonomy element which defines its meaning
- The reporting period
- The numeric unit (if a number)

So now you have your filing, your taxonomy, and DM, and you are ready to build your instance document. The process is to map, model, tag, and package.

- **Map** Analyze and document the associations between specific financial reporting concepts and the UGT.
- **Model** Build or update an extension taxonomy specific to the reporting entity.

- **Tag** Associate the financial reporting facts with the proper taxonomy concepts.
- **Package** Prepare, review, and validate the files and deliver.

Future releases of Disclosure Management are expected to provide the following key features:

- Collaborative document creation
- Document life cycle management
- Assignments and workflow
- Version control
- Rounding and cross-footing
- Report rollover
- More output formats
- Edgar
- iXBRL

Conclusion

When you build reports, you need to make sure you follow best practices, not only because it ensures that your reports perform as well as they can, but also because it will reduce the maintenance you will spend each month keeping them working well. In this chapter, we covered a strategy for building and developing reports. This will help you get the most from your application.

CHAPTER 5

Data Integration and Testing

nce you have the shell of your database, and have started writing reports, you will need data in the system to validate that you have a good build and good performance. Data is what this is really all about. Good data in the system will make all the difference. The better the data quality coming in, the better information you will have, and the better decisions you will make. It drives everything in the tool. But first you have to get the data into the application.

There are many kinds of data you can load into HFM. It is most common to load numeric values like what would be expected for the trial balance, or supplemental data. This data is primary to the system, in that it is always needed to report the financials. There is data that supports the financials, and that is supporting data. For example, there is cell text that could be loaded to a given cell. There are documents that could be attached to cells. Intercompany Transaction data, Journal Entries, and Annotations are all supplemental to the trial balance data. There are, of course, data values that we cannot load into HFM. They are often requested, but the system currently will not support it; for example, transaction data, date-oriented data, or unstructured data.

Most projects will need to pull data from many sources. These many sources are often very different, each with different formats and fields. In fact, the more sites and entities you have, the more types of data feeds you will see. There are many different ledgers, offline worksheets, data marts, and warehouses. There are many options for getting the data in, with many kinds of bells and whistles. Some can automate; others can help with metadata, and allow drilling into the source data. Each tool offers different benefits, and some tools offer overlapping features. With so many options, it is hard to see what the right tool is, and when to use it. Fortunately, Oracle offers tools to help with getting data into HFM.

Some of the options are simple, like Smart View, Web Forms, or the use of a flat file to load data directly. These offer quick and simple ways to get data into the application, but they often require some manual manipulation or data entry to get it to work.

If you are looking for full-featured automation, validation, and auditability, then you are looking at one of the feature-rich tools. Many of these tools are often referred to as ETL tools. This stands for Extract, Transform, and Load. The extract phase involves having a hook into the source systems, and identifying what data it should pull. Then the data must meet an expected pattern or structure. If not, the data may be rejected entirely or in part. The transform phase maps the data to the destination, through mapping or rules. The load phase writes the data to the destination, HFM in this case.

When HFM was first released by Hyperion Solutions, the only ways they provided for you to load data were through a flat file, using the Excel add-in or Hyperion Application Link (HAL). Using Excel to load data presents problems. There are too many opportunities to modify the data and mapping. There are really no controls or reliable ways to back it up. These Excel files often need to be saved on a server, where anyone with access can see all the data loaded.

HAL was powerful, but it was a platform. It was a tool that needed to be implemented for each client from scratch. That was a major issue. Each solution was unique to the team that designed and developed it. That meant when you had a major change or update, you needed to get the people who built it to come back and help you. The other issue is that it could be as complex as you wanted to make it, and it was made complex.

Hyperion did offer Data Integration Manager (DIM) for a short time. This was built on the Informatica tool. DIM was not widely adopted for two reasons: Hyperion acquired Upstream Software and the WebLink product, and after the Oracle acquisition of Hyperion, WebLink was later renamed Financial Data Quality Management. People did not really have time to learn DIM before it was hurried out the door for the two products people use now.

Upstream offered the very successful product WebLink, which provided exactly the sort of end user–oriented tool that HFM customers wanted, whereas DIM requires a very high level of technical expertise to develop and run. Oracle then later replaced DIM with the standard across all Oracle tools, Oracle Data Integrator (ODI).

WebLink was rebranded as Financial Data Quality Management (FDM; yes, only three letters) and Oracle added Oracle Data Integrator (ODI) to the suite of Hyperion applications. While you still have the simple options of forms, Excel add-ins, and flat files, FDM and ODI offer feature-rich options.

The Right Tool for the Right Job

FDM and ODI together offer a full solution for those customers using Hyperion Business Performance Management solutions. Each product has strengths that should be leveraged to provide customers with a best-of-breed solution for data integration and transformation. The best solutions are never one or the other, but the right mix that maximizes reliability and auditability and improves the data quality. But which one should you use and when?

FDM is a financial data integration platform that delivers a web-based data collection solution that is focused on both finance and end users. This framework provides prebuilt process and logistical support as well as visibility to all aspects of the data integration process. Key Sarbanes-Oxley controls and processes are "out of the box" in FDM. If you want a packaged solution, this is the answer. Also, data quality and integrity is ensured through data validation and quality checking against target systems. FDM has a great user interface, which makes it a great tool for end users, whereas ODI is not. FDM is designed for use over the web, which helps to bring in data files from all over the world. FDM is not as powerful as the best ETL tools when it comes to large volumes of records to load, whereas ODI is.

FDM offers a process and reporting that helps get data loaded by reporting the details of the mapping and data file process. The financial requirements defined by Sarbanes-Oxley require increased audit and process controls delivered by FDM "out of the box." FDM also has tremendous flexibility via VBScript to solve the most complex data movement and translation problems.

For companies with multiple locations, multiple source systems, and multidimensional mapping requirements, FDM will help drive down the cost and time of implementation cycles of HFM as well as speeding adoption and increasing ROI. Typically, FDM is used for loading Hyperion Enterprise and Hyperion Financial Management; however, FDM can also be an excellent solution for Hyperion Essbase and Hyperion Planning.

ODI is a data integration and business process automation tool that dramatically reduces the time and expense of integrating source data with the Hyperion Business Performance Management suite. Designed specifically for IT or application power users, ODI enables end-to-end connectivity with one or more data sources, 100 percent business process automation, and broad data source connectivity including purpose-built adapters for transaction processing applications from vendors, such as SAP, PeopleSoft, J. D. Edwards, and Seibel. ODI is built for each client's needs for that project, offering a framework to build integration solutions that suit exact business needs.

You can build either tool to achieve complete process automation. Adapters are available for each tool to integrate with all Hyperion packaged and tailored-made applications to support data and metadata exchange.

The choices are not one or the other. In fact, the best solutions will include the best features of each tool. Organizations are looking to leverage the integration strengths of ODI along with the "packaged" out-of-the-box functionality of FDM. Examples includes organizations with a central ERP for U.S. operations and a variety of GL systems across the globe. FDM can call ODI integration capabilities through ERPi to read in the ledger data while utilizing FDM's Data Pump to provide a seamless method for loading pure GL source files that come from all over the world through zero-footprint web interfaces. Then you can take advantage of functionality providing key Sarbanes-Oxley controls including: financial data transparency, end-user visibility, and audit trail to source data, automation, batch processing, process monitoring, mapping consistency, and data quality checks. When both tools work together, they can offer a better solution than either alone.

Data Flow

Each company has its own set of databases and systems that also impact the decision of what tool or combination of tools work best. The first principle, and the most important principle you should adhere to, above anything else, is to reduce the number of reconciliation steps. Some companies have a data mart they want to use as the source of all the data they have, and they need the consolidation tool. Or, for whatever reason, they do not want to source the data from the ledger. If that company understands that they are giving up some functionality, such as the ability to drill into the data they are loading, it is not the worst thing they could do. Assume you have several feeds coming into the data mart. Then you want to have those feed directly into HFM. Now you have created many feeds that must be reconciled, and HFM must be reconciled to the mart. There is a cost to that. If the drill-through functionality is not required, or valued, then isn't it a better option to load directly from the data mart?

I would still explore sourcing directly from the ledger. One should never dismiss functionality, or disregard a clear product direction. However, when a company forces a consolidation tool into a data flow, and it creates places where you have to do additional reconciliation, to make sure that the data does in fact tie out at each spot, then that creates work that is not value added.

Linear data flows that do not double back on to other systems are the easiest to maintain. The best systems are easy to explain and transparent. Complex data flows that double back and load back into something else create timing issues, mapping problems, and other issues. Even if you can automate the validation of the data between the systems, you can create problems. Automation sometimes creates a sense of security, which allows mistakes to flow from one system to another.

Another consideration before you decide on a tool: You should look at the data to be loaded. How is the data that will be loaded going to be dispersed in your environment? Is it centrally located or is it decentralized? Centralized data environments would have only one or two general ledger systems, where most data to be loaded into HFM resides. In this situation the data loading, mapping, and validation can be controlled by a centralized team. Decentralized data environments have many general ledger systems or sources of data, typically spread out across many remote locations. Decentralized data often creates the impossibility of having a centralized group manage mappings. The ownership of mapping and validation has to be pushed to the sites. The central core application team has to focus on managing the effort. As this chapter covers the tools you can use to load data, it will highlight where some tools handle each of these functions better than the others.

Oracle Hyperion Financial Data Quality Management

Oracle Hyperion Financial Data Quality Management (FDM) is a packaged data transformation tool that feeds financial data to HFM, Planning, and Essbase. FDM is a great tool for accountants and end users. It has some nice features that help with audit and reconciliation. It has the ability to see a history of the mapped data. FDM helps users, administrators, and auditors to investigate, identify, and correct errors. There are controls and validations you can build in to make sure the data being loaded is good. You can get adapters to load to HFM Planning and Essbase, or pull from many types of sources. The FDM tool is best suited for supporting decentralized data, although it can be used for centralized sources.

This tool uses a very intuitive interface that makes it easier for nontechnical users to load and map files. The interface is zero-footprint–based, meaning there is nothing to install on users' machines. This simple interface allows users to load, map, and validate data in a uniform and controlled process, by stepping through each step of the process. Anyone who has used this tool will tell you how simple it is to see the fish work their way through loading the data.

What are the fish, you say? The fish walk users through the steps they need to do to get data into the system. The fish are icons used to symbolize the movement of data "upstream," which is a play on the original company's name. Figure 5-1 shows the Financial Data Quality Management web interface and the fish. The basic FDM process includes six steps:

1. Import source data.
2. Validate source data against mapping tables.
3. Export source data to a target system.
4. Consolidate target system data.
5. Validate target system data.
6. Review and validate internal financial control.

Why should you use FDM? The value of FDM is that it is a packaged solution. All of the data is loaded into a central repository that contains all source data and maps. This allows you to drill down and drill through, providing an audit trail to the data loaded into the system. Within this database, FDM archives all of the source files, error logs, and load files,

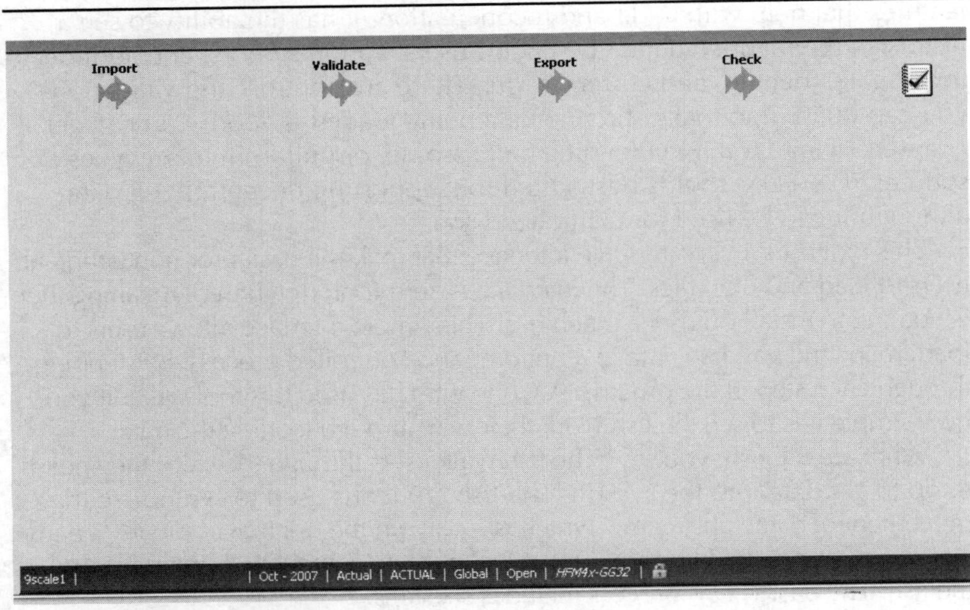

FIGURE 5-1. *Oracle Hyperion Financial Data Quality Management web interface*

so you can go back to them at any time and see what was loaded and by whom.

You can load many periods and automate the loading into batch jobs.

You can create control questions and use the certification feature that helps you comply with sections 302 and 404 of the Sarbanes-Oxley Act. Users can load additional data, view spreadsheet journals, and see the data broken out by the source in the reports.

There are full sets of prebuilt reports that allow you to monitor the loading of the data into your applications. You can see just about everything you need for FDM in these reports.

FDM uses maps and tables to translate a source dimension value to HFM dimensions. Maps are created for each HFM dimension (Account, Entity, ICP, Line Item Detail). Within each dimensional map, there are four map types—Explicit, Between, In, and Like. These maps run in a specific order. The order is

1. Account
2. Entity
3. ICP
4. Line Item Detail

Since you have this sequence, you can map other dimensions based on the results of another dimension's mapping.

Fewer source dimension combinations result in fewer maps being required. The result is faster FDM data processing.

Within a dimension map, the map types process in the following order:

1. **Explicit** A single source dimension is mapped to a single target dimension. Explicit maps are the most efficient and straightforward type, and hence the fastest. However, Explicit can result in increased maintenance.
2. **Between** A range of source dimension members is mapped to a single target. Wildcards are not supported in Between maps.
3. **In** A noncontinuous list of source dimensions that maps to a single target dimension. For example, 9000, 9001, and 9002 map to revenue. These are the slowest of the mapping options, so they should be used sparingly.
4. **Like** Source dimensions are mapped using wildcards in place of actual characters. For example, all accounts that begin with 9 are mapped to Revenue (9* = Revenue). Like maps support only two types of wildcards, asterisks (*) and question marks (?). The question mark represents only one character. An asterisk is used to represent one or more characters. So "9*" would mean any number of characters beginning with 9, while "9?" would mean any two characters beginning with 9.

For all of these reasons, it is very unusual to see HFM without FDM. It provides so many benefits to getting data into HFM, in such an easy way.

Oracle Data Integrator

Oracle Data Integrator (ODI) is a full-featured data integration platform, whereas FDM is a packaged tool. ODI is made for infrastructure people. To that end, ODI covers all data integration requirements: from high-volume, high-performance batch loads, to event-driven, trickle-feed integration processes, to SOA-enabled data services. ODI is a much more technical tool, and not something typical end users would interact with. ODI works best with centralized data. Figure 5-2 shows the main desktop of Oracle Data Integrator.

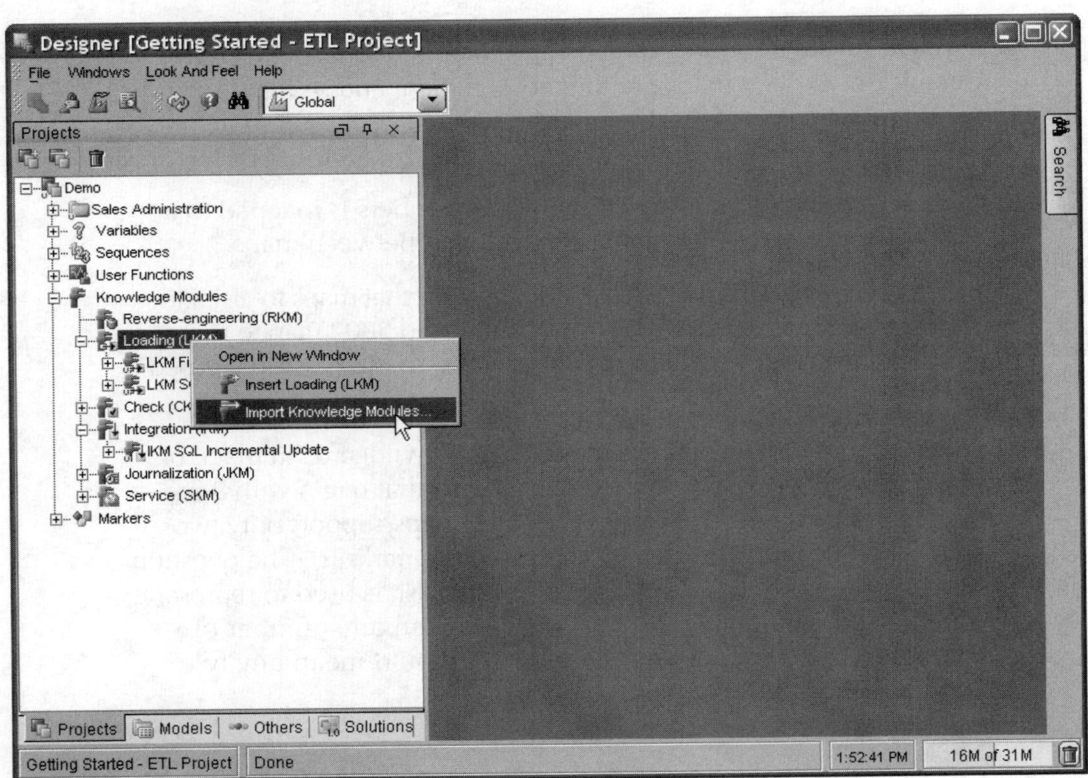

FIGURE 5-2. *Main desktop of Oracle Data Integrator*

ODI is used to move and transform information across the information system. ODI, like HAL, is a development platform for integration processes. ODI is a real ETL tool. It uses a process that leverages existing systems. This is why ODI needs the set of adapters to integrate with the system. You use different Oracle Data Integrator graphical user interfaces to access the repositories. Security and Topology are used for administering the infrastructure, Designer is used for reverse-engineering metadata and developing projects, and Operator is used for scheduling and operating run-time operations.

The central component of ODI is the master repository. In this repository all configuration information about the IT infrastructure, the metadata for all applications, projects, scenarios, information about the ODI infrastructure, and execution logs are stored.

The developers will work in this repository to define metadata and business rules. They create processing jobs that are run by the Agents. The Agents coordinate all of this through all the existing systems. These Agents connect to available servers and request them to execute the code and then record the messages back in the repository.

Most HFM (and Planning) users are already aware of the ability to drill back from HFM through data grids and data forms into the supporting FDM detail. Release 11.1.1.3 also provides this functionality from both Smart View and Financial Reporting, thus further tightening the integration of HFM with FDM.

The ability to drill back directly from Smart View and Financial Reporting makes data analysis much more simple and straightforward, because users will no longer need to re-create their analysis in a data grid to perform drillback. Drilling back from Smart View and Financial Reporting is similar to doing it from HFM in that the drillback must be initiated from a base intersection. This can be confusing to some clients as they do not fully realize that drillback to FDM can only occur at the base members. FDM only loads its data to base members or intersections inside HFM, so that is why drillback cannot be initiated from parent members.

The drillback takes users to an FDM launching page, where they see the amount balance. Users can then drill down into that balance to see all of the general ledger or source accounts that are mapping into the HFM account. It is very similar to the functionality that exists in FDM's Validate step, where you see consolidated values and then can drill down into the source accounts that map into that value, along with the mapping rules and source document that the values are associated with.

ERPi

ERP Integration Adapter for Oracle Applications (ERPi) is a module of Oracle Hyperion Financial Data Quality Management, which enables you to perform the following tasks:

- Integrate metadata and data from an Enterprise Resource Planning (ERP) source system into an Enterprise Performance Management (EPM) target application
- Drill through from the EPM target application and view data in the ERP source system
- Write back budget data to the source system from any Oracle Hyperion Planning, Fusion Edition, Oracle Essbase ASO, or Essbase BSO application

ERPi isn't really an add-on to FDM. In fact, you don't have to have FDM to run ERPi. ERPi is an interface that sits on top of ODI. So you must have ODI. Then ERPi integrates with FDM and EPMA to move data and metadata respectively into HFM. Obviously then, this is a tool for centralized data. This is not something you would configure for many sources of data, especially if they are remote.

This creates a framework for moving information from the source systems into HFM, Planning, and Essbase. Now there is a seamless integration from source systems into HFM. This creates the ability to move from one number back through its mapping to the source of the data, a full audit trail. As the product matures, more ledger systems will be added, even non-Oracle-owned systems.

Drillthrough vs. Drillback

Drilling back to source systems was, for the longest time, the holy grail of consolidation reporting. Finally it is something that is not only possible, but common with the Oracle EPM platform. But what do people mean when they say "drill"? Over time, the terms "drill back," "drill through," and "drill down" have been misused or used interchangeably. But each means something very different. Now that FDM, ODI, and ERPi allow this, each term means something very important.

These terms should not be used interchangeably. This is important because the term should tell the user where you are looking to see the data. Am I talking about going to just FDM, or am I talking about going back to your ERP, and will that suffice?

Planning users can drill through to FDM to view the sources used to load the Planning intersections. Intersections that have been loaded by FDM or ERPi are flagged to indicate that they contain a drillable region.

To drill down means to find the detail within the application hierarchies within the HFM, Essbase, or Planning dimensionality that comprises an aggregated or consolidated value. For example, you could drill from total company to each business unit. Drilling down is going from parents to children in the hierarchy. The user does not have visibility to the data beyond what is in the application.

To drill back means to go from the data in HFM, Essbase, and Planning and view the detail of the records that were mapped and loaded into the system. Depending on the mapping complexity, that could be easy to see or not. But the mapping and source file ultimately resulted in the numbers loaded into the applications. Drillback was added to FDM in the 9.3.1 series. A user can see the pre- and post-mapped values by linking into FDM. The EPM products pass a POV back to FDM along with the user's ID, and they can see what numbers were loaded to that target cell along with the mapping information. The user now can see the file that was loaded and the mapping, but not the source transactions that would have been used to create the load file.

Drill-through allows users to see the source transactions that were mapped into the balance account in HFM, Essbase, or Planning. This means we can see beyond the values that got loaded into FDM, and actually query back into the source GL transactions. This is accomplished through ERPi and has been available since Release 11.1.1.3. In this case, the drill process goes from EPM into FDM, and then from FDM, the POV information and user ID are passed all the way back to the ledger system, which launches a general ledger report or ledger window that provides the transactions.

Drilling further down or navigating to other data from this point depends on your ability to do this in the ledger.

Starting in Release 11.1.1.3, the FDM documentation (see the 11.1.1.2 and 11.1.1.3 readme files) has merged the drillback and drillthrough to simply be drillthrough. You will notice that in HFM 11.1.1.3, the previous "Audit Intersection" menu item has been replaced with "Drill Through to FDM." But each does mean something different.

Converting HAL to FDM or ODI

If you were one of the early adopters of HFM, then you would likely have the early data integration solutions. When HFM was first released by Hyperion Solutions, the only ways you could load data were through a flat file, using the Excel add-in or Hyperion Application Link (HAL). HAL is a platform, like ODI. When pulling large amounts of data and pushing it into the Hyperion tools, HAL worked very well. There were tools to help with mapping and updating the data. HAL was built for IT professionals, though, and not really built for people in accounting and finance who did not have a programming or IT background. The result was that HAL was positioned as a solution where it really didn't make sense, or worse, where complex custom scripts and programs were required, ones that would have made it impossible for the people in accounting and finance to manage the application without fear that the HAL expert who set up the integration would not be able to help in an emergency.

Now HAL is no longer supported by Oracle. And since the new tools can offer so much more, this is not an upgrade. This is an opportunity to fix issues you have and build something that you can use to expand the parts of the toolset you like. You should take advantage of this opportunity. The first place to start is to look at the data and metadata process you have and build a solution that fits that.

This won't be like the first time you sat in the design meeting and had to completely trust that your consultant understood your requirements. And to be fair, how could they? Knowing what you do now about your process and how the tool has evolved, could you say that you really knew what your requirements were? But so here you are, ready to take these lessons and really do it right.

The best thing you can do when thinking through the new data design is to be sure to remember that you need to use the right tool for the right job. The best data solutions are ones that include a variety of approaches. That could be FDM and ODI. That could also mean you expand your use of Web Data Entry Forms.

Supplemental Data

When you're loading data, it is common to not be able to pull all of your information from the ledger system. Or, you may not want to build a big integration for something like a couple of accounts, or some light supplemental data. You may be fine with just keying in the data. The most import thing to do when preparing to do this is to always remember: Don't touch ledger data that you have loaded. You can do this in one of a couple ways. You need to add a section called Supplemental, and make that a group of accounts that you will be loading. You never want to load data directly into the accounts that are fed from the ledger.

So when you are ready to load data, you have a couple of choices. You could use spreadsheets, Web Data Entry forms, or grids. You could always use some combination of the three. But I would almost always recommend using Web Data Entry Forms (WDEFs). WDEFs don't need anything on the client machine, so they can be rolled out quickly. They can prevent users from navigating to other intersections where they should not enter data. They can also include a check sum total to make sure the data loaded is reconciling to the amounts entered.

As a best practice, whenever you load data through a WDEF, you should always have a validation. That validation can be as simple as checking whether the total of the values entered reconciles to some summary line in the application. That validation can also be complex, such as checking other variances, and ensuring that the number is within some threshold. But using validations, even if you do not use Process Management, ensures that the data you are manually entering meets some basic check and eliminates many of the common issues you would expect with having a person type in the data.

Journals

So when you absolutely have to make changes that impact the general ledger data you submitted, you need to have a way to post amounts, and still see what was sourced from what. Whenever you want to make changes to a source system, you want to have controls on who is making and approving those changes. You want to have the descriptions and details behind that information. The Journal module provides all of that. However, Journals in HFM are not like journals in ledger systems. Journals are really just another way to get data into the system, with a couple of exceptions. Unlike WDEFs or grids, journals provide system reports to view that give you a trail of the changes made. There is also a simple interface to help users post the journals. You can create balanced journals, unbalanced journals, recurring journals for future periods, or auto-reversing journals to create reversing journal entries. In addition, you can use journal templates to post journals that have common adjustment information. Figure 5-3 shows the Journal module.

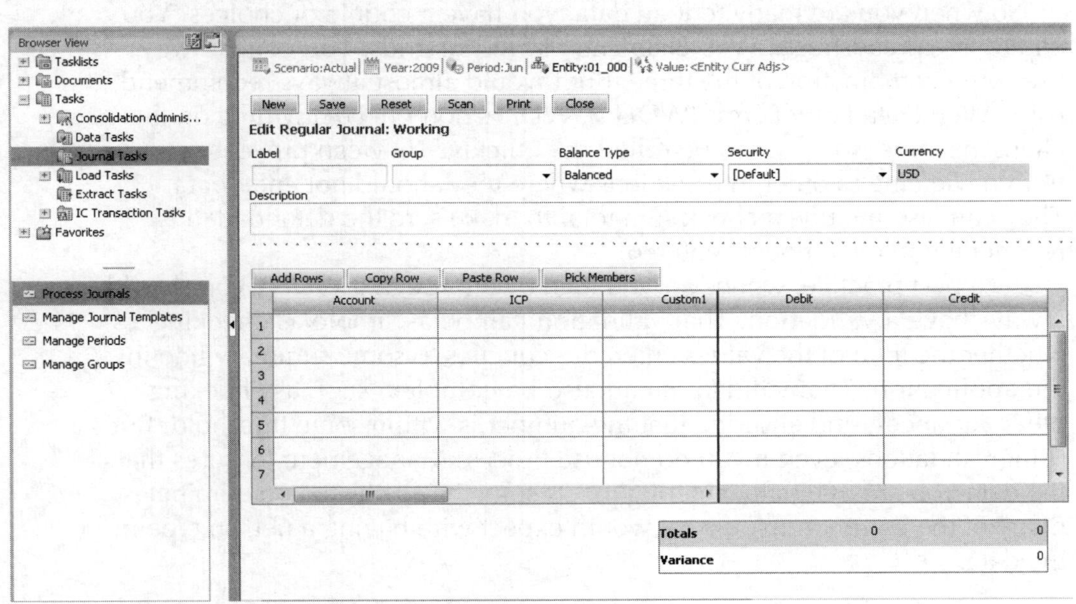

FIGURE 5-3. *Journals*

Hyperion journals allow users to manually enter data and retain some documentation or backup—an audit trail. In a way this is like journals in a G/L system, which creates some of the confusion. But one big difference is in the way HFM displays and stores data in future periods. Remember there is a scenario setting that determines how HFM will handle missing data values for Adjustment members. It is these values HFM uses as a starting point when a journal is posted. If these values are not in balance, then the adjustment entry will not be in balance, even if the journal was. Problems are especially common when journals are posted with balance sheet and P/L accounts in the same entry when the missing data as set to periodic.

Journal data is accumulated when it is loaded.

Data from a journal is entered as a year-to-date amount even when the default view is set to periodic. When a journal is posted for a period, it is added to the YTD values in that period. This is the case even when the values are derived. Therefore the "missing zero" plays a key role in how the journal will work. You should note that journals are the only place in HFM where you must define the data as debits and credits.

Balance accounts, like Assets and Liabilities, always show a derived value of zero in the future periods whether the "missing data as zero" is set to periodic or not. The problem occurs with income/expense accounts.

Another major consideration with Journals is when posting to any Value member above Parent Currency Total. At any one of these nodes in the value dimension, you are referring to a parent-and-child combination of the entity structure. That entity relationship is very important to the journal. It tells the journal where it should be layered into the data. If that relationship of the entity changes, then the node changes, and then the journal is referring to a metadata relationship that does not exist. These journals become invalid.

Another consideration for journals is when you post journals below Parent Currency Total. This is when you post journals to Entity Currency Adjust and Parent Currency Adjust, as these journals are attached to the entity and the currency. So if you change the currency of an entity, you would create an invalid journal. If you must change the entity, then you must rebuild the entity and reconstruct all journals associated with the entity for all years, scenarios, and periods.

There is an option that you may be somewhat familiar with when loading metadata and it is called Check Integrity. One problem I have with this as an option is just that—it is an option. There really isn't a good reason why anyone would want to load journals or metadata that creates these issues. You should *always* have this option selected, and do not load the metadata without it.

The reason the option box exists at all is that some metadata changes in some applications can take a very long time to load. Factors like the number of journals you have can make this an issue. Before HFM loads the metadata changes, it validates that each one of those journals will not be made invalid. Only in a *very* rare event would you choose to skip this check. But okay, you did it and you have invalid journals. How do you clean this up? I am sure you have found that those invalid journals cannot be unposted and deleted through the user interface. And if you have them, you are likely getting random and mysterious error messages. Invalid journals also block the extraction process (Unexpected Error: 80040880 occurred). Since you cannot extract the invalid journals, your first option is to rebuild the application. But that may not be a reasonable option. Besides, all journals would have to be re-created from scratch in the new application since it is not possible to extract them.

Here is a methodology for customers who wish to rebuild their application:

1. Back-up the application in the database.
2. Extract from the application all the elements: security, metadata, rules, lists, data, and journals.
3. Identify the Scenario/Year/Period where extraction of journals is not possible. These Scenario/Year/Period contain invalid journals.
4. For each Scenario/Year containing invalid journals, identify the journals to be re-created.
5. After verification, the invalid journal details can be deleted manually.

6. Apply steps 4 and 5 to identify and delete invalid journal templates.
7. After deletion of invalid journals and journal templates, extract journals from remaining Scenario/Year/Period.
8. Re-create a new application and reload all files extracted from existing application
9. You will then need to re-create the journal that was deleted.

Data Loading Validations

A common problem people have with all the different tools and overlapping functionality is choosing what tool they should be using for what. Many people who are experts with each tool don't help in this regard because they often hear the question as "Can I do this?" and not "Should I do this?" As the old saying goes, if you are a hammer, then every problem looks like a nail.

A very common question is where the data validations should happen. You could have validations in HFM as part of Process Management, and you can have them in FDM as part of the loading process. But this seems redundant. Why not have these validations in one or the other? First, each offers validations but at different times. FDM validations should be done for loading the data. HFM validations should be focused on the consolidation.

There are solutions that load the data through FDM, run a consolidation from FDM, and then pull data back into FDM to perform a check. This is not a best practice on two counts. First, in a well-designed flow, you should never have data looping back over. Anyone who has worked with large-scale data migration or integration projects will tell you that is a huge mistake. Second, you should never force the system to do something it was not designed for in order to meet some perceived benefit. In this case, the perceived benefit is that it is easier to do it in one tool over another, or that doing it both ways is too much work. The fact is that they both use VBScript to accomplish the validations. Also, each tool is doing something specific with the data, so why would you force the data-loading tool to validate the consolidation?

Data Relationship Management

As you consider your data strategy, you should also consider your metadata strategy. There are many options for updating the metadata, such as ODI and ERPi. But Oracle offers another tool that can expand your ability to update the databases and structures beyond even the Hyperion tools. The key to that offering is Data Relationship Management (DRM). This was formerly known as Master Data Management (MDM). It was built on a product developed by a company called Razza. DRM functions as a hub where structures are maintained, analyzed, and validated before moving throughout the enterprise. DRM also offers automation and validations.

One of the first things you will notice when using DRM is how familiar it is to EPMA. But DRM is not EPMA. There are some big differences.

The following are capabilities of Data Relationship Management:

- Manage change of business master data across enterprise applications
- Consolidate and rationalize structures across source systems
- Conform dimensions and validate integrity of attributes and relationships
- Synchronize alternate business views with corporate hierarchies
- Key features include
  - Versioning and modeling
  - Custom rules and validations
  - Configurable exports
  - Granular security
  - Change tracking

The following are capabilities of EPM Architect:

- Unify and align application administration processes across the Oracle EPM system
- Import and share business dimensions in the Dimension Library

- Build, validate, and deploy applications in the Application Library
- Load and synchronize data into and between EPM applications

You want to consider using DRM when you need a centralized change management of master data for enterprise applications including ERP/DW/EPM. DRM will also give you the following:

- Configurable data model and business rules for metadata creation and validation (this is a key consideration, as EPMA does not offer this)
- A way to compare hierarchies and synchronize them
- Automated and calculated attributes
- Validations
- An auditable environment for automated ongoing governance
- Versioning and rollback of changes
- Integration to workflow

Validating Your Data

The one part of any project that involves volumes of data that can never be underestimated is the data reconciliation. It will always take much longer than you plan. It will always be much more work than you think. And that is true no matter what you think. I have heard it all before. "My data is pretty clean." "We rebuild all the time, and don't have problems." You have issues with your data. You just don't know what they are.

That's one of the most understated benefits of doing an implementation with a tool like HFM. You will find all of your data problems. You will see them because you are taking the parts of data you are seeing now and looking at them in new ways. If there is a flaw in the data, it comes out when you do this data reconciliation.

So, why is it so much work? The biggest reason is that this is the first time as a user of the system that you have to sit down and navigate through the database. This is the first time you will realize that the parent entity is the sum of its children's Contribution Total, no matter how many times you heard it before, or the fact that you just read it here. The light bulb will go off, and you will realize how this database really works. So until you get the dimensionality, you will be learning as you go.

Sometimes the data changes so significantly that it creates more work validating that the system is working as you would expect. For example, deciding to report monthly from quarterly impacts the translation and roll forwards. Sometimes the added dimensionality of using custom dimensions and details creates new details that may have never even been in a report before. This can take time not only to validate, but also for the team to conceptualize.

The next reason this will take longer is: the truth is that this is not glamorous work. In fact, it is tedious and time-consuming. So it is easy to get distracted and pulled away to do something else.

The only way to sit down and work through the data reconciliation work is to roll up your sleeves and get to work. But you need a plan. You need to first decide at what level you will be doing your data reconciliation. Is every account necessary when you know they sum to the parent? Or do you only need to do that once or twice and then move on? I would recommend for each account and custom dimensions to go to the parent entity after consolidation and ensure that the children are rolling to the correct parents, and the data values are flowing correctly. Once this is done, there is no sense in continuing to do it.

Next, you need to build some tools to help you in the process. The first is a Smart View spreadsheet that should include all accounts for the HFM application. These accounts will include all levels in the hierarchy and will be organized into groups based on what they are providing (P&L, B/S, Calculations, and Statistical). This spreadsheet will be the primary tool you will use to reconcile. Why use a spreadsheet and not a grid or report? You can build quick calculations right on the face of the spreadsheet. That helps you find if parents are not rolling correctly or if adjustments need to be made. Spreadsheets are also common tools for other products, which you might be able to pull data from to help move reconciliation along. This flexibility makes it much easier to build adjustments and make corrections. Figure 5-4 is an example of such a spreadsheet. The periods to be reconciled are columns, and the entities that should be validated are each row in the application.

	A	B	C	D	E	F	G	H	I	J	K	L	M	N	O	P	Q
1													C:\DOCUME~1\ADMIN~1\LOCAL!				
2	HFM Data Reconciliation Schedule											=	Data loaded				
3												=	Data validated				
4		Ver 1.01	20 Dec 06									=	No Data load needed				
5																	
6																	
7								Jan	Feb	Mar	Apr	May	Jun	Jul	Aug	Sep	Oct
8								05	05	05	05	05	05	05	05	05	05
9																	
10					ACTUAL												
11	PWC_Con																
66	Misc																
67		9922															
68		TLG															
69			9923														
70			EFG														
71				Misc_AUS													
72					9906												
73					9907												
74					9908												
75				####													
76				9983													
77				Misc_HKG													
78					9979												

FIGURE 5-4. *Reconciliation spreadsheet*

The second tool you will need is a set of reports, or information you have gotten from the source system to which you can reconcile. It absolutely needs to be verified that this is the same as the data you are loading. It also needs to be at the correct level of detail to which you are reconciling. Let me tell you, it is a nightmare to try and reconcile to something that you can't drill into. If possible, you should build something that helps you with reconciliation in the spreadsheets you built. You can use the simple functions in Excel to speed the tedious ticking and tying.

As you prepare to load the data, you want to make sure you have a full set of data to start reconciling. Have the rates and ownership data loaded into the system. Have your trial balance and roll forward data completed. You should enter overrides and beginning balances. HFM requires a start period to load the beginning balances before you load the first full year of data in the application.

Now you are ready to reconcile the data. You want to stick to your plan. You can break this up across a team, but you should follow the following steps.

The first step to reconciliation is to validate all base accounts and base customs for a data load file until you are comfortable that the mapping from your ETL is correct. This is usually no more than two to three periods of data. But once you are sure all the base accounts are correct and mapped, you are ready to see the data aggregate and consolidation in HFM.

The second step is to validate parent accounts and customs for a set of entities. This is discussed to ensure that the structures you have built are in fact what you need. You may need to build subtotals using Excel functionality where the consolidating points differ between the old and new hierarchies. The calculation accounts will also be aligned to ensure that the old and new are correct and any changes to the calculation methodology can be identified and explained. Key accounts will be identified (with auditor assistance) that will be the same between the applications at the higher levels that will be used to validate the consolidation points.

The third step is to make any base-level adjustments. You will likely find issues at this point. Hierarchies might have been reported incorrectly, or changed over time. Do not make the mistake of building things in HFM for the way things used to be. The structures will make it harder to make changes in the future. It will make general maintenance and upgrades harder. It will create more work that really has no value going forward. You should not waste time building a structure for old reporting or issues. Post a journal and move on. And knowing the audit features and reporting of journals, you can see how this is a preferred way to get the data into HFM. So, it is less work and yields a better result.

The fourth step is to validate the translation. Depending on how you were doing translation before, you may see differences. It is important to remember that it is not just rate but methodology that can change. The methodology of translation only affects the flow accounts. All balance sheet accounts will use the rate at the end of the period that the balance is in. The flow accounts (revenue, expense and cash flow) should translate using an average rate. The average rate can be an average for the year, or for the month. Fortunately, HFM can translate using both a year-to-date average and a periodic average. The periodic method is called Periodic Value Add (PVA). This periodic translation is done each month, so the sum of the months would yield the year-to-date translated amounts. You have to have all current months of a given year to see the correct translated amounts. For example, if you were translating using the periodic method, you would need all twelve months.

Certain accounts add difficulty because, at the end of the previous year, the data was translated at last year's closing rate, so current period opening balances need to show the same value as the prior year's closing. Other accounts need to translate at historical rates. Dividends in the profit and loss account use the rate as of the date they were declared.

It is possible that you are taking advantage of an upgrade or rebuild of HFM to redefine your translation methodology. And if that is the case, you would expect translation differences. You have a couple of ways to handle the changes in translation for history. You can build something for the way the accounts used to be translated, but that is not a best practice. It's the same as when you were reconciling base members; it will make general maintenance and upgrades harder. You could try to post adjustments, but depending on what level you choose, you will find there are many entries that need to be made. You could just load translated values for historical periods. I would recommend that approach since it will be easier to reconcile. You can turn on translation for periods when the translation is what you will use going forward.

Reconciling translation is another place where reconciling more than a handful of periods will give you diminishing returns. The translation is just a set of rules. Once you have ensured that the translation is working, you should move on. Then you can be sure the only variables you have are the currency rates and how you decided to handle historical overrides for equity accounts. Doing any more than this is like making sure 1 plus 1 equals 2, over and over again.

The next step of the reconciliation is to reconcile parent entities. You should start at a group of lower entities. You can see a group of entities and the data you loaded consolidate here to the parent entity. Then you can move to other entities higher in structure. The historical reconciliations will take place at all top-level names within the entity structure and at specific legal entities within the structures you defined. This is one place where I would reconcile every period of data.

A second area of testing will occur when the reports are converted to the new chart of accounts. Next, you will take hard copies of the reports printed out, tied out with tick marks, and collected in a binder that will be reviewed and signed by either internal audit or the controller.

These steps will validate both the base-level data mappings as well as consolidation points in the financial statements. It is a thorough approach that minimizes working over the same data again and again. You should note that it is possible that all aggregation or consolidation points cannot be validated due to the changes in the structures where there may be different accounts rolling together or some points may not exist any more. So with those spots, you will need to spend extra effort.

Also, calculations may have changed due to the new chart or a new standardization of the calculation criteria, and these differences will be explained. Many of the old calculations are also invalid or not used any more and have been deleted from the functional chart of accounts. For these instances, you should have a reconciling report that shows and explains these differences as a new report. Fortunately, the spreadsheet you use to reconcile can be used to document this.

Once you have your reports and the data is signed off, you should lock the historical periods. You do not want anyone making any changes to these periods, even by accident. You should also make full data extracts of all the periods and save those with a set of the reconciliation reports as .pdf. This with the binder and sign-offs should satisfy any audit or review of the project.

Historical Data

When considering how much work is involved with building out the application, you need to ask yourself, "How much historical data should I load and reconcile?" Yes, it is some work, but this reconciliation step serves two significant purposes. First, it trains your core team to support the application. Just the process of reconciling historical data helps people understand the system and troubleshoot for most of the common issues. Working through those common issues will ensure that they are ready to support the application after the reconciliation is done.

The second benefit of reconciling more periods of data is that it functions as a test of the rules and data load process. The more periods you load and reconcile, the more sure you can be that the rules are ready for the close, and that you can handle data mapping issues. With rules, much of what you wrote and developed is written based on assumptions and expected data sets.

What happens when those expected data sets change? What happens when the assumptions change? More than likely the rules will fail. So the best thing you can do is run more periods of data through the system. This is also true for the data integration you built. The structure does change over time, by varying degrees depending on your business and process. So when new accounts are added, how does your system respond? Even if the data integration accounts for these changes with dynamic mapping, then it is still helpful for the team to see this work, and be ready to reconcile the data in these new members.

Still, you may find that you want seven years of history in your application for audit or tax reasons. There is no reason why you cannot start with a number of periods and then backfill from there. With that said, many people elect to load and consolidate two years of data for the application and build back from there. The benefit here is that you would be reducing risk to the project. You have fewer data values to work through. Two years for the implementation seems to be the best option for most people. That meets the majority of required reporting for the go-live. It also is not so few as to cause uncertainty that the application is ready for production use.

It is likely the history you load has changes that will be calculated in your new system going forward. This is different than just seeing different accounting treatments or structural changes. For example, this is seeing posted allocations written to the same accounts you are pulling from for other data. So if I were going to re-create that allocation in HFM, I would double the allocation for history. So how should you handle changes in history that you can't exclude from the load? For these issues, you should turn off the rules until you reach periods you can test. Then treat the rules you cannot validate as if you were adding them post go-live. You should test the calculations against the data set in your development environment, and then merge into production.

For some historical changes, people want to see the data as if there were no changes, that is, changes in the system like an acquisition, a merger, or a restructure of entities or debt. One way to accomplish doing this is to build a Pro Forma scenario. This is really just another scenario where you can load data with different attributes. For example, you could load a full year profit and loss statement, instead of the months that were loaded. Now you can see what the company would look like if you had that company the whole year.

Over time you may want to store the data in your application somewhere else, thinking the database is too big or that it is affecting performance. You do not need to archive data in HFM. Having many years' worth of data will not impact the performance, and besides, it will increase the size of the database.

So if there is a proven and reliable approach to reconciliation, why do people fail here? Why is it so hard for some people to reconcile their data? Often it is a combination of factors. When there are data issues, the consulting team can only go so far. The business users need to take control of this process. You cannot bring in a ton of external people to work on the data. They will take longer than you think to get up to speed, and then they will leave with the knowledge. Hiring consultants is very expensive. You need to assign people who will be supporting the application and put them on this phase full time. If dates start to slip, you need to make sure there are no bottlenecks. For example, the users are finding issues and all taking them to one person to resolve. The group needs to work on a concentrated effort to complete this critical task.

It is true this is where most people struggle. But with a good plan and procedure, any team can work through these issues.

Ongoing Account Reconciliation

The process you used to reconcile the periods of your historical data can and should be used to reconcile the data loads each month. Yes, after each load you absolutely need to check that the load worked and the data was consolidated successfully. You can minimize the effort by having some plan of attack. So for each load, you need to rerun your reconciliation process. You may find that you can do this at a summary level.

You should also create a process for reconciliation for each feed downstream of the application. You could be moving data from HFM to a Planning or Essbase application. You could be moving data from HFM to a data warehouse or data mart. This reconciliation process would not be very different from the ongoing data-loading reconciliation. Each time you have an integration of data, you need to have some method for validating that the systems do in fact reconcile. When you employ a tool like Financial Close Manager, you can even audit and track these reconciliations, ensuring that your process has integrity.

Data Validations

The basic validations you should have in the data-loading process will help you with reconciliation issues. For example, the first one every application should have is an "out of balance" validation. Before data gets loaded into HFM, you can be sure the trial balance is in balance.

Extended Analytics

Hyperion Financial Management introduced a new feature called Extended Analytics in version 3.0. Extended Analytics allows the administrator to extract data to a "star schema" or flat file that can include any of the Hyperion Financial Management metadata and data. The star schema can then be used by Essbase Integration Services (EIS) to create one or many Essbase cubes.

Early versions of the functionality had performance limitations. The versions since system 9 are remarkable in how well they perform. You can now move large amounts of data. I would still limit the extract to the current period for a given scenario. It is still not recommended to extract the entire application. If you consider only the leaf or base members of any hierarchy existing in the application, the system has to build all the parent levels. That can take some time. Still the performance is now so good that it is not uncommon for people to pull all Actual data for a given month.

Currently, Extended Analytics supports Oracle, SQL Server, and DB2 RDBMS. Extended Analytics can only be used to "push" data into the star schema, which means that you can create the star schema and use EIS to create Essbase cubes, but any changes made in Essbase or the star schema will not be read back into HFM.

This allows the administrator to take a snapshot of the data and metadata from HFM. You can pull that data into a data mart or warehouse. You can also use that summary data you may have in HFM to see that detail or transaction level from another system does, in fact, reconcile. You can also use Essbase to do more analysis or management reporting. For example, the EIS Administrator can create Essbase cubes for the budgeting, sales, and marketing departments with only the information that pertains to that group.

Figure 5-5 shows the Star Schema Link screen.

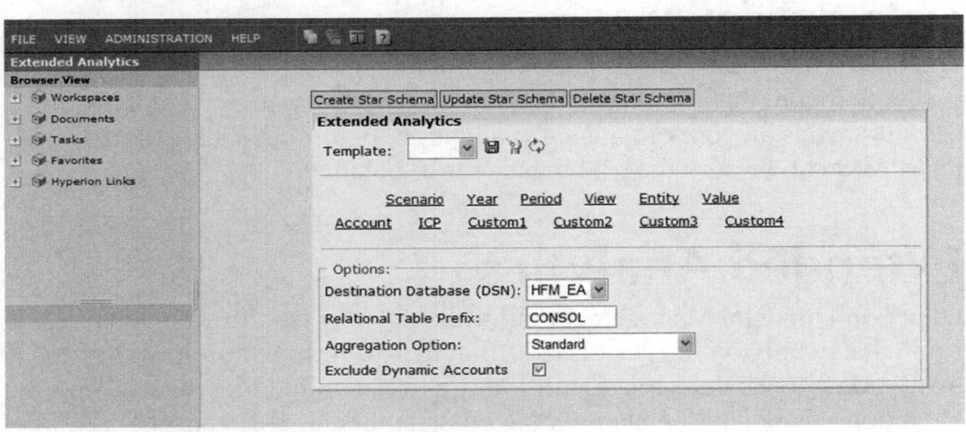

FIGURE 5-5. *Star Schema Link screen*

Since version 4.0, improvements to the Extended Analytics offering introduced new extract types, like the ability to save Extract Query criteria and access Extended Analytics from the Hyperion Financial Management web interface. If you have not seen EA in some time, some of the new User Interface Updates include

- Ability to create templates (Extended Analytics Query)
- Selection of the Extended Analytics DSN (in case of multiple database tables)
- Aggregation Options:
  - Standard Extract (Original Star Schema extract)
  - Metadata Only
  - Selected Metadata Only
  - Essbase
  - Data Warehouse
- Exclude Dynamic View Accounts (the default is to exclude)

The Aggregation Options give you options for the fields that will be extracted in the tables.

- **Standard Extract** The Standard schema creates 14 tables (13 dimensions and 1 data).

  The Standard schema tables include parent information, descriptions, user-defined fields, dimension sharing, ICP, and dimension member leaf information, as well as the default currency.

- **Metadata Only** The entire metadata structure will be exported using the standard schema. The standard 14 tables will be created, but the fact table will not be populated with data.

- **Selected Metadata Only** The metadata structure that is selected by the administrator will be exported to the standard schema format. The resulting information in the standard schema will only contain the members that were selected. For example, the hierarchy of the east region will only contain EastRegion and its children.

- **Essbase** Creates a star schema that only contains the base information. The aggregations are performed after EIS is used to create the Essbase cube. The star schema is made up of the same tables as the Standard Extract; however, it also contains a base table for each metadata dimension.

  Beginning with HFM 4.0, the Comma sample application includes EIS XML examples for SQL Server, Oracle, and DB2, that can be imported into EIS, allowing the administrator to see how the new extract can aid in building Essbase cubes.

- **Data Warehouse** Exports the Hyperion Financial Management dimensions and data in a normalized hierarchy schema. This means that all the levels for the hierarchy should be contained within the same table.

With so many options, you might not be sure which method to use. A good guideline to follow is

- Use the Standard schema if you want to see the effects of shared members (data explosion).
- Use the Data Warehouse schema if shared members are not required.
- Use the Essbase schema if you want to externally aggregate the data or only want access to the base data for a selected POV.

Moving Journals and Elimination Data

When loading data from Extended Analytics, you can select your Value dimension. This is helpful when you want to move only the elimination or adjustment data. For example, you would want to do this when you have made the determination that the book of record is not HFM. You would need to move any values calculated in HFM out to some other system. Now that Extended Analytics allows for moving to a flat file or a SQL database, there should be integration with any system.

Conclusion

Data reconciliation needs to happen for any change of significance with the product. Why so many people struggle with it and others don't is often the result of some combination of data issues, lack of commitment, lack of resources, historical issues, and a poor plan. You can ensure your success by knowing what to reconcile and when with the process laid out in this chapter.

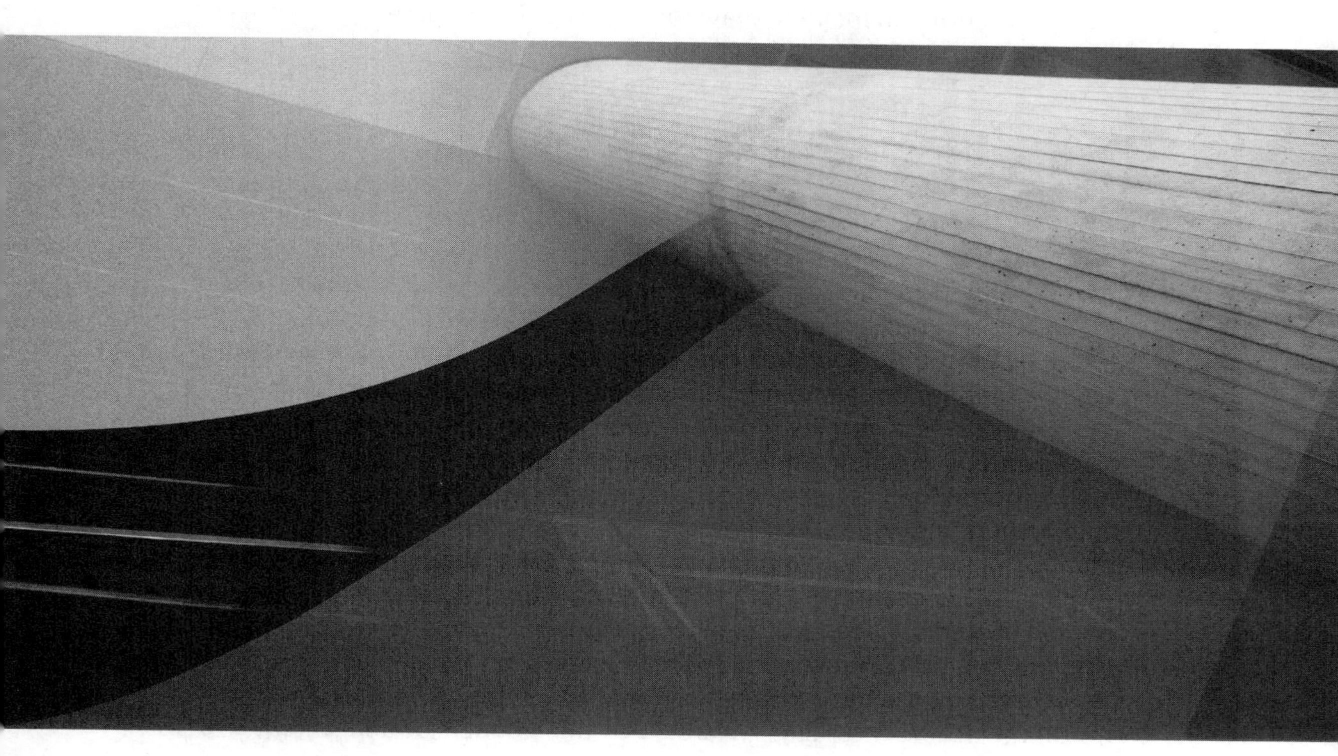

CHAPTER 6

Supporting Your Application

nyone who is planning to buy or take on a project and is getting HFM is concerned about what needs to be done to support the application. How do you organize the team who built this application to support the users going forward? Who are the people whom you need to identify? And what are they doing?

Some companies have full-time infrastructure people supporting the HFM application. Other companies have three to five man-days a month. The reason for such a difference has more to do with how they are trying to manage the application, and issues with the design more than anything else. So what is the recommended approach and why?

In this chapter, we will cover the best approaches and tools for the team to support the application. We will cover a change control process that will minimize issues and not impact functionality or usability. We will also cover common support issues and how to resolve them. Finally, we will list common error messages and steps to resolve them. While not a full list of possible errors, these pages will serve as a guide for helping you find and resolve many of the most common issues. Appendix A provides a list of error numbers and messages generated by the Financial Management Error Lookup tool.

Support can be broken out into two distinct elements: IT Support and Admin/Functional (development for HFM, FDM, Reports, and the supporting tools). Sometimes companies refine the Admin/Functional role into two groups, an analyst (finance/functional data owners who will continue to steer the application content) and a pure administrator (maintenance for HFM, FDM, Reports, and the supporting tools). The size of the team and how you define these roles relates to the complexity of the application and the number of users. The complexity of the application is not just rules, but the whole close process. The more complicated the process surrounding the close, the more steps and issues you will have to manage during the close. Applications with 20 users might only have a single part-time administrator, and support "as needed" from IT, while a company with 3,200 users might have four administrators, six analysts, and a full-time team of four infrastructure resources, eight regional administrators in different regions of the world, a DBA for a few days each month, and a finance team of several people serving as subject matter experts. Knowing what it will take to manage your application should be a goal during the parallel testing you would do before you are live with the application. You can estimate, but you will be able to confirm during this test.

Finally, for customers who have HFM and Planning with more than 100 users, it is common to see two teams—one for each, HFM and Planning.

Planning to Support Your Application

So why is it so important to think about the team you will be involved with in the design and build? Because not only are they building the application, but they become the default choice for supporting after the project is over. The skill set needed to administer an HFM application is very valuable. Good administrators can be hard to find in more remote cities. You won't have to look further than the team you have to support the application.

So, as the consultants are ready to leave, and the testing is done, you are ready to support your application, right? Supporting the application starts all the way back in design. At each step you should consider the fact that you will be doing this work. Document the issues and resolutions; document your data recon process. Document what works for parallel and what didn't.

Some best practices for project documentation include having an issue log. You should be keeping track of every issue you have during your project and its resolution. Issues usually come back, and having that knowledge is important to resolve the issue. Also, many of these problems, while they don't appear so, can be inter-related. For example, you may be having timeout issues, and you can't figure out why the web settings do not allow for tasks to complete. Then you realize later that a database setting is resizing the database, causing certain tasks to time out. Finally, these issues and the resolution with your training materials become the foundation for your desktop procedures.

So, you didn't do this when you implemented your project? It is not too late. Get in a room with your team and start this log. Build your knowledge base to support the issues unique to your environment. It is never too late or too soon to start writing these procedures.

IT Support

If you are the infrastructure person, or if you manage those people, you need to sit with a good infrastructure consultant and do an install of the product suite. Don't let a team come in, while you miss your opportunity to learn. The team should show you the tricks of configuration, how the products interact with each other, and where you can expect to find issues.

All installations should have scripts or BAT files you can use to start and stop services. A good installation will include reviewing database procedures. For example, you should never have the database growing by a percent. Instead, make sure your application database grows by some number of megabytes. After the installation, it will work fine either way. But as the database grows, the quick growth of 5 percent of 100MB becomes the slow traumatic growth of 5 percent of 100GB. This causes timeout errors and other issues.

You also need to make sure you back up your databases. Yes, this includes backing up your development instance. This will help the team do faster restores when they make the catastrophic errors you would expect in development. The cost of not backing up your development instance would be losing all the project work to date. While good consultants will make occasional extracts, I would not take that risk.

The following procedure is necessary to back up and restore a single application that resides in a Hyperion Financial Management database. All applications and data within a single Financial Management instance are stored in a single schema. So, if you have seven applications, there will be seven application sets located within that database. The typical backup procedures for the applications include having all users logged out of the system and taking a full backup of the database. This will affect all users in all applications for the Financial Management installation. In order to back up a single application without affecting other users in the system, you must follow the procedures in the following lists.

To back up the application, follow these steps:

1. Disable connections to the Production application in question in the Financial Management Administration Web Client.

2. Create a new database in an RDBMS located on a non-Production server.

3. Copy the Financial Management application with the HfmCopyApplication.exe utility (located in the Hyperion Financial Management server directory) from the source Production database to the target Backup non-Production database.
4. Re-enable connections to the Production application.
5. Back up the target non-Production database.

To restore the application, follow these steps:

1. Restore the application from your backup mechanism to the new non-Production database that you created in step 2 of the backup process.
2. Disable connections to the Production application in question in the Financial Management Administration Web Client.
3. Copy the Financial Management application with the HfmCopyApplication.exe utility from the source Backup non-Production database to the target Production database.
4. Re-enable connections to the Production application.
5. When performing steps 1 through 4, it is important that you *do not* restore any database to the Production server, or *all* application data will be overwritten. So, when you restore the database to the non-Production database, all data in that database will be overwritten.

Admin/Functional Support

The administrator is not only the key resource for your project, the right person to support your application after you have taken it live, but he or she is also critical to the system. The most common questions people seem to ask are first, where should this person sit? Not where should they physically sit, but should the person be in an IT role, or a Business Functional role? I think the question comes from the fact that at some point they have seen some scripting, and that means coding, and that usually means an IT person. The reality is that the level of scripting is that of writing a macro in Excel. This really is not programming. So it is easier to teach a business person how to write these types of scripts, than it is to teach an IT person debits and credits. Frankly, there are accountants out there who don't know debits and credits. The administrator needs to know enough to ask the next question. That person needs to understand "what is the end game," so they can think of how that works within the whole system. For example, let's say a business user comes and asks for a roll forward to be added to the application. They are very specific about what they need and the accounts. A good administrator who understands the business process will think to ask about a validation to reconcile it to the trial balance. They will ask about the filings or management reports that are impacted. They will also know who in the accounting team might need to weigh in on who should have access, whether it is something all sites need to do, and how it impacts the close. It turns out that adding accounts and updating a roll forward are a very small part of the request.

The second question people ask all the time is, "How much time is this going to take?" That is when I give my safe consultant answer, "It depends" (that answer gets me out of so much trouble, I frankly don't know what I would do without saying it). Still, it is the truth. It does depend. It depends on who the administrator is in your company. If the person understands the close process, and what users really need, they spend less time trying to understand how people are using the system. It depends on how much work you took on during the project. If you only loaded one year of data, they will be pretty busy loading data for months later. It depends on your company. Is the company culture one that requires buy-in from users and fills days with meetings of large groups of people who need to reach a consensus? Then it will be much longer.

Most administrators have another job. They are not just the HFM administrator.

I get the chance to talk to auditors at different companies, and when I tell them what I do, we start talking about HFM. Many have told me that when they had a question about the consolidation, they found the only person who really knew how it was calculated was the HFM administrator. Even if the administrator doesn't know the way it "should be" done, they know how it is "currently being" done. So, think about the person who is doing that work. They become not only critical to the application, but critical to your close and your business.

Change Control Processes

If you have a system and do not have a separate environment, you are just about asking for a crisis. Every mission-critical application, which HFM is, needs to have some controlled environment to manage changes that need to be made to the system. You need to test changes before you make them. Change control is the formal process used to ensure that changes to a product or system are introduced in a controlled and coordinated manner. A good process makes you think about what changes you want to make, and how you can ensure they are done right.

Financial Management should always have multiple environments. At a minimum, there should be two: a development/test and production environment. Each should have its own separate hardware. If possible, you should break the development and test into two, so there would be three environments (development, test, and production) with the test and production having identical hardware and software configurations. Any patches for any software could be tested thoroughly in the test environment before they are applied to production. Change control manages the migration of changes from one of these environments to another.

You do need to have people with administrator rights in the production application in order to use certain functionality. If you find you just can't have this because of security concerns in your application, then you need to plan for this by having the people who do have administrative rights to the application provide the reports or detail to your administrator. For example, your administrator may not have administrator rights in production. You may have an IT resource take this role in order to segregate duties in the production environment. That means the administrator cannot view task audit reports or data audit reports. So plan for this, and have your IT user be prepared to send these reports or information to your administrator.

The question everyone asks is, "What are things we should test, and what are the things we should let users do directly?" I answer that by making the distinction of which application changes could make the system not functional for the whole set of users, as opposed to getting an error on specific tasks. In other words, if I get an error writing a bad grid, then only I will get an error when I try to use that grid. If I write a bad rule, I can prevent all users from running any calculation or consolidation.

Tasks that should be tested before being loaded into production include:

- **Rules** See the chapter about rules in this book (Chapter 3). Data explosion and poorly written rules can impact your application just about more than anything else.
- **Metadata** Following naming conventions and reliable procedures for adding members will help with issues. Still, something as careless as promoting a base member to a parent could cause you to face clearing all the metadata from your application. Renaming parents could cause reports to fail.
- **Lists** Since lists impact both rules and metadata, these can be important.

Oracle HFM System Logs

When supporting the application, you need to know where you can find the messages that tell you how your application is performing. The error messages appear in a couple of places. The main places are

- The HsvEventLog.Log file under the HFM application server's \Hyperion\logs\hfm folder
- The HFM_ErrorLog table within the relational store (Oracle HFM schema)
- Windows application events
- Audit and task logs
- User interface

If you aren't familiar with HFM, it can be difficult to understand what these messages are trying to tell you about your application. Unfortunately, there isn't a list of the errors that you can refer to and see what is wrong. More importantly, there isn't a list of errors that tells you what the resolution is for each error. In this section, you will see most of the messages you could get, and what the resolution most likely is. I will try to emphasize the term "messages" rather than "errors." Some of the messages are errors, but the logs contain a lot of information about how the system is performing. They also capture quite a few transactions, such as failed logins or the execution of Calculate and Consolidate. You should refer to the latest EPM installation documentation provided by Oracle for more information about EPM logs and troubleshooting.

You will get errors. You can count on it. When you do, you will need to get the information that will help you. But just as important is to be able to help the people who want to help you. When you call support, you will want to give them the best information so they can provide the most likely cause of the issues. So you will need to know where to find the issues.

The first thing you should know, without question, is what version you are running. You can click on the About HFM menu option, and then click Show Details to reveal details for each of the installed modules and products, as shown in Figure 6-1.

HSV Event Log

The first and best place to start reviewing system messages is the HFM event log. There is a wealth of detail in this log. Each application server will have an HsvEventLog.log file under the \Hyperion\logs\hfm folder. There are no options for increasing or decreasing the events or level of detail captured in the HFM event logs. It is also important to note that the HFM web servers will have an HFM log. This can be useful to trace problems that may appear on the web tier but not on HFM, the application tier. The messages are stored in XML, so the HFM_ErrorLog table requires the reader to query and interpret the XML. This should help you appreciate how valuable the HFM Error Log Viewer utility is to interpret these messages.

This file can be very tough to read. It is a string of complex tags and code that really doesn't tell you anything. Luckily for us, Oracle provides

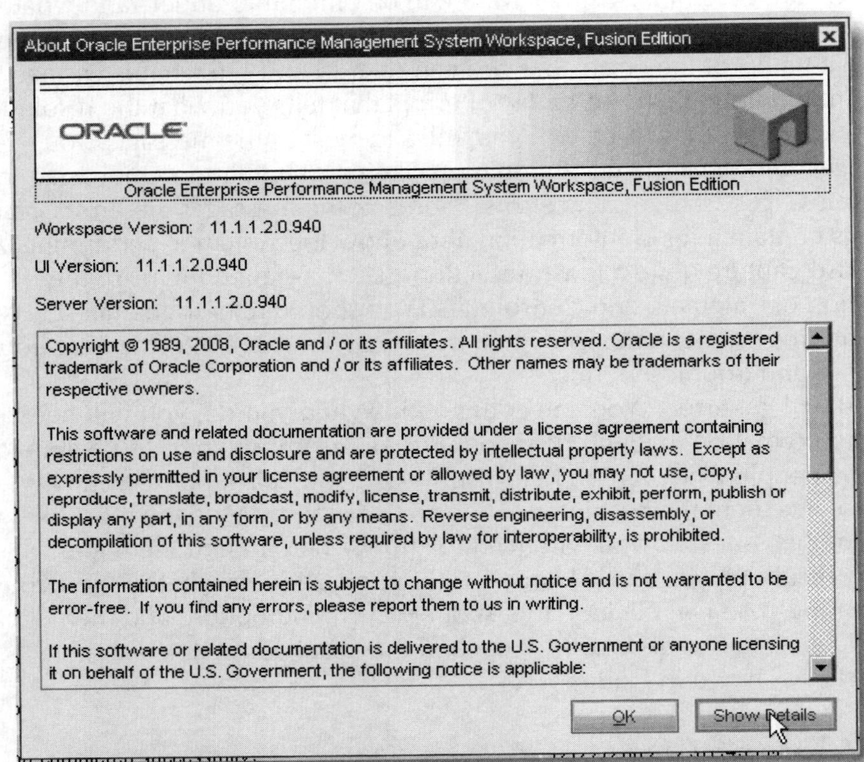

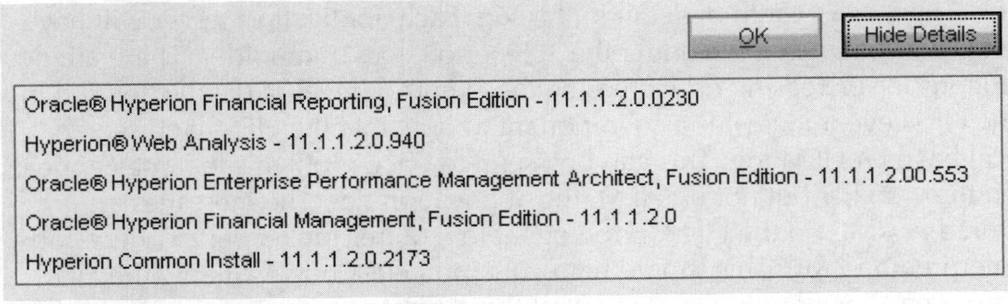

FIGURE 6-1. *What version are you running?*

a utility to read this file, the HFM Error Log Viewer utility (under Consultant Utilities wherever the HFM client is installed), which not only displays the messages in human readable format rather than XML, but the events themselves must be translated from the hexadecimal codes into English messages. Figure 6-2 shows the default location for the utility. For 64-bit applications, you will see a "_x64" suffix; there will be no suffix for 32-bit applications.

Since this HsvEventLog.log file can get so big so quickly, and because it is a text file that is being created, you want to figure out how to manage its size before it is too big to deal with and not affect the users. The system needs to open this file to write to it, and then close the file when done. A large file takes time to open and close. This impacts performance. It is a best practice to rename the file as soon as it reaches about 20MB. I recommend renaming the file with the application and dates. HFM will just create a new file when it sees that the old file is gone.

It is good to extract the log files from the application and rename them using the same convention as the HsvEventLog.log. Then clear the logs in the application. This should be done monthly, after the close is complete.

It is really a better practice to set this up to run on the server, without any users involved. This ensures that the backup is done and archived correctly and safely.

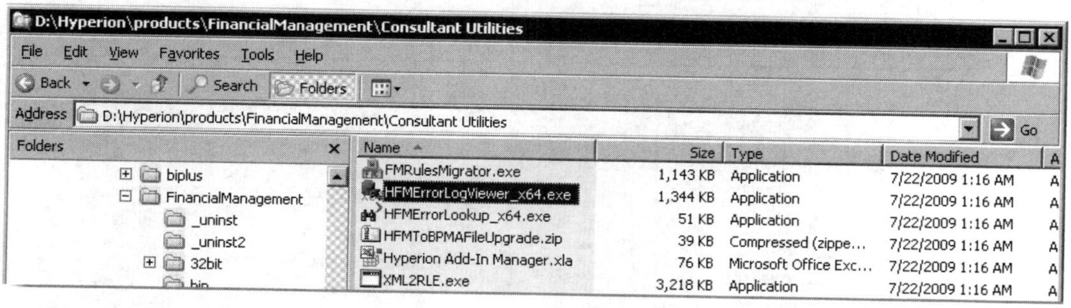

FIGURE 6-2. *Where to find your utility*

HFM Error Log

The System Messages module located in the web client (under the Administration menu) also provides a way to see this detailed information. While the Error Log utility provides the most detailed information, the web System Messages can be accessed by any application administrator via the browser without a viewing utility. Figure 6-3 is the menu option to view these errors.

Just like the other files, this HFM_ErrorLog table needs to be archived, although you will need to do this with either the HFM Event Log utility or SQL commands. This is another table that can affect the performance of HFM if left unchecked.

The Error Log table contains error information as created within the Hyperion Financial Management application server and Win32 client components. This information is centrally stored in the database. You must use the web-based management screen to view the errors stored in the database. Figure 6-4 shows the fields of this table.

Windows Event Log

The next place you can find system messages is in the Windows event log. To see these, though, you need to first have access to the system, and second, you need to understand that the messages are about the services and not functional issues in HFM. Figure 6-5 shows an example of this log.

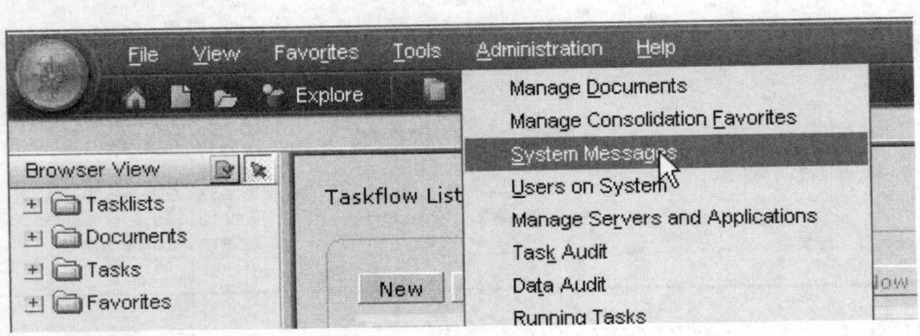

FIGURE 6-3. *System messages on the web*

HFM_ERRORLOG	Data Type	Allows Nulls	Description
SGUID	nvarchar	NOT NULL	Unique Identifier
LLOGTYPE	smallint	NULL	Logging Action Type
DTIMESTAMP	float	NULL	Error Time Stamp
SSERVERNAME	nvarchar	NULL	Application Server Name
SAPPNAME	nvarchar	NULL	Server Component Name
SXMLERROR	ntext	NULL	XML Error Tree

FIGURE 6-4. *HFM error log*

These errors can be overwritten just by the Windows Server policy, so if you wish to save this or record this information, you need to update Windows.

When you first start the application, a "Registry" record is the first thing logged. This message is written to the event log every time an application starts up on one of the servers. Once the last user has logged out of the application on the specific server, the HsvDataSource.exe process will terminate on its own. When the first person logs on, there can be a delay to starting HFM, and the services that are starting are one of the causes.

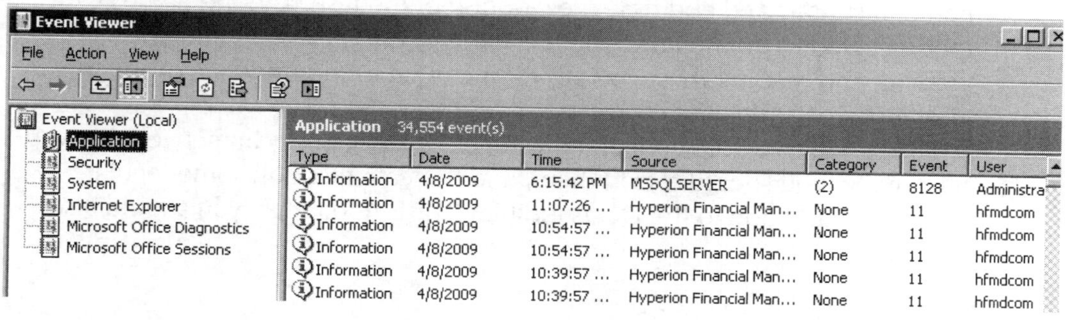

Event Viewer

File Action View Help

Event Viewer (Local)
- Application
- Security
- System
- Internet Explorer
- Microsoft Office Diagnostics
- Microsoft Office Sessions

Application 34,554 event(s)

Type	Date	Time	Source	Category	Event	User
Information	4/8/2009	6:15:42 PM	MSSQLSERVER	(2)	8128	Administra
Information	4/8/2009	11:07:26 ...	Hyperion Financial Man...	None	11	hfmdcom
Information	4/8/2009	10:54:57 ...	Hyperion Financial Man...	None	11	hfmdcom
Information	4/8/2009	10:54:57 ...	Hyperion Financial Man...	None	11	hfmdcom
Information	4/8/2009	10:39:57 ...	Hyperion Financial Man...	None	11	hfmdcom
Information	4/8/2009	10:39:57 ...	Hyperion Financial Man...	None	11	hfmdcom

FIGURE 6-5. *Windows event log*

To minimize this impact, you can set the HFM Service on the application server to "Automatic." This service will then keep the processes running. Since each application will be available, you should see multiple HsvDataSource.exe processes, one for each application.

If the first user login takes longer than a minute without the HFM management service running, this is an indication of a problem in the environment. It could be caused by extensive HS.NoInput rules, a delay in establishing a connection to the relational database, or a problem establishing a connection to the external authentication provider(s).

Audit and Error Log Tables

There are two tables in HFM that keep track of what the users are doing. These tables are grouped to contain user tasks and data entry changes. They are called

- <APPNAME>_DATA_AUDIT
- <APPNAME>_TASK_AUDIT

The Data Audit log records the changes to the data and time-stamps the change. In addition to tracking the data changes a user makes in the system, the Data Audit log tracks the server, the username, and an activity code.

The Task Audit table is used to log tasks performed by a user on the system. This table stores the user, session ID, activity code, application name, task start and end time, description of the task, and the name of the module used to do the task. There is another error-viewing utility for viewing and reading these log tables. It can be found under \Consultant Utilities, alongside the HFM Error Log Viewer.

These tables, while containing valuable information, can get very big very quickly. So you should export them, and truncate them on some regular interval. In addition to the Data Audit and Task Audit logs, you should also monitor the HFM_ERROR_LOG. The HFM_ERROR_LOG and TASK_AUDIT are both always enabled and will constantly grow, unchecked. The DATA_AUDIT can be turned off.

As with the other log files, when these tables get too big, viewing them can be slow and can consume valuable system resources. They need to be extracted and cleared periodically as well.

Oracle HFM Errors and Common Causes

This collection of errors is by no means a comprehensive list of every error you could get within HFM. Most errors are intuitive with metadata, and easily resolved. However, there are some that require some additional knowledge to identify the issue. Unfortunately, some of the errors are very technical in nature and the descriptions are not clear. So, the following pages provide a list of errors and possible resolutions. I have grouped them as Windows interface errors and the Error Log errors. The Windows interface errors are ones you will get while administering and maintaining the application. The Error Log errors are ones you will find in the HSV event log.

Windows Interface Errors

As you navigate around HFM, some of the messages you get will be very intuitive. You might get a message "Member already exists," for example, when trying to add metadata with the same label. The system won't let you do that, and the message is exactly what you would expect. It is my hope that these messages will at least get you in the right direction, and give you more information to get your application back up and healthy.

Unexpected Error: 8004023B

What it means This message would appear when loading or extracting metadata from the HFM application. This usually means there was some problem with a previous file loaded, and it has created a problem with the tables that prevents you from extracting or loading the metadata. This message may also occur when you open metadata files with the WIN32 interface. If you get this error while trying to view the metadata file after extracting it, it may be a semicolon in a metadata description, or a character that could be construed as a field delimiter. Try saving the file in .xml format instead of an .app. If this works, it is because the XML provides proper escape codes around these characters. The following illustration shows an example.

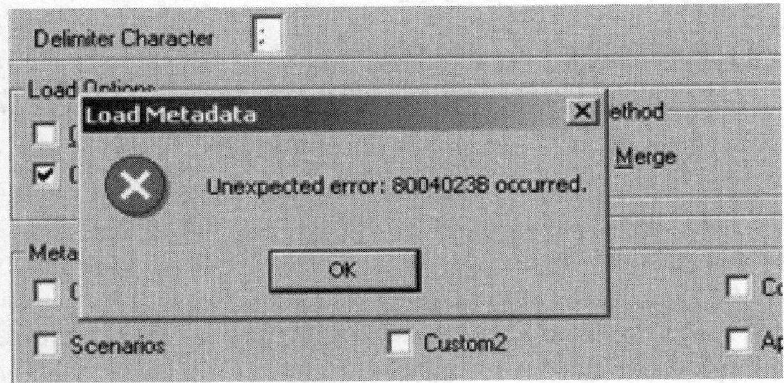

How you fix it The application will need to be restored to a point before the issue occurred, or rebuilt. You can avoid this issue by ensuring that you never deselect the check integrity option when loading data.

Common Rule Error

What it means There is an error in the rule file, as described. The error message may appear when running Translate, Consolidate, or Calculate from within the WIN32 grid or WDEFs. An example is shown in the following illustration. The rules either have an invalid variable, a syntax error in the VBScript, or some other issue within the rule file.

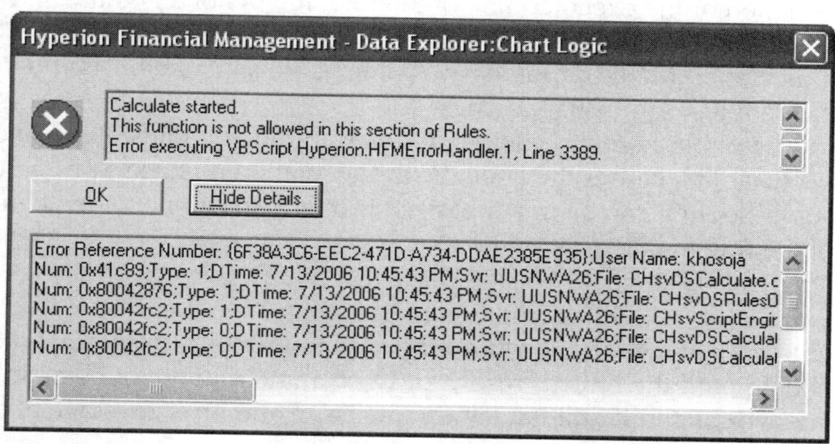

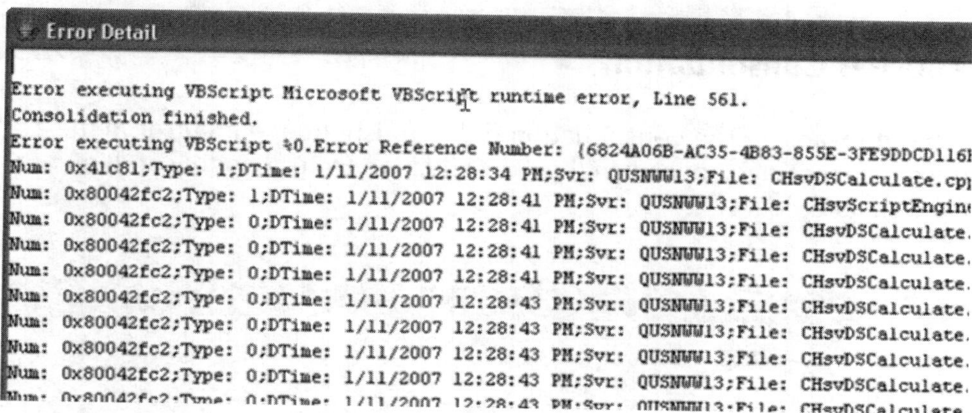

If you get any error that says "Error Executing VBScript" when running any Calculate or consolidation, it would be an error in the script created, which is either in the rules or member lists; that is, if you can create the error by performing the same action. I consolidate, I get a VBScript error.

The error message will give a line where HFM believes the error to be, but it is not a line in the rule file itself. These lines are either the line of code where it failed or the executed line of the rule. It will not tell you where to see the problem. You have to dig into the rule file and find the issue. When using Calculation Manager, there isn't a line at all, so it can be a bit harder to find where the error is happening.

To start troubleshooting, you need to start turning off parts of the rules and find what line causes the issue. With Calculation Manager, this part of the troubleshooting can be much easier, since it is so simple to deploy only parts of the rule file.

How you fix it The rules will require an update, and then you reload and run the task again. All users will not be able to Calculate, Translate, or Consolidate until the error is resolved. Users may or may not be able to continue working, but will have the same issue and error message at the intersection of data where this error occurred.

Aborted Consolidation

What it means The consolidation didn't finish, due to an error in the rules. The message appears in the Consolidation Status window and in the task audit log.

Oracle Hyperion Financial Management, Fusion Edition - Financial Management Progress - Windows Internet Explorer

Running Tasks

Stop Task	Activity	Progress	Status	Start Time	Description
	Consolidation	47%	Aborted	4/5/2011 7:53:12 AM	(Actual;2011;Jan-Jan;Total_Company) Calculated :

Auto Close

How you fix it The intersection where this happened needs to be identified and the issue in the rules resolved. It is some issue with the rules, and you need to continue running the consolidation, translations, and calculations until you find the exact intersection of the issue. It is at that point where you will find you get the different "common rule error" described earlier.

Aborted Rules Load in Calculation Manager

What it means The rules were not able to load in Calculation Manager due to some errors. The message appears in the application library when you try to deploy rules that have some issues.

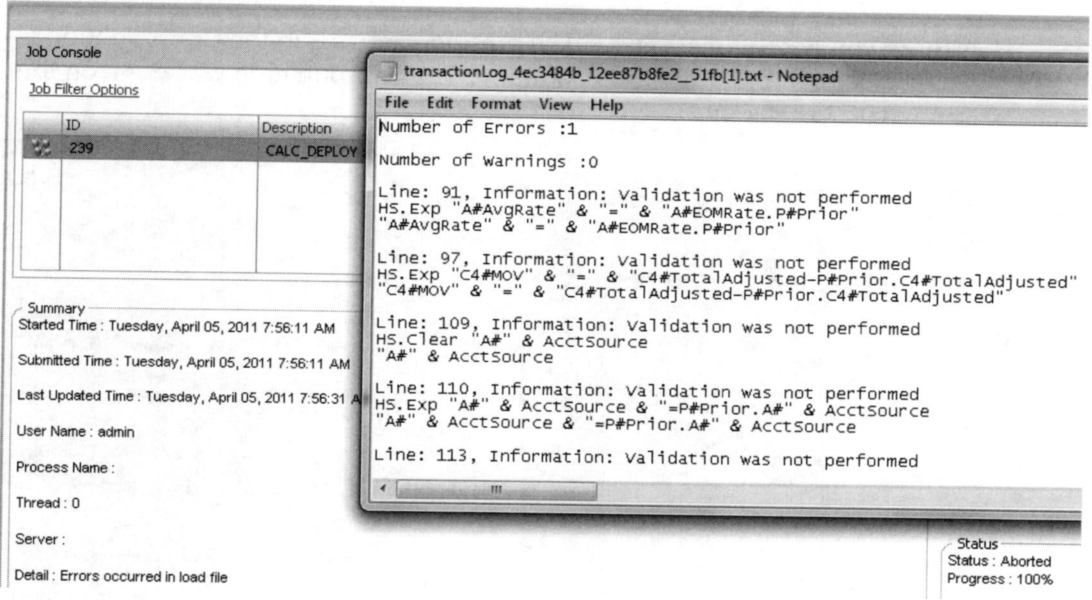

How you fix it Find the invalid line of code or rule and resolve the issue. It would also be a good idea to validate all of your rules before trying to redeploy.

HsvData2 Object Error

What it means When running a consolidation, you get an error: "An unknown error has occurred in the HsvData2 object" with a description of: "Value violated the integrity constraints for a column or table" and the following problem: "Cannot insert duplicate key in object." HsvData2 errors are typically HFM engine-related errors. These should not be overlooked.

How you fix it To solve this error, delete invalid records.

Overlapping Consolidation

Where you get the message The message appears in the Consolidation Status window and in the task audit log. The consolidation was done on the same entity or parent.

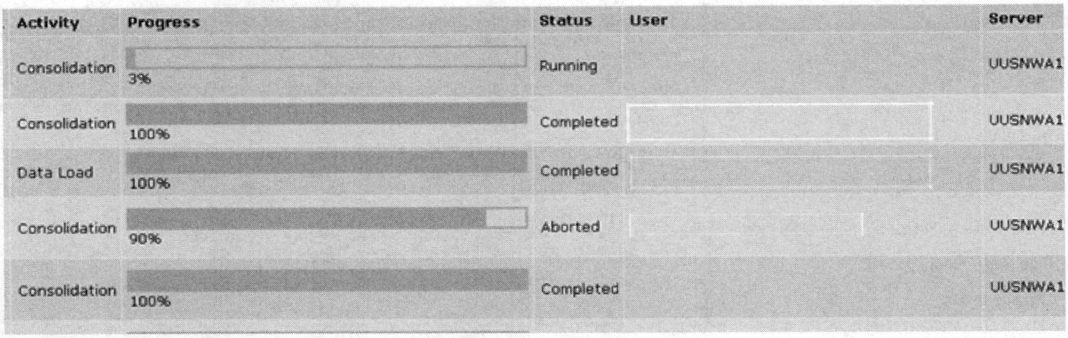

Activity	Progress	Status	User	Server
Consolidation	3%	Running		UUSNWA1
Consolidation	100%	Completed		UUSNWA1
Data Load	100%	Completed		UUSNWA1
Consolidation	90%	Aborted		UUSNWA1
Consolidation	100%	Completed		UUSNWA1

How you fix it The consolidation must be allowed to finish. There will be a significant performance impact to the consolidation. This actually isn't an error in the sense that there is something that needs to be fixed in the system. This is a very helpful message in the sense that it is keeping you from creating issues. The issue is that you are asking HFM to do something it is already doing. However, it does mean your users are not clear on how the consolidation should work. They should not be overlapping consolidations.

Metadata Grid Error

What it means This error could appear when opening or loading a grid. The metadata has changed, and the grid is no longer valid or has an issue.

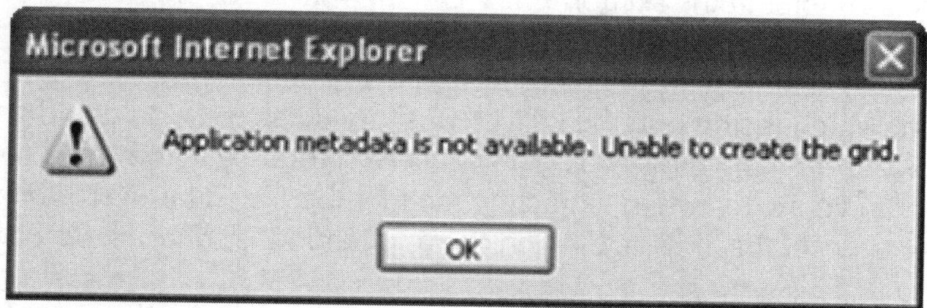

How you fix it If the metadata has changed, please rebuild the grid. If the metadata has not changed, try logging off.

Unknown Error

What it means When in the application, in the web browser, and trying to complete a task, the system was unable to complete the request. This is typically outside the control of HFM.

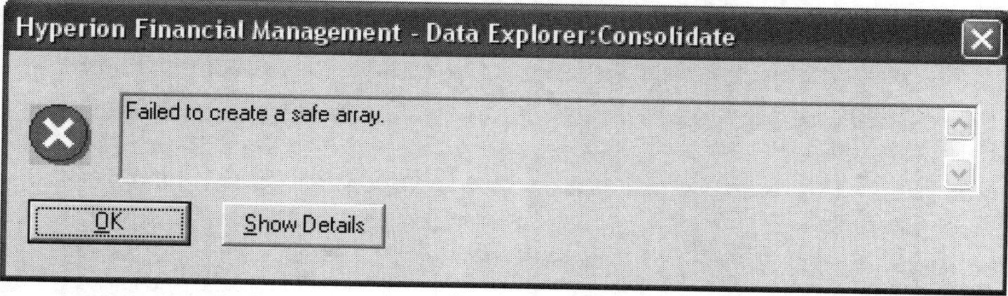

How you fix it Log off and log back in. If the problem persists, contact Oracle support. You will need to dig deeper into the HFM and operating system messages to see if something outside of HFM is affecting your usage.

Safe Array Error, 0x80040211

What it means This error can appear when using grids. The cause can be many things; to identify what it is, please review the HSV event log as described later in this chapter in the section "HSV Event Errors and Codes." This can occur when a user is trying to open the Process Control module. When this happens, there are likely issues with some corruption in the default Process Control grid definition, which is stored in the HFM repository database. You could get this error as well when opening grids. This is likely caused by a corrupted member list. You can verify this when extracting the member list; it has a size of zero. You may also get this message when the application is suffering from data explosion.

As you might gather at this point, this error message can mean a lot of things. Unfortunately, none of what it indicates is good for your application.

How you fix it The resolution of this issue will require advanced help. Please contact Oracle support immediately.

Metadata Not Available

What it means The error appears when trying to run a grid. This means that the metadata was changed while you were trying to view or update the grid.

How you fix it Refresh the grid.

Parent/Child Error

What it means The error can appear in either grids or WDEFs. The Point of View is incorrect and needs to be updated.

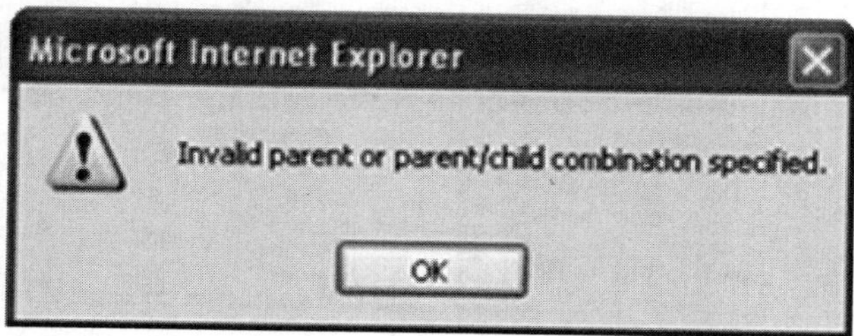

How you fix it The parent is not valid for the current child. It does not appear in the structure.

Unable to Process Request Error

What it means There was a communication error in the system for your request. The system could not respond to your request.

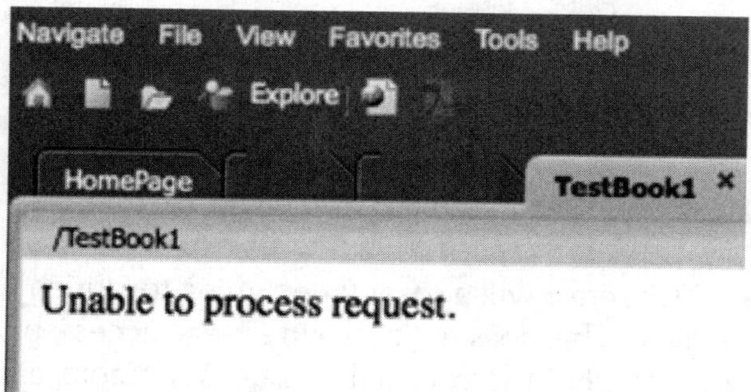

How you fix it Log back in to the system and retry. If the error persists, contact Oracle support to log the issue.

Server Not Found Error

What it means This error will appear when trying to launch HFM. The server is either unavailable or not accessible.

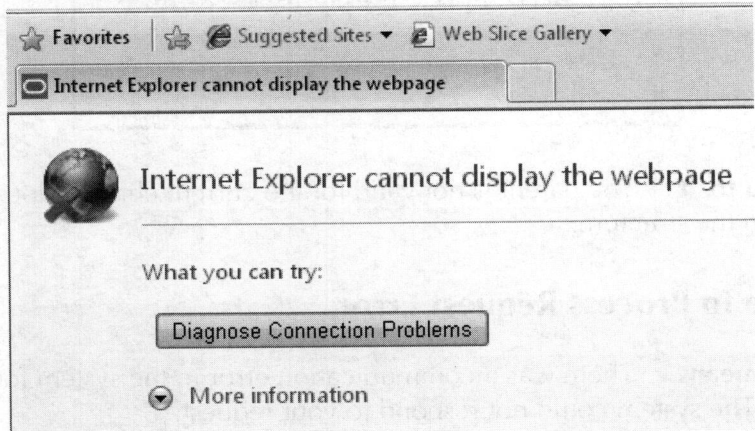

How you fix it Ensure that you have access to the network. If the problem persists, it means the application is down or blocked.

Access Denied

What it means This error will appear when trying to launch HFM. The server is not accessible. This does not mean the users' access, but a problem with access between the EPM servers. If this issue is sporadic, ask the Windows Server administrator to look at the Windows System messages for sporadic DCOM errors on each of the servers. If these are visible, there is a common fix for the Windows operating system, which is documented in the HFM readme file.

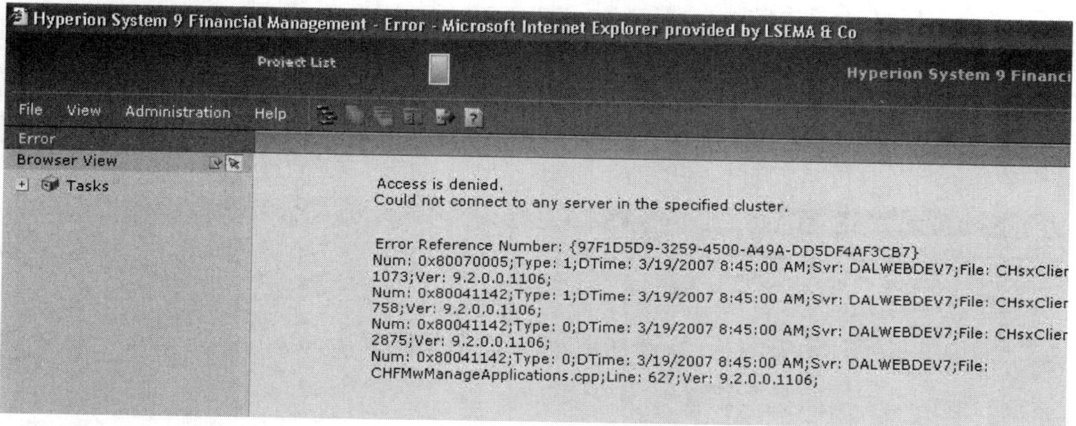

How you fix it This is a technical issue; the IT department needs to review security for changes.

Cannot Configure System Error

What it means This error can appear when trying to access HFM. The system configuration has changed.

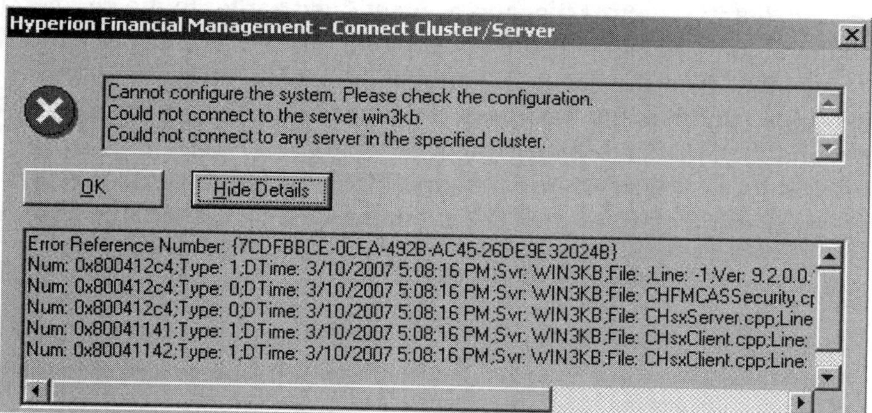

How you fix it Contact the IT group so they can confirm changes with the configuration and setup.

Translation Error Running ICP Report

What it means This error appears when running the ICP report. This means there is an issue with the translation required for the ICP report.

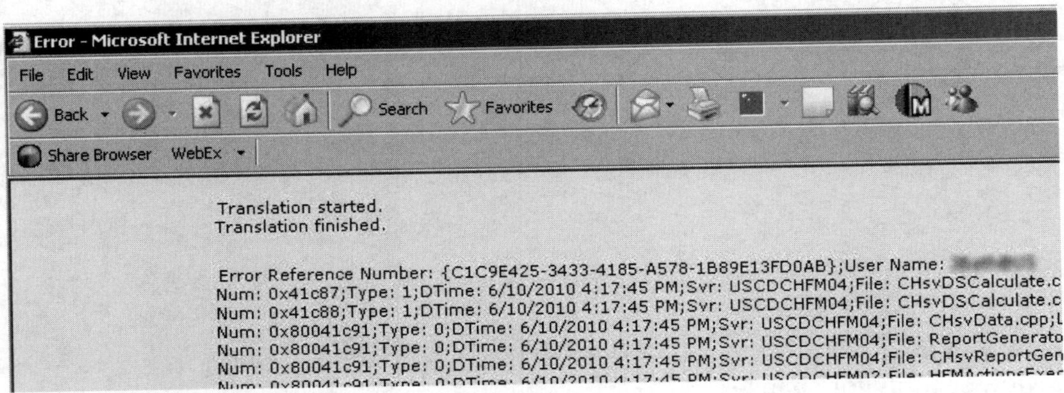

How you fix it There is an error in the Sub Translate section of the rules.

HSV Event Errors and Codes

The HSV event log is a text file, and as mentioned earlier in the chapter, is very difficult to read. Figure 6-6 is a sample of this file. You can see it is not in a format that is easily readable. Fortunately, Oracle provides two tools to help you read and identify the errors: the Financial Management Error Look up tool and the Financial Management Error Log Reader.

The first tool is the HFMErrorLookup.EXE file. When you run this on the server, you can quickly see the HSV event log in a clear, readable format.

```
Information*11*hypfmp*07/24/2007 16:27:50*CPrimaryClusterController.cpp*Line 141
<EStr><Ref>{574D5BB0-50EE-4DFF-B8A2-FE7FEEE744FA}</Ref><User/><DBUpdate>1</DBUpd
*
Warning*11*hypfmp*07/24/2007 16:27:50*CPrimaryClusterController.cpp*Line 1421*<?
<EStr><Ref>{BA29AF54-3420-405C-B6BF-FA86A75EDE66}</Ref><User/><DBUpdate>1</DBUpd
*
Information*11*hypfmp*07/24/2007 16:29:44*CPrimaryClusterController.cpp*Line 281
<EStr><Ref>{759D4499-6BE4-4009-AD2A-96444F9C4BB1}</Ref><User/><DBUpdate>1</DBUpd
*
Warning*11*hypfmp*07/24/2007 16:29:44*CPrimaryClusterController.cpp*Line 2825*<?
<EStr><Ref>{82FD785D-AD3A-4682-8EFB-A8DC398588E3}</Ref><User/><DBUpdate>1</DBUpd
*
Information*11*hypfmp*07/24/2007 16:30:00*CPrimaryClusterController.cpp*Line 141
<EStr><Ref>{D705FD4D-D76A-41B9-912E-C40C91573DB9}</Ref><User/><DBUpdate>1</DBUpd
*
Warning*11*hypfmp*07/24/2007 16:30:00*CPrimaryClusterController.cpp*Line 1421*<?
<EStr><Ref>{0D8E41B8-E1D7-4B91-878E-78DEB5198B8E}</Ref><User/><DBUpdate>1</DBUpd
*
Information*11*hypfmp*07/24/2007 16:30:11*CPrimaryClusterController.cpp*Line 141
<EStr><Ref>{9C3F54D4-D45D-476B-A014-EA202A8AC233}</Ref><User/><DBUpdate>1</DBUpd
*
Warning*11*hypfmp*07/24/2007 16:30:11*CPrimaryClusterController.cpp*Line 1421*<?
<EStr><Ref>{C50FB4E4-C610-4406-AB4E-45C56FD62A42}</Ref><User/><DBUpdate>1</DBUpd
*
```

FIGURE 6-6. *HSV Event log text file*

When you open the log file with the HFMErrorLog Viewer, you see each message by type with a summary and date. Figure 6-7 is a sample file with errors. Along the toolbar are some common options, like New and Print. There are also some uncommon buttons, but they serve an important purpose like connecting to HFM. You can filter by messages, warnings, and errors. Messages are identified by the comment icon, with the exclamation point. Warnings are the yellow triangle with an exclamation point. Errors are identified with a red circle and white X.

When you have an error, you may find that you are getting a code that begins with "0x8004." It is not possible to know what all these numbers mean, so Oracle provides the Financial Management Error Lookup tool. When you enter the code, it returns a plain English explanation of the issue. It does not necessarily tell you what is the cause or resolution of the issue.

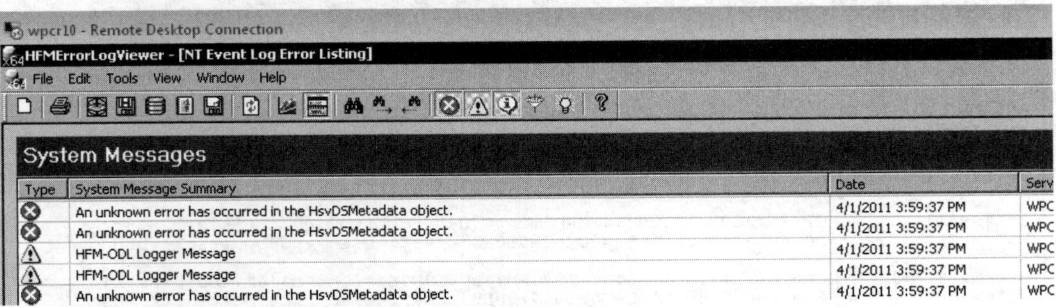

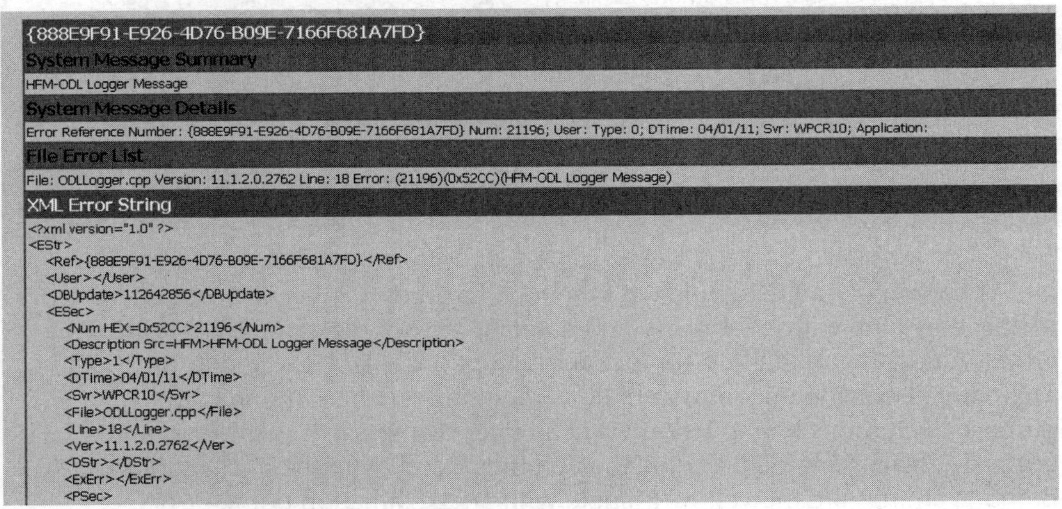

FIGURE 6-7. *HFMErrorLog Viewer*

Figure 6-8 shows what the tool will look like on your screen. There are many errors for which this tool will not provide an explanation. Those errors are very generic and often hard to diagnose. Appendix A provides a full list of the errors this tool would return.

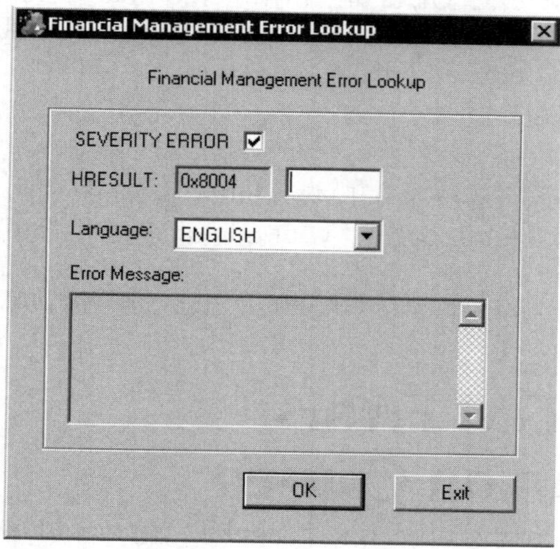

FIGURE 6-8. *Financial Management Error Lookup window*

0x80042080

An unknown error has occurred in the {HFM_EXCLUDE}HsvDSDataCubes2{/HFM_EXCLUDE} object.

What it means This error usually means the Background POV is not valid, and this can happen when you copy an application.

How you fix it This is a technical issue, and requires support to update the SQL tables.

0x80045E95

The installed version of {HFM_EXCLUDE}DB2{/HFM_EXCLUDE} does not meet the requirements for this version of {HFM_EXCLUDE}Financial

Management{/HFM_EXCLUDE} and the Intercompany Transaction module. The IC database objects will not be created. {HFM_EXCLUDE}DB2{/HFM_EXCLUDE} version detected:{HFM_EXCLUDE} %0{/HFM_EXCLUDE}

0x80040e57

The user is unable to log on to HFM and they get the following error: ""An error has occurred. Please contact your administrator" "String or binary data would be truncated."

Usernames are limited to less than 64 characters in HFM.

Oracle FDM Errors and Common Causes

While the purpose of this book is to cover HFM, it would be a mistake not to talk about some common FDM errors and tests too. There are very few HFM applications that do not make use of FDM. When used with the functionality of HFM, FDM becomes a very valuable tool. So it would be a mistake not to cover FDM errors and some of the basics. This book cannot cover every issue that you could encounter. It is important to note that most errors are logged to the user error log. This can be found in the Logs directory in the outbox of the application. It is called *UserName*.err. Other log information is also contained in the application log, which is written to an FDM DB table.

This is helpful for the administrator when a user has an error. It can be found for that username in the outbox\logs directory. Any error returned in FDM that includes the text ".cpp" is actually an HFM error that FDM is reporting. This is an indication that the integration to HFM is not working properly.

Some other errors you might or your users might find are described in the following sections.

Error with Import Script

What it means The import script is not correct, or could be related to a change in folder permissions. You should check your scripts assigned to the import format.

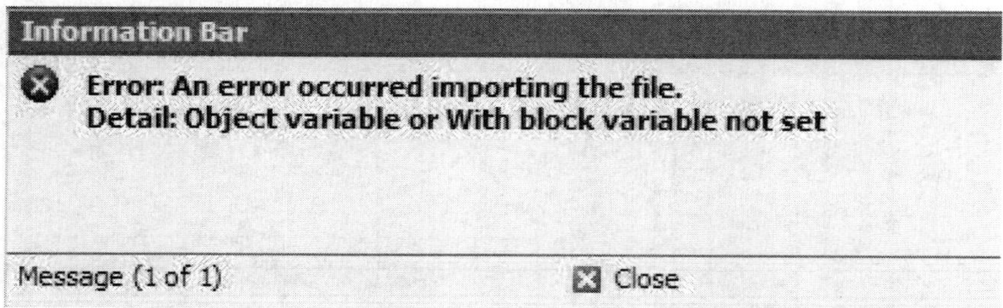

Error When Trying to Validate Data

What it means The FDM application is having a connection issue on the client side. Add FDM to your list of trusted sites.

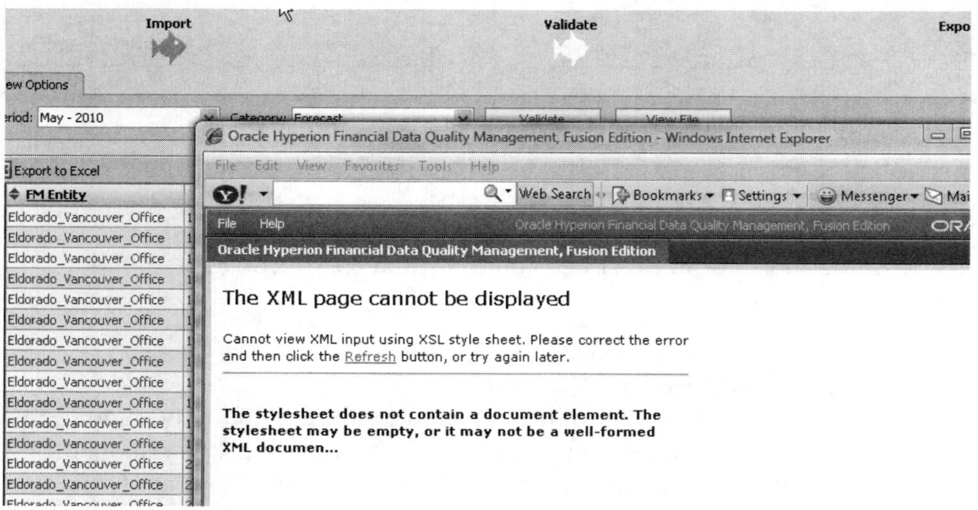

Error with Multi-Load Screen

What it means The Multi-Load screen with Error Check did not load. Update your files to ensure they are correct, and then reload.

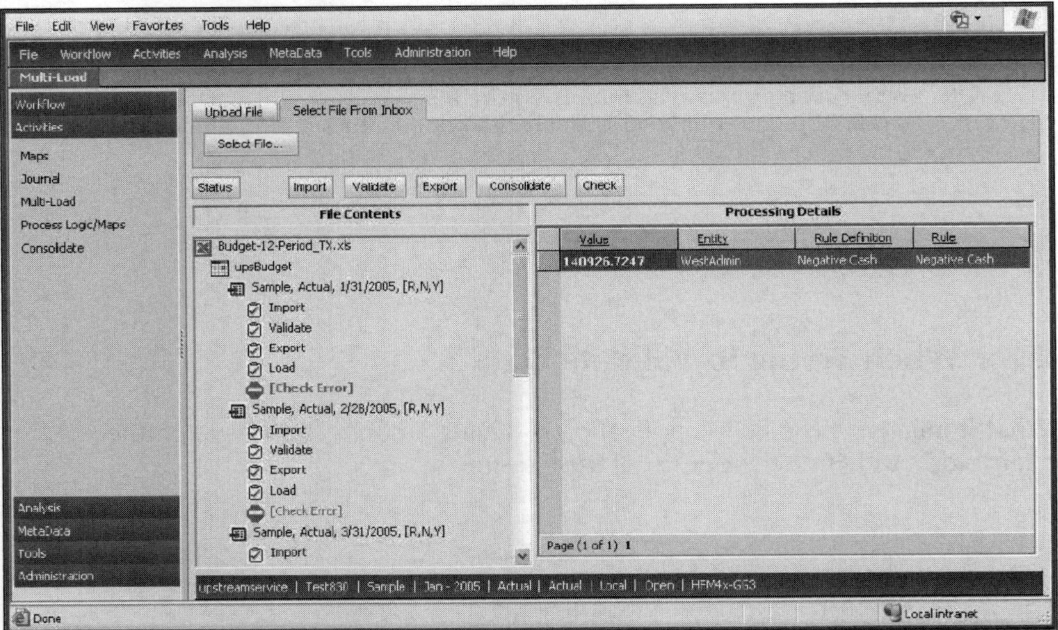

Testing FDM Integration

Some of the most common issues can be isolated by testing some of the basic functions of FDM.

Target Application Integration

Log on to the application, go to the Metadata option in the menu, and then click Control Tables. When you double-click the year, a list of years will drop down. Select a year from the list and click OK. Click Update Grid to save the change. If the years do not populate, you are not able to integrate with HFM from FDM.

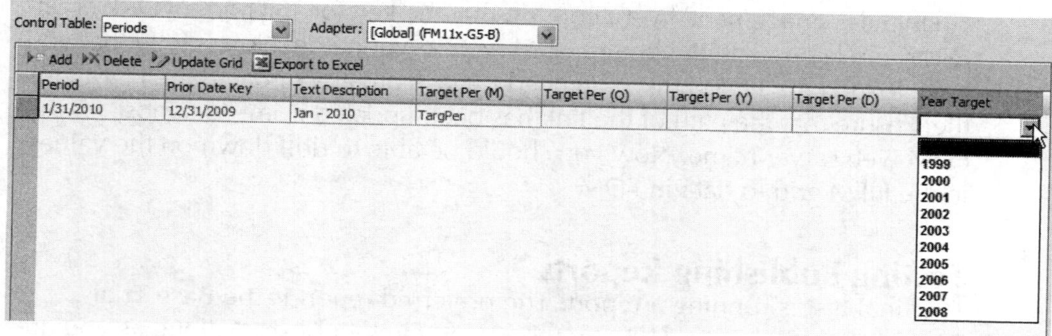

How you fix it If this happens, you need to make sure your integration settings are correct. If you don't find an issue, or changes don't resolve it, then you need to review the System log for DCOM errors. Any DCOM errors would indicate the configuration was done incorrectly during the install. If you have imported multiple adaptors, select the second (and subsequent) adaptor from the Adaptor drop-down. Confirm that the list of years populates for that adaptor.

Testing Export to Excel

The next test is to verify that the Export To Excel functionality is working properly. First, you should click the Export to Excel button at the top of the grid, and save to the desktop. If the Export process appears to hang, either the Excel installation was never initialized, or Smart View is active for the FDM service account.

Testing Workflow

You should next test the workflow. This is simply seeing the data file you are submitting migrate through the Workflow menu. Simply import a file, then click the area under Validate. The intersection validation report will display in a new window. There should also be a white fish icon under Validate.

Testing Drillback

To test HFM drillback, first confirm that the registry is properly updated on the HFM app server. Under HKLM\Software\Hyperion Solutions\Hyperion Financial Management\Web, confirm that the key for "HyperionFDMServer" exists and is populated with the FDM web server name. Next, verify that you have loaded the FDM Link. You need to have already updated the FDM Link file. Ensure that the path of the link has been updated from "localhost" to the FDM web server name. Now you should be able to drill down on the values in the HFM grid to data in FDM.

Testing Publishing Reports

The final test is running a report. The preferred report is the Base Trial Balance Reports. But select any report and click Publish. As long as you are prompted to save the PDF or the report opens in a new window, this test has been passed.

At this point, provided you did not get any application or system errors, you should be confident that FDM is tested and ready to use. These tests are good to run when you are having any issues since they cover the product's core functionality. This helps identify other symptoms that might help isolate the issue.

Relational Database Structure

At the heart of the HFM application is a set of tables that hold the data HFM needs to handle reporting and validations. Understanding these tables, even at a high level, is important to help you maintain the system. There are Data tables, Metadata tables, and System tables.

Data Table Overview

First, you have to understand there are both tables that are specific to the application and tables that are specific to the database. The Data tables contain the data required to configure an application and maintain the financial data pertaining to that application. Data tables have the application name, a three-character designator defining the use of the table, and then the period ID and the year, separated by underscores: for example, "COMMA_DCE_3_2011." Security Tables have a "HSV_" prefix, then the application name, then the table function, separated by underscores: for example, "HSV_COMMA_SECCLASSES." A unique set of data tables exists for each application in the system.

The data tables consist of the following tables:

- DCE (Entity)
- DCN (Node)
- DCT (Transaction)

The DCN and DCE tables contain the dimensions not in the table names, Entity, Value, Account, ICP, Custom1–4. There are two more fields for each period loaded, Input and InputTransType. The dTimestamp field is used to identify the time of the last change. The actual data is stored in a column named "Input." The InputTransType represents a binary flag for the status of the data.

This is another reason for never having a daily application. Let's say an application has 12 periods, and then there would be 12 Input fields named dP0_Input through dP11_Input. However, if there are 365 periods, then there would be 365 Input fields named dP0_Input through dP364_Input.

Line-item Detail and Cell Text Tables

Each of these functions requires tables. The Line Item Detail uses the LID table. And the Cell Text table, which contains cell text information, uses the TXT label. They use the same format as the DEC tables.

Consolidation Status Tables

The consolidation tables consist of the following tables:

- CSE (Entity)
- CSN (Node)
- CONSMETH (Consolidation Method)

The CSE table stores the consolidation data at the entity level. And the CSN table stores the consolidation data at the Node level. Both tables contain one lPer and one dTimestamp for each period in the application.

Since the CSE table could be for any currency, it has a field for currency, And since you need a Parent to identify the Node, the CSN table contains the Parent.

Statutory Consolidation Tables

The Statutory data tables are container tables used to help speed the calculation of data, and they are

- Reports Transaction Data (RTD)
- Reports Transaction Source Data (RTS)
- Entity Transaction Table (ETX)

Journals Tables

Adjustment journals consist of several different tables. They are

- Journals Master/Detail tables
- Journals Templates Master/Detail tables
- Journals Group tables
- Journals Period Status tables

The Journal tables are Scenario-Year–based tables. So this is like the data tables; you could have Actual 2000, 2001, 2002 for the application.

Ancillary Data Tables

The following tables are used to store binary data:

- BINARYFILES
- USERPARAMS
- ATTACHMENTS

Certain data used to operate the system is stored as binary data, for example, application settings, member lists, and rules data. HFM stores each of these as BLOBs (Binary Large Object) in the BINARYFILES table. The USERPARAMS table is just like the BINARYFILES table. However, the USERPARAMS table is used to store user-based information (such as Extended Analytics settings, Web Data Entry Form settings, Web Based Report Files, and so on). The ATTACHMENTS table is a link table used to link documents to specific data cells.

Some other tables are the Reports (RPTS) table, which contains Report Definition information. The Process Flow (PFLOW) table contains the process flow settings. The PARAMETERS table contains the configuration information.

Metadata Tables

The Metadata tables are used to store properties and attributes of each of the 12 POV dimensions. They follow a similar naming convention as the data tables. For example, there are 12 Metadata tables for each application, one for each dimension, so for the COMMA application, you would find a "COMMA_ENTITY_HEADER" table. The POV dimensions are Scenario, Year, Period, View, Entity, Value, Account, ICP, and Custom1 through Custom4.

Each POV dimension has the following four metadata tables associated with it:

- DESC
- HEADER
- LAYOUT
- ITEM

Application Security Tables

All the System tables begin with "HSX_". Then they have some name that describes what they contain. Application tables use the application name as a prefix, followed by the function of the table. For example, the Security tables used to maintain user/group access and rights are stored in the following tables:

- SECCLASSES
- SECCACCCESS

Intercompany Transaction Objects

If an application uses the Intercompany Transaction (ICT) tables and Stored Procedures, the following tables will be included. These ICT tables are new since HFM 4.0.

- The ICT_CURRRATE table stores the mapping of currencies to rates.
- The ICT_ENTITIES table stores map entities to transaction status.
- The HFM_ICT_NUMBERS table only exists in MS SQL Server and IBM DB2 installations and is used to maintain a matching number set used in transactional processing.
- The ICT_PERIODS table stores the mapping of currencies to rates.
- The ICT_REASONCODE table stores custom-defined match reason codes.
- The ICT_SEQUENCE table only exists in MS SQL Server installations and is used to maintain the next unique identifier for IC transactions.
- The ICT_TRANSACTIONS table stores the transaction data.
- The ICT_VERSION table stores and maintains ICT schema version information.

System Table Overview

When a database is first created, a set of common system tables is created for all applications in the database. The Hyperion Financial Management Properties table contains system-wide property settings.

Data Source Table

The DATASOURCES table stores the applications contained in the database.

Clustering Tables

The Clustering tables consist of the following:

- **HSX_CLUSTER_CONT_INFO** The Controller Info table stores each application server that is running an application; an entry exists along with the timestamp of the last time the application server communicated with the database server.
- **HSX_CLUSTER_CONTROLLERS** Contains the App Server that is responsible for maintaining data synchronization.

Activity Tables

The Activity tables consist of the following:

- **HSV_ACTIVITY_KILL_USERS** Tracks user sessions that are to be discontinued.
- **HSV_ACTIVITY_NO_ACCESS** Users who have restricted access to one or all systems and one or all applications.
- **HSV_ACTIVITY_SESSIONS** Tracks active sessions within the system.
- **HSV_ACTIVITY_USERS** Tracks the users of the system.
- **HSV_USERS_ON_SYSTEM** Tracks the users on the system.

Invalid Records

Over time, as metadata is changed, it is possible that records in the database will become invalid. For example, if data is entered for an account, and later after data is loaded to that account, then it is deleted from metadata, all the records for this account will become invalid. The data will continue to survive in the application, but it will not be accessible from the application or any reports. This speeds the metadata updates.

But as your application ages, it is important to periodically delete these invalid records. This should be done after big changes to your system. But it will not remove all of these invalid values. Using Delete Invalid Records will delete invalid members' records but not invalid intersection records. Invalid metadata members are members that existed at some point and had data loaded against them or calculations performed. As in our example earlier, you have an account called WesWelker that records the number of touchdowns. Then you delete the account WesWelker. The number of touchdowns would still be in the database. This could be deleted safely by using Delete Invalid Records. Invalid intersections are intersections of accounts and customs that were valid at one time, populated with data, and now are no longer valid. For example, you add an account called Garnet, and you attached the Custom1 dimension to break out detail, like blocks, steals, and assists. But then you remove that custom dimension. In this case, the members themselves continue to be valid for the application, but the specific intersections are no longer valid. This type of issue happens when either the CustomXTopMember relationship changes or a parent-child relationship changes. You cannot resolve this by using Delete Invalid Records.

If you have performance issues related to these invalid intersections, the only resolution is to rebuild the application. And I do not make this recommendation lightly. It could be significant work, and some process data would be lost. However, the issue will not go away until this is done.

Starting Services

Of all the things you could do to help resolve an issue, sometimes it is just as simple as stopping and starting the servers. You should refer to "Starting and Stopping EPM System Products" in the *Oracle Hyperion Enterprise Performance Management System Installation and Configuration Guide*. This will give you the details that are specific to your version of HFM.

Unfortunately, it is not as easy as flipping a switch. There are some things you need to know when starting and stopping your application services. The first thing is that the main Windows processes of an HFM application server are HsxService.exe, HsxServer.exe, CASSecurity.exe, and HsvDatasource.exe. These are the processes that are running on your server.

When you start your application, a process called HsxService.exe starts and appears in the Windows Task Manager. The HsxServer.exe, CASSecurity.exe, and HsvDataSource.exe processes are also started, but for each application. These will run until all users have completely logged out of the application.

If your application does take a long time to start, you can change the setting of the Windows service for HFM to Started from Automatic. If the Windows Service starts automatically, the application server will prelaunch each application, which will then be "active" and already started when the first user attempts to connect to the application. The reason this is set by default to Automatic is that when you have it set to Started, all applications are running whether they are in use or not. This can consume more resources than you intend.

The reason this can take longer in some applications is that metadata dimensions get very large, when an application server or database is under heavy load, or when the rules file of the application contains a large number of NoInput rules.

CASSecurity.exe is critical, as it serves as an interface between HFM and Shared Services. It handles some of the authorization and authentication processes of HFM, as well as security-related features while the application is running. After changes in the external provider data, users will have to log off and back on to recycle the CASSecurity.exe process.

Sometimes it appears that HFM has frozen or locked up. Forcing a shutdown of the browser does nothing to reset these processes. You should always stop the processes in a very specific order. You should start with stopping the Financial Management Windows Service (HsxService.exe) in the Windows Services. Then for each application, shut down the HsvDataSource.exe. If the HsvDataSource.exe is using high CPU, or consistently for a long time, you will likely find database issues when terminating this process. Finally, stop the CASSecurity.exe process and any HsxServer.exe process. You need to do this process for all servers in your environment, before trying to bring the application back up again.

Life Cycle Management

Life Cycle Management allows you to migrate application components called *artifacts* from one application to another and from one environment to another. Most commonly people group the LCM tasks into eight task groups:

- **Explore and Search Artifacts** The LCM tool provides an interface to explore, view, search, migrate, export, and import artifacts. The application and repository artifacts are grouped into categories so they are easy to filter through.
- **Migrating Security** The LCM Console enables you to bulk-export users, groups, roles, delegated lists, and assigned roles.
- **Migrating Individual Artifacts or Dimensions** The LCM Console functionality allows the administrator to select a single artifact or dimension for export and import.
- **Migrating an Entire Application** The LCM Console functionality allows migrations of artifacts when the source and destination are on the same network. If they are on separate networks, then you can leverage the file system, or you can have two instances of Shared Services communicate to the same file server location.
- **Compare Applications and Folders** Every administrator needs to be able to find differences between two applications. Comparisons can be done at the application level or folder level. You can view these comparisons in the Shared Services Console or save them as a report (CSV file).
- **Migration Status Report** The LCM Console functionality allows you to view the status of your migrations.
- **Saving and Loading Migration Definition Files** The LCM Console functionality allows you to save your definition of your migration as an XML file. This allows you to repeat a migration or run a "lights-out" migration using a third-party scheduler.
- **Application Auditing** The LCM Console functionality records every action that is taken within LCM and logs it to an Audit Report. Administrators can filter the log based on certain criteria and print it.

Here are some things you should be aware of when using LCM:

- LCM doesn't support clusters.
- LCM doesn't support parentheses ( ) in form names.
- LCM doesn't support global variables with limits set in them.
- Report Name Length is a maximum of 131 characters less the folder name.
- Form folders get reordered on migration. You can work around this by manually adding the form folders before importing the forms.
- For reports, you must manually update the data source.
- Members don't come over with certain special characters.

Task Automation

The Task Automation module provides a web-based tool that allows you to create a series of tasks to be run together. When you have commonly done tasks or routinely done processes, a task flow can help you. This tool is very simple to use. You need to go to the menu and select Administration | Manage Task Flows. You can automate the following with Task Automation:

- Allocate
- Calculate
- Calculate Contribution
- Translate
- Consolidate
- Load Journals
- Extract Journals
- Load Data

- Extract Data
- Execute Journal Action
- Extended Analytics
- Process Management Action

A task flow is a series of tasks, which are placed into a "stage." Within each stage, "links" are created to define "actions." For example, some actions assigned to a link might be ending the task flow if an error is encountered, or continuing to the next stage if the stage is completed successfully.

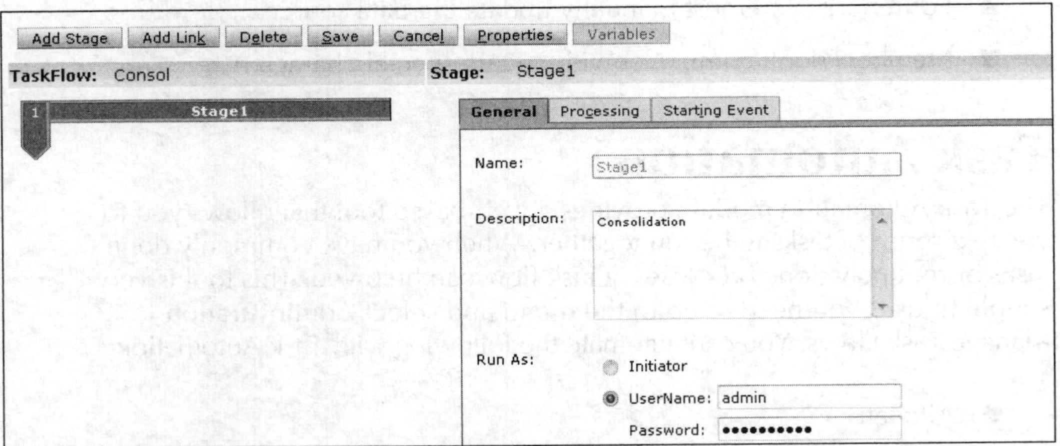

The tip for having task lists you can manage is to start with good naming conventions. As with many other features of HFM, you need to put some thought into the naming convention or maintaining this will be a nightmare for you. As with other labels in HFM, you cannot use any special characters. All of the names should be intuitive, in that they tell you what the stage or link does. Stage and link names are limited to 30 characters. Since only the first few characters appear in the graphics, it is a good idea not to use long prefixes. For example, if you wanted to consolidate actual, you might choose "ACTCons - Consolidate Actuals."

As you add a stage, you will need to define the General, Properties, and Starting Event parameters. The General tab, shown in the previous illustration, allows you to put in your label and description, and also the username and password required to run the task. The Properties tab allows you to create the task.

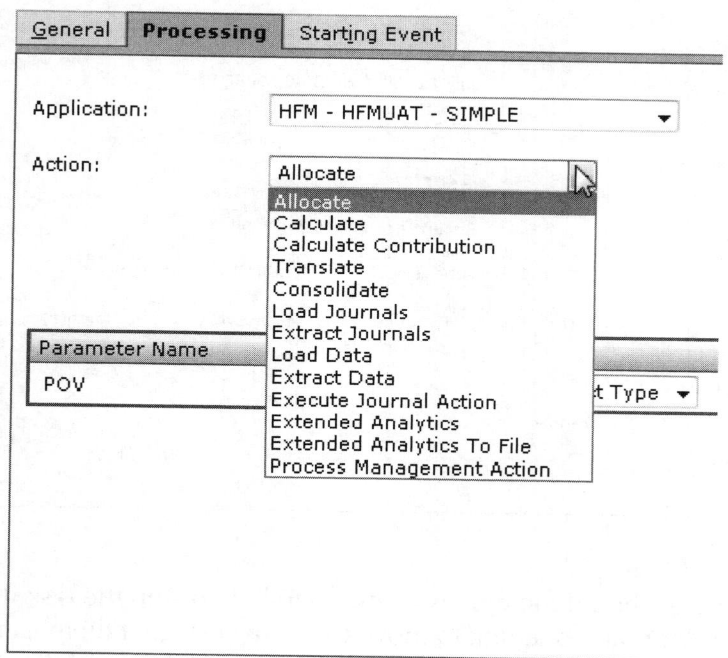

Some tasks require that parameters be defined for them to work correctly. So, when possible use the Edit Text option to create your point of view for your tasks. This is called a "URL," but when you select Edit, you can create this within a graphical interface. The Starting Eventtab allows you to schedule or manually launch the task flow. You would select Disabled from the drop-down menu to run the task list manually. In order to schedule the task, select Scheduled Event from the drop-down menu and fill out the required information.

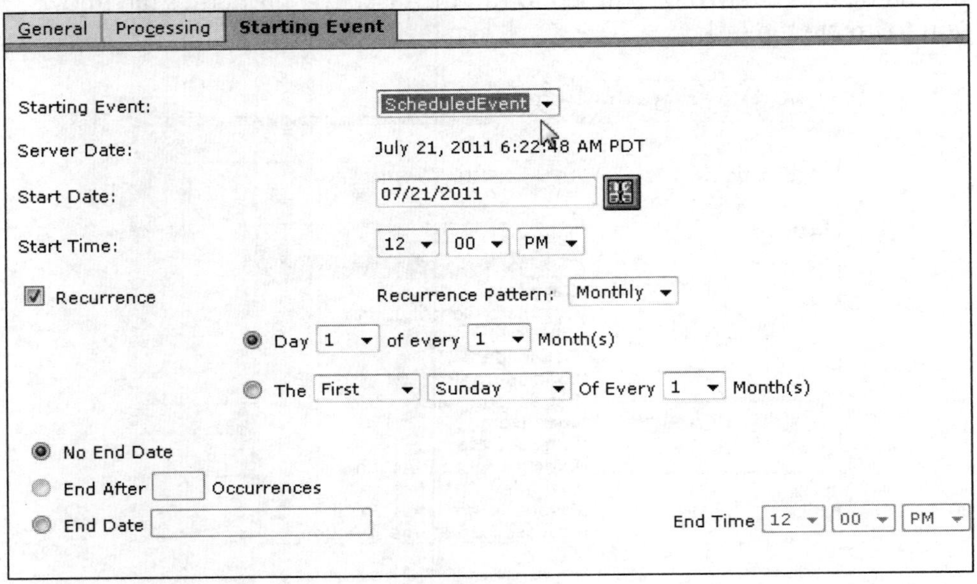

Every stage should include two links: one link to stop the task flow if there is an error, and one link to move to the next stage if there is not an error. The last stage should also have two links to end the task flow, one for if there is an error and one for if there is not an error.

You should add each stage in the order in which you expect them to run, and build your links within those stages. To add a link to a stage, select the stage so that it is highlighted on the screen, and then select the Add Link button.

Since every task flow has a user ID and password that you assign in the first stage, you need to control who can run the task flow. The security section of Task Automation controls who has the rights to run a given task flow.

Other Information Sources

As part of every maintenance agreement, Oracle provides access to information and support to help administer the HFM system. You should keep a local copy of all documentation for the release of your software that you are running with the same version installation files.

- The Installation Documents and Readmes: Installation documentation, new features, known issues, configuration issues, recommendations, and troubleshooting information.
- Product documentation and Administrator and User Guides.
- Oracle support online at the "My Oracle Support" site: https://support.oracle.com.
- Patches and downloads are available from the Patches & Updates tab on My Oracle Support.

Upgrading and Patching Your Application

When you are ready to upgrade your application, you need to start with planning. The most common mistake people make is underestimating the testing effort and project planning. The truth about upgrading an HFM application is that it can be very easy. You have to remember that all the application forms, structures, and rules are stored in the SQL database. So when you upgrade the database, it should have everything you had in your application before you started. Oracle provides a schema update utility that adds the fields or new tables that an upgrade might require. So after the install and the update to the database, you should be done, right? Well, at least you're done with the technical effort. The rest of the project is planning and preparing to support the end users and minimize the impact of the upgrade on them.

You should always start an upgrade by looking at the scope type of the upgrade. As soon as you try to use the upgrade as an opportunity to add new functionality or features, you are adding risk. Consider that you can't do both at the same time; you will upgrade, test, and then make the changes. You really don't get the benefit of using testing to test both the upgrade and new functionality added.

Once you have the scope defined, you need to consider the strategy for moving the hardware. Ask yourself, is this an "in place" upgrade, or will you have new hardware? You need to figure out how the servers will be updated. Consider the time you need to install updates and third-party software. Smart View may need to be updated as well. That will likely require some time to get the new version out to the end users.

And since all of these servers are moving around and getting updated, you will need to have a blackout period on all application changes. You need to have the users—and if possible, all changes—suspended until the work is done. Since you have a good change control process in place, you should be able to manage this easily.

Finally, consider the impact on the end users. Do they need to be trained? What is the impact on their business process? What is the change to the user interface? Most upgrades need some training for the end users. This can be best done by a series of web-based training sessions.

Conclusion

Supporting the application does require some planning and effort. Oracle provides many tools to support you. We covered the best approaches and tools to support the application. You can see how having a change control process will minimize problems. If you are organized, and have the right team in place, it is not overwhelming to support the users.

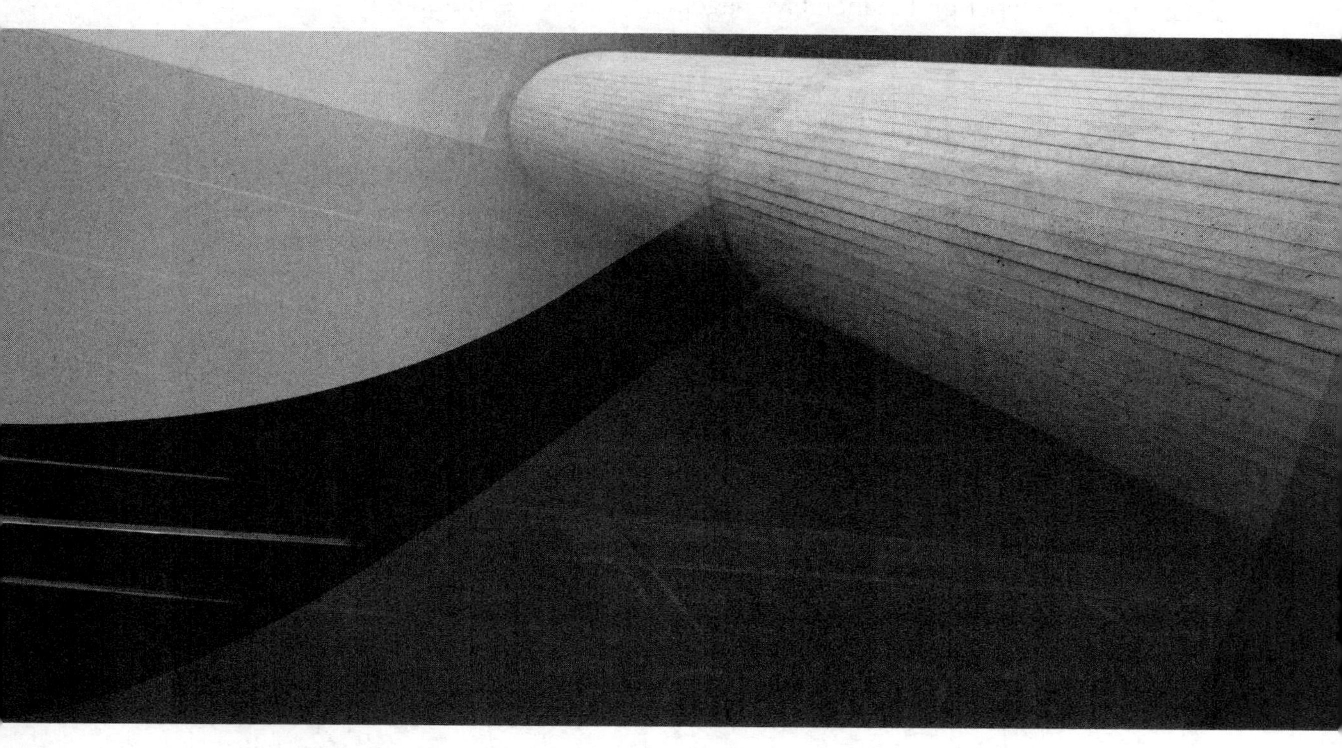

CHAPTER 7

Tuning Your Application

ver time your application may get slow, or freeze, or you may see other issues. If you don't follow best practices, issues are sure to arise. Even when you do all the right things, it is possible for your application to stop performing well. An application that seems to perform well might be tuned to run better. That makes users happier, and helps you extend the investment you have in Financial Management.

First, you need to figure out how you measure performance for the tool. Then you need to understand how the drivers for the components of HFM perform. Once you have an understanding of these two main concepts, you can address concerns that end users have. You will also be able to bring a much deeper understanding to your design and build. Knowing how even a small change can affect performance might help you understand what the full impact of that change would bring to your application.

With something to measure, you can impact the system and see how that metric changes during your test. This type of testing of the application and environment is often referred to as *performance testing*. Performance testing emphasizes a measurable characteristic or function. For example, how fast are consolidations? This is a quantitative test we can measure. This tells us where issues might be, and where to focus our effort to improve the performance of the entire system. Qualitative tests that measure scalability, high availability, and interoperability are sometimes included. When we do these performance tests, we stress the system under an expected load, and then bring it to the breaking point.

There are five areas to look at when troubleshooting an application that is performing poorly:

- **Server capacity** Number of servers, quantity and speed of processors, available memory.
- **Network performance and capacity** Bandwidth, network utilization, and network security.
- **Platform and third-party software** Relational databases, Java application servers, web servers, client/server operating system, and browsers.

- **HFM application design** Subcubes, volumes of data, and rules.
- **Business process** How are the users using the system? We look at three areas here. They are user activity, rate of user activity, and user concurrency.

Understanding Key Performance Drivers

"This seems slow" is not a very helpful comment. It isn't even a problem. It is just a complaint. For anyone in support or consulting, it can be incredibly frustrating. But you have to get past that frustration and uncover the issue. When someone states a complaint, instead of an issue, then it is clear that there is frustration, and some upset about how the application is performing. What is not clear from a statement like that is the cause of that upset. There isn't even a starting point, or any place to go when someone says that. The person supporting that user now has to drill into what the issue is. "What is slow?" "What are you doing?" "Has it been this way for some time?"

"Slow" is a relative term. What is slow for one person might be fine for another. It depends on what they think they should see. What was the system they were using before? What are the expectations? One person might think opening a report in 20 seconds is completely unacceptable, while another will think that is fine.

When you are either supporting users, or logging a case with Oracle support, you need to consider what are the pieces of information that will help them resolve the issue? Relative terms are not a starting point. A specific difference, such as "It used to take ten minutes and now it takes an hour," is so much more helpful. Error messages and logs are other tools. Before you roll out your application, you should gather benchmarks for how the application is expected to perform. Benchmarks are measurements that you can use to compare system performance. You should have a battery of tests that you can run any time.

So what are the things you should measure? This will determine the tests that make the most sense. First, you should test the things that drive the perception and user experience. That starts with the logon. Then you should go from there, and focus on the main tasks, thinking of how your users navigate and operate throughout their use of the application. The main tasks will be as follows:

1. Log on.
2. Open a grid.
3. Open, create, and post a journal.
4. Run rules—for one entity, then all entities, and one period, then all periods:
   - Calculate
   - Translate
   - Consolidate
   - Allocate, IC Transactions, Equity Pickup, other special rules
5. Data loading
6. Extended analytics

You know you have one of six places to look for your issue. As you progress closer to finding the problem, these metrics will allow you to measure success. The rules were "slow." So you ask, "What is slow?" It is running at about 35 minutes for this one entity. You check your baseline, and you see it was 10 minutes when you went live.

So, before you start digging into the issue, you must establish a baseline. The problem might be a changed web setting, data explosion, or zeros in the database, but first have the information that will help you identify where to look. The baseline for data and rules will help you see the impact of your data set and rules. Consider running these tests when the application is at its best. What was the application doing when it was implemented? If you rolled out an application with consolidation times of 45 minutes, it might not interest you that it now takes 55 minutes. I can tell you there are people who would find 55-minute consolidations completely unacceptable. It is a good practice to record these times in your testing documentation.

So if these times are slow, you need to know what your options are for improving performance. The volume of data is a significant driver on the performance of the application. Refer to the discussion of subcubes in Chapter 3. The size of that cube, even with all the enhancements and memory management Oracle has added, drives many of the tasks listed earlier.

The reality is that you are unlikely to change your data set for an application that is either far along in the build, or rolled out to end users. You also likely don't want to lose any functionality or reports. So what are the levers you can pull to change the application or improve how it is performing? I can tell you most applications have consolidation times between 15 and 45 minutes, to consolidate one period of data. With over 100 applications I have personally worked on, all have fallen into that range. It is not a bad thing when it does take longer than 45 minutes to consolidate. If you absolutely need the data that pushed the application to even an hour or two, then you may have to look elsewhere to improve the application. It is not wrong to have a large application, but you should just have a valid business reason for it. You don't want to have the machine cranking away while the user is waiting for no good reason. And you must make sure the users of the system have a reasonable expectation. Now, if you have components of your reporting that are optional, you might consider removing them. There might be better tools than HFM for what you are trying do. You could remove that tax provision from the application, if it drops your consolidation times by 15 percent.

Rules are a significant driver on the performance of the application. Not understanding the use of Dynamic Consolidation members and using consolidation rules, when they are not needed, will add at least 10 percent to your consolidation times. One poorly written rule could cause data explosion. If you had a rule like HS.Exp "A#ALL = 4" in your file, you would fill your database with garbage data that served no purpose but to slow the system and frustrate your users. The rules baseline you should take is to run a full consolidation with "no rules." This is not doing any calculations at all, but instead running the system with the default rules for both translation and consolidation. So when we say "no rules," a more accurate statement might be "no custom rules."

Typically we see most HFM applications consolidate between 0.25 and 2.0 seconds per entity. There should be some specific reason for applications that take on an average 10 seconds and higher per entity. It's possible that the data volumes are high, the rules are inefficient, or there are a large number of complex rules to meet the business's needs. If you don't think you have anything particularly complex or involved, then you likely have an issue.

Using a Reference Application

What if you didn't know to run these baseline tests before you had the problem? You didn't have time, or just didn't think it was a good idea at the time. You always have the option of using a reference application. A reference application is simply a sample application you can run by comparison to your application. When troubleshooting issues within an application, you can use a reference application to help determine how yours is performing by comparison. There are some great sample applications in the folder called Sample Apps. That might be a good place to start. You will not see every issue or problem in any one application. But having an application that you know should perform a specific way removes application design from the list of possible issues. This will let you focus on hardware and the network. Or if you made a change to your application and it seems to cripple your application, then try it in the reference application, and see if the impact is the same. If the reference application is having the same problem as your production environment, maybe it is not the application, but the environment.

Identifying and Resolving Problems

If you can eliminate possible causes of an issue, then you can narrow down what the cause could be. If I can remove environment, network, third-party software, and so on, as possible causes, I can narrow down what needs to be done to resolve the issues with my system.

Can you see the error happen when you do something in the system? Can you re-create the issue? Does the error happen in both development and production? The more variables you can take to form the equation, the easier it is to resolve the issues. You should know what your users are running for operating system, web browser, and everything they could be running on their machines. In fact, it is helpful when a company has a strict installation policy. Sometimes you have people who are reporting issues, and complaining that the application is slow or unresponsive. If you are lucky enough to see what they are using their machine for, you find a rat's nest of software, plug-ins, and junk software installed.

During a project you may consider creating an end-user survey. This helps you gather and inventory the user systems, contact information, locations, and other valuable information. This will help not only with planning on the project, but rolling out updates and planning outages. It is a good practice to follow.

Oracle support can be a valuable tool in working through an issue. I am surprised how many people who pay for maintenance often ignore and have an issue with their database will not call Oracle support for help. Earlier in the chapter I explained the value of a reference application. The Oracle support team will often try to re-create the issue you are having, to help work through it. This is a valuable exercise too. Always read the Readme, the installation documentation, and the extensive additional documentation Oracle provides. Also, review the posts in the forums for more information.

There are some steps you can work through when first troubleshooting an issue, to help gather the information that will help you isolate the issue:

- Is the problem single user or multiuser? Is it during a certain time of day?
- Benchmark everything based on a single-user consolidation. If the problem is multiuser only, could the issue be overlapping consolidations?
- Confirm that the latest service fix or pack has been applied. Ensure that no new updates have been made to third-party software.
- Verify that every piece of software is using the correct supported version.
- Make sure that antivirus software is not being run against the database objects or files.

- Avoid running backups during consolidations.
- Firewalls between the tiers may present problems for DCOM.
- Check the event logs to see if database connections are being created or re-created.
- Review the metadata of the application and compare to best practices defined in this book.
- Rules can be the greatest source of performance problems.
- Look at the event log for signs of problems.
- Zeros cause unnecessary calculations and increase the size of the database.

Server Capacity

When sizing your hardware, it is critical that you identify and consult with a qualified Oracle infrastructure consultant. This should be someone who has done several installations, not someone who just works with Oracle generally, but the Hyperion products suite specifically. The installation process has become more and more complex over time and should not be viewed as "just another install." There are many issues and problems you can encounter, and it is helpful to have a knowledgeable person to guide you through the first installations.

When sizing your hardware, if you had to pick one place where you would not want to skimp, it would be the application server. The application server is the workhorse for HFM. It does all of the work, handling security, managing the subcubes, generating forms, and so on. For example, the HFM consolidation performance is directly linked to the speed of the processor along with the amount of memory required for caching on the application server. The server's memory and processors will draw the most scrutiny when anyone is designing or reviewing the hardware. Hardware has individual performance characteristics and when combined can be configured in ways that change those characteristics. A good infrastructure consultant will specify what hardware you should use down to the CPU level. Most configurations will assume physical environments.

If you are considering virtualized environments, the CPU and memory requirements need to be met on a one-for-one ratio between virtual and physical servers; otherwise, you can expect worse performance than a comparable physical environment.

Memory Requirements

So do you have enough memory on your application server? How much do you really need? Since the creation and use of the subcubes is what drives this, you need to look at the size and number of those cubes. While it is very difficult to know exactly what the number will be, you can estimate the number of cubes, then the size of those cubes.

You can start by looking at the sizes of the subcubes of your application. You can do this by calculating the number of records for each combination of account, ICP, and Custom 1 through 4. You can look at these same dimensions for the top entity. This should be your most dense subcube, meaning that the top entity will have more intersections of data populated than any other entity. Since the data records are what drive the size of the subcube, this will be the largest. This is a good number to know.

Now you can take the number of populated intersections, and multiply that by 120 bytes. That is the size of that subcube. Once you have a good sample of subcube sizes, you can then estimate the average size of those cubes. Ideally, you want to imagine the worst case, that all cubes would be in memory at the same time. Those cubes would be created for each value dimension they are viewed in; at a minimum, Entity Currency, Parent Currency, Proportion, and Contribution. Cubes would be created for each combination of the Year and Scenario. So, if you have three years of Actual data and two years of Budget, then you would have five Year and Scenario combinations. If you take this number of subcube records multiplied by bytes, multiplied by the number of cubes created, you are left with a large number of bytes. Convert this to the amount of RAM required to store that much data.

Data should be in HFM's cache, and also in the database server's cache. Whenever the data is not in cache at the time a user needs it, whether for reporting, data entry, load, or consolidation, the server must take time to get this data and bring it into the cache.

Memory and 64-bit Software

The term "64-bit" refers to a class of memory and architecture and the software that runs on them. In a 32-bit Windows environment, each server process has access to only 2GB of the 4GB virtual address space. The Windows operating system usually reserves a portion, 2GB by default. You can reduce the amount of memory Windows has access to to 1GB, leaving 3GB for HFM. However, even if a machine has more than 4GB of virtual memory, no more than 3GB will be available for any given single process.

In 64-bit systems, this restriction is practically nonexistent (for now). This "new" architecture (super-computers in the '70s took advantage of 64-bit architecture) has such a high memory limit that most processors cannot currently access such a limit of memory.

Since memory is so important for HFM, this is good news for the larger applications. Since subcubes are what drive the application performance, and if they are in memory they can be accessed quickly and efficiently, it would make sense that the more we can load into RAM, the better the HFM experience would be for the users. This is less exciting for users who have no plans to reach the limits of the 32-bit application. As long as the memory footprint fits in the 32-bit address space, then the Financial Management's server memory will hold all necessary records of the subcubes in memory. Then there would be little benefit for those applications to move to 64-bit.

But possibly you are reading this section of the book because you are at that limit. Or perhaps you have already blown by those limits and are looking for some relief. Consider the size and number of your subcubes. Are you there? Is it a problem that you think moving to 64-bit will address? You may have reasonably sized subcubes and many users. Or you may have few users, but very large cubes.

It is possible that you went ahead and built a weekly application, even after I told you in this book that was a really bad idea. But if you did and you are struggling, you would certainly benefit from having a 64-bit application.

Another benefit of moving to a 64-bit application, if you have an application with this large memory footprint, is that these applications will rely more on a caching file, and shift the memory requirements to the disk and database. This will put a burden on the network and the relational database server.

Available Physical Memory	MaxNumDataRecordsinRAM	MaxDataCacheSizeinMB
4 GB	4,000,000	500
8 GB	10,000,000	1500
16 GB	30,000,000	4500
32 GB	60,000,000	9000

FIGURE 7-1. *Memory settings*

Financial Management's default memory settings are optimized for the small- to medium-size applications that would take advantage of a 32-bit environment. The majority of applications will not need to change this setting. If you did move to 64-bit, you would need to make some registry changes. The relevant registry settings are MaxNumDataRecordsInRAM and MaxDataCacheSizeinMB, which need to be created or changed in [HKEY_LOCAL_MACHINE\SOFTWARE\Hyperion Solutions\Hyperion Financial Management\Server] in each application server's Windows registry. Figure 7-1 shows suggested settings from Oracle for these settings. If you are planning on running multiple applications on the server, then you need to divide the Total Physical Memory installed on the server by the number of Financial Management applications to determine the "Available Physical Memory" for each application.

Maintaining Your Registry

The registry contains key settings that determine how the HFM applications run. Earlier we discussed the memory settings. One word of caution: changing these settings is not for the faint of heart. Oracle's default setting works well for the vast majority of applications. You should only plan to make any changes to the registry with the direct help or supervision of a certified expert in these parameters. You should absolutely make sure you follow good change control procedures and test thoroughly any change you make to your application.

The following are the default settings in the Registry.

MaxNumDataRecordsInRAM Determines the maximum number of records that can be maintained in RAM.

HKEY_LOCAL_MACHINE\SOFTWARE\Hyperion Solutions\Hyperion Financial Management\Server

- **Value:** MaxNumDataRecordsInRAM
- **Type:** DWORD
- **Data:** 1000000 (Decimal) (default setting)

MinDataCacheSizeinMB This setting represents the minimum size of the data cache in megabytes. A higher number for this setting will reduce the number of DataCache growth attempts and hence reduce memory fragmentation. Typically it will grow 25MB maximum at a time.

HKEY_LOCAL_MACHINE\SOFTWARE\Hyperion Solutions\Hyperion Financial Management\Server

- **Value:** MinDataCacheSizeInMB
- **Type:** DWORD
- **Data:** 130 (Decimal) (default setting)

MaxDataCacheSizeInMB This setting represents the maximum amount of memory that the Financial Management application server will allocate to store the cell values and cell status. If more memory is required by the system, then the cell value and cell status will be paged out to disk based on least recently used (LRU) logic. If you are experiencing performance issues because of paging, you can increase MaxDataCacheSizeInMB to minimize paging. This value should be more than the total memory usage allowed by MaxNumDataRecordsInRAM, so that the system does not page out the cells to disk unnecessarily. If you set MaxDataCacheSizeInMB too low, you will run out of memory required to store data records and begin paging.

HKEY_LOCAL_MACHINE\SOFTWARE\Hyperion Solutions\Hyperion Financial Management\Server

- **Value:** MaxDataCacheSizeInMB
- **Type:** DWORD
- **Data:** 260 (Decimal) (default setting)

MaxNumCubesInTemporaryCache (0–10000, default 100) This setting is the maximum number of subcubes kept in memory during data retrieval (grids, WDEFs, reports, and so on). If you have very dense cubes, you can lower this number to alleviate high memory usage during data retrieval (WDEFs, grids, reports). Consolidations are not affected by this parameter. This setting applies to Releases 11.1.1.3, 9.3.1.4, and 9.2.1.2 only.

MaxNumCubesInRAM (100–500000, default 30000) This setting is the maximum number of subcubes that can be held in memory at any given time. You can lower this setting to help with high memory usage for sparse applications. This setting applies only to Releases 11.1.2 and 9.3.3.

MaxNumConcurrentConsolidations This setting controls the number of concurrent consolidations allowed per application server. This can be set from 1 to 8; additional consolidations above this number are queued in the system.

NumConsolidationsAllowed This setting controls the number of consolidations allowed per application across all the application servers. The default value is 8 and the range is 1 to 20.

Network Performance and Capacity

If you are experiencing issues running your HFM application over the network, you can take steps beyond increasing the bandwidth to improve performance. I can tell you there are several applications that work all over the world, and work well. If you are having network issues, they can be resolved if you have the skills in-house, and the will to resolve them.

One of the ways you can help the HFM application is to use compression. For the less tech-savvy, think of the application "zipping" a file, making the amount of data transferred much smaller than it would be otherwise. If this is such a good idea, then why not use it all the time, right? Well, because it does take some effort to compress those files. If you have a very slow network, or limited bandwidth, you would see a benefit of compression because the trade-off would be less. So for that reason, if you are using HFM over a LAN, it is not recommended to enable compression/caching for HTTP servers. It is only recommended to enable compression/caching when EPM applications are used over a WAN and remote users are accessing from high-latency locations.

Platform and Third-Party Software

First, do not let Windows tell you what you should be doing. It is not uncommon for a new patch or security fix to be released even though it has not yet been thoroughly tested against the EPM product suite. And unless you have some desire to be part of the beta team for this testing, you should wait until you know the impact. Problems are not that common, but when they happen, it is usually bad. One release comes to mind right away. When Internet Explorer 8 was released, it was pushed on the user community as a "critical update," and was part of the auto-update feature in Windows. The update for IE8 was not a small change, like many of the security updates that preceded the release. It was a major change to how the browser worked. This change caused problems with many web sites and tools. The EPM suite was no exception and did not work completely in IE8. Unfortunately, it was very difficult to roll back to an earlier version of IE. So people were forced to install and use Mozilla Firefox until an upgrade to the newer version or patch could be installed. It was a mess for many people.

Do not turn "Automatic Updates" on—this can lead to undesirable results (that is, an outage, error messages, and performance issues). You should leverage your environments to make updates (Windows patches, utility patches/updates). They should be applied in a standard testing order, and follow your change control, just like everything else—DEV, QA, PROD.

If you are very concerned about a patch, you could patch both DEV and QA immediately, then aggressively test, then patch PROD when the DEV and

QA testing has been completed. You should not expect that Oracle would be able to test and validate every version, patch, and release. The volume of changes to all of the software that interacts with the Oracle software is too great for even a company the size of Oracle to thoroughly test and certify everything. Oracle publishes the supported platforms for each new release, and service fixes are also supported as long as the third-party vendor asserts full backward compatibility. Regardless, you should test each new service fix and service pack before applying the same change into production. That is true if they come from Oracle or a third party.

When running virus software, you should avoid scanning the entire Hyperion directory (on all of the Hyperion servers). You should be sure to schedule your scans to occur at periods of low usage or outage time periods. Some people have experienced situations where the antivirus program has contended with the Hyperion software.

Oracle HFM Application Design

It is important to make sure that your application follows the principles of good design. If you are still having issues, you have options to fine-tune the application and its features.

Subcubes as described earlier in Chapter 3 are critical to a well-performing Financial Management. Subcubes impact just about everything that HFM does, including grids, forms, reports—everything. Processing through subcubes happens while they are stored in memory, so the larger the subcube, the bigger the hit on performance.

Rules that are poorly written will do more to kill HFM performance than just about anything else. One of the biggest problems with rules is that they rely so much on the data set they are running on. So you can test and validate with your data continuously, but not capture every possible error. Some rules are poorly written, and will still perform well because the data set does not expose the problem. Rules can also create zeros that can fill and choke the database over time. These zeros increase the size of the subcubes.

When possible, migrate ratios and simple calculations to the Dynamic section of the rules. Not only do these rules work better for calculating totals, but they are not part of the consolidation. Let's say, something like a set of metrics for a couple dozen ratios, but for 500 products, and for 100 regions in your customs. You could be generating hundreds of thousands of records you don't have to store. If you have many of these calculations, you can see some benefit of taking the calculations and data out of the system.

Rules, as powerful and dynamic as they are, can populate many more intersections than you intend. This is called data explosion, and it is bad. Often the only way to completely resolve the issue is to rebuild the application or have a very experienced person work through the tables.

You should periodically look at the base data and top entity extracts of data and ensure that you do not have more than 10 percent of the data populated as zeros. When you do, you likely will have some issue with either loading zeros, or rules loading zeros to the system. Loading to or calculating zeros in a Financial Management application is absolutely not recommended. Zeros are stored as data, and they will take space up in the database, which increases the database size and can affect performance.

If you do not require the Data Audit feature, you might want to consider turning it off. If the Data Audit table is larger than 10GB, then you can see performance issues with your HFM application. Alternatively, you can take measures to maintain the tables. They should be truncated, and if you wish to store the history, then save that outside the HFM database.

Another issue occurs when HFM is not properly shut down. Temporary files may remain after reboot. To maintain peak performance, it is recommended that you delete all *.db.* file names from the Financial Management Server Working folder before launching Financial Management.

It is a good idea to watch the size of your HsvEventLog.Log file. This text file is under the HFM application server's \Hyperion\logs\hfm folder. You should occasionally take that file and archive it. When you remove the file, HFM will create a new one when it finds it is missing. There are tables in HFM that need to be actively maintained—the error log, task audit, and data audit. You can refer to Chapter 6 for more information about maintaining these tables. But you should know that as they grow, they require more resources to open and write to.

You should never use Consolidate All. When you choose this consolidation option, HFM ignores the status flags and will change entities' status from NODATA to OK. Why is this a problem? Well, whenever you run another consolidation, you will run it on entities that do not require consolidation and will have rules running, which can inadvertently create zeros in the database. Consolidate All should be secured so that only a limited number of people can use this feature. Consolidate should be used most of the time, and it is the most efficient, because only entities that require logic or consolidation are updated by the system. The Consolidate All with Data option should only be used to change status from OK SC to OK after metadata and rule changes.

If you are using Lifecycle Management (LCM) and experience an out-of-memory exception in the Internet Information Services (IIS) web server, then open IIS and change the following settings for HFMLCMservice:

1. Right-click on HFMLCMService Application Pool and open the Properties page.
2. Select the Recycling tab, and under Memory Recycling, set these values:
   - Maximum virtual memory (in megabytes): 1000
   - Maximum used memory (in megabytes): 800
3. Click the Health tab and change the Shutdown time limit to 10800 seconds (3 hours).
4. Click on Apply, then OK to close the Properties page.
5. Perform an IIS reset.

It is actually fairly unusual for an application to have table structure issues, unlike HFM's predecessor, Hyperion Enterprise. Hyperion Enterprise (HE) used a proprietary flat-file database, and only in later versions was enabled for SQL. HE was not known for a robust integration with SQL. HFM was built to work with SQL, and it does so very well. But in cases when you have issues, Oracle provides an index utility that will inspect the indexes on the database tables. The utility will examine the indexes on the database tables and compare them against the required indexes. You may want to use this tool after a database migration, database restore, or some other task where the validity of the indexes may be in question.

The index update utility operates in three modes. The first is to examine the existing database table indexes in a Financial Management application and generate a report outlining any potential problems that may exist. The second option will generate a report and a file of SQL commands to drop and re-create any possibly missing or incorrect indexes. The third mode generates a report and instantly executes the commands to drop and re-create indexes.

You should avoid having entities with a single child. That means you should not have an entity with one entity as a child. When you do this, you create places where duplicate data is created, and that will take time to consolidate and will take space in the database. Even when the parent entity and child are of different currencies, you will have nodes of the Value dimensions that overlap. When a single parent-and-child entity is of the same currency, it will contain the exact same data. There is no difference between the data in the entities.

When you are pulling values forward from a prior month, you need to identify the correct scenario, account, and so on. People often forget here that pulling the right scenario is just as important. A commonly used approach is the use of a dynamic variable called the "source_value." This variable would change depending on the current point of view. If you are at Entity Currency, you would want to pull forward Entity Currency Total, so you can capture all journals made in the prior year. If you were at the Parent Currency, you would want to pull forward the Parent Currency Total, so you would capture journals there. So let's say your point of view is Entity Currency, and you determined that at the beginning of your rule file by using a variable called "pov_value." As you look at Figure 7-2, you can see how the value in "pov_value" variable determines what is to be used in the "source_value."

Once you have determined the source value, you can use it within the rules to make sure the same rule will pull from the correct source value dimension. Here is an example of a simple line of code with the "source_value".

```
Hs.Exp "A#BegRE = A#EndRE.P#Last.Y#Prior" & source_value
```

The other benefit of using of the "source_value" variable is that values in journals from the prior year do not need to be pulled forward in the "ADJ" value members. Since the adjustment members of the Value dimension will

```
'****************************************************************************
'Many calculations are run at the entity and parent level.  We typically write
' rules to populate the <Entity Currency> and <Parent Currency>.  The issue is
' that the data that we want to draw from is in the <Entity Curr Total> and
' the [Parent Total].  These statements help to determine the right hand side
' of the equation.

'If at the Entity Currency
If pov_value = "<Entity Currency>" Then

    'Make the data source Entity Currency Total
    source_value = ".V#<Entity Curr Total>"

    source_valueUSD = ".V#USD Total"

'If at Parent Currency
ElseIf HS.Value.IsTransCur = True Then

    'This determines what currency we are translating to at the moment
    translate_to = HS.Value.Currency

    'Take the currency (like USD) and add Total to back to get the new
    ' source ie: USD becomes .V#USD Total
    source_value = ".V#" & translate_to & " Total"

'If at the Proportion node
ElseIf pov_value = "[Proportion]" Then

    'Make the data source the Contribution Total
    source_value = ".V#[Contribution Total]"

End If  'Value
```

FIGURE 7-2. *Source value*

not run any rules until a journal is loaded, or a Force Calculate is run, this can be very helpful. If you need journal data to be pulled forward, but don't want to worry about the adjustment members being excluded, this is a good rule to have.

But with every benefit there is often a cost. This is no exception. When you have the source_value variables, you must use Consolidate All with Data whenever journal entries are made. The Consolidate All with Data option will ignore the status flags of the entities as long as they have data, and will consolidate those members. This is required because of the order of operations in rules within the value dimension, since the source value is pulling from the Total members of the Value dimension. The issue is that after data is loaded and a consolidation is performed, data in all entities, all value dimension nodes, would be "OK." If later someone posted a new journal entry, a normal Consolidate would only run rules on the affected <Entity Curr Adjs> nodes, and *not* the <Entity Currency> nodes. The rule that is pulling from Entity Currency Total is in Entity Currency, so it would not update. Only by running a Consolidate All with Data when using "source_value" would you be able to ensure that the rules are updating correctly.

Finally, pay attention to the size of documents you attach to your cell. Oracle recommends that you attach no more than three documents to a cell, and that each document be smaller than 100K.

Identifying Design Issues

If you had a good design to begin with, this may be less of an issue. Often there are changes or updates you could not have known about, but were added to the application along the way. It can create problems. The trick to identifying design issues is simple. It is simply to evaluate the impact of any change on the size of the subcube and the rules.

Each change should be reviewed with a discriminating eye. Ask these questions:

- What will this do to the size of our subcubes?
- Do we need this?
- Will we be writing many values to the database?

Most companies require a change control process, but even if you don't have one, you should consider taking the time to go through one for an evaluation. Then you can put concrete answers to these questions.

I would also recommend following the guidelines in Chapter 2.

Identifying Rule Issues

The rules in HFM have only recently added a mechanism for calculating the per-rule calculation times. However, this requires you to use Calculation Manager. You can select the Enable Timer option for each rule, rule set, or component. This will record the time each rule takes to run in the log file. This can be very valuable in determining where your rules are spending time calculating. It is very easy to do as well; just make sure that you select Enable Logging for the rule you wish to see, and from the System View, make sure you choose Set Logger as shown in Figure 7-3.

If you don't have Calculation Manager turned on, you can view the Task Audit and tell us how long a consolidation or translation took. But if you are having issues, you may want to drill down a bit further and determine where the issue is specifically. If that is the case, you might want to add a WriteToFile statement in the rules file. This is basically a simple routine you can paste into your rule file, as shown in Figure 7-4. Once this is in the rules, you can pass all kinds of information to the routine and it will write it to a text file you can read.

So you can pass your point of view, variables, the number of records written as zeros, and so on. You can check if, during your rules, you are recalculating values unnecessarily. All of this is very helpful in troubleshooting and working to isolate issues.

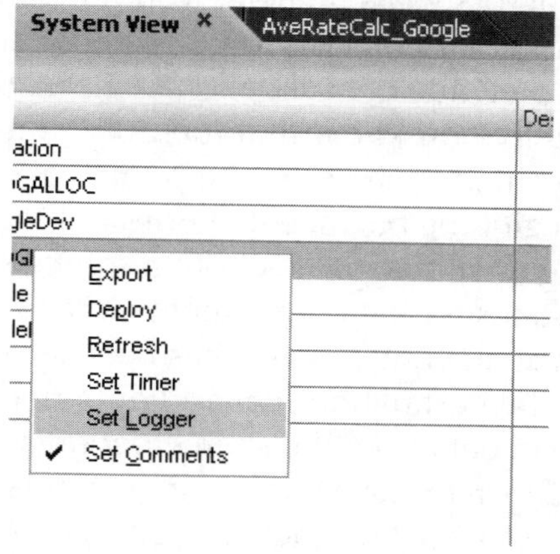

FIGURE 7-3. *Set Logger option*

```
Sub WriteToFile(text)
On Error Resume Next
    Const ForAppending = 8
    Set fso = CreateObject("Scripting.FileSystemObject")
    Set tf = fso.OpenTextFile(LogFile, ForAppending, True)
    tf.writeline text
    tf.Close
On Error GoTo 0
End Sub
```

FIGURE 7-4. *WritetoFile example*

Unfortunately it is not a good method for getting any accurate time for each rule's part of the processing. That is because it adds a lot of processing time to the consolidation that we're trying to reduce, sometimes by 25 to 50 percent. It can be used, however, to identify what rules are taking much longer than others to run, which does help identify where an issue may be.

The application should make use of the HS.ImpactStatus function to facilitate copying data from one scenario to another, as well as simplifying the roll-forward rules across years. Imagine you run consolidation in the year 2011, and the status has changed to OK. Then you post a journal in 2010. When you complete the consolidation in 2010, normally there is nothing that would let you know that the 2011 data needed to be consolidated again to reflect changes in the prior year balances. You could find yourself with a beginning balance that does not reconcile with the prior year balance. So using the ImpactStatus from a source scenario or period will change the calc status for the current entity in a future period or parallel scenario to "CN." Once an entity's status has been set to "CN," upon the next consolidation of the destination scenario or period, another set of rules can be executed to read data from the source period/scenario.

It is also not a good idea to leave this rule in your rule file in any production environment. Regardless of what precautions you take to be sure it is off, by its presence alone, it can be turned on inadvertently and impact the performance of your application.

Business Process

There is an old joke among system implementers: "The system would run great if it weren't for these users." Sometimes users do things that you did not expect. Or they use the system in ways that it really isn't designed for. A good example of this is having users dump volumes of data into Excel worksheets. First, because they think they "need" it, and second because they are not as comfortable with using HFM.

If you have a poor business process or user activity that impacts the system, you need to address it. Start in this example by asking them to explain why they are doing this, and then offer functionality they can't do in Excel. For example, show them how the data is consolidated and has information aggregate in ways they can't easily do in Excel.

Diagnosing Performance Problems Using Monitoring Tools

Using a tool like Oracle Application Testing Suite (ATS) or Load Runner by HP, you can simulate the expected load during the close, and watch for issues with each aspect of the application. When running this testing, you must start with good test scripts and descriptions of what you intend to do with the system. Are you planning to run reports, post journals, and so on?

These tests should focus on doing the validations that will ensure your hardware and your network can handle and maintain the highest load you can expect, while making sure you can grow with the system.

Conclusion

With a good design and good practices, you may never need to spend a large effort tuning your application. But in cases when performance is not as expected, you can identify the issues and then pursue the options to fix the problem.

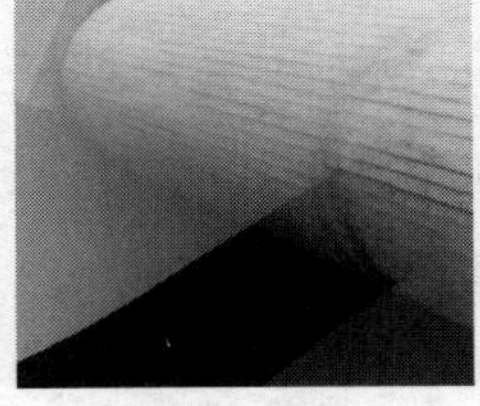

CHAPTER 8

Case Studies

Each project brings its own unique challenges and people. Company culture, attitude, budget constraints, and perceptions all drive the outcome of a project before it even starts. Goals get created at the beginning of projects, sometimes to sell the need for getting this tool, and often whether those goals are met or not is decided on far more than the design or functionality of the tool. People determine the success of a project. This chapter will share some of those experiences. Some of the stories are compilations, not just one client's story. All the names and details have been changed. But all of these stories are based on my experiences over the past ten years. There is a lot to learn from these stories. You can see what works, and what does not.

I will tell you this: The success of an implementation and support of the application has much more to do with people who will own the application than just about anything else. No consultant who comes in will know the business better than the people who work there. The best you can hope for is that the consultants really know the product and can help you navigate the bugs and issues that will inevitably come up. While some companies are better at some things than others, the basic implementation process for software is just about the same for every consulting company, from boutique to major global consulting firm. Any decent certified consultant will bring best practices and proven approaches to the project. But the biggest risks to an implementation of HFM are the parts of the project the business owners of the application own. Hence the client team that is assigned to the project is critical.

As you will see, data and data reconciliation are always the point of a project where things can go sideways. Data is the common issue in all of these case studies. It is critical that you overplan for this effort. No matter how much time you plan for this effort, I can tell you it will not be enough. Remember, this will likely be the first time you are working directly in the application, and even finding numbers for the first time can be a challenge.

In some of these stories, you will hear about administrators who aren't committed full time to the project. If you are not involved, then you will have a harder time reconciling data. You have to be involved. This product absolutely does not lend itself to "turn-key" implementations. You can't ask the consultants to just go build this, and then expect to just take ownership. Understanding how this application works is one thing, but understanding how *your* application works is critical to being able to support your close. When you have an administrator who isn't dedicated to this, and to learning about it, you are at risk.

I am amazed how project management is so often the first thing people will look to scale back on a project. Some of the issues either could be avoided or at least managed better with good project management. Managing a timeline, tracking issues, and working to a budget are important things to do. As you will see in my project examples, it is one of the things people regret not considering as an inclusion. Scope creep and changes are a common risk. Basically there are two common causes of this change in scope. The first is that people start to see the data and think of new ways of viewing and analyzing their data. You can spend months doing design work, and still not have the team understand how the data will look once it is in the system. Nothing is better than touching and seeing the data in the system. But what happens on a project when these changes are pushed through without understanding the impact? The second cause is often that people see something or think they need something that was not identified during the development of the requirements. When you sit and detail what you need for your application, you need to both list what you want and prioritize your list. The goal of gathering requirements is agreeing on what you will build during the project.

Other project management issues come from poor communication. This is another point of a project where people tend to underestimate the effort needed. It is much more work than you think to make sure there are open lines of communication, as these examples will show.

With so many things that can go wrong, how do people manage to get these applications up and running? How do these projects even stand a chance to go live? The next couple of case studies should help give you some insight into the experiences of other companies. You can learn from their mistakes and successes. What worked and what didn't work for them? Every project presents its own set of challenges and issues to overcome.

An Electronics Group (AEG)

An Electronics Group (AEG) is a California-based company specializing in software and consumer electronics.

Company Profile

The company is well known, mostly for their explosive growth over the past ten years. As with many companies in the Silicon Valley, their fortunes change quickly with new technologies and competition. Five years ago, AEG launched a tremendously successful cell phone product that swept through the market. This has allowed them to expand into other products and software. Before the project began, AEG announced a major acquisition of a competing software company that offered competing cell phone technology. This acquisition highlighted the fact that AEG was not ready to handle another acquisition of this size.

Success has brought good and bad results to the company. It has grown so quickly that the processes for closing that work for a small company don't work any more, and are filled with risk.

- Five hundred users
- Established in 1996; the premier supplier of cell phones
- Revenues in 2010: $15 billion
- Estimated project budget $1.2 million

Business Situation

This company does not have as much history as some other companies. They only went public six years ago. As a result, they don't have a tremendous amount of historical data, or processes that have been in place for many years that cannot be changed. The accounting systems were really made for a company of a much smaller size. No one anticipated the growth they enjoy today.

As we began the project discussions, it was clear that there was no process for managing the consolidation. Reports were built on an ad-hoc basis and not validated against other structures, like those used in the data warehouse. Reconciliation between the reports from the consolidation and external reporting team often did not reconcile with reports from detailed systems. Proving that they do in fact tie takes so much effort to identify the issues that they never bother to do it.

The processes AEG uses to close, which might have been fine for a much smaller company, just don't work any more. Systems have grown almost in silos. Then data that is coming from one application will not reconcile to other systems. This causes quite a bit of embarrassment for the controller.

In an effort to fix having all these systems reporting different numbers, AEG embarked on implementing SAP across the whole company. But as this project started, it was clear they were not ready to take this work on. The SAP implementation has been filled with delays and issues. It isn't the history of data, but trying to define what the business will look like and the metrics they need for the whole company. The result is that each department head, from sales to operations, is trying to meet every need they have for the application in SAP. It has just turned into a big mess. Regardless, the controller is left without a system that can handle reporting and the consolidations.

The Team

The client team is made up of people across the company. The project manager comes from the IT group with a strong background in ERP systems. It is clear from working with him that his experience with ERP frames everything. Every issue or problem that comes up is related to "the way we do it with our ERP upgrade."

The client needed to be reminded constantly that experience with ERP system implementation is relevant to EPM implementations only to the extent that it requires managing financial data. The users are often different pools, and the project definitions, milestones, testing approach, and methodology are all completely different. Applying an ERP methodology to EPM systems often creates unnecessary conflict and increases costs, and ultimately results in an upset client.

AEG had a very strong project sponsor. He had been with the company since it became public. He knows that for the accounting and finance department to move forward they must improve the processes they have in place. It is also a major risk for him and his job. Just last month, because of a reconciliation issue between a set of reports, the numbers were not distributed one day during the close. It was a major embarrassment.

AEG assigned two people from the accounting group to work as Subject Matter Experts (SMEs). Unfortunately, both are working full-time jobs. This presents problems because they only get to work on the data or application after 6 P.M. The consulting team is coming from Arizona, and so loses two days coming and going each week. This limits the time they can work together. Since the business processes are really not clear, the close is completely dependent on what these two people know.

The project team recommended they identify resources for the project and backfill for them. Instead, the project team got a temporary resource. This was an issue right away, since the temporary resource did not know the product or the company. It is much more effective to backfill the finance job and have the permanent staff participate in the project, especially performing data validation.

The administrator is not defined. They have a posting, but only two candidates ever came forward. One was believed to be qualified. However, after she was hired, it was painfully clear that she had overstated her qualifications. Basic tasks were beyond her. It was up to the consulting team to pull the project sponsor aside and tell them the issues.

The external consulting team consisted of four people. The lead consultant was very experienced and would take on all functional work with the administrators. He delegated some of the light work to a junior consultant. There was a project manager assigned to the project. And the lead and junior consultants identified an infrastructure consultant to be used as needed for the project.

Accounting Challenges

The biggest issues came from the lack of availability of the SMEs. Since they were not available or reliable in any way, it was very difficult for the team to get answers to questions to resolve the data reconciliation. The SMEs would not sit and work with the consulting team. This left them working in a vacuum, with no direction. The consulting team would have to take best guesses at certain things and report back to the SMEs when they could.

Physically sitting with or near the implementation team is important to the project's success as it encourages better knowledge transfer and better communication. In typical IT projects, the IT team gathers requirements and then periodically meets with the finance team sporadically throughout the build. In these cases, the finance team has lost valuable time in terms of learning the system. In almost all cases managed in this way for HFM, the project costs escalate and adoption is poor.

The SMEs felt that the system was being implemented to marginalize them. They had made subtle comments that if HFM were implemented, they would be fired. They really looked to sabotage the project when they could. They did this in subtle ways, like insisting on changes to the system regardless of whether they were in scope during the design, or in more overt ways, such as setting up meetings and not attending them.

It was so bad at one point that one of the SMEs came in to work drunk, smelling strongly of alcohol. The project manager needed to go to the project sponsor and make them aware of the issue. The SME was escorted off the property, but was back at work just a couple of days later. The fact was that they needed this person desperately to close the books.

It was later determined that one of the SMEs was very ill. This made having the knowledge these two people documented and made part of a system even more critical. So many projects underestimate the value of fully documented processes. Good documentation can take weeks to develop, but it is your best bet to hedge against the risk of changed resources and turnover.

Besides the personalities, there were major accounting inconsistencies. Because of the growth in the company and the reliance on these two people, they had many "workarounds" and issues that only the two of them seemed to understand. They would either not explain clearly or dismiss questions about consistency and approach.

Intercompany transactions were one of the biggest challenges. While most of the company was on SAP, the process was not working. They spent a great deal of time managing the intercompany issues each month. They needed a better process.

Infrastructure Challenges

AEG had a tremendously strong Infrastructure group. They were able to provide resources and support throughout the project. The IT team and CIO were very influential. They had quite a bit of influence over the business processes as they affected systems. The CIO came from a large company and was very experienced. The IT group insisted on providing a project manager to the team. He was new to this type of implementation, but was confident he could drive the project to resolution. One benefit was that they were not afraid to escalate issues to the project sponsor. However, he was not about to cross the SMEs. He wanted to move forward in the company, and making enemies with two people he perceived as in a powerful position was not something he was going to be engaged in. This would make him press the consulting team more to compensate for the issues of the project.

At first the IT team was not on board with the project, but had to get on board when it became obvious of the personnel risks. They learned this firsthand when they implemented their own data warehouse project. The IT team envisioned that the data warehousing project with a BI reporting solution would be able to handle the reporting for the whole company. It was very expensive and time-consuming. Because of the work they did, they felt very strongly that it needed to be part of any data reporting solution at AEG.

Solution

The IT team found a software selection company to help with the software selection, and very wisely told the selection company that they would not be implementing the recommended software. Many companies will take the advice of the software selection company, which is more than happy to implement their recommendation. AEG would only take the advice of a company if they could be sure the advice was not tainted. They then took the recommendation and put the project to bid. AEG elected to move to Oracle Hyperion Financial Management (HFM) consolidation system for the following stated reasons:

- **IFRS** AEG will be reporting IFRS and USGAAP in the near future.
- **More dimensions** More dimensions result in richer standard and ad-hoc reporting.
- **Easy-to-use web interface** HFM web front-end includes web grids for online data analysis and Web Data Entry Forms to simplify manual data entry.
- **Oracle Hyperion Smart View for Microsoft Office** A common reporting interface for Essbase and HFM that works from within MS Excel, Word, and PowerPoint.

- **Oracle Hyperion Financial Reporting** AEG will be able to create high-quality reports delivered in a variety of formats: HTML, PDF, and Excel for both Essbase and HFM.
- **Shared Services** Hyperion Financial Management is a member of the Oracle Hyperion Enterprise Performance Management (EPM) suite. As such, it uses the Shared Services interface for managing security for all Hyperion applications. AEG administrators will be able to use Shared Services to efficiently manage user access to HFM, FDM, Essbase, and the central reporting repository.

Intercompany matching was a real problem. They had started an internal intercompany matching project already. The first problem is that the history was so bad that they might never get it all resolved in the ledger. The second problem is that despite most of the company being on SAP, each site that was using process management had a validation to identify an issue with the intercompany matching. With the use of the intercompany matching report, they were able to see differences in the intercompany balances as the data consolidated. This was very helpful for them to find and resolve the intercompany issues. Now instead of someone finding an issue, and it taking a day for the response to come back from corporate, the users were taking control of the issues before the issue even got to corporate.

It was critical that during the project the consulting team get invested in finding and bringing in an administrator. The team found a local resource who did not want to travel and consult, but just work locally. Having a string administrator that could help drive the project from the company side reduced risk significantly. Also, it was important that they did not have to invest in training the administrator.

The project manager needed to focus on managing the scope. When issues were brought up by the SMEs, they were tabled for a later phase. The application was very ambitious at first, but as the project risks became clear, the project manager pulled back on all scope. The SMEs were not happy with this approach, so it was very important that this request came from the project sponsor.

For training, because we had over 500 users, we chose a "train the trainer" approach. Each site had a resource who helped manage the close and work with the location. We brought those people on site in California to train them on the product, and then gave them the materials to go back and train the people at their sites. The success and how it was perceived was really dependent on the trainers selected. Some were better than others.

Benefits

AEG found a superior system that will deliver an efficient end-to-end consolidation solution with flexibility to scale to AEG's continued growth. The system will

- Deliver a fully automated consolidated process from revaluation through to generation of reports within a two-hour time limit.
- Automate acquisition GLs with ability to drill through to source transactions.
- Automate reporting to alert users of any failed processes.
- Immediate and seamless IT support should the system experience problems and delay the close process.
- Enforce compliance with staggered close deadlines.
- Enable users of reports to run and generate these reports on a self-service basis.
- Integrate with current AEG data warehousing structure.

Anticipated

AEG expected to see much better reporting and see the reporting structures stabilized. It was also important to get the accounting to be consistent and reviewed. This was the first time the company was able to document how the close took place.

AEG also expected the audit fees to be reduced. The auditors would spend much less time chasing the SMEs asking for answers to questions.

Unanticipated

Some of the benefits were not really unanticipated, more like unstated—the absolutely biggest was the reduced risk of SME issues. Having a system and a resource they could rely on changed the close as much as anything they could have done. While they did not get every benefit they planned on during the sales cycle, this proved to be the most critical as one of the SMEs had become too ill to continue working and left the company.

Over time they added some of the out-of-scope items and were able to build on the project. This gave them more time to adopt new functionality and understand what they were adding. During this time, they understood the changes each made to the system and were able to expand the value even more.

One of the most common benefits is the list of issues they found with the data that they were able to resolve. For example, they were using different translation rates for each legal entity, and translating cash flow with a different rate and methodology than the income statement. They decided this approach was not GAAP and although it was not material, they needed to change it.

Products and Services Used

- HFM
- Hyperion Financial Reports
- Hyperion Smart View
- Financial Data Quality Management

Henri and the Bean's Toy Emporium

Henri and the Bean's Toy Emporium, headquartered in Colorado, leads the midstream segment as one of the nation's largest distributors of toys.

Company Profile

As a major toy distribution company, Henri and the Bean needs to view data by channel and region. They have some complex ownership issues fueled by the fact that toy distribution can have very slim margins.

- Toy distributor to regional toy stores
- One hundred and fifty users
- Twelve billion dollars in revenue

Business Situation

Henri and the Bean was undertaking an implementation of HFM and was falling very far behind schedule. They were moving on the project as they were spun off from a national children's toy store. The former parent company was divesting this distribution branch and spinning them off as their own company. The parent company was using Hyperion Enterprise to do the corporate reporting. The deal was to be final in September, and external reporting needed to be ready to go. They needed to have the application up and live with no room for error. They had the existing corporate enterprise application they could leverage. But the consolidation system was not the only system that was going through this. They were working through a complex PeopleSoft implementation that was consuming a great deal of resources and effort. It put the consolidation system much more at risk.

The application required very complex ratios, and they were well defined. The application had complex ownership, though. The spinoff created a complex structure with a holding company and cross-ownership and equity issues. It would take days to calculate the eliminations in detail for each entity.

They expected to have between 100 and 150 users accessing the application when they go live. The project timeline was set for 12 months.

Finally, since the company is structured globally, the users are all over the globe. With data feeds coming from each of the remote locations, they needed to create a global support center that could support the close and any issues people will have. They called this a "center of excellence."

Technical Situation

Henri and the Bean's current environment runs older computers that are no longer capable of handling the bandwidth necessary for maintaining the business. New hardware is being bought as needed, but they are trying to be careful not to spend money frivolously even if the money will be capitalized.

The Team

Since the PeopleSoft implementation was consuming so many of the resources, the client team consisted of one single person. This required the client team to be strongly augmented with very senior functional consultants. The most junior person on the consulting team had been doing implementations for no less than ten years. It is very difficult to have an EPM project run concurrently with an ERP implementation.

The consulting team consisted of two functional consultants and a senior FDM resource.

Accounting Challenges

The company has extremely complex ownership issues. This type of rules and accounting is frankly among the most complex and requires a truly dedicated expert to support the build and maintenance of the application.

Infrastructure Challenges

There were many infrastructure issues, beginning with the initial installation and the environment not meeting technical specifications. The specifications of the hardware were written without consulting any experts. During the flurry of buying servers for the PeopleSoft environment, wrong or incorrect hardware was acquired. The following problems were encountered during the initial installation, which caused additional effort:

- Servers were not ready on Day One when the infrastructure resource arrived in Denver.
- The database for the Production application was delayed.
- Memory on the application servers was 2GB and running very slowly for the installation; the specifications called for 12GB.
- The development environment was built with virtualized environments (VMs) and very slow (underpowered).
- The HFM server had to be reimaged because the FDM workbench would not work (Microsoft OS issue).
- Because of debugging network issues that were supposedly fixed but were not, the new network required was behind schedule.
- More than anticipated complexity in solidifying metadata (for example, SOW assumed straightforward PeopleSoft metadata vs. definition of a department roll-up and product hierarchy)

Solution

The consulting team took over the project by starting with a redesign focusing on the Hyperion Enterprise application, including Hyperion Reports/Hyperion Retrieve for production reporting and HAL for data integration. This was the tactical plan. All work that was built and defined at this point was documented and saved for the HFM design that was to happen after the company spinoff. Strategically, the plan was still to move to HFM, when resources and hardware issues could be addressed.

The issue here was that they needed an *immediate* consolidation system. Since user access and time were both at a premium, changing into a new system should not have been the priority.

During the project, all of the users who needed access to Budget and Forecast data realized they would want access. This created an issue for the project team. First, they were flooded with reports and requests. Second, there was not a planned budget for training the additional users. The team was forced to change gears and strategy for training. They moved to a "train the trainer" approach so they could cover the entire set of end users.

We continued to lay out a migration plan for the company to ensure that they would be able to migrate when the time was right. Since the Hyperion Enterprise application was already stable and in place, it was very easy to stand up and get data into, so the reporting could move forward. This allowed the infrastructure team to clean up and resolve the issues with the hardware and complete a much more thorough network testing.

With the high number of users but with the company focused on other priorities, we had to choose the "road show" training approach. The road show approach involves creating a team of trainers, at least one client and consultant resource, to travel to remote sites and train users at their locations. We could not find more resources to help us train. We had to visit each site and deliver the training. The number of sites was not quite too many, but it was some effort. The team broke into smaller teams of one consultant and one client resource.

Benefits

The consolidation system status went from critical to complete in four weeks. The "at-risk" project was saved, and completed so quickly we were able to conduct an extra parallel ensuring go-live success. The consulting team ensured that there was plenty of time for extra parallels to ensure that the system was "close ready."

So while they did not get an HFM application as quickly as they hoped, the interim Enterprise application satisfied the ongoing user requests while the team separately built out the HFM system.

This saved hours and days of manual effort by automating many of the consolidating entries. Since the work was so well documented, the team was able to move rather easily over to HFM after the dust settled. Administering the system was not a problem either with this approach. There was not a new system to learn; they already knew not only Hyperion Enterprise, but that application in Hyperion Enterprise. They picked it up and ran with it with not much effort.

Anticipated

Risk was significantly reduced. The company was able to focus on the other critical tasks they needed to do.

Unanticipated

The PeopleSoft implementation benefited as well. First, there was a reliable way to report externally, so that issues with the PeopleSoft project would not impact the consolidation. Second, there would be less competing of resources for the two projects. The finance team was able to focus. Since resources could be more focused after the ERP project completed, project costs were able to stay relatively the same. The timeline was pushed out though, from an original 7 months to 12 months.

Products and Services Used

- Hyperion Enterprise
- Hyperion Enterprise Reporting
- HFM
- Hyperion BI+
- Hyperion Smart View
- Hyperion Application Link (HAL)

Putty's Pet Food

Putty's Pet Food is a company on the East Coast that specializes in gourmet dog and cat foods.

Company Profile

Putty's Pet Food offers high-end products that are sold in larger department stores globally. Their extensive portfolio of brands includes the well-known "Beef and Broccoli" for dogs. Of course everyone knows the jingle, "There really is nothing like Putty."

- Fewer than 50 users, centrally located
- Nine hundred million dollars in revenue

Business Situation

Putty's Pet Food, like many companies, has complex requirements and relies on disparate information from end users. Disruption in the financial reporting process is something that would be devastating for the company. Yet there are business needs that require migration, including ongoing support from Hyperion. This needed to be done with as little risk as possible.

Putty's has some very complex allocations, which they calculate by brand. Since they use celebrity dogs and cats to advertise the foods they sell, they pay large royalties from the corporate group. Advertising and marketing play an important part in driving the brand of Putty. Those costs are then spread out down to the local sites that distribute and sell the products. As Putty's Pet Food prepared for the project, they revealed that these allocations were written within a massive Excel worksheet. The problem is that the spreadsheet has broken links, wrong formulas, and is a nightmare to maintain. Building the allocations is critical to the success of the project.

Technical Situation

Technically, the environment is very simple. The servers are average size because the number of users is moderate. While allocations were discussed during the hardware scoping call, this was done with a technical resource that the salesperson was able to make available for the call. No one with functional expertise was able to review the allocations for their potential impact on the design, and specifically the hardware.

The Team

Since the number of users was not large, the team at Putty's was confident they did not need to assign a full team. They did have a solid resource to add to the team, a young woman who knew the calculations very well and could explain what needed to be done. She was critical to many processes at Putty, and had no ambition of maintaining the application. She was perfect in many ways to help us build the application, but would not stay through the project. All infrastructure resources were scheduled during the design meeting for the project.

The consulting team was reflective of the number of users. One senior consultant was on the project. During the sale, some people recommended having more resources to handle the rules work. In fact, one company recommended having a "rules expert" assigned to the project. This created some confusion during the sales cycle because there was a large variance between estimates. Where some tried to estimate the allocations out in detail, others only provided an allowance for the completion of the allocations since they could not accurately scope them.

The selection team at Putty's realized that just taking the lowest bid was probably not the right course, but they were not completely sure who understood the calculations and the complexity. Fortunately, the one resource was very strong with the rules in the system.

Accounting Challenges

Did I mention allocations? The rest of the application was really so simple. The work involved in building the allocations took far longer than anyone could have thought. The biggest reason was that the allocations were not as well defined as they thought. Once the team dug into the spreadsheet and found all the issues, it was clear that the way they had been doing the allocations was not the way they had thought. This caused a delay, as the team wanted to take a step back and think about how they should really do the allocations. The second delay was trying to figure out how they should handle the history of data they had reported already.

Infrastructure Challenges

Once the allocations were defined, they were built for far more intersections than what was done in Excel. The rules were very complex, and pulled data from many intersections. This created many large subcubes. The performance of the application became terrible. This was a big disappointment to the Putty team. They thought from the earlier calls that the servers would be more than enough for the 50 users who would be accessing the system.

Solution

The Putty SME who was assigned to the project just wanted to see the rules completed. She really didn't care how they were written. She was very content with them being a "black box" within the application. Her thinking was that "the rules should just work," so it was the consultant's responsibility to make them work. She would run a report and send it over to the consultant with errors just highlighted.

The problem was that since she knew the allocations so well, she could have helped give guidance for how the rules were not working. In the long term, if the folks at Putty were going maintain the application, she needed to sit with the consultant and build them together. This was a potentially huge risk to the project. The team then had to document the allocations incredibly well, and that took time.

The application performance was a real issue, since the allocations adversely impacted the subcube size. The company had to take a long look at the servers, and bring in application tuning experts to help them evaluate what could be done. The team decided to add some hardware, have a consolation-specific server, and tune the registry settings. That mixed approach worked very well and cut the times by half.

Since there were problems with the historical data, they had to make a decision of how to handle the historical data. Historical data should be something you load and reconcile to, and not build structures and rules to support. The decision was made to build rules to change the allocations based on the periods anyway. Now the numbers of allocations were effectively doubled. The effort to reconcile the data was doubled. Maintenance of the application going forward was made more complex. This was a mistake. They made this decision against the recommendation of the consultants on site, because they believed the history needed to be re-created in HFM, not just forced in.

The solution was to limit the intersections the allocations were running. Second, the team pressed to identify a second resource to help maintain the application. Once this second person was up to speed, they were able to help get the data reconciliation going.

As the project slowed because of the performance issues, and allocation issues, the Putty team needed to identify ways to reduce scope if they were going to have any chance of getting the application standing up. But the Putty team wanted *everything*. This created a rift. The Putty team and the consulting team really are in the project together. They both have to see the project be successful. Such a rift should not have happened.

Since there was only one person on the team, there was not a project manager. There were a lot of project issues that could not be addressed as a result. The team was not communicating effectively. Having a more frank discussion about scope would have benefited the entire team. Since the consultant was so focused on build and the complexity of the rules, they could not manage the budget. In fact, the result was that the consultant just billed without regard to the budget. With the performance issues, there was no one to track issues with the infrastructure team and drive issues to resolution.

This project was at risk for most of the implementation. The only thing that saved the project was the dedication and hard work of the consultant. He was able to complete the allocations and save the implementation.

Since many of the users were close to the main office location and the number of users was manageable, the project team chose the classroom training approach. They were careful not to have more than 20 people in each class. The production environment was used to train the individuals on the system, by making a copy of the production application.

The data and infrastructure issues were too much to manage in the budget and eight-month time line. Troubleshooting and working the issues added two months and 20 percent to the project costs.

Benefits

HFM has a "zero footprint" for end users' machines, so updating those machines is much easier. Obviously, some of the users required Smart View. So while those users do in fact have install, they now can update many of the Smart View spreadsheets on their own after the training, eliminating the need for additional consulting.

HFM provides Putty's with more dynamic drilldown capabilities within the delivered end-user interface, especially as related to ad-hoc analysis conducted by financial analysts. This was completed in less than a week, minimizing the project risk and causing no disruption to the reporting process.

Anticipated

The allocations were able to be part of the database calculations. They performed quickly and were much more controllable and auditable. Moving out of Excel was also a huge win for the team.

Unanticipated

Although the transition to HFM was painful, the confidence the Putty team had in the financial statements after the project saved them hours of time validating the allocations. Also, they had not realized how much time they spent handling rounding and footing with the reports. Many of the reports they had were handled by a junior accountant who would spend a long time footing and plugging the reports.

Products and Services Used

- HFM
- Hyperion BI+
- Hyperion Smart View
- Hyperion Application Link (HAL)

Fictus Corp

Fictus Corporation, headquartered in New England, develops and manufactures high-performance bicycle accessories.

Company Profile

Fictus operates manufacturing facilities in the United States, France, Belgium, and China. Sales offices are located around various countries around the globe, including Japan, Taiwan, Korea, China, and Singapore.

- Twenty users, spread around the globe
- One hundred million dollars in revenue

Business Situation

The problem Fictus faced was that the consolidation was done in Excel. Inventory and sales data were kept in a data mart. The sales and inventory databases did not reconcile easily. The main reason was timing. Since orders were coming in constantly, if the reports were created at different times, they would never reconcile. The team at Fictus decided they needed to develop an automated consolidation application and replace a home-grown data warehouse with a purpose-built data warehouse that would allow for faster accurate reconciliation of data.

They saw the reporting features of the Hyperion tool set and decided it would be best to deliver all these solutions via the web utilizing Hyperion Reports and Hyperion Analyzer. This would require a standardized set of reports that could handle the current and future requirements of the company.

Technical Situation

Fictus's reporting and consolidation process was based on a set of Microsoft Excel spreadsheets and general ledger reports, which lacked appropriate controls and procedures. In addition, the financial close took numerous days of effort. The home-grown data warehouse was not linked to the financial reporting, and discrepancies in the data would typically exist.

Although the number of current users was relatively small, they also needed a strategy for implementing a solution across the entire company that would accommodate the growth and development they are having. They began the project with fewer than 10 users total in the corporate reporting group. While they had three remote sites that would be reviewing data, they would have fewer than 20 users across the entire company accessing the system. Hence, the hardware requirements were very light for this project.

The biggest concern would be how to support a high-availability system globally from a small town in New England. This project would not get the support or resources it would at a multibillion dollar company in Silicon Valley.

The Team

The team at Fictus could not have been more perfect for this project. They had a great understanding of the issues that come with software implementations. They did have a very tight budget, though. So they relied on internal resources as much as they could to deliver the project.

The team consisted of the controller, two data reconciliation resources, and the administrator. The consulting team consisted of only two people, a very senior resource and a junior resource to write reports and help with data reconciliation.

Accounting Challenges

The budget was the biggest concern. They could not ask for "just another 100K," and this created problems for the consulting team. If there were unforeseen issues with the project, like bugs, accounting discrepancies, resource issues, or any change in the business, there would not be an option of asking for more money.

Fortunately, the team at Fictus understood the project analogy of the "three-legged stool," with each leg being functionality, cost, and time, and you would only get to pick two. As issues came up, the team made decisions within the timeline, or functionality. They got everything they wanted, just not all in Phase One. The team was able to manage this by overcommunicating to the end users. They were able to let people know how market and business decisions were affecting what was coming and when. By working closely with the consulting team, they were able to minimize completely in some cases any "throwaway" work in this approach.

One of the biggest challenges was the mistakes and issues found with the data in the PeopleSoft ledger. In addition to people booking entries where they should have had some kind of validation rules to prevent entry, people were also selecting different rates to translate data than they should have been. The design of the ledger did not support the reporting they really wanted to accomplish either. The chance to rethink what they wanted for the company was a big departure from the reporting they had built in PeopleSoft. We had to focus on what HFM could do, though, and resolving the sins of a bad PeopleSoft design was not what we could do.

The thing is, as in any system, we cannot create data. We can only take what was coming in and work with that. If the dimensionality and depth of the data was lousy, then we were stuck with lousy. However, we did look for opportunities to pull from subledgers and use Web Data Entry Forms to collect as much as we could to augment that data. No, we didn't resolve every issue. But the team did manage to address many issues, like a better and more accurate fixed asset report.

Infrastructure Challenges

Solving the support issues for the infrastructure team was a real challenge. There were not the resources that one might hope for when planning a global, high-availability system. The first step was to break the support into a type. We broke into both functional and technical. The team was able to identify by region a resource that would be available in normal working hours to act as a point of contact for issues. That person would resolve accounting and basic questions. If it required the work of the administrator, they would log a request for someone from the business to respond when they got the message. The technical resource would do things a bit differently. If it was a simple issue of logging on, or access, this would be routed through the support desk.

System-down issues would be answered by an on-call IT resource during the close, the critical time of the system. Non-close issues would be answered first thing the next day.

The other issue was the politics of legacy systems that this new tool was replacing. The IT team was very invested in the existing system. First, they had spent quite a bit of time building and supporting it. They were proud of it. Second, it was somewhat an issue of job security. The legacy system was owned and maintained by the IT group, and the users were all in Finance. In the new approach, they would share the ownership between both IT and Finance. How this would be defined created some concern.

Solution

First, the consulting team successfully designed and implemented Hyperion Financial Management and Hyperion Essbase system, utilizing a Web Analysis dashboard to deliver the solution to the company. The team developed the foundation of a purpose-built data warehouse that would allow drilldown analysis and that is scalable to meet the future analysis needs of the company. HFM would pull data from PeopleSoft for the full trial balance, and then translate, eliminate, and consolidate the data. The data would also be fed from PeopleSoft into a staging table built in Oracle. Essbase would then dynamically create cubes from those tables for detailed sales and inventory data only.

One of the biggest challenges was creating a process to reconcile the data between these systems. But the solution drove the project team to a simple resolution. Since the new data flow created two data paths from the same source of data (PeopleSoft), Smart View templates that could pull both HFM and Essbase data were created that highlighted reconciliation points between the systems. The users could quickly reconcile the two systems and see that sales and inventory did in fact tie to the financial data. Since both feeds were pulled at the same time, timing differences with the data disappeared.

With reconciliation being such a big issue, extra care was put into defining a set of validations they could run on their data. These validations were set up as described in this book. With so few users, you wouldn't think they would need process management, but the use of this tool and the validations improved data quality more than they expected.

As the project team moved forward, they developed protocols for issues, and segregated duties between the groups. The IT team found that the new system not only required just as much support as before, but they learned a new skill set that increased their value beyond the company. The company was not stuck with a static in-house system anymore. The reporting reconciled.

With a small group, so spread out geographically, and obviously cost being a concern, the team chose web-based training. Although it was the least effective, the project team planned for additional support issues as a result and managed that during the parallels.

Benefits

Since the reconciliation times dropped so much, this solution was able to help shorten the close. The close did not shorten by as much as they had hoped. The biggest reason was that although they were spending less time validating numbers, they focused on the quality of those numbers. The result was not the savings they had hoped for during the close process, but a much better understanding of the data and the business. This was much harder to justify as part of the ROI, but very valuable nonetheless.

For the first time, management reporting and external reporting had the same source data and reconciled. This saved those days of answering questions and reconciling data. They finally had eliminated the manual processes, including running monthly reports and creating and reconciling many independent spreadsheets. This eased the administration by the Corporate Finance Reporting department. They did not have to fight to get reports completed by the deadline.

Controlled processing of last-minute adjustments of GAAP consolidated results—the solution can receive a journal-based entry and reconsolidate the legal and management consolidation structures within a 30-minute window. This had other ramifications, such as

- Reduced turnaround time for restatements and organizational changes
- Reduced time in the external audit process
- More robust reporting than was possible in the PeopleSoft solution they had in place

Anticipated

They expected this would improve the turnaround time and responsiveness of the team. The biggest benefit was their ability to do real value-added work on the data. They could finally focus on changes in the data, asking deep accounting questions to make sure they were reporting accurately and completely.

Unanticipated

The project did take much longer than they thought to complete. The data was the biggest obstacle to overcome. The team at Fictus had no idea how many issues were pervasive in the underlying data. Once they worked through those issues, the quality of ongoing data problems dropped off significantly. They added more validations over time, and with the use of threshold accounts as described in this book, were able to continue the gains long after the project was completed.

Products and Services Used

- Hyperion Financial Management
- Hyperion Reports
- Hyperion Analyzer
- Hyperion Application Link Advanced
- Hyperion Essbase
- Hyperion Essbase Integration Services

Conclusion

Not every project goes well. In fact, if I am ever on a project without any issues, I will be writing a book about just that experience alone. You and everyone else will have issues. The true measure of the implementation team is how they handle these issues. Do they panic and over-react? Do they throw resources at it without thinking? Or do they manage the communication, and work patiently and stay focused to find the right solution? People who do the latter are much more likely to be successful.

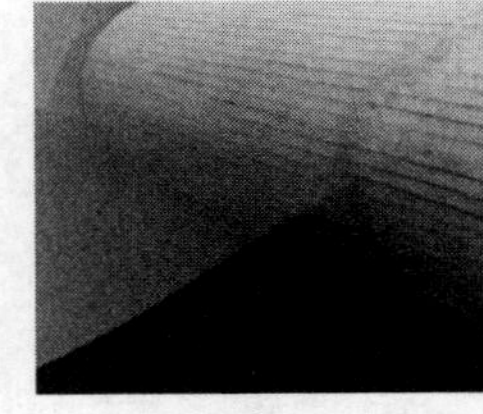

APPENDIX A

Oracle HFM Errors and Event Codes

The HSV Event Log of error codes is a text file, and as mentioned in earlier chapters, it is very difficult to read. From any one of the error logs, you can expand into the details. On the details screen you will see an Error Message Number; this is in the System Details. Those error message numbers are helpful in researching what the issue might be caused by. This appendix shows the errors and codes you may see while using HFM.

0x80042A00 An unknown error has occurred in the HsvDSSystemChange object.

0x000411C1 Sticky server attempt failed. Reverting back to randomly picked server [%0].

0x00041C8B Error loading rules from the database.

0x80040200 An unknown error has occurred in Oracle Hyperion Financial Management.

0x80040208 Error occurred while writing cube data.

0x8004020D Unable to allocate %0 bytes of memory.

0x8004020E Error occurred while creating %0 object.

0x8004020F Error occurred while querying the interface of %0 object.

0x80040213 Error occurred while connecting to the database.

0x80040214 Error occurred while initializing the ADO.

0x80040222 Unable to support the present version of database.

0x80040223 Unable to get the database version.

0x80040224 Unrecognized database driver.

0x80040227	Error creating SQL table(s).
0x8004022D	A function call was made to the following uninitialized object: %0.
0x80040235	Error occurred while accessing %0 object.
0x80040236	Error occurred while initializing %0 object.
0x8004024F	The Extended Analytics component has not been initialized correctly.
0x80040251	A general error occurred while trying to obtain a database Reader/Writer lock.
0x80040252	The database driver suggested in the provided UDL is invalid or of an unknown type.
0x80040253	A general error occurred while working with the database.
0x80040255	The database locking system has not been correctly initialized.
0x8004025C	An unexpected database error occurred. Check event log for details.
0x8004025F	A communications failure occurred in CSS.
0x80040262	A general error occured in HfmRenameIntegrity.
0x80040600	An unknown error has occurred in the HsvADMDriverACM object.
0x80040605	Unable to enumerate member lists.
0x80040606	Unable to enumerate member lists.

0x80040680 An unknown error has occurred in the HsvDataExplorerACM object.

0x80040740 An unknown error has occurred in the HsvDBManagementACM object.

0x80040743 Unable to clear the data objects.

0x80040744 Unable to clear the input data objects.

0x800407C0 An unknown error has occurred in the HsvEssbaseACM object.

0x800407C4 Can't initialize OLAP engine.

0x800407C5 Can't log in to OLAP engine.

0x80040840 An unknown error has occurred in the HsvFileTransfer object.

0x80040880 An unknown error has occurred in the HsvJournalLoadACM object.

0x80040885 An error occurred while trying to initialize the security.

0x80040900 An unknown error has occurred in the HsvJournalsACM object.

0x80040980 An unknown error has occurred in the HsvMetadataLoadACM object.

0x80040A00 An unknown error has occurred in the HsvReportGeneratorACM object.

0x80040A04 An error occurred while enumerating style sheets.

0x80040A05 An error occurred while enumerating reports.

0x80040A80 An unknown error has occurred in the HsvRetrieveACM object.

0x80040AC0 An unknown error has occurred in the HsvSecurityLoadACM object.

0x80040B40 An unknown error has occurred in the HsvSharesCalculationsACM object.

0x80040BC0 An unknown error has occurred in the HsvStarSchemaACM object.

0x80040C40 An unknown error has occurred in the HsvUserPrefACM object.

0x80040CC0 An unknown error has occurred in the HsvWebACM object.

0x80040D40 An unknown error has occurred in the HsvWebFormGeneratorACM object.

0x80040D45 Computed Year out of range.

0x80040D47 Computed Period out of range.

0x80040e57 User unable to log on to HFM and they get the error: "An error has occurred. Please contact your administrator" "String or binary data would be truncated."

0x800412C0 An unknown error has occurred in the HsxAuthentication object.

0x800413C0 An unknown error has occurred in the HsxDSNs object.

0x800413C2 Can't initialize OLAP engine.

0x800413C4 Can't log in to OLAP engine.

0x80041440 An unknown error has occurred in the HsxDSSecurity object.

0x800414C0 An unknown error has occurred in the HsxSecurity object.

0x80041540 An unknown error has occurred in the HsxServer object.

0x800415C0 An unknown error has occurred in the HsxServerImpl object.

0x800415C6 Error occurred while initializing the data source.

0x800415C7 Error occurred while enumerating the data sources.

0x800416C0 An unknown error has occurred in the HsxService object.

0x80041700 An unknown error has occurred in the HsxSQLHelper object.

0x80041701 An error has occurred while reading the default database tablespace information from the HIT Registry object. Tablespace information will be defaulted.

0x80041900 An unknown error has occurred in the HsvDataSource object.

0x80041904 Failed to load database connection parameters from HIT registry.

0x80041906 Failed to load database connection parameters from NT registry.

0x80041A00 An unknown error has occurred in the HsvDataSourceImpl object.

0x80041B00 An unknown error has occurred in the HsvDSCalcStatus object.

0x80041C80 An unknown error has occurred in the HsvDSCalculate object.

0x80041C8F	VBScript Engine could not be initialized.
0x80041C90	VBSG conversion failed.
0x80041E80	An unknown error has occurred in the HsvDSData2 object.
0x80042080	An unknown error has occurred in the HsvDSDataCubes2 object.
0x80042081	Subcube Paging SubSystem could not write record.
0x80042082	Subcube Paging SubSystem could not read record.
0x80042083	Subcube Paging Subsyterm could not delete record.
0x80042084	Subcube Paging Subsytem had error.
0x80042200	An unknown error has occurred in the HsvDSJournals object.
0x80042380	An unknown error has occurred in the HsvDSMemberLists object.
0x80042400	An unknown error has occurred in the HsvDSMemberListScript object.
0x80042480	An unknown error has occurred in the HsvDSMetadata object.
0x80042680	An unknown error has occurred in the HsvDSOrgByPeriod object.
0x80042780	An unknown error has occurred in the HsvDSReports object.
0x80042800	An unknown error has occurred in the HsvDSRulesOM object.

0x8004282D	Invalid number of parameters specified for the function.
0x8004283A	The Index value is out of range.
0x80042857	Error initializing the Rules engine.
0x80042859	Error loading rules from the database.
0x80042884	DataUnit already initialized. Duplicate Initialization.
0x80042900	An unknown error has occurred in the HsvDSSQL object.
0x80042903	A failure occurred during notification of system change.
0x80042A80	An unknown error has occurred in the HsvDSSystemInfo object.
0x80042B40	An unknown error has occurred in the HsvDSTransactions object.
0x80042BD0	General error in the HfmFileStream object.
0x80042C00	An unknown error has occurred in the HsvADMDriver2 object.
0x80042C01	The Financial Management driver failed to initialize.
0x80042C02	The Financial Management driver cannot connect to server %0.
0x80042C03	The Financial Management driver cannot open a connection to Financial Management.
0x80042C05	The Financial Management driver cannot enumerate applications.
0x80042C07	The Financial Management driver cannot find the server.

0x80042C08	The Financial Management driver cannot get dimension information.
0x80042C09	The Financial Management driver cannot get function information.
0x80042C0B	The Financial Management driver cannot get the member information.
0x80042C0C	The Financial Management driver cannot get the member property information.
0x80042C0D	The Financial Management driver is unable to get meta-metadata information.
0x80042C0E	The Financial Management driver cannot retrieve the selected data query.
0x80042C0F	The Financial Management driver is unable to get data grid information.
0x80042C10	The Financial Management driver is unable to close operation.
0x80042C12	The Financial Management driver is unable to perform transaction.
0x80042C13	The Financial Management driver failed to initialize.
0x80042C14	The Financial Management driver cannot set cell POV.
0x80042C15	The Financial Management driver had an error with line item detail.
0x80042C17	The Financial Management driver failed to write data.
0x80042C18	The Financial Management driver had an error with document attachments.

0x80042C19	The Financial Management driver had an error with Drillable URLs.
0x80042CC0	An unknown error has occurred in the HsvHALDriver object.
0x80042CC2	Error occurred while initializing temporary load file.
0x80042DC0	An unknown error has occurred in the HsvHTTPListenerACM object.
0x80042E40	An unknown error has occurred in the HsvLoadExtractOptions object.
0x80042E80	An unknown error has occurred in the HsvLoadFileConverter object.
0x80042EC0	An unknown error has occurred in the HsvMDArrays object.
0x80042F40	An unknown error has occurred in the HsvMetadataXML object.
0x80042FC0	An unknown error has occurred in the HsvScriptEngine object.
0x80042FC2	Error executing VBScript %0.
0x80043040	An unknown error has occurred in the HsvSharedAppData object.
0x80043041	An error has occurred in the HsvSharedAppData object because of a prior version.
0x80043340	An unknown error has occurred in the Resource Manager object.

0x80043380	An unknown error has occurred in the HsvCalculate object.
0x80043400	An unknown error has occurred in the HsvData object.
0x80043480	An unknown error has occurred in the HsvDataCubes object.
0x80043580	An unknown error has occurred in the HsvMetadata object.
0x80043600	An unknown error has occurred in the HsvProcessFlow object.
0x80043680	An unknown error has occurred in the HsvReports object.
0x80043700	An unknown error has occurred in the HsvSecurityAccess object.
0x80043780	An unknown error has occurred in the HsvSession object.
0x80043800	An unknown error has occurred in the HsvSystemChange object.
0x80043880	An unknown error has occurred in the HsvSystemInfo object.
0x80043902	Could not access the database provided in the UDL file. Please make sure database server is running and the UDL file is set properly.
0x80043B00	An unknown error has occurred in the HFMSchemaUpgrade object.
0x80044102	Open Application [%0] failed.
0x80044243	Client object session must be set to perform this action.
0x800442C0	An unknown error has occurred in the Financial Management Error Handler object.
0x800442C2	An error has occurred while trying to update the database.

0x800447C1 An unknown error has occurred in the HsvSecurityAdminACM object.

0x80045340 An unknown error has occurred in the HsvClusterController object.

0x80045342 The HsvClusterController object m_cReadWriteLockArray is being released while locks are still in the array.

0x800453C0 An unknown error has occurred in the HsvDSDocuments object.

0x800456C0 An unknown Load or Extract error has occurred.

0x800458C0 An unknown error has occurred in a Reports Object.

0x80045940 An unknown error has occurred in a Journals Object.

0x80045B41 The following %0 of %1 tasks failed to stop: %2

0x80045D00 An unknown error has occurred in a HsvSystemActivity Object.

0x80045E00 General error in HFMICACM object.

0x80045E01 IDS_ICACM_FAILED_MVBP

0x80045E40 General error in HFMICM object.

0x80045E80 General error in HFMDSICM object.

0x80045E81 Requested intercompany transaction not found in database.

0x80045E95 The installed version of DB2 does not meet the requirements for this version of Financial Management and the Intercompany Transaction module. The IC database objects will not be created. DB2 version detected: %0

0x80045F40	Data Layer general error.
0x80045F41	Data Page general error.
0x80045F42	Data Page was not initialized.
0x80045F49	Database Statement general error.
0x80045F4A	Database Statement not initialized.
0x80045F4C	Database Statement used after the end of database data stream.
0x80045F50	This driver type is not supported by Database Retry.
0x80045F56	Database Object general error.
0x80045F58	Database Retry general error.
0x80045F59	A SQL error occurred on the database which prevented a command from executing. Contact the system administrator to review the specifics of the error.
0x80045F5A	DLDataSource object general error.
0x8004604B	Error initializing licensing: %0.
0x80046052	Could not initialize Licensing Server. Error: %0.
0x80047167	Grid action requires a valid session. Either session is not set or it is not initialized.
0x8004733C	A failure occurred while processing an ACK message!
0x8004733D	Response buffer processing failed!
0x8004733E	Buffer processing failed. This may be due to insufficient memory!

0x8004733F	Unable to allocate buffer memory!
0x80047340	Unable to allocate a new client context. The new session will not be accepted.
0x80047341	Unable to allocate memory to hold the query string!
0x80047346	A failure response was returned in response to a client submit message!
0x8004735B	DME Listener Socket Error: A general socket error occurred while processing incoming data.
0x8004735C	Stream processing failed!
0x80047360	Task processing failed!
0x80047530	A general error in the HFMwAwbHandler object has occurred.
0x80047921	General failure in the HfmAwbAgent object.
0x80047927	Financial Management migration failed.
0x80047F26	Reading contents into file failed with unknown cause.
0x8004B780	An unknown error has occurred in a HsxADO Object.
0x8004B782	The object does not exist or is not visible to this database user.

APPENDIX B

Examples of Common Oracle HFM Rules

Even if you have a good sense of what the rules are for your application, this section has a good set of examples I have used in applications. There are some rules that every application has. You don't need to reinvent the wheel. In fact, most consultants start with some rules that they wrote, or someone else wrote for them.

Good code is more than just formatting efficient lines of code. It should be very easy to follow and maintain. I have seen some rules that very good consultants have built, but the client who was to own the application could not even begin to understand them. The first thing I hope you get from this appendix is an understanding of how to simplify your rules, and still have them work well and fast.

This appendix describes rules that every application should have. They are just about the standard you might expect to see anywhere. The second hope I have for this appendix is that you can take these examples and add to your investment with HFM. If you never got to that cash flow and still want to have one, or if you want to add to your list of validations, this will help you understand the work involved.

Formatting

Good formatting is critical to writing a good rule file. Formatting includes proper spacing, indenting, and naming conventions. You should always indent when you're writing scripts. Each line should have some comments. You can provide an explanation of what each section of the rules file is built to accomplish by adding lines that begin with an apostrophe and are considered "commented out" or commentary.

When using Calculation Manager, you should have a consistent and clear naming convention. The description should be intuitive and brief. For the naming convention, use short prefixes. Consider something that identifies rule sets, rule objects, and rule components. These practices will create easily read flow charts and rules within the graphical user interface of HFM. Writing scripts with VBScript requires more careful work with the formatting.

Your comments should be clear and in plain English. It should be intuitively obvious what the rules are doing, how variables are used, and the purpose of the calculation. The comments should include a history of the changes. The content of your comments should just about be able to stand by itself as a document.

If you are writing in VBScript or in objects with Calculation Manager, it is absolutely a best practice to complete every line of commentary. You want your rules to be as well documented as possible. The best rule file will not require an administrator's guide to follow; each line will be clearly documented. Well-written rules have at least as much commentary as rules. There is absolutely no performance impact to having more comments in the file.

Variables

There are many common members you will call again and again. For example, you will likely need to check if the entity is translated. Instead of calling these members over and over again, you can create a variable, and populate that variable with the member. In Figure B-1, you can see a set of examples of variables. The variable names are simple and not overdone. So, while they do not follow a strict naming convention, it is clear what they are intended for, and that is the most important thing.

Notice that while this file does not seem to follow a naming convention as described earlier in this book, the variable names follow two of the most

```
' -- Populate variables that represent the Point Of View and entity status
' Component Name = Variables_CLIENT

' -- current entity
pov_entity= HS.Entity.Member()'' -- current entity
' -- parent of current entity
pov_parent= HS.Parent.Member()'' -- parent of current entity
' -- current scenario
pov_scenario= HS.Scenario.Member()'' -- current scenario
' -- current value
pov_value= HS.Value.Member()'' -- current value
' -- current year
pov_year= HS.Year.Member()'' -- current year
' -- This is the number not the name
pov_period= HS.Period.Number()'' -- This is the number not the name
' -- are we at Parent Currency
is_parent_cur= HS.Value.IsTransCur()'' -- are we at Parent Currency
' -- are we at Parent Currency Adjust
is_parent_cur_adj= HS.Value.IsTransCurAdj()'' -- are we at Parent Currency Adjust
' -- is this a base level entity
is_base_ent= HS.Entity.IsBase("","")'' -- is this a base level entity
Nones= ".I#[ICP None].C1#[None].C2#[None].C3#[None].C4#[None]"
Tops= ".I#[ICP Top].C1#TOTC1.C2#TOTC2.C3#TOTC3.C4#TOTC4"
StartYear= "2004"
EntityDefCurrency= HS.Entity.DefCurrency("")
pov_Currency= HS.Value.Currency()
```

FIGURE B-1. *Variables*

important guidelines we have defined. First, the variables are self-descriptive. The "pov_" tells you that the dimension defined is part of the Point of View. The second guideline this file adheres to is that the variables are not named any of the reserved key words; for example, a name like "pov_entity" is used instead of "entity." Variable names should be intuitive and help you read the rule file.

When building your variables in Calculation Manager, you should also consider putting similar variables in a group. In this example, you could group the "pov" variables together as a POV group. See Figure B-2 as an example of how you might set up a variable in Calculation Manager.

Calc Manager requires a little more work when defining a variable. First, the syntax is different in that variables are presented in braces, such as {x}=10. Since the braces are not valid in VBScript, they are removed when the file is created. Calculation Manager groups the variables into two groups, execution and replacement. Execution variables are populated

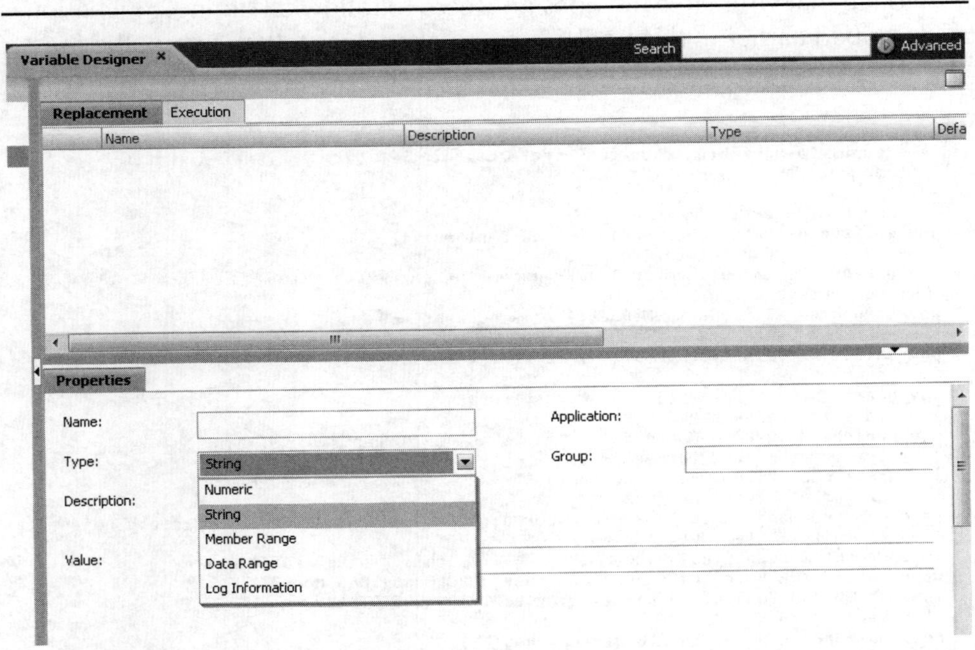

FIGURE B-2. *Defining variables in Calculation Manager*

when a rule is run or when the calculation is performed. Replacement variables are static for the entire scope; they are typically used as a replacement for part of components or strings within the script.

Calculate Rules

The first and probably the most commonly used subroutine in HFM is Sub Calculate. These rules are run up to eight times in the Value dimension, so more often than not, this will ensure that you will be able to run the rules you intend to at the right point of the consolidation. That doesn't mean that the easiest path is the right option here. If you can, you should put your rules in a subroutine and refer to them where it makes sense. If that is Sub Calculate, then you should put them there.

There are some commonly used rules you should put in the Sub Calculate routine, though, and we will cover them in the next section of this appendix.

Out of Balance

The first rule you should think about having in your application is a simple out-of-balance rule. This rule will help you identify when your balance sheet is out of balance. Your assets always equal your liabilities and equity, you say? But in the unlikely event that they don't reconcile, you will need this. Okay, it will happen all the time, and this is the easiest check to make in your system. You should have this rule no matter what. This calculation should run only at the Entity Currency member of base entities and adjustment Value members. It would then aggregate up the Entity structure during consolidation.

You will have to create a name for this account. In Figure B-3, I have selected the account name "Out_of_Balance." I would also point out this first rule is written in Calculation Manager. The amount within the Out_of_Balance account represents a mismatch of entries between the Assets and Liabilities of the balance sheet and should be reconciled so that it falls below an acceptable threshold. Since the Out_of_Balance account is flagged as IsCalculated, a Clear statement is not required. You do not want the Out_of_Balance account to consolidate up the organization. You want to check at each spot if it is still in balance. When you set it up to consolidate, it is not telling you that the trial balance is in balance except at the base entities.

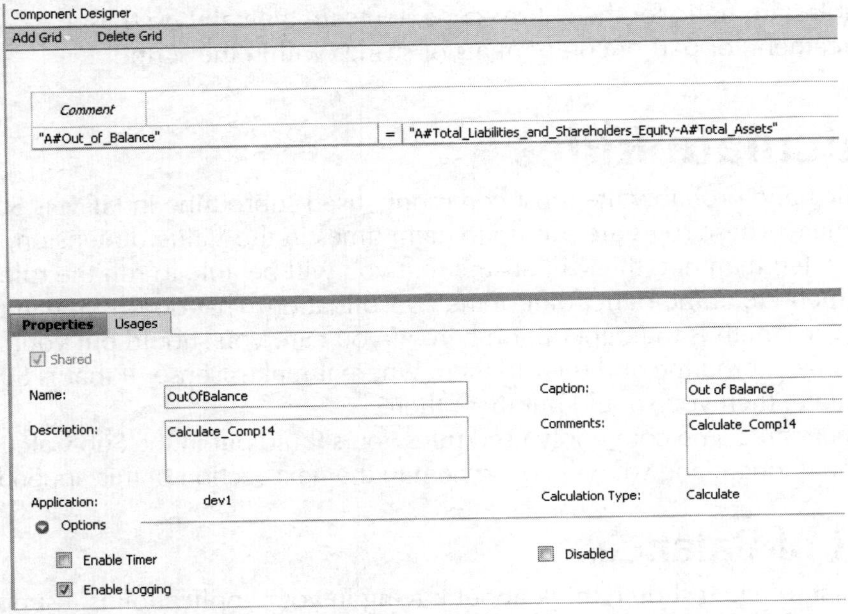

Component Designer
Add Grid Delete Grid

Comment		
"A#Out_of_Balance"	=	"A#Total_Liabilities_and_Shareholders_Equity-A#Total_Assets"

Properties Usages

☑ Shared

Name: OutOfBalance Caption: Out of Balance

Description: Calculate_Comp14 Comments: Calculate_Comp14

Application: dev1 Calculation Type: Calculate

Options

☐ Enable Timer ☐ Disabled

☑ Enable Logging

FIGURE B-3. *Out of balance*

CTA and Currency Translation

The next most common type of rules people would have in their application is rules to handle CTA and currency translation. Before I show these rules, it makes sense to review how to calculate CTA.

What is CTA? CTA stands for Cumulative Translation Adjustment or Currency Translation Adjustment. It is an entry in a translated balance sheet in which gains and/or losses from translation have been accumulated over a period of time. The CTA is required under the FASB No. 52 rule.

A simple example would be one where you had an opening balance sheet with the following (opening period rate is 1.5):

Cash	LC100 × FX of 1.5 to get	US $150
Notes Payable	LC(50) × FX of 1.5 to get	US $(75)
Equity	LC(50) × FX of 1.5 to get	US $(75)

At the end of the year, if nothing changes except that you paid off the note with the cash, paid an expense of Local Currency (LC)20, and the Foreign

Exchange rate (FX) rate moved to 1.6 (current period End of Month [EOM) rate), you would have a current period trial balance of 80.

Let's assume an average current period rate of 1.55. In reality, exchange rates change daily, but we generally use an average rate to measure income statement items and always use the ending rate to measure the balance sheet as a point in time. The FX impact on any specific balance sheet item is an estimate because we do not measure each transaction of the activity balance separately.

Expense	LC20 × FX of 1.55 to get	US $31
Net Income	LC(20) × FX of 1.55 to get	US ($31)

(Current end of period rate is 1.6)

Cash	LC30 × FX of 1.6 to get	US $48

(Cash decreases of 50 to Notes, and 20 to expense)

Notes Payable	LC(0) × FX of 1.6 to get	US $(0)
Equity	LC(50) × FX of 1.5 to get	US $(75) (not impacted by FX)
Current RE	LC20 × FX of 1.55 to get	US $31 (average rate at a loss)
CTA		US $(4) (to balance)

The easiest way to calculate this Currency Translation Adjustment (CTA) balance in the rules is to calculate the difference between the total assets and the total liabilities and equity. The assumption is that if your balance sheet is in balance in local currency, then after translation, any out-of-balance condition that exists must be a result of that translation. So, you can then take that out-of-balance amount and know that it will exactly equal your CTA. This is just like the Out of Balance calculations. This works because you are using the Out_of_Balance account as shown in the preceding tables. When you use that account, you can be sure your balance sheet is always in balance. So if your balance sheet is in balance, you need not worry that you could overstate your CTA.

The CTA calculation runs only after translation. It is then aggregated up the Entity structure during consolidation. This calculation is performed after translation instead of during translation because it requires all other accounts to be translated prior to its calculation. Therefore, it is called from Sub Calculate when IsTrans = True instead of being called from Sub Translate.

If you do feel that you want to calculate each part of CTA to build a proof, that is not as hard as it seems either. In Figure B-4, the rules that break out each part of the CTA components are shown. You can see how simple it is, but this example assumes that each balance sheet account has two custom members, one for the beginning balance impact and one for the movement impact.

To calculate the FX on beginning balance:

- The CTA on cash is the change in the FX rate of (0.1) × BOY cash of LC100 = US $(10).
- The CTA on liabilities is the change in the FX rate of (0.1) × BOY liabilities of LC(50) = US $5.
- The CTA on equity is the change in the FX rate of (0.0) × balance of LC(50) = US $0.

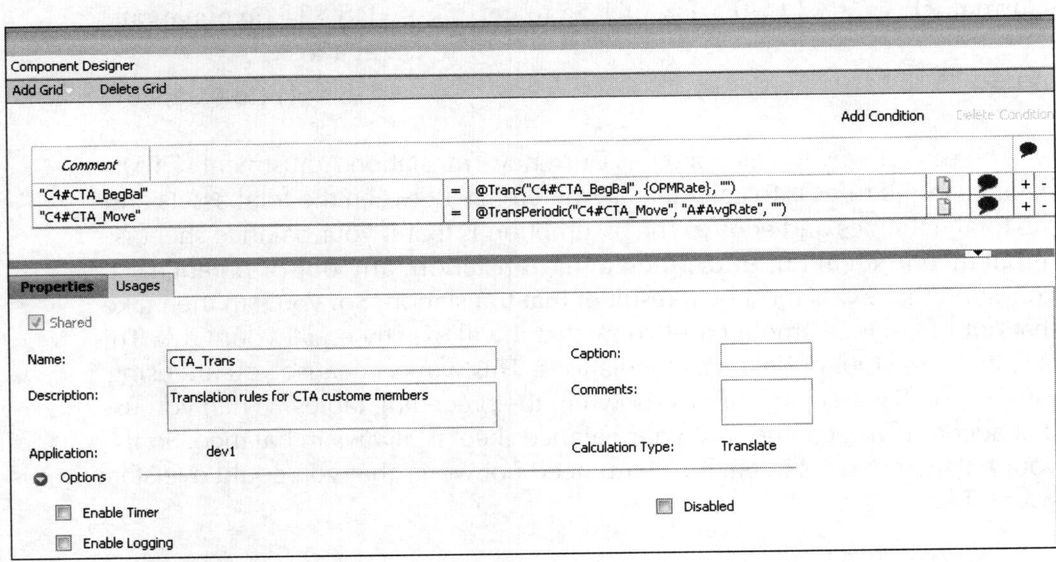

FIGURE B-4. *CTA proof*

To calculate the FX on activity:

- The CTA on cash is the change in the FX rate of (0.05) × movement of LC 70 = US $3.5.
- The CTA on liabilities is the change in the FX rate of (0.05) × movement of liabilities of LC(50) = US $(2.5).
- Total FX impact of $(4) is $(10) on cash, $5 on liabilities, and the rate of the movements of $1.

Retained Earnings

Retained earnings are the percentage of net earnings not paid out as dividends, but retained by the company to be reinvested in the business. It is found in the shareholders' equity on the balance sheet. The logic is a basic roll forward. It has several components:

- **Ending Retained Earnings** This is the sum of the other components.
- **Beginning Retained Earnings** This is equal to the Ending Retained Earnings of the prior year-end.
- **Current Retained Earnings** This is equal to Net Income.
- **Dividends** Percentage of earnings paid to shareholders.

The Retained Earnings calculation copies the amount from Account "PROFIT_LOSS" (Net Income) to Account "39998" (Current Retained Earnings). The second part pulls the amount from Account "RETAINEDEARNINGS" (Prior Year End Retained Earnings) to Account "39999" (Beginning Retained Earnings). Figure B-5 shows how you should set this up in Calculation Manager. This calculation would run only at the EC member of base entities and adjustment Value members. It is then aggregated up the Entity structure during consolidation.

If you wanted to build these rules in the VBScript option, you would use the example in Figure B-6. You can see in this example how we specify where this rule would run, by limiting the calculation to run in Entity Currency only.

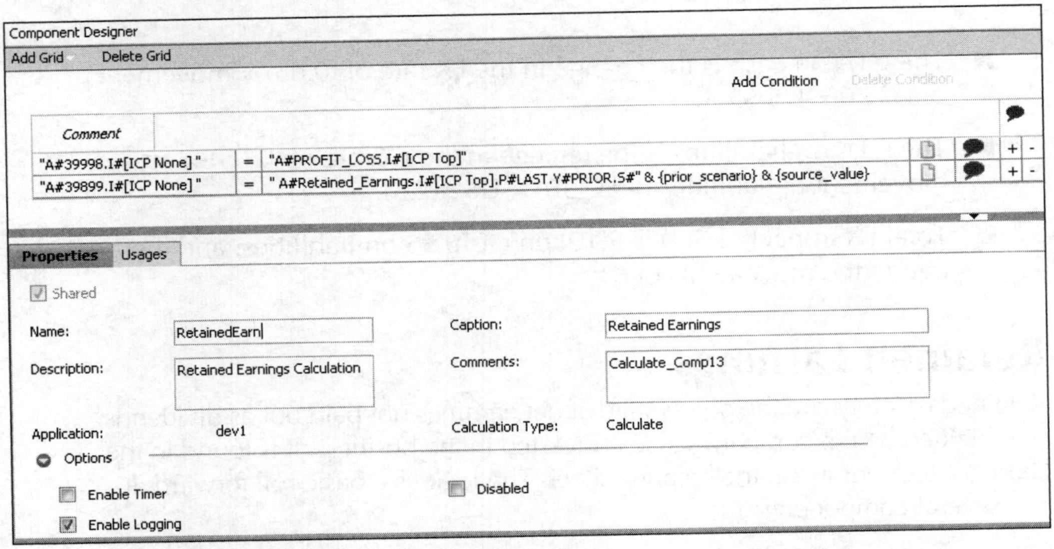

Component Designer

Add Grid Delete Grid

Add Condition Delete Condition

Comment		
"A#39998.I#[ICP None]"	=	"A#PROFIT_LOSS.I#[ICP Top]"
"A#39899.I#[ICP None]"	=	" A#Retained_Earnings.I#[ICP Top].P#LAST.Y#PRIOR.S#" & {prior_scenario} & {source_value}

Properties Usages

Shared

Name: RetainedEarn

Caption: Retained Earnings

Description: Retained Earnings Calculation

Comments: Calculate_Comp13

Application: dev1

Calculation Type: Calculate

Options

Enable Timer

Disabled

Enable Logging

FIGURE B-5. *Retained earnings*

Validations

You will want to test that certain conditions are true while consolidating your data. This type of rule works to make tools like Process Management more useful, but *every* application should have validations. The best approach was first done by one of the technical editors of this book and myself on one of the very first HFM projects. I know it is a pretty good approach since years later,

```
' -- Retained earnings
If pov_value= "<Entity Currency>" OR is_parent_cur Then
     ' -- Calculate_Comp13
     ' Component Name = RetainedEarn_CLIENT

     HS.Exp "A#39998.I#[ICP None] " & "=" & "A#PROFIT_LOSS.I#[ICP Top]"
     HS.Exp "A#39999.I#[ICP None] " & "=" & "A#Retained_Earnings.I#[ICP
Top].P#LAST.Y#PRIOR.S#" & prior_scenario & source_value
End If
```

FIGURE B-6. *Retained earnings in VBScript*

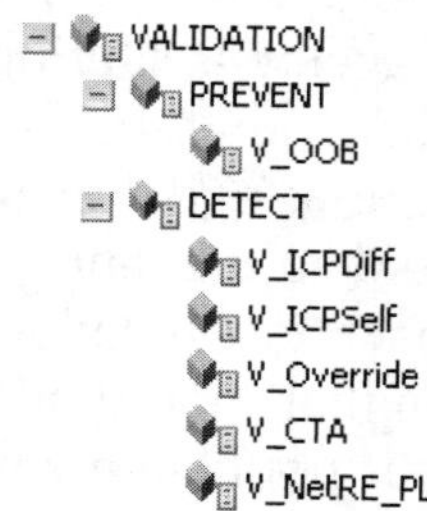

FIGURE B-7. *Validation accounts*

at a meeting on best practices, a large firm presented this concept as a best practice.

First, you should group your validations by type, Prevent and Detect. Prevent validations are validations that you intend to stop the close. These are Accounting 101 basic mistakes, ones that are so egregious that you want to stop the close until they are resolved. This includes things like if your balance sheet is out of balance, or if a roll forward does not tie to the balance sheet. Detect validations are ones that there might be a valid reason for, and you want to make the users aware of the issue, but you do not want to stop the close. Figure B-7 shows an example of how this might be set up in the dimension editor of EPMA.

The Prevent account will be your validation account in the application settings. The Detect will only show up on a report. But you will need rules to make this work. The concept here is that the Prevent account needs to be zero. Since it is a parent account, it is the sum of its children. You will write a rule for each child to test some condition. Look at Figure B-8, and see what a simple balance sheet check might look like in VBScript. Now you can go crazy checking all kinds of rules.

```
If is_base = True And pov_value = "<Entity Currency>" Then

        HS.Exp "A#BalanceSheetValidation" & nones & " = " & _
        "A#Assets.I#[ICP Top]" & tops & "-A#LiabEquity.I#[ICP Top]" & tops
End If
```

FIGURE B-8. *Out of balance in VBScript*

Validation accounts are important to have, and especially important if you plan on using Process Management. During the review process, when the user will try to promote the data unit to a higher level, the system will check if the account for validation is equal to zero. If that is not the case, the system will not promote the data unit and a message will be displayed to the user. In the common approach to validation accounts, the script checks to see if there is some condition that should be resolved. If there is a number present, the validation account is populated with a one. The validation accounts aggregate to a parent account. That parent account must be zero for data to be promoted. You can build these validations for any type of check. Figure B-9 shows how they could look in Calculation Manager. The rule components here (V_OOB, for example) will write a "1" to the validation account if the "Out of Balance" condition is true.

It might be agreed that having data submitters reconcile to the penny is not the best use of their time. So it is very common to utilize threshold accounts. The validations that I described should not be enforced if the amount is below the threshold in USD. You would create a threshold account, put what you want to test in that account, and refer to it in

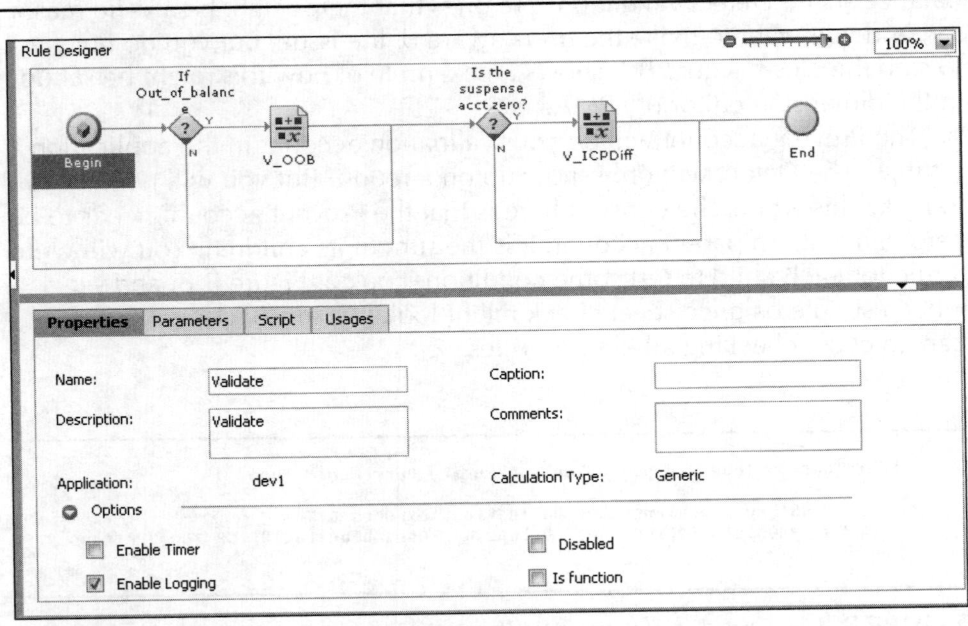

FIGURE B-9. *Validations*

your rules. You would check in the rule if the outage is greater than the amount in your threshold. The rules can determine the correct local currency.

When you write the validations in VBScript, it is a good idea to group the entire validations within a Sub Validation procedure. Figure B-10 shows multiple validations within the Sub procedure. The benefit of taking this approach is that you can take this rule out of the file by simply commenting out the call for Sub Validate. With Calculation Manager, it is much easier to exclude the rule, and take it out of scope. You would simply remove the rule from the rule set.

From an HFM design perspective, a separate account hierarchy is set up to total all the Validation accounts, grouped between Prevent and Detect validations. The Prevent hierarchy will include those validations that would prevent entities from promoting or submitting data to the next level.

There are some common validations everyone seems to use:

- Balance sheet out of balance
- Total of balance sheet roll-forwards = Balance sheet balance
- ICP plug
- Historical overrides check

```
Sub Validate(bLog)
    'ID:4

            ' -- out of balalnce
            If HS.GetCell("A#Out_of_Balance") <> 0 Then
                ' -- Validate_Comp46
                ' Component Name = Out of Balance Validation

                HS.Exp "A#V_OOB " & "=" & " 1"
            End If
            If HS.GetCell("A#13110") <> 0 Then
                ' Component Name = ICP Diff Validation

                ' -- Test if ICP accounts eliminate correctly
                HS.Exp "A#V_ICPDiff" & "=" & "1"
            End If
End Sub
```

FIGURE B-10. *VBScript validations*

Cash Flow

Cash flow is not complicated, but envisioning how it might work in HFM can be if you are new to the system. If your cash flow has the two sections I have described, you are on your way to making this report much easier to manage.

There is no application that can completely automate the cash flow statement. Since it is not that difficult, there really is not a reason to have a cash flow statement. However, HFM can offer four very important reasons to include cash flow:

- Automate the change in balances, and pull values from the income statement and roll forwards.
- Accurately calculate the effect of the exchange rate on the change in cash.
- Validate the cash flow statement, like other financial statements.
- Ensure that the cash flow is backed up and locked down with the trial balance and supporting schedules.

To calculate the cash flow statement, there are really only two parts. First, at entity currency, take the change in cash from each balance sheet, income or roll forward account, and write that to the corresponding cash flow account. You should make the cash flow accounts income type. The reason for this is that they will translate using the same rate and methodology as your income statement. The reason for income instead of expense is to have them show correctly on a report, if you use better/worse functionality. If you do this, you will have all of your cash flow accounts translated correctly and reconciling to the trial balance.

As part of calculating the change in cash, you should always pull beginning cash and ending cash from the balance sheet. This will set you up to do a simple validation later.

The second part of the cash flow is the effect of the exchange rate on the change in cash. The simplest calculation is to just multiply the change in exchange rates by the opening cash/cash equivalent balances to get the impact of FX. The first part is the foreign exchange on the opening balance of cash. You would need to take the beginning cash and multiply that by the change in the opening rate and current end of month rate. The second part is to take the activity in local currency on the cash flow statement and multiply that by the difference in the average rate and the current end-of-month rate. Then add the first and second parts together. Any other approach, since not recommended in FAS95, really should have a validation to ensure that it is working as intended.

Many people use the Custom1 dimension (or some available custom dimension) to calculate the FX impact by *each* Cash Flow account. This was an approach that was introduced to me by Bob Nelson, a long-time expert in consolidation tools and accounting. Most every cash flow approach used in HFM now is a variation on his original approach. The benefit is that you would be able to see detail by line in the cash flow statement, like FX impact by balance sheet account. The top-level member of the Custom1 dimension for Cash Flow must be assigned to each Cash Flow account (CFTop is this example). Figure B-11 illustrates three elements below the CFTop total (parent level).

- CFNet (Cash Flow Net) represents the raw change in data for each account (for example, change in accounts receivable).
- CFFX represents the calculation of the FX on the Cash Flow account.
- CFGross (Cash Flow Operations) represents the total of the raw change in the cash flow plus the Foreign exchange impact.
- CFAdj will capture all reclasses and adjustments to the application. This will be a parent member, as the adjustments will roll to a total adjustment.

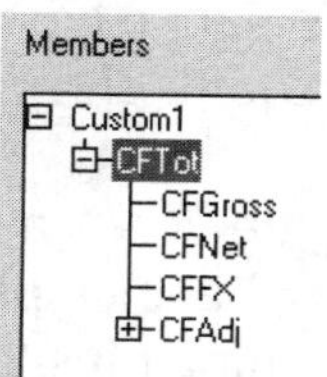

FIGURE B-11. *Cash Flow customs*

The Aggregate weights for CFGross, CFAdj, and CFFX should be set to 0. The aggregate weight for the CFNet element should be set to 1. To correctly capture the Cash Flow, rules will be written specific to the entity currency value dimension and the parent currency dimension.

Of course, you should have a validation added to the application if you are trying to build cash flow within HFM. It is simply, "Does the change in cash equal the change in activity of the cash flow?" You can test this in a couple of ways, but basically the formula is

Cash - Cash, opening period = change in cash from Activity + Financing + Investing

You would insert your account names in the preceding formula and determine a validation account, as in this example;

```
HS.Exp "A#V_CFCheck = A#CF_Chng – A#CF_ACT- A#CF_FIN–A#CF_
INV"
```

In doing this, with the way I am recommending calculating the currency effect of the change in cash, you can be sure that if this validation works, you are calculating the correct foreign exchange impact.

Roll Forwards and Movement Accounts

Every balance sheet has beginning retained earnings. I am sure you have that in your ledger, too. So why should you not just load that value? The reason is to ensure that the beginning balances do not have unexplained adjustments. It also sets you up for a validation on the beginning balances, but we will cover that in validations. One of the nice things about HFM is the ability to combine flow and balance type accounts and have each behave the correct way; flow accounts show periodic change and balance accounts do not.

The rules for this calculation are very simple: just specify that the closing balance is the sum of the opening balance plus movements.

Write a rule that takes the opening plus the movement, and write that to the closing:

```
HS.Exp "C1#Close = C1#Open + C1#Move"
```

You could also make the C1#Close the parent account. And that would not require a rule. Then you could attach the custom dimensions to each account you want to roll forward, even every account on your balance sheet.

However, for your beginning balance, you should consider something else. You want to make them dynamic, meaning that regardless of the period, they pull the right amount. Also, you want to consider the impact on currency changes. Look at the example in Figure B-12. You can see how you must run the rule twice. The rules run once for entity currency and then again if the currency changes.

So why can't you just say if it is equal to parent currency? The reason is that there really always is a parent currency. It is just a pointer to the currency. And if the parent currency is the same as the entity currency, it does not really fix what you are trying to do. You are trying to test whether translation happened. And to do that we would use the rule "IsTranCur." If you needed to test whether the adjustment member is translated, you would use IsTransCurAdj.

If HS.Value.IsTransCur = True Then

So let's look at how the rules might be impacted from the scenario dimension. In Figure B-13, we are addressing another issue with pulling beginning balances. We are considering "what is the correct scenario" to

```
Sub Calculate
        'Rules run at base entity and at local currency
        If HS.Entity.IsBase("","") = True And HS.Value.Member = "<Entity Currency>" Then

             'Pull NetProfit into RetainedEarnings
             HS.Exp "A#RetainedEarnings= A#Netprofit"

        'Rules also run at translation
        Else If HS.Value.IsTransCur() = True Then

             'Pull NetProfit into RetainedEarnings
             HS.Exp "A#RetainedEarnings= A#Netprofit"

        End If 'If HS.Entity.IsBase("","") = True And HS.Value.Member = "<Entity Currency>" Then
End Sub
```

FIGURE B-12. *Retained earnings in VBScript*

```
Sub Calculate

        If UCase(HS.Scenario.Member) = "FORECAST" Then

            strSourceScenario = ".S#FORECAST"
        Else
            strSourceScenario = ".S#ACTUAL"
        End If

        'Rules run at base entity and at local currency
        If HS.Entity.IsBase("","") = True And HS.Value.Member = "<Entity Currency>" Then

            'Pull NetProfit into RetainedEarnings
            HS.Exp "A#RetainedEarnings= A#Netprofit" &  strSourceScenario

        'Rules also run at translation
        Else If HS.Value.IsTransCur() = True Then

            'Pull NetProfit into RetainedEarnings
            HS.Exp "A#RetainedEarnings= A#Netprofit" &  strSourceScenario

        End If 'If HS.Entity.IsBase("","") = True And HS.Value.Member = "<Entity Currency>" Then

End Sub
```

FIGURE B-13. *Pulling from the correct scenario*

pull from. In actual, it does not need to be called out because it hasn't changed. But for the budget, we want to use actual for our ending balances. To do this we use a dynamic variable. Based on what scenario the rules are running, we would set our opening scenario. If it is Actual or Budget, the rules should pull from the Actual scenario. If it is running in the Forecast, then pull from the Forecast.

The two considerations, translation and scenario, should always be considered when pulling beginning balances.

Roll Forward

Retained earnings are basically just a roll forward. The purpose of roll forward rules is to pull the ending balances from the prior year into the beginning balance of the current year. It also pulls forward any prior period adjustments to beginning balance. So you can use this approach not just for retained earnings, but also fixed assets, debt schedules, and others.

If you have many roll forwards, you should build the common components into a custom dimension. As shown in Figure B-14, Ending Balances (ClosingBalance) should be the parent member of the beginning

```
If pov_scenario = "ACTUAL" Then

    HS.Clear "C1#OpeningBalance"
    HS.Exp "C1#OpeningBalance = C1#ClosingBalance.P#Last.Y#Prior"

ElseIf pov_scenario = "BUDGET" Then

    HS.Clear "C1#OpeningBalance"
    HS.Exp "C1#OpeningBalance = C1#ClosingBalance.P#Last.Y#Prior.S#Actual"

End If 'pov_scenario = "ACTUAL"
```

FIGURE B-14. *Roll forward rules in customs*

balance (OpeningBalance) and the activity. The roll forward logic then performs two calculations: (1) in the first period of the year, it pulls data from the ClosingBalance member from the last period of the prior, and writes to the OpeningBalance member; and (2) in all other periods, it pulls the prior period's OpeningBalance member (which include beginning balance adjustments) and copies it to the OpeningBalance of the current period.

When it runs in the first period on a base entity, it will only run on the EC member pulling from the ECT member of the prior year. This allows all journal adjustments from the prior year to be pulled into the EC of the current year.

Copy Scenarios

Often, people want to have a copy of data in one scenario in another. This can be for several reasons, for example, building forecast data, constant currency analysis, or pro forma reporting. This is something we can do very simply in HFM.

In certain circumstances data could be copied between scenarios. For example, Actual periods will be copied into the Forecast scenarios once those periods are closed. Or Actual data could also be copied into scenarios; different rates where they will be translated at a constant rate to allow for comparison across scenarios without the impact of exchange rate changes being a factor.

Take a look at Figure B-15. The rule itself is quite simple. In fact, the first thing to note is the use of the keyword ALL. By using this keyword, you don't need to loop through any members or build anything very complex.

```
If HS.Scenario.Member = "Forecast" and HS.Getcell "A#CopyFlag" = 1 Then
    'Rules run at base entity and at local currency
    If HS.Entity.IsBase("","") = True And HS.Value.Member = "<Entity Currency>" Then

        HS.Clear "A#ALL"
        HS.Exp "A#ALL = S#Actual"

    End if
End If 'HS.Scenario.Member = "Forecast" and HS.Getcell "A#CopyFlag" = 1
```

FIGURE B-15. *Copy scenario*

Using this keyword is very efficient. The second thing to note is the use of the "Copy_Flag" account. This is an admin account that requires a value of one to be entered, or the copy will not run. This gives the administrator the ability to turn this rule on and off without reloading the rules. This is helpful during the close.

This rule should run at base entities and for Entity Currency only as well, as you can see it is added to the rule file. You could use a rule like this for not only copying Actual into the Forecast scenario, but also copying Actuals into Constant Dollar scenarios. Then you can be sure the data in a Actual scenario at Budget rate scenario is the same base data as in the Actual scenario; just be sure to not overwrite the rates in the [None] entity.

Impact Scenarios

Impact the calculation status of specified scenarios so that when a consolidation is run in those scenarios, the proper data is copied into them.

In these certain circumstances, data will be copied between scenarios. For example, Actual periods will be copied into the Forecast scenarios once those periods are closed. This rule ensures that when data is entered into the source scenario, the calculation status of the same intersection of the destination scenario will be impacted. This tells HFM that when a "Consolidate" or "Consolidate All With Data" is run in the destination scenario, it will run the rules that copy the data into that intersection regardless of whether or not there is already data in the destination.

As shown in Figure B-16, Impact Status rules can slow down consolidation times, so they should be controlled by triggers when possible. An Account trigger called "ImpactCopy" or something similar should be used to control

```
If HS.Scenario.Member = "Actual" and HS.Getcell "A#ImpactCopy" = 1 Then
    HS.ImpactStatus "S#Forecast"
End If 'HS.Scenario.Member = "Forecast" and HS.Getcell "A#CopyFlag" = 1
```

FIGURE B-16. *Impact scenario*

when Actual data impacts the Forecast scenarios. If you wanted to make the trigger work globally, you would set the trigger on in the "[None]" Entity. In this case, this rule will run only on all Entities with a value in the flag account when a consolidation is run.

HS.ImpactStatus Functionality

You might notice that the rules seem to always seem to pull data from other points of view (Year, Scenario, Period, and Value). That is true, with only a couple of exceptions. The Impact Status rule is one of those exceptions. This rule can go to another point of view and change the status of that entity to be impacted. Consider this typical example: You want to have a rule that determines the opening balance for an account (Retained Earnings). Now assume that at some point you might need to go back into last year's data and make changes that affect the ending earnings of that year.

Since there is no link between the current and prior year, after changes in last year have been made, the status of the current year will continue to show OK. In order for the change to be reflected in next year's opening equity, users typically would have to go into the subsequent year and run a Force Calculate because the entity would have a status of OK. However, you don't want to do that. In fact, if you are asking users to run Force Calculate in your application, you could have a problem. But since we cover that in another chapter, let's stick to the ImpactStatus. If the change were in the first period of a year, that would impact all future periods where there is data in the same year. However, crossing subcube boundaries (year, scenario) is not assumed, for performance reasons. To do this, you must use the HFM function ImpactStatus. This enables the system to impact data across subcubes.

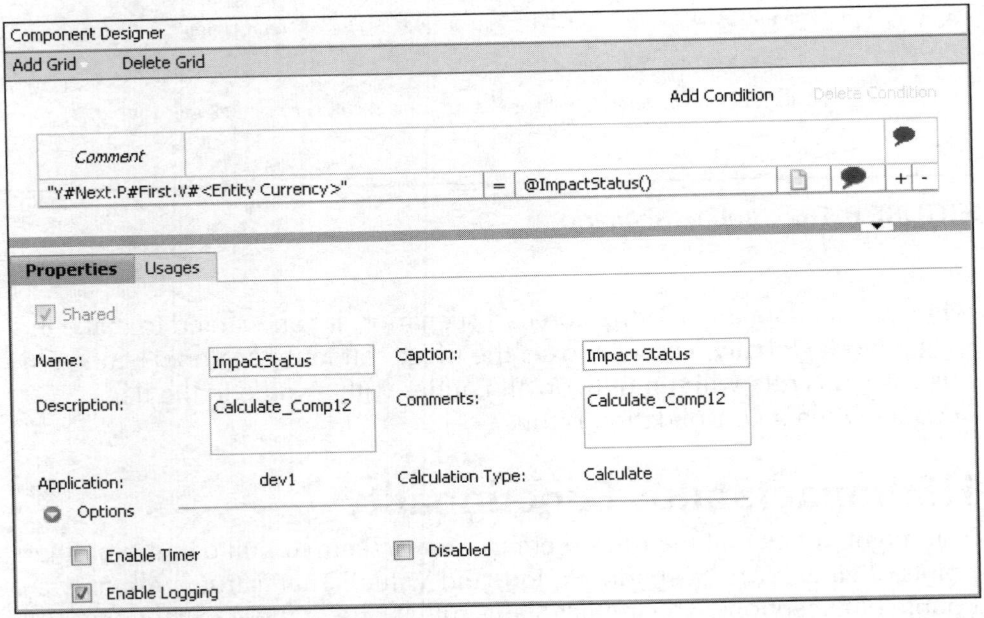

FIGURE B-17. *Impact status*

The HS.ImpactStatus rule allows you to impact another period and across year boundaries. Figure B-17 shows the rule that will impact the next year if there is some change that could affect current period ending balances that will need to roll into the opening balances.

You would do this using any combination of valid Scenario, Year, Period, Entity, and Value dimension members. If the scenario is the same, the year and period combination must be equal to the current period or future period. If no value member is specified, it is assumed to be current:

```
HS.ImpactStatus"S#Scenario.Y#Year.P#Period.E#Entity.V#Value"
```

NoInput and Input Rules

There are times when you need to prevent input for a cell for a given period, entity custom, account, and so on. The NoInput rules allow you to do this. They are very straightforward. You just need to write these rules

```
Sub NoInput()

     HS.NoInput "S#BudV1.A#Sales"
     HS.NoInput "S#BudV2.A#Sales"

End Sub
```

FIGURE B-18. *NoInput rules*

with the NoInput subroutine. Take a look at Figure B-18, and see how easy NoInput rules are. The only risk you have is that you must be aware, when creating loops, of how many NoInput rules you are actually running. I have seen people create billions of loops on the same five or six NoInput lines. In such a situation, you can expect the performance of loading the rules file and starting up the application to be unusually long. This is when the array created from the NoInput rules is created, and if you have many NoInput rules, it will take time to work through them all.

You can avoid using these rules by thinking more about your metadata. For example, you can refine your custom top member in the Accounts dimension. This setting will limit what custom members are valid for an intersection of an account. You could also change the ICP Top member to ICP Entities. This would make ICP None not a valid intersection for the intercompany accounts.

Security can help eliminate the need for using NoInput rules. You can limit access to accounts, customs, scenarios, entities, and so on.

NoInput rules prevent data input into cells, thus reserving the cells for calculations. To write a NoInput rule, use the NoInput function and an argument to specify the cells in which you want to prohibit data input. You can use the NoInput function multiple times in a NoInput rule to prohibit data input into several nonadjacent cells. You may have some accounts in which users should be able to input data for some intersecting dimension members and not for others. For example, you may have supplemental data that applies to only one location but not another. You can simply add a NoInput rule to prevent the location form accidentally entering data. This can be very helpful.

The rules are not any more complicated in Calculation Manager, as shown in Figure B-19.

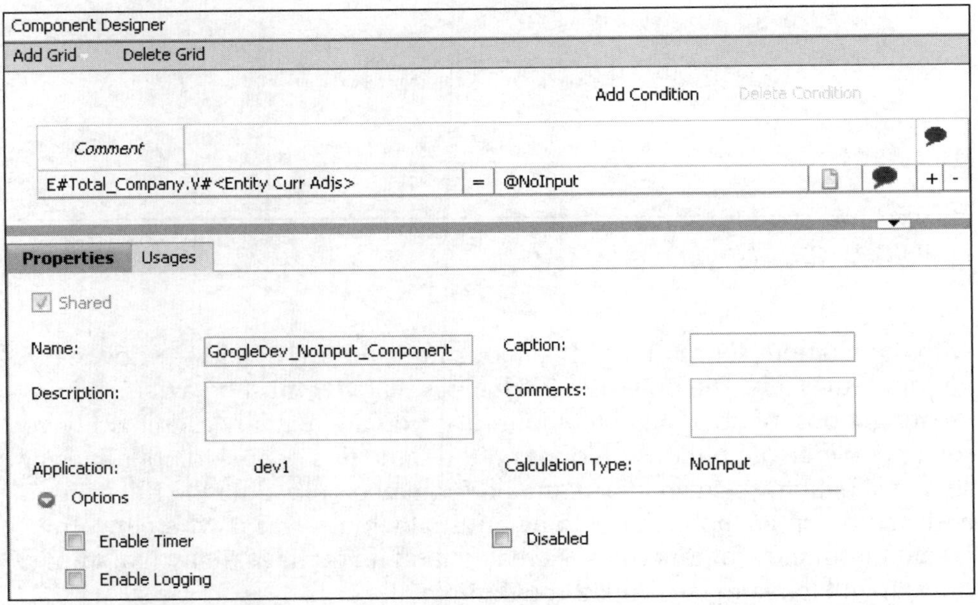

FIGURE B-19. *NoInput rules for Calculation Manager*

Now look at Figure B-20. Writing input rules really is not much different than writing NoInput rules. One thing that is different with how they work, though, is the cells you can make valid for Input. You make base accounts and customs at parent entities available for input.

```
Sub Input
   HS.Input "E#NewHampshire.A#Headcount"
End Sub
```

FIGURE B-20. *Input rules*

Dynamic Rules

Dynamic accounts are dynamically calculated when the data is requested. The values are not stored; they are calculated "on the fly." Most commonly, you would see these as ratios. Parent totals for accounts, custom dimensions, and time periods are calculated dynamically; they are not aggregated from children. These rules are some of the easiest rules to write. Since they only run when called, they have no impact on the database, and so the only risk is a bad grid or report when run. People get into trouble with these rules by just not understanding the limitations. Look at Figure B-21 to see an example of Dynamic rules. The underlying script would look something like Figure B-22.

Use these guidelines to make sure that your rules work well:

- The right side of the equation must reference the same Scenario/Year/Entity combination. This means you cannot reference prior year amounts in your calculations.
- You can use HS.Dynamic only in the Sub Dynamic procedures.

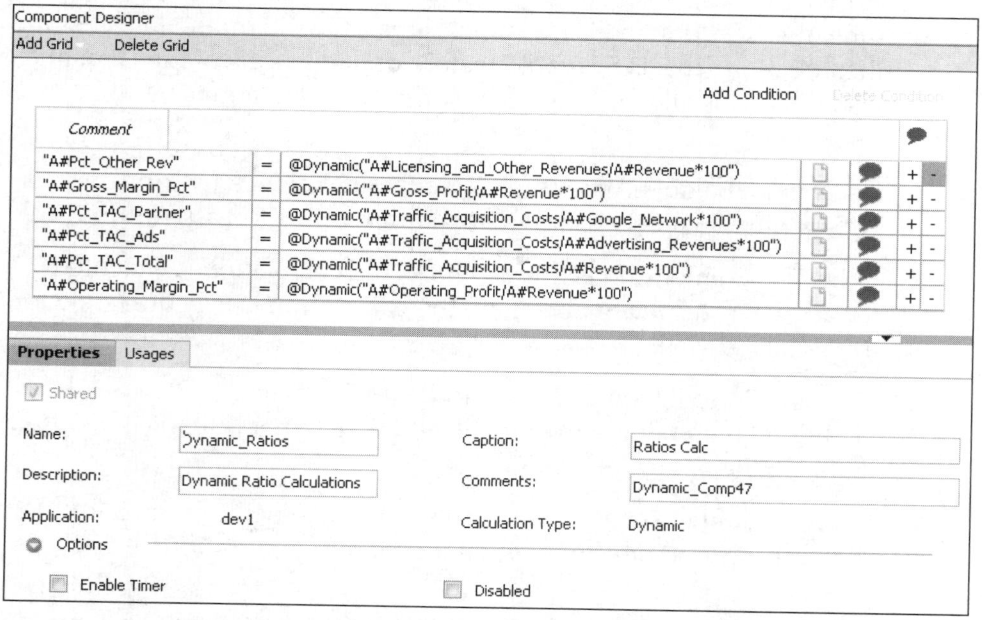

Component Designer

Add Grid Delete Grid

Add Condition Delete Condition

Comment		
"A#Pct_Other_Rev"	=	@Dynamic("A#Licensing_and_Other_Revenues/A#Revenue*100")
"A#Gross_Margin_Pct"	=	@Dynamic("A#Gross_Profit/A#Revenue*100")
"A#Pct_TAC_Partner"	=	@Dynamic("A#Traffic_Acquisition_Costs/A#Google_Network*100")
"A#Pct_TAC_Ads"	=	@Dynamic("A#Traffic_Acquisition_Costs/A#Advertising_Revenues*100")
"A#Pct_TAC_Total"	=	@Dynamic("A#Traffic_Acquisition_Costs/A#Revenue*100")
"A#Operating_Margin_Pct"	=	@Dynamic("A#Operating_Profit/A#Revenue*100")

Properties Usages

Shared

Name: Dynamic_Ratios Caption: Ratios Calc

Description: Dynamic Ratio Calculations Comments: Dynamic_Comp47

Application: dev1 Calculation Type: Dynamic

Options

Enable Timer Disabled

FIGURE B-21. *Dynamic rules in Calculation Manager*

```
Sub Dynamic_Rule7(bLog)
    'ID:8

            ' -- Dynamic_Comp47
            ' Component Name = CLIENTDev_Dynamic_Ratios

            HS.Dynamic "A#Pct_CLIENT_Com" & "=" & "A#CLIENT_Properties/A#Advertising_Revenues*100"
            HS.Dynamic "A#Pct_Partner_Rev" & "=" & "A#CLIENT_Network/A#Advertising_Revenues*100"
            HS.Dynamic "A#Pct_CLIENT_Site" & "=" & "A#CLIENT_Properties/A#Revenue*100"
            HS.Dynamic "A#Pct_Partner_Rev_Tot" & "=" & "A#CLIENT_Network/A#Revenue*100"
            HS.Dynamic "A#Pct_Other_Rev" & "=" & "A#Licensing_and_Other_Revenues/A#Revenue*100"
            HS.Dynamic "A#Gross_Margin_Pct" & "=" & "A#Gross_Profit/A#Revenue*100"
            HS.Dynamic "A#Pct_TAC_Partner" & "=" & "A#Traffic_Acquisition_Costs/A#CLIENT_Network*100"
            HS.Dynamic "A#Pct_TAC_Ads" & "=" & "A#Traffic_Acquisition_Costs/A#Advertising_Revenues*100"
            HS.Dynamic "A#Pct_TAC_Total" & "=" & "A#Traffic_Acquisition_Costs/A#Revenue*100"
            HS.Dynamic "A#Operating_Margin_Pct" & "=" & "A#Operating_Profit/A#Revenue*100"
End Sub
```

FIGURE B-22. *Dynamic rules in VBScript*

- HS.Dynamic is executed for the current Point of View for Entity, Scenario, and Year.
- You cannot use conditional statements with dynamic rules.
- Only dynamic accounts are valid on the left side of the equation.
- Dynamic accounts cannot be used on the right side of the equation.
- Only the Account and View dimensions are valid on the left side of the equation. This is a favorite feature of many users of the Dynamic accounts. This allows you to have different calculations by frequency.

  A#OpeningBalance.V#Periodic = A#EndingBalance.P#Prior
  A#OpeningBalance.V#YTD = A#EndingBalance.P#Last.Y#Prior

- If the View dimension is not specified, the calculation is executed for all views. If View is specified, the calculation is executed only for the specified view.
- HS.View.PeriodNumber, HS.Period.NumPerInGen, and HS.Period.Number are the only valid HS statements that can be used in an HS.Dynamic calculation.
- As with all other sections in the rules file, statements in the Sub Dynamic section are executed sequentially.

The Sub Dynamic routine can hurt performance if not used correctly, even though it doesn't write values to the database. First, you must know that the Sub

Dynamic rule runs automatically and cannot be halted. The Sub Dynamic routine will run either at application startup or during rules load time.

If you had a rule that used a constant, for example, you could populate millions, billions, or even trillions of intersections with that constant (just like the rule for the HS.EXP, where all intersections are populated with some number). When this happens, you can't load a new rule or metadata file into the afflicted application until the errant dynamic rule errors or completes.

Translation Rules

Translation is not a difficult concept. You have revenue you earn in multiple currencies, but you need to report it in one of the parents. You have transactions that need to be translated into the functional currency of the entity. That process is called "revaluation." Since HFM does not have transactional detail, revaluation must stay in the ledger. Once in the functional currency, the data can move into HFM. Your application should have functional currency by legal entity for many reasons. Once functional currency is in HFM, the translation process can progress.

One of the benefits of HFM is that it was built to be GAAP neutral. You can calculate the translation as you need. However, for the benefit of this appendix, let's assume US GAAP. This approach is also valid for IFRS. So it will serve as a good example of the rules for translation.

Balance sheet accounts use the rate at the end of the period that the balance is in. This year-to-date method is called VAL. The flow accounts (revenue, expense, and cash flow) should translate using an average rate. The average rate can be an average for the year, or for the month. Fortunately, HFM can translate using both a year-to-date average and periodic average. The periodic method is called Periodic Value Add (PVA).

- The VAL method translates the entire balance at the current period rate.
- The PVA method:
  - Translates just the YTD change from the previous period at the current period's exchange rate.
  - Adds this to the previous month translated balance.

Certain accounts add difficulty due to the fact that at the end of the previous year, the data was translated at last year's closing rate, so current period opening balances need to show the same value as the prior year's closing. Other accounts need to translate at historical rates. Dividends in the profit and loss account use the rate as of the date they are declared.

Calculating these accounts at different rates isn't difficult. Either use the Hs.Translate in the Sub Translate, or in the Sub Calculate section, use the HS.Exp function to override the values that would normally be translated. Hence, these are called override rules, or just overrides.

The differences arising from these treatments of the different types of data are taken to a reserve called "CTA," or cumulative translation adjustment.

When consolidating, the Sub Translate procedure runs when entity and parent currency are different, and actually converts the data from one currency to another. The Sub Translate procedure will be called other times as well, when you are not consolidating, but when the source and target currencies are not the same, for example, when you run the intercompany matching report.

Translation Best Practices

If you haven't picked up yet on a couple of these rules, one of the key points is that HFM can't create data. The data coming in has to be at the right detail, and clean—or you will have problems. One of the strengths of HFM is its ability to translate. It is a mistake not to load functional currency into HFM. The functional currency is required for many external reports, and not including it prevents you from having one source for the data.

FX Calculations

So how should you do foreign exchange calculations and calculate the cumulative currency adjustment? You have two choices: you can calculate each piece or back into the number. (Please note I do not say plug, which doesn't mean that it isn't a plug.)

So if you wanted to calculate each piece of CTA, you would need to calculate two parts for each account on the balance sheet. For the foreign exchange impact in a roll forward, it is basically the same calculation.

- Effect due to change in rate on opening balance:
  - Prior period balance in local currency multiplied by end-of-month rate
  - And then subtract
  - Prior period balance in local currency multiplied by end-of-month rate for the prior period

- Effect due to balance sheet activity:
  - Current balance sheet activity in local currency multiplied by end-of-month rate
  - And then subtract
  - Current balance sheet activity in local currency multiplied by average monthly rate

It is absolutely important to build this out in a custom for one reason. You can use these values by account to be your CTA proof. But all of this assumes you have local currency by legal entity.

Overrides

Not all accounts will translate using the default rules. As per US GAAP and IFRS, certain accounts (investment and equity are most common) need to translate at a historic rate. The override is the approach used to "override" the translation, when we don't want to translate using VAL or PVA, but some historical rate. To do this translation, we have two options:

- **Override rate** Enter a historical rate.
- **Override amount** Enter the value you want to see at translation.

The approach you might choose between the two depends on what you are more comfortable with and the system you have in place. The work involved between calculating a rate or the override amount is really the same. Each has the same shortcomings, where you may have to enter multiple values. However, many people still prefer the "override amount." The reason is that the override amount is easier to follow in HFM. You see what you entered, and you see that value appear at translation. Second, you don't have to deal with any rounding. What you enter is the value at translation.

To build a rule with the Override Amount approach, you have to make a set of override accounts. For an account that is translated at Historical/Spot rates, an amount representing the post-translated value of that account will be stored in a separate account called an Override account. An individual Override account will exist per each historically translated account and per each currency into which data will be translated. For example, if during consolidation, data is translated into USD and also into EUR, then the account "17000" should have two corresponding Override accounts, "17000_USD" and "17000_EUR." Currently, this application is only translating into USD.

In each period, a user will manually enter an override amount into the Override account that represents the post-translated value of the activity that was posted in the account of that period. For example, if the value in the account "17000" of a EUR entity changed from 1400 to 1600 between January and February, then an Override amount of USD 315 is entered into the account "17000_USD" corresponding to that EUR 200 of activity. If an amount of USD 2210 already existed in that Override account, then it will be added to it to get a total value of USD 2525 for the "17000_USD" account.

The USD 2525 will override the result of the default translation of the EUR 1600 in account "17000."

This rule will run after translation occurs. For the currency into which data is being translated, this rule will pull the appropriate Override Accounts that contain data and override the corresponding IS or BS account with this data.

What accounts will use this rate depends on what you choose for your translation method. It could be many or only a handful of accounts. Most people will look at this and not even really know there are different methods. Translation method is the approach used to translate your accounts, and the approach for handling the impact of this translation. Even the two most commonly used methods are not set in stone. It is possible to even use combinations of the two, even for just certain entities.

Current vs. Temporal Translation

The two most commonly used methods for translation are the Current-Rate method and the Temporal method. Basically, IFRS and US GAAP require that the Temporal method be used only in cases where you are reporting in a local currency other than functional, or if the functional currency is considered hyperinflationary.

- **Current-Rate method** (also known as the Closing-Rate method) Assets and liabilities translate at the current rate of exchange on the date of the balance sheet. Items in the income statement, which represent flows over the accounting period, are translated at the exchange rate at the times of accrual, or more commonly a weighted average exchange rate over the accounting period. Dividends and other distributions are translated at the exchange rate at the time they were paid.

- **Temporal method** Monetary assets and liabilities (cash, liquid securities, and accounts payable and receivable, debt) are translated at the current end-of-month rate. Nonmonetary assets and liabilities (fixed assets and inventory) are translated at historical spot rates. Hence there are no capital gains or losses from these accounts. Income state items are translated at the average exchange rate unless they are directly associated with nonmonetary items (depreciation or cost of inventory).

You would need a rule to either translate these accounts at historical rates, or capture overrides for them. Since neither is easy, this should be considered when attempting to employ these approaches.

It is worth noting that HFM can do even this type of complex translation. Well, there are even a couple of acceptable approaches. The first approach is to use customs to capture overrides. You would just need to use a custom member, preferably one that is already being used for the entire trial balance, but with not many members, to capture the historical override for each account. This would be a different approach than typical overrides since you are doing so many. For typical overrides, you might create an account for each override you are creating. But you don't want to do that here, because you could wind up creating so much of your chart of accounts that it would be a mess. Next, you would write a rule that basically looks to see if there is a value in the override, and if it is there, uses that amount as the override.

Writing an Override Rule

The rule is tricky here. Since it is complex, let's think through what we are trying to say first. We can use the "commentary method" again. Basically the rule should say:

Did it translate? If so, then…

    Get a list of the override accounts; these are children of a parent called Override.

        Is this an account that should have an override? If so, then…
        Is there an override? If so, then…

Write the override to the account that needs to be at the new rate.
If there is no override then…
Take the change in the balance, translate that using the current month rate and add that the prior months YTD balance.
End
End
End

Now look at Figure B-23, and see how each line of our plain English becomes the rules for our overrides. Notice how the commentary becomes the explanation of the rule. It's pretty straightforward to follow what you are trying to accomplish.

You should consider building rules like this. It takes what would be complicated and makes it something you can logically follow. This might be a rule you would shy away from building on your own, because it seems too complex, but each line is not overwhelming, and the commentary helps you follow what is happening and where. Most everything has been covered

```
'Did it translate?  If so, then...
If HS.Value.IsTransCur = True Then
    'Get a list of the override accounts; these are children of a parent called Override
    aActList = HS.Account.List("Override", "[Base]")
    For a = LBound(aActList) To UBound(aActList)
    'Is this an account that should have an override? If so, then...
            strDetinationAccount = Right(aActList(a), 5)

            'Is there an override? If so, then...
            strOveride = HS.GetCell("A#" & aActList(a))

            If strOveride <> 0 Then
                'Write the override to the account that needs to be at the new rate
                HS.Exp "A#" & strDetinationAccount & "= A#" aActList(a)
            'If there is no override then...
            Else
                'Take the change in the balance, translate that using the current
                'month rate and add that the prior months YTD balance.
                HS.Exp "A#" & strDetinationAccount & "= A#" strDetinationAccount & "P#Prior"
            End If
            'End
    Next
    'End
'End
```

FIGURE B-23. *Override rule with commentary*

in this chapter, so you have the tools to start. Soon you will be writing rules much more complex than this!

Allocation Rules

There are several types of allocations, but basically we can group them into three main types.

- **Name** Data allocation from one entity to many related entities.
- **Account** Data allocation from one account to many related accounts.
- **Time** Data allocation from one period to a range of periods.

Each type can use a different method for allocation:

- **Percent** Allocate the data to destinations by multiplying it by percentage values for those destinations.
- **Value** Allocate the data to destinations by multiplying it by ratios that are calculated by dividing specific values for destinations by a value representing all destinations.
- **Factor** Allocate the data to destinations by multiplying it by some factor for those destinations.
- **Total** Allocate the data to destinations by multiplying it by ratios that are calculated differently than in the Value method. The ratios are calculated by dividing specific values for destinations by the sum of those destinations.

So now that you have the concepts, you need to identify the allocation you are building, so that you are ready to write out the rules you need. For example:

For only base entities and entity currency, this rule will
  Pull from Total Operating Expense (Account Type)
  And write to my allocation accounts by the Percent account (Percent Method)
End rule

All the functions you can use in the Calculate routine, you can use in the Allocate routine, except Impact Status, OpenDataUnit, and Round. So when writing an allocation rule for the first time, you want to think about how you are getting your data.

I also tend not to use or recommend the Sub Allocate routine or the HS.Allocate function. There are some issues with it that make it not always the right tool. For example, if you use the HS.Allocate function, you will find out that it does not take currency as consideration. Also, Sub Allocate is very sensitive to any point of view changes. So you might find that the allocation you want to build is better suited for Sub Calculate.

The most important thing to consider when writing allocations that use another entity as the basis of the allocation is that you need to be sure the source entity is calculated and consolidated before you run the allocations. Unfortunately, you cannot control the sequence of execution for entities within HFM. So, the application administrator should have a process of allocation to be executed in a sequence. That is, make sure that all other calculations are complete before the entity basis allocation is calculated.

Using the Impact Status rule would help here, as long as the rule is focused and does not impact every other entity in the application. Performance would suffer if this was done.

Consolidation Rules

Consolidation is the process of gathering data from child entities and aggregating the data to parent entities. When you run a consolidation, each child's contribution to the parent is derived by using the default application calculations, and the results are written to the Entity Currency member of the parent. You can use the default or write your own consolidation rules. The power of being able to write your own rules is that you can control what accounts move from the Parent total to the Proportion and Elimination members of the Value dimension.

The best place to start with writing your own consolidation rules is to use the rules provided in the Sample Applications folder. This folder is found on the server where the install took place. When you select the "Y" option in the application settings, you will need to add a subroutine like that provided, as shown in Figure B-24.

While rules are also provided for Calculation Manager, it is scripting objects and has not been updated for the graphical view yet.

```
Sub Consolidate() 'consolidation rules (if app does not use default this section is used to consolidate
    Dim MyDataUnit
    Dim lNumItems
   Dim dPCon

    Set MyDataUnit = HS.OpenDataUnit("")

   dPCon = HS.Node.PCon("")

    lNumItems = MyDataUnit.GetNumItems

   for i = 0 to lNumItems-1

      ' Get the next item from the dataunit
    call MyDataUnit.GetItem(i, strAccount, strICP, strCustom1, strCustom2, strCustom3, strCustom4, dData)

      ' See if this is a consolidatable account
      If HS.Account.IsConsolidated(strAccount) Then

         ' Proportionalize this account
         call HS.Con("",dPCon,"")

         ' see if we should eliminate this account
         call Eliminate(strAccount, strICP)
      End If

   next

End sub
```

FIGURE B-24. *Consolidation rules*

The following steps describe the procedure that Financial Management uses to calculate the child's contribution to the parent for each account:

1. Check the IsConsolidated property of the account to verify that it should be consolidated.
2. Apply the consolidation percentage in the PCON account to the data in the Parent Total member. The Parent Total member is the sum of the Parent Curr Total and Parent Curr Adjs members. If there is no data in the PCON account, use 100 percent.
3. Write the result to the Proportion member of the Value dimension.
4. Run the Sub Calculate procedure for the Proportion member.

During the consolidation of the data, there are times when eliminations will need to be run. And when the conditions are valid, as described in the following list, the account is eliminated.

- The account is IsICP.
- A PlugAcct is defined.
- The ICP member of the Value dimension specifies an intercompany partner.
- The specified Intercompany partner is a descendant of the current parent.

If the criteria are met, the rule calculates the elimination:

- Write a reversing entry for the data in the Proportion member to the Elimination member.
- Write an entry for the data in the Proportion member to the Elimination member of the Plug account.

Figure B-25 offers an example of the elimination rules you can start with from the sample application folder.

You cannot specify a source for the Hs.Con function. The source is always the Parent Total member of the Value dimension for the current scenario, year, period, and entity. When the HS.Con function is used within an OpenDataUnit function, the source values are provided from the current item in the data unit. The other great thing the HS.Con will do is recognize account types. If you are writing to a destination account that has a different debit/credit attribute from the source account, the system reverses the sign in the destination. For example, if the source is a Revenue account and the destination is an Expense account, the sign is reversed.

```
Sub Eliminate (strAccount, strICP) 'intercompany elimination rules

   Dim CanEliminate
   Dim strPlug
   Dim dPCon


   CanEliminate = TRUE
   NegatePlug = FALSE

   If (StrComp(strICP, "[ICP None]", vbTextCompare) = 0) Then
      CanEliminate = FALSE
   ElseIf (HS.Account.IsICP(strAccount) = FALSE) Then
      CanEliminate = FALSE
   ElseIf (HS.PARENT.ISDESCENDANT(HS.PARENT.Member,strICP) = FALSE) Then
          CanEliminate = FALSE
   'ElseIf (HS.PARENT.ISDESCENDANT(strICP,"") = FALSE) Then
      'CanEliminate = FALSE
   Else
      strPlug = HS.Account.PlugAcct(strAccount)

'HS.Parent.IsDescendant("I#[ICP Top]", "")
      If (strPlug = "") Then CanEliminate = FALSE
   End If

   If CanEliminate Then

      dPCon = HS.Node.PCon("")

      call HS.Con("V#[Elimination]",-1*dPCon,"")

      call HS.Con("V#[Elimination].A#" & strPlug,dPCon,"")

   End If

End Sub
```

FIGURE B-25. *Eliminations*

In Figure B-26, we take this example and add a slight twist. With the HS.Con function, we can specify a custom we might want the eliminations to map to. So, if we had an application that was tracking the source of data, and we wanted the elimination to write that member, we would add something like this example. The elimination data would be in the custom member called "AutoElim."

```
Sub Eliminate
    bCanEliminate = True

    If (HS.Account.IsICP(sAccount) = False) Then
        bCanEliminate = False
    ElseIf (StrComp(sICP, "[ICP None]", vbTextCompare) = 0) Then
        bCanEliminate = False
    ElseIf (HS.Entity.ISDESCENDANT(pov_parent, sICP) = False) Then
        bCanEliminate = False
    Else
        sPlug = HS.Account.PlugAcct(sAccount)
        If (sPlug = "") Then bCanEliminate = False
        End If

    If bCanEliminate = True Then
        Call HS.Con("V#[Elimination].C4#AutoElim", -1 * dPCon, "")
        Call HS.Con("V#[Elimination].C4#AutoElim.A#" & sPlug, dPCon, "")
    End If 'bCanEliminate = True

End Sub      'Eliminate sub
```

FIGURE B-26. *Auto eliminations*

Conclusion

The rules are so important for HFM. If they are simple, well written, and easy to follow, you will have fewer problems and more flexibility as your business changes. Keep your rules clean and simple. Document every line of code, or every object in Calculation Manager. Finally, test thoroughly any changes you make.

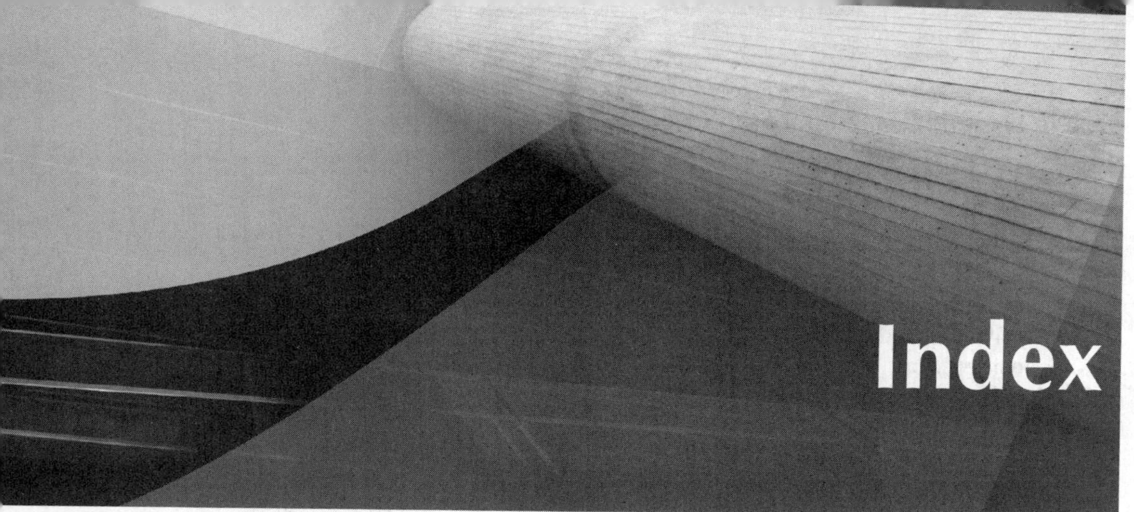

Index

C

D

E

F

G

H

I

J

L

M

N

O

P

S

T

U

V

W

X

Y

Z

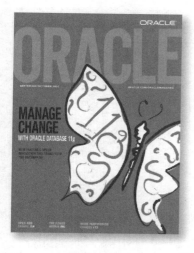